DATE DUE

DEMCO 38-297

CARL AKELEY

CARL AKELEY

Africa's Collector, Africa's Savior

Penelope Bodry-Sanders

PARAGON HOUSE
NEW YORK

First edition, 1991

Published in the United States by

Paragon House
90 Fifth Avenue
New York, N.Y. 10011

Book design by Jules Perlmutter/Off-Broadway Graphics

10 9 8 7 6 5 4 3 2 1

Library of Congress Cataloging-in-Publishing data
Bodry-Sanders, Penelope, 1944–
Carl Akeley : Africa's collector, Africa's savior / by Penelope
Bodry-Sanders.—1st ed.
p.   cm.
Includes bibliographical references and index.
ISBN 1–55778–243–1 : $19.95
1. Akeley, Carl Ethan, 1864–1926.   2. Zoological specimens—
Africa—Collection and preservation.   3. Wild animal collectors—
United States—Biography.   4. Taxidermists—United States—
Biography.   I. Title.
QL31.A5B63 1990

590'.92—dc20
[B]   90–49528
CIP

Manufactured in the United States of America.

Frontispiece: (facing title page) Carl Akeley with elephant skull and tusks collected by his wife Mickie on their 1905 expedition for the Field Museum of Natural History.

DEDICATION

*For my personal troika, Judy Rasmuson, Mary Fussell,
and Blair Brown, without whose vigilant love and support I could
not have found my way.*

CONTENTS

ACKNOWLEDGMENTS

This Akeley biography has been helped, supported, and encouraged by many people. It is with delight and joy that I remember and acknowledge them. The first person I wish to thank is Vernette Akeley Armstrong, Carl Akeley's niece, who provided me with access to her own private archives and, more importantly, has been a loving presence and supporter throughout. To her sister, Joyce Akeley Folsom, I also add my thanks. To Patricia and Lot Page, I am indebted not only for access to the journals and letters of Delia and Carl, but also for valuable insights into their relationship. Lot was fortunate to have known both Delia and Mary Jobe, and he unreservedly shared his perceptions of the Akeley wives. Both Patty and Lot have been warm and hospitable, opening up to me not only their archives, but their lives as well. I would never have considered writing this biography were it not for the encouragement of David Hare, who constantly assured me I "had a story to tell."

Many professionals have generously provided me with assistance. To Alan Isselhard, Clarendon town historian, who not only shared his knowledge with me but researched information as well; Karl Kabalac, archivist, Rush Rhees Library; Karen Zimmerman, archivist, I.D. Weeks Library, University of South Dakota; Ivan Saunders, archivist, Saskatchewan Archives Board, without whom I would never have found Vernette; Janet Baldwin, librarian, Explorer's Club; Philip Schiavo, owner, Roman Bronze Works, who gave me access to the records of Akeley's bronze sculptures and allowed me to roam freely among Akeley's plaster casts; Kathleen Baxter, photo archivist, Smithsonian Institution; and Mary Ann Johnson, archivist, Field Museum of Natural History, who was truly unflappable and generous in the face of enormous demands, I owe heartfelt gratitude.

Acknowledgments

Other authors have graciously given support and information: To Errol Trzebinski; Elizabeth Fagg Olds; Richard Milner; Pascal Imperato, M.D., who was exceedingly generous in giving me medical information and sharing research information assembled for his forthcoming biography entitled *Across the World: The Lives of Martin and Osa Johnson*; and Dawn-Starr Crowther, who is researching the life of Mary Jobe preparatory to a published biography of her, I owe an enormous debt of thanks. To writers John Heminway, Jack Flam, and George Schaller, I express my deep gratitude for contributing statements attesting to Akeley's legacy.

At the American Museum of Natural History, I have been given exceptional support. I wish to thank Nina Root, library chairwoman, for giving me the opportunity to embrace and serve the archival collections that gave inspiration for this biography. Her belief in me was a sustaining force in my life for a long time. Thanks are also due to Guy Musser and Helmut Schmidt in Mammalogy for giving me access to the accession records; Ray de Lucia and Stephen Quinn for help in examining dioramas in a more critical and appreciative way; Denis Finnin, Diana Shih, Carmen Collazo, and especially Andrea La Sala, who offered continued help and encouragement. Andrea was a generous, assiduous assistant who worked untiringly to clean up the loose ends of research for me. Without the support of my boss, Todd Nielsen, I would not have made my pilgrimages at all. He gave me not only the opportunity to go, but the time as well. Additionally, he has been a champion for the Akeley project for years.

I wish to thank Frank Marino and Olympus Camera Corporation for their generous loan of excellent camera and video equipment for my Akeley African pilgrimage of 1988/89. I also wish to thank Alistair Ballantine and Sue Blais of Abercrombie & Kent, Int., who supported the pilgrimages as well.

In Africa, there were many who helped with my research: To Dedan and Nancy Kinuthia, David Njau, David Markham, David Sugden, Cynthia Downey, Allen Ker, and especially N'gan'ga Kinuthia, I owe my gratitude. N'gan'ga acted as Kikuyu intrepreter on my expeditions to find "Bill's" family, and was also willing to discuss the painful subject of racism with me. I extend my gratitude to Bill's son, Joseph Gikungu Mbiru, for giving me insight into Akeley's relationship with his father. I also wish to thank Rosamond Carr for her hospitality and thoughts on Delia and Mary Jobe, as well as on gorilla hunting. I express my appreciation to Felician Nizenimana for his efforts on my behalf, and to Jean Marc Panossian, manager of the Izuba Meridian, for hospitality on my research missions. It is to Laurence Bajeneza that I owe the most. He was my companion on both Akeley pilgrimages, and the periods of time during which we traveled, talked, and laughed will always remain highlights of my life.

To the following people I express appreciation for individual acts of kindness and assistance: Rob Tucher, Fred and Debbie Tucher, Bob and Ramona Fussell, William D. Campbell, Carol Ferguson, Gretel Cummings. Adding to this list, I wish to thank the backers of the Akeley Grave Project: Vernette Akeley Armstrong, Joyce Akeley Folsom, Blair Brown, David Hare, Lois Meredith, Dorothy and Frank Bodry, Mary LeCroy, Mary Genett, Carol Tucher, Carol Levy, Ann Prewitt, Harry Blumenthal, Joseph Nell, Stella Hardee, Linda Goldman, Meg Wagner, Jack and Ruth Eagan, John and Judy Dircks, Bob and Peggy Sloves, Dick and Muriel Pederson, Michelle Saks, Ed Koss, Joan Kedziora, Rose Somodi, Ralph and Adie Bannett, Barbara and Arthur Simon, Greta Pofcher, Marge and Howard Cohen, Lee MacNeil, Macklyn and Monta Humphrey, Makabuza Kabirizi wa Nzigiye, Margaret Jones, Joseph Cuadrado, and Albert Lehman. There are no words equal to my gratitude to Laurence and George Rowbottom. Without these extraordinary, loving companions, the project could never have been accomplished.

I wish to extend deep thanks to my colleagues and friends who read, in whole or in part, and commented on the manuscript—Mary Genett, David Hare, Mary LeCroy, Lois Meredith, and Anne Sullivan, who was one of the biography's first and most avid supporters—for their valuable questions, suggestions, and encouragement. I wish to thank my good friend Donna Olson for assisting in the insertion of final edits and rewrites and offering me valuable comments. To Carol Tucher I owe my most profound appreciation for reading different versions of the entire manuscript, assisting with the tedious details of notes and bibliography, and maintaining a sense of humor and enthusiasm throughout. To my literary agent, Elizabeth Knappman, I extend my thanks for introducing me to the wonderful staff of Paragon House; and I wish to thank Andrew DeSalvo, my editor, for his enthusiastic support from the beginning.

On a personal level, I would like to acknowledge the undying belief in me that my parents have expressed. They have supported me through various lifestyles, some of which troubled them, because of that belief. Thanks, Mom and Dad. Thanks, St. Thomas Aquinas. Special thanks to Philip Zabriskie, whose counsel, encouragement, and love helped me to believe. Thanks to Richard Sanders. The Akeley obsession that has consumed a vast amount of my energy for several years has been very hard on my family. I have often been distracted and otherwise engaged. It is to my family that I owe my most heartfelt gratitude: to my step-daughter Kate, my son and pilgrimage companion Kipling, and especially my husband Mackarness Goode (incidentally the great grandson of G.B. Goode), for their perseverance, patience, support, love, and understanding.

PROLOGUE
Murwanashvaka:
The Trek to Akeley's Grave

I felt as if my heart had just blown a hole in my chest. A split second before, a blinding light had cut through my brain and I was nauseated by the pain. Sweat seeped into my eyes as self pity and exhaustion flooded over me. I felt weak and stupid.

I was climbing Mt. Mikeno in Zaire, on the last leg of a bizarre pilgrimage at an enormous personal expense to a grave that I knew was empty; and at that moment it seemed, even to me, like real folly. My eleven-year-old son, Kipling, was scrambling up the mountain ahead of me, looking back occasionally at the "hell of cockle he clamored through," but always pausing to help me over an obscured root or fallen tree that crossed the buffalo trail we were following. Comfort and ease had long since ebbed, drained away along with the splendid romance of our journey. Now it was just hard work.

Laurence Bajeneza, our Rwandan guide, led us up higher and higher into the rarified air. I had to stop for another slug of water from my canteen and felt the throbbing vessels in my cheeks. I tried to catch my breath with some semblance of nonchalance as he explained exactly where we were—Kabarozi, "Poisoner's Ridge," a place where local murderers were dangled over the edge to extract their confessions. Poisoning was the popular method of murder in these parts. I slipped again in very black, very wet buffalo dung and felt like sobbing. Laurence asked if I was all right. "Oh yes," I lied. Night was falling fast, as it always does near the Equator, and we were faced with finishing our journey in the dark.

The magnificent *hagenia* and *hypericum* trees loomed around us. These huge giants, strewn with bearded lichen and covered with enormous pads of moss creating a fairyland by day, were now transformed in the fading light into a Grimm's nightmare of tangled vegetation and monstrous arms. We'd been climbing for almost five hours.

You can't talk when you're climbing mountains—first, because it takes too much energy, and second, because the gasping sounds that punctuate your speech reveal how out-of-shape you really are. So you are forced inward. A strange process begins; layers of mental baggage wash away with your sweat. A growing purity is just around the bend; you can sense your mind and soul becoming more focused, streamlined, essential. Through a forced economy of thought and desire, you start getting your priorities right. And yet, a funny combination of thoughts and sensations also bubble to the surface. Flashes of reality and fantasy mingle like a dream.

Kanyamagufa, a steep depression, was constantly to our left, keeping me somewhat rooted in the present. The name means Canyon of Bones. There are three local theories about this name: One says that floods career into the canyon, taking with them every living thing; another refers to the guilty poisoners' crashing death on the canyon's floor. The last theory speaks to the human remains of a terrible intertribal battle that was staged before anyone can remember. But no matter—you had to stay sober in spite of the thinning air and pay attention to where you stepped, lest your bones end up in the canyon as well.

In 1921 there were other murders in this canyon: gorilla murders; three of them. They were pretty awful, as gorilla murders always are, but in this particular case the animals' murderer, in an ironic twist of fate, became their savior. It was his grave that we were going to find. His *empty* grave. No gorillas lived here now, but the mountain was sometimes visited by a grand old silverback named Bishitsi. I hoped we would find evidence of him and his family near the grave; it would make a good story.

As we sloughed onward in the dim light, we paused for the last time before our final push to our destination, 10,300 feet above sea level. Our resting place was called Mau Mau Camp, so-called because an English-speaking naturalist camped here during Kenya's Mau uprising, euphemistically called The Emergency. He had nothing to do with Kenya's problems, his sights were on gorillas not guerrillas, but the association stuck in the minds of the local people. We were told that the naturalist was George Schaller, one of my own heroes, following in the footsteps of that first naturalist capitivated by the elegance, power, and beauty of the species called *Gorilla gorilla beringei*.

However, Schaller never camped anywhere except Kabara, our destination. Schaller himself suggested that the English-speaking camper might have been Alan Root, a wonderful Kenyan filmmaker—but at that moment I hardly cared. The last light was being squeezed out and now we were moving mostly by instinct.

We reached our destination and campsite at about 7:15 P.M., and went immediately to the grave as our porters built small charcoal fires to warm us. As Laurence, Kipling, Mzee Ndisetse (a park ranger and tracker), and I stood at the open pit, a wave of mixed emotions swept over me. I knelt down to send up a prayer as much for myself as for him, hoping that it would permeate the meadow of Kabara—Place of Rest—and touch the god that lived there.

A few tears slid down my cheeks and my son touched me in a comforting gesture. I felt an odd suspension of life and sensed a strong camaraderie between those of us who had made the climb and come to that remote place. Laurence said that I was "murwanashyaka"—"someone who wants something very badly." But Laurence and Kipling were in there too; the first because he was (and is) a kindred spirit and the other, my son, because he didn't want to miss the action. It was all so unreal that in a strange way I wasn't even present. I tried to absorb and experience every possible feeling, but fatigue and poignancy overwhelmed me. I also felt a strange sadness, as if I had found and lost something very quickly, before fully understanding it. It was like waking from a dream exuberant because you had found some vital key to a problem or situation—only to forget the dream immediately.

What an odd quest. Carl Ethan Akeley, 1864–1926: Who was this man who, though long dead, still held such a powerful fascination? I could rattle off the facts about him; I could even instill admiration and love for him in others. Yet I had come halfway around the world to discover who he was and I wasn't even sure why. I'd come to Africa to find something—an understanding of his obsessions, his hopes, his failed loves, his tenderness, the sum of his parts—and maybe, just maybe, in writing his story I'd understand myself and life around me a little bit better.

I had told Laurence the stories of the gorilla murders in great and gory detail, and he urged me not to write about them because they would taint the reputation of this man, who ultimately became their savior. But of course it all has to be told, because all of it is what makes the man so splendid. He was a man—only a man, but a man who accomplished more things in his lifetime than ten men usually do. Adventurer, African explorer, inventor, movie maker, author, sculptor, museologist, conservationist, and taxidermist: not a bad resume.

He was also husband to two talented women, a reckless driver, a workaholic, a scotch drinker, a sweet and touching man with those he loved, and a monster to his enemies. He cursed like a Marine, dazzled children, could be so distracted he would wear mismatched shoes and rumpled suits, was deeply cherished by his friends, loved Africans, and was a racist. He was all of it: a combination of disparate entities. And I wanted to see it all. I needed to come to this place called Kabara to find something that would enlighten me.

Akeley had died tragically in this saucerlike meadow on the saddle between Mt. Mikeno and Mt. Karisimbi in 1926, when he came here to study gorillas. He was buried in what was thought to be an impenetrable grave, but in 1978 someone ransacked his tomb and scattered his remains about the meadow. I had speculated often about the desecration, thinking alternately that the grave robbers were looking for treasure or that they were seeking human bones for their sumu pouches, which were used as amulets for good or evil.

I stood in Kabara thinking about those bones, and his restless spirit seemed to roam on the eerie wind. The sweat that soaked my clothes now made me shiver in the chilled night air. We went into the three-room building that had been built in the 1970s as a research station for the Frankfurt Zoological Society. We ate some dinner, drank some beer, and Laurence, Kipling, and I shared one room as the Mzee and the seven porters huddled near a charcoal burner in the next, talking and laughing. Symptoms that felt like malaria overwhelmed all of us—freezing cold chills one second, the next a heat from deep within as if we were being microwaved. I knew enough not to worry about these effects of altitude sickness, but in spite of Laurence's reassurances, I was certain that the fumes from the charcoal stove would kill us slowly and imperceptibly during the night. In my semi-dreamlike state, the irony of that possibility amused me, and the thought was almost seductive. But we didn't die; we didn't even sleep. None of us. Once again, fact, fantasy, Akeley, monsters, God, birds, gorillas, grey cave walls, that odd wind outside, and unfamiliar sounds all zigzagged and echoed through my brain.

We rose at dawn and went again to the grave pit, where Laurence nonchalantly delivered some astonishing news. There were, in fact, a skull and two arm bones in the pit. The revelation sent a new chill through me.

I had requested information about the feasibility of visiting the grave site in 1987. To this end, Laurence made a trip to Kabara in February 1988. The Africans thought that he was crazy—climbing Mt. Mikeno in search of the bones of a colonialist *muzungu* (white European) whom they thought had been killed by a wounded gorilla. But Laurence, a gregarious man of steaming intensity, is independent and willful. He was curious himself about Akeley and thought he'd take a look at Kabara and have his own adventure.

Laurence made the trek with Sebihaza, his guide-companion and the son of Muguru, the Batwa gorilla tracker who served Akeley in 1921 and 1926. Sebihaza had heard his father tell of his experiences with Akeley many times, and related these stories to Laurence prior to my arrival in Africa. I owe an enormous debt to Laurence for the facts, as Sebihaza died but weeks before I came to Zaire—a loss that deeply affected me.

Akeley's grave had probably been looted for treasure as I suspected, but the circumstances were quite different than I had imagined. The vandals were not necessarily grave robbers. A rash of vandalism had swept through the rural areas in the 1960s. The perpetrators sought stakes buried in cement, which they believed were markers for buried treasure. The early European colonists, especially the Germans, had marked off their property with these stakes. During the civil upheavals in Rwanda and Zaire, caused by the "winds of change" sweeping over most of Africa before independence, Europeans scattered frantically across both borders, disoriented and terrified, to escape the violence leveled against whites. The local peoples in the rural areas thought that the Europeans were running around in search of the buried stakes because they had hidden money at their bases. In spite of an official campaign at the grass-roots level to educate the local people and halt the vandalism, nearly every visible stake in cement was uprooted. The rumor was still alive in the late 1970s, when Akeley's grave was desecrated.

Akeley's grave was covered with a slab of cement and was originally surrounded by a stockade of wooden stakes. In 1971, David Salseth, the young son of a missionary, camped in Kabara and found the crumbled remains of Akeley's original gravestone, constructed in 1926. He identified the grave by piecing together Carl Akeley's name. Salseth, familiar with Akeley's story, beautifully restored the grave at that time. Seven years later, the jungle had done its work, but not so totally as to obscure the grave from potential vandals. Ironically, if the grave had remained in its decrepit state, Akeley's tomb, invisible, would probably have remained inviolate. But it was not to be. Someone ransacked the grave.

The pit yielded no treasure, but the skeleton was disinterred and the remains left there on the earth's surface. An unidentified person found the skull and put it on the table inside the research building. When making rounds with Sebihaza, the game warden found the skull. Sebihaza, knowing the Akeley story well, suggested that the skull was Akeley's.

He took the warden to find the grave. The arm bones lay near the excavated tomb. Sebihaza reburied the remains himself, adding more earth and stones to the pit. The incident took place in 1979, and I wonder if Sebihaza knew even more, and was trying to protect the culprits. But he is dead now and his son, Dunia, knows nothing.

The fact that the skull and arm bones were still in the pit had a profound effect on me. The fact that they had been dug up, tossed aside, held, touched, examined, felt, and reburied moved me. They added an immediacy and reality to the proceedings. Somehow I was rather enjoying the poetry of my "wandering spirit of Kabara" theory. It appealed to my Irish soul. I was enjoying the fact that Akeley was probably enjoying it too. But now the rules had changed. I was less able to spin off into fantasy with real bones facing me. My God—he really was a man, flesh and bone. The notion was almost shocking.

Prologue

I wanted to touch those bones myself, dig through the earth and hold them. Maybe I'd even take one home and put it in my collector's cabinet with all the other bones, maybe even light a candle. But of course I didn't; I was afraid, nervous. Instead, I asked my friends to send money to rebuild the grave. Our sense of humanity admonishes us, like our first Neanderthal brothers before us, to bury our dead. I hear the voice within and Akeley's vulnerable remains bother me. I think of them often. But I would venture to say that Akeley likes them just the way they are.

And so I have all of Africa to remind me of Akeley. She really symbolizes him at his essence: on the edge, exciting, violent, bright and dark, charming, bigger than life, touching, in harmony, at odds, parched and burnt-out. He was full of heart like her own heart-shaped land mass.

But I keep thinking of those bones. No metaphor—they are very real and they hold for me a fascination and a vivid reminder that Akeley was really just a man. There was no enlightenment at Kabara, no song from the Muse to make my job easier. There was only a skull placed indignantly on a wooden table and a couple of bones. But they admonished me to inspect the stuff of Akeley's life in a more profound way. Here, then, is Akeley's story.

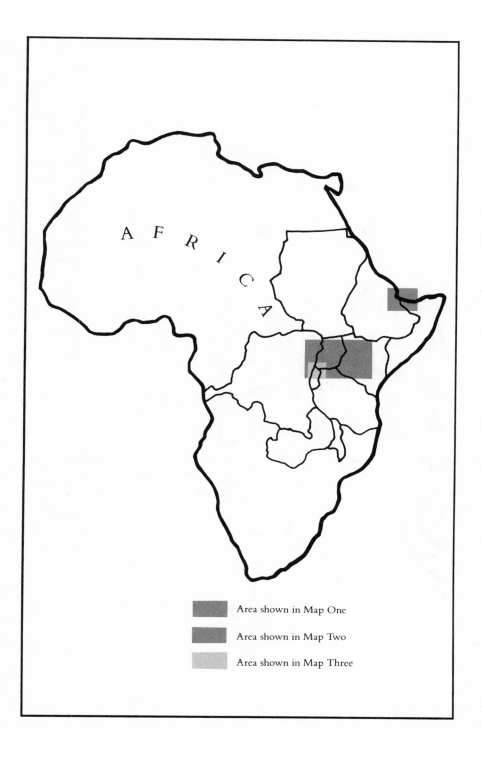

Area shown in Map One

Area shown in Map Two

Area shown in Map Three

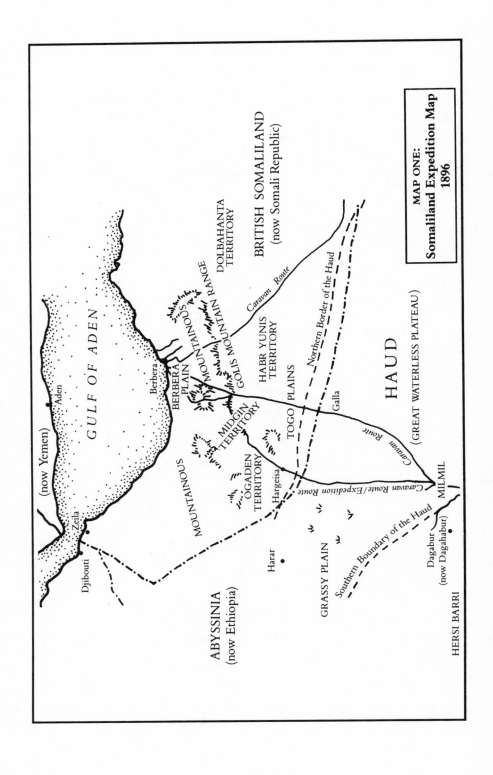

MAP ONE:
Somaliland Expedition Map
1896

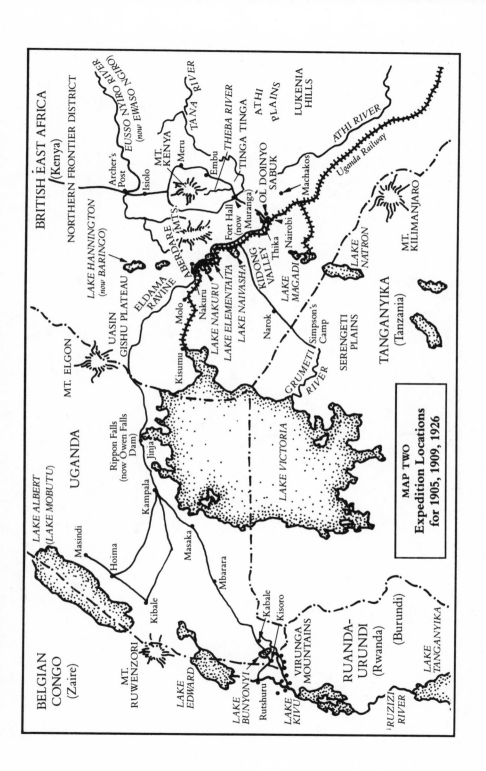

MAP TWO
Expedition Locations
for 1905, 1909, 1926

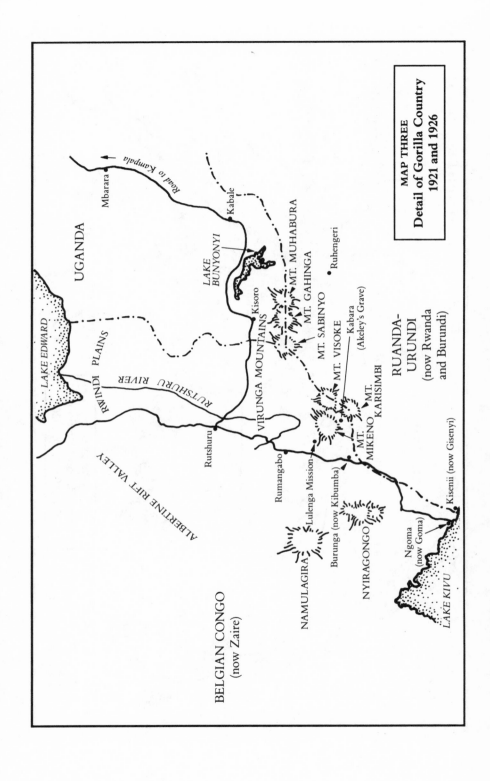

MAP THREE
Detail of Gorilla Country
1921 and 1926

UGANDA

LAKE EDWARD

Mbarara

Road to Kampala

Kabale

LAKE BUNYONYI

Kisoro

MT. MUHABURA

MT. GAHINGA

MT. SABINYO

Ruhengeri

RWINDI PLAINS

RUTSHURU RIVER

VIRUNGA MOUNTAINS

MT. VISOKE

Kabara
(Akeley's Grave)

MT. KARISIMBI

MT. MIKENO

Rutshuru

ALBERTINE RIFT VALLEY

Rumangabo

Lulenga Mission
(now Kibumba)

Burunga (now Goma)

NAMULAGIRA

NYIRAGONGO

Ngoma
(now Goma)

Kisenii (now Gisenyi)

LAKE KIVU

RUANDA-
URUNDI
(now Rwanda
and Burundi)

BELGIAN CONGO
(now Zaire)

BEGINNINGS

Afric is all the sun's and as her earth
  Her human clay is kindled. Full of power
For good or evil, burning from its birth . . .
  —Lord Byron, "Don Juan"

CARL AKELEY was not born in Africa. In fact, he only went to Africa five times and spent, all totaled, less than five years of his sixty-two-year life there. But he was Africa's son. She nourished him like a mother, animating him with passion and burning purpose. Akeley's life and work caught fire after his first expedition to the "dark continent." Until then his technical abilities developed steadily, but his artistic spirit did not find full expression. After his fateful first safari, Carl Akeley's epic obsession centered on revealing and representing Africa's boundless mysteries and treasures. Guy de Maupassant, who "felt attracted to Africa by an overwhelming need," eloquently expressed what the continent has always symbolized for westerners, "[it is a] kind of door through which one leaves known reality to penetrate another unexplored and dreamlike reality . . ." Many people never experience this need, but many do. Carl Akeley did. Africa became for him an ideal, an inner landscape, a mother lode of power, mystery, peace, and beauty. Akeley felt the need to capture the essence of Africa, to fix it in some tangible, visual reality, and in doing so possess it. The Arabs have a proverb: "Once you have drunk of Africa's waters, you will drink again." The proverb is more a challenge or a contract than a prediction. The continent dares you to remain untouched by it.

By reviewing his African expeditions and artistic accomplishments we can gain a fuller understanding of who Akeley was. The sheer volume of his

1

contribution provides a rich field to explore. However, Akeley gave us little to help us know him, besides his actions and the spatial representations of what compelled him. He was called Africa's "biographer" and "poet." Indeed he was, but in a visual sense. He was not a particularly verbal man, and left behind little evidence of what he thought and felt. His "voice" is faint in the literature that bears his name, as his stories were rendered by ghostwriters or interpreted by his second wife. His life, then, becomes a huge and complex puzzle that must be pieced together by examining the reactions of the world around him and by listening to the people who loved and loathed him. Occasionally his voice comes through the business or expedition logistics in his journals or letters, and when it does, its clarity is stunning.

Of Akeley's youth and family relations we know little. What we can examine is his early life in the context of the environment in which he grew, his family relationships, and three incidents which seriously influenced his life.

On May 19, 1864 Clarence Ethan Akeley was born to Julia Glidden Akeley and Daniel Webster Akeley on a fifty-eight-acre working farm in Clarendon, New York. Clarendon was a small hamlet, about six square miles, in Orleans County just south of Lake Ontario. The land is basically flat and wide open, with occasional low hills, and in those days, one could still see evidence of Iroquois burial mounds bulging up from the earth's surface. The surrounding land is swampy as a result of glacial meltwaters, and is rich in Silurian fossils.

When Akeley was born, near the end of the Civil War, Clarendon was probably one of the stations on the Underground Railroad due to its proximity to Canada. Polly's Tavern reputedly hosted individual and family groups of southern blacks looking for freedom from slavery. The citizens were proud to do what they could to help the anti-slavery movement. The same community, however, expressed bigotry towards Irish Catholics, who had immigrated to Orleans County from their homeland to escape the potato famine. Some Clarendon residents found sport in provoking the "Pope-loving ignorant savages."[1] Irish and Catholic were synonymous, and they were not fully accepted for decades. Akeley's family was anti–Irish Catholic, yet Akeley's first wife would be of that background.

The indigenous Iroquois Indians also made the townspeople uncomfortable, often terrifying them by appearing on their doorsteps to beg for food. In the early 1820s the Indians had supplied the townspeople with venison, bear meat, and beaver pelts, but as the Indians had hunted out the beaver population, "they, in turn, had been hunted out by the white man,"[2] wrote David Sturgis Copeland, Clarendon's historian. The Iroquois were soon forced onto reservations.

The 1825 completion of the Erie Canal, which passed through nearby Holly, brought good fortune to Clarendon as it opened up an avenue by which the town's vast quantities of limestone and produce could be marketed to the outside world. But by 1888, Copeland was lamenting the fact that the land and citizenry of Clarendon had lost their charm and virtue, when in the town's youth, "simplicity and originality walked hand and hand unfettered by the tyranny of public opinion" and gossip. Then, he wrote, "Clarendon was as a child, open and honest in her thought and action."[3] Enterprise and progress brought prosperity to the town along with the attendant social problems of development. But even more, the Civil War had changed the town, turning innocence into cynicism.

Clarendon's cultural vista was tinged with shades of the spiritualism movement as well. The practitioners, it was believed, could communicate with the dead through a series of coded signals. The local movement had started when a couple of teenage girls in Rochester—the Fox sisters—interpreted rappings on a window as spirits trying to communicate with the living. The girls were probably clairvoyant, as they successfully assisted local policemen in forensic work, and as their reputation grew, so did the number of their followers.

These diverse points of view combined to form a fascinating collective intelligence, conscience, and morality, providing the spiritual ambience into which Akeley was born. Most of his neighbors were white, Anglo-Saxon Protestants; hard-working, respectable, family-oriented individuals with a decided leaning towards puritanism. Many of the old families had come from New England, especially Vermont and New Hampshire—in fact, the town was named after Vermont's Clarendon.

Carl Akeley knew very little about his own family. "I know father was born somewhere in Vermont," he wrote. "Then it seems that the family trekked west and as near as I can make out there were a bunch of kids and somewhere in western New York my dad fell out of the wagon and they went on and left him. He was taken in, and when quite a young man married the daughter of the farmer for whom he worked."[4] The farmer was Thomas Glidden.

Thomas Glidden was born in Unity, New Hampshire in 1803 and had moved with his family to Clarendon in 1817. The Gliddens date back to Devon, England; Charles Glidden immigrated to Boston in the 1660s, and the family moved to Portsmouth, New Hampshire, where it remained through three generations. One of the sons of the fourth generation, Captain Jacob Glidden, decided to pack up his family and move west. He, his wife and four sons left Unity, New Hampshire, stumbling on Clarendon, New York and setting up house in 1817.

Akeley's maternal great-grandfather, Jacob Glidden, had the spirit of a pioneer, willing to take on hardships to open up virgin territory, gambling on the success of a new and unknown enterprise. "Glidden first put up a shanty of fifteen by twenty feet with a bark roof and only one room, with no upstairs . . . Glidden made a bedstead of poles and divided them with curtains, having some natural modesty. The fireplace was on the ground in the corner and the smoke escaped through a hole in the roof."[5] Jacob Glidden and his sons cleared ninety acres of land, planting them and coaxing the earth to produce. His son Thomas bought a piece of land nearby, with the financial assistance of a neighbor, David Matson. Thomas (1803–1888) married Emma Crosby, another neighbor, in 1827. She died at age twenty-one after only three years of marriage. In 1831 Thomas remarried the daughter of David Matson, Betsey. This second marriage produced two daughters. One of Thomas's daughters, Julia, fell in love with and married the farm hand, Daniel Webster "Webb" Akeley. Carl Akeley's brother, Lewis, would later credit Carl's intuitive and creative fire to the Matson blood, calling it "the spark which disturbed the clod."[6]

The Glidden clan was not enamored with Webb Akeley. He was outspoken and contemptuous of the Clarendon community in general, especially as personified by the Gliddens, whom he felt were hypocrites. Akeley found the exception in Thomas Glidden, whom he respected and loved as a father. Thomas Glidden was a rebel, "a man who knew his friends in any time of the highway of life; full of hospitality, and above all hypocrisy and cunning."[7] Glidden ignored his family's opinion of Webb Akeley, embracing him and blessing Akeley's union with his daughter.

After Julia and Webb were married they lived next door to her father's home. Thomas had wrested a good living from the land, and had given the fifty-eight-acre piece of property to his daughter—perhaps as her dowry.

Besides his inclination to say what was on his mind (a characteristic strongly visited on his son, Carl), Webb Akeley was remembered by the community as a man of "stirling" qualities—honesty heading the list of virtues—who was deeply kind and affectionate in his family relationships. The family regularly attended services at the Universalist church and Webb served as one of its trustees when Carl Akeley was a boy.

When Webb Akeley was conscripted to serve in the Civil War in 1862, he paid a neighbor one thousand dollars to serve in his place. His granddaughter would write that "he feared for the welfare of his little family."[8] Three of Webb's brothers served, one killed in the war. While it was a fairly common practice to hire surrogates to serve in one's place without apparent stigma, it is not quite clear why Webb Akeley chose this course. He had only one child at the time—Lewis, born in 1861—and his wife was not solely dependent on him, surrounded as she was by a large family. He might have been a pacifist, or he might have been a coward. For whatever reason, he refused to fight. What we do know is that his decision cost the family a great deal in morale and finances. The family suffered financially for years as a result of the debt, as one thousand dollars was a fortune in those days. Lewis wrote that "there were years in which father did well to pay the interest on the obligation."[9]

Carl Akeley's mother, Julia, inherited her father's idealism and spirit. She was a "sensitive woman who loved poetry and beauty."[10] Like her mother before her, Julia taught school in Clarendon. She quit teaching after the birth of Lewis, and would have scant opportunity to express her aestheticism in the difficult years that followed. Financial hardship plagued the marriage. Webb dealt with the problems better than his wife did; but then they were paying off a debt of his own making. Julia was miserable. Their poverty, exacerbated by the contrasting lifestyles of better-heeled Glidden clan members, embittered her. She pushed and nagged her husband to improve the family's position and quality of life.

Julia Akeley had seven boys, four of whom survived infancy. The timing of the other infant births and deaths was crucial to Carl Akeley's early development. In 1866, when Carl was two years old, Julia had another son, Walter, who died after one year; when he was four, Winnie, another son, was born, but died after two months; and when Carl was five, Julia gave birth to another boy who either died immediately or was stillborn. The impact that these pregnancies, births, and deaths (one a year for three consecutive years), had on Julia and her family is important. If she wasn't reeling from gestation or postpartum depression, she was grieving. Her young, impressionable boys must have thought that they too might die. The feelings of loss and grief permeating the household, and their confusion about the situation, was devastating to Lewis and Carl. They had no control over the events or over their parents' sadness and frustration. As small boys they watched their mother as she navigated, in her own bitter unhappiness, a world not to her liking. Carl Akeley, a toddler, needed his mother for affection and comfort; Julia, drained and sad, had little to give him. These, his formative years, were emotionally difficult times, and Carl grew solitary and introspective.

Webb wanted to leave Clarendon, oppressed by the "old clay lump we called a farm"[11] and the hard life. He dreamed of moving west, where they could all make a fresh start together. But his Civil War debt and Julia's refusal to leave her family killed the dream. Julia's sons, who considered her manipulative and "spoiled," held her responsible for the family's unhappiness.

But Julia's decision to stay was not an easy one. On the one hand, the move was attractive: It was an adventurous and romantic opportunity to make a fresh start with her husband and boys. Other Gliddens had relocated successfully to the west, so there was a precedent. And it was agreed that her husband could succeed there. Webb Akeley's rebellious and independent qualities, like those of her father, were no secret to Julia, and were essential qualities for pioneering. On the other hand, she resented Webb Akeley. She wanted to make him pay the price for plunging them into debt and poverty. She refused to move, which had the desired demoralizing effect on her husband. She was also afraid to leave the solace and security of her family.

The family stayed on in Clarendon, caught up in what Lewis later called "an utterly hopeless agricultural situation" in which his father found no economic independence. Julia, in turn, condemned herself to an emotional prison in which she grew more miserable and crustier, badgering and bickering with her husband in an atmosphere of impotence and frustration. Webb and the children felt bitter about the decision for many years.

Julia successfully gave birth to two more sons, Ward in 1871, when Akeley was eight, and Thomas in 1875, when Akeley was eleven. Of these four sons, Lewis was the most outspoken about the Akeley family. It is through his eyes that we see these early relationships. Lewis was quite different from his brothers in that he was more articulate—a scholar, writer, philosopher, and an overtly sensitive man. He lived to be one hundred years old, and for many years was a renowned educator at the University of South Dakota. He started as a professor of natural science in 1887, was promoted to dean of the College of Engineering in 1908, and after his retirement in 1933, became a lecturer in philosophy until his death in 1961. He was the only brother who had a successful marriage; those of his siblings ended in divorce or abandonment.

Lewis Akeley's insights into his family usually combine the objectivity of a scientist and the poignancy of a poet/philosopher. His opinions shed a great deal of light on incidents and relationships in Carl Akeley's life. In private correspondence he often refers to Carl's early years as truly tragic. On the other hand, he believed that those "dreadful years . . . gave his genius its stimulus; all genius has been nourished by struggle and poverty."[12]

Lewis suggested late in his life that his father was "plenty ignorant" and was not totally without blame for the "injustice" manifest in Carl Akeley's youth.[13] Webb, however, loved his boys with warmth, affection, and respect. "Mr. Akeley was a jovial, friendly man, fond of children, exceedingly proud of his boys, especially Lewis and Carl."[14] His father admired Carl's mechanical genius, astute nature, and odd sense of humor.

Webb wanted to see his boys escape from the environment that he himself hated. He taught his sons to be honest men. "I do not care what they become," he said. "They can be Catholics for all I care, or atheists. The one thing I hope for is that they become men." The literature of the day is filled with definitions of what a "real" man should be. The qualities advocated for men at the time were not strictly masculine—they were human virtues: "courage, hard work, self mastery, intelligent effort . . . 'Only those are fit to live who do not fear to die and none are fit to die who have shrunk from the joy of life and the duty of life.' " (inscriptions on the walls of the Roosevelt Memorial Hall at the American Museum of Natural History) These particular masculine virtues were articulated by Carl Akeley's idol, Theodore Roosevelt, when Roosevelt was writing about youth and manhood. Webb, a product of his time, expected each of his sons to be a man, "no mere pretender to manhood, . . . or anything with a streak of yellow."[15] This notion rings a hollow note, given Webb Akeley's Civil War story. The boys, too, sensed his hypocrisy. Carl, especially, would have difficulty with notions of courage later in his life.

Webb Akeley's influence on his sons cannot be overestimated. They enjoyed his companionship and preferred their father over their mother, but Webb could have gone a long way towards helping his sons understand their mother's pain, and he seems not to have done that. Granted, they were times that cannot be judged from a twentieth-century perspective; men and women were not as apt to express their emotional life then as they are today. But for years Carl seethed with deep resentment toward his mother, and a little understanding might have helped everyone get on better. Carl, by nature, was less capable than Lewis of letting go of grievances; he tended to harbor and nurse them, adding to his own unhappiness. Lewis was a more understanding and compassionate man than Carl. He felt sympathy and sadness for their mother when he saw her "deprived of all conveniences for living, disappointed, [living] a hard life."

All the boys worked the farm. Chores on the Akeley farm included planting, cultivating, and harvesting crops of wheat, corn, oats, barley, beans, and Canadian thistles. The boys also tended the cows, hogs, and fowl, but the task they enjoyed the most was picking apples and making cider. Clarendon was at that time the leading producer of apples in the state, and Webb and his two oldest boys looked forward to the yearly autumn ritual— the "men" alone together in the field. It looked as if Carl would make a fine farmer; he had a real understanding of the earth and loved the animals.

When Carl was fifteen, his relatives from DeKalb, Illinois invited him to the Midwest to work on their farm during a school break. Joseph Glidden, the inventor of barbed wire fencing, had once lived in Clarendon. On a return visit he had been impressed with Carl, admiring the boy's strength and dedication to his chores. He put Carl to work milking fifteen to twenty cows, morning and night. It was Carl's first taste of life outside of northwestern New York, and while Carl had trouble with the Gliddens, he loved the Midwest.

Many years later, Lewis would comment to Carl how tragic it was that their father had not forced the issue of moving west. Carl replied that if indeed the journey had been made, he would have become a farmer. He actually felt fortunate to have grown up in the oppressive atmosphere of his youth, for it had stimulated him to leave it.

Carl was a solitary, reticent boy who preferred the companionship of wild fauna to other children. As uncomfortable as he was with people, Akeley loved the countryside and the nuances of the seasons: the crunch of frost tightening the matted grass under his feet; the sharpness of spring's sunlight hitting his face as it rounded the horizon, coloring all in its path a surprising pink; the exuberant vitality of summer's life; and the sweet/sour smells of autumn rising and falling with changing winds. Most particularly, he loved

7

the creatures, especially the birds. His naturalist tendencies were fed constantly as he roamed Bergen swamp, Oatka Creek, and the numerous fields near his home. Squirrels, muskrats, foxes and the great diversity of birds fascinated him, and observation taught him patience. He learned how thrilling it could be to simply watch creatures and their behavior in their natural habitat; to make a connection, a discovery. He would sit for hours and concentrate on a bird building a nest or a predator poised and patient at a potential victim's front door—watching the watcher. He roamed the fields alone, sometimes playing hookey from school. He hated school, which surely rankled his mother, the ex–school teacher.

Akeley went to the Cowles School, a one-room schoolhouse about a half-mile from his home. The room was dark, and the smell of the oil that was used on the floor permeated the air. The walls were painted a dark color so that they would not show dirt and the windows were covered with green shades. A wood or coal burning stove stood in the front of the room. Students in the front roasted; those in the back froze. Classes lasted year round with two breaks in the calendar: one in the fall so that the children could help harvest the crops, the other at Christmas.

Cowles had a reputation for discipline. Often, misbehaving boys were sent outside to fetch their own switches. One teacher taught all the students whose ages ranged from six to fourteen. The various grades rotated to the front benches for their lessons as the rest of the student body completed written assignments. In all his years at Cowles, there were two teachers that Akeley loved—both were men who seemed to understand him and respect his quick mind, irrespective of the fact that he failed to apply it to his studies. They encouraged Carl to learn the very basics of education, reading, writing and math.

According to one of Akeley's schoolmates, Jennie A. Cowles, Carl was a "quiet, fairhaired, rosy-cheeked boy known to his schoolmates as 'Clarence' or 'Carlie' . . . and he did not shine in his recitations."[16] An old friend of the family, Elizabeth Martin, observed, "No parental pleadings or commands could overcome the desire to rid himself of schoolbooks, and the four walls of a schoolroom. But the jibes and jeers of those who saw him as a truant and a lazy boy so entered his sensitive soul that he never in later life wished to return to his childhood home."[17] Three events in Carl Akeley's youth were particularly important and noteworthy. The first concerned a dog—a pointer—that abruptly and happily crossed his path one day. Carl tried to find its owner, and when he couldn't, accepted the dog as a gift from the gods. He fought with his mother for permission to keep the dog, and she relented under pressure from her husband. Carl and the dog remained inseparable for about a year.

Carl's only friend outside of the family was Osman "Oz" Mitchell. He was an older man, a farmer who had fallen on bad times and served as the town mailman. A brilliant naturalist, Oz taught Carl all he knew about the creatures of the field, sky, and stream, including how to hunt them. He also helped Carl train the pointer to become a top-notch bird dog.

Mitchell loved the solitary Carl and gave him much more than hunting prowess—he gave him a sympathetic ear when times were rough for the boy. He was an "unspeakable comfort" for Carl, whom he considered a "lost soul."[18] They spent hours in the field together, training and talking. Much later in his life, when Akeley finally consented to return to Clarendon around World War I, the only person he asked to see was Oz, who had just recently died.

The dog was Carl's companion and treasure. He was proud of his work with the dog, proud that he could trust the dog to obey his every command. Training his dog made Carl feel powerful, in control of things.

Once Carl and Lewis took the pointer with them to what is now the Iroquois National Wildlife Reserve, in the Tonawanda Swamp on Lake Ontario, to watch the sky blacken with migrating birds, especially Canada geese. They tied their buckboard to a tree in the woods and put the dog under a blanket in the back. Carl trusted the dog to stay in the wagon simply because he told him to. The brothers returned to find the dog gone.

Carl was devastated. The boys searched for the dog, but soon faced the futility of their hunt, and gave up. On the ride home, Carl struggled with disbelief and grief. Lewis, acutely aware of his brother's pain, offered consolation to his unconsolable companion.

Carl was a master at controlling his feelings with only momentary spasmodic bursts of temper or other emotions. But he was brokenhearted, and a deep depression enveloped him for months following the incident. Even as an adult, he blamed hunters for stealing the dog. No one can doubt that he felt a profound sense of loss, but his pain was exacerbated by his own sense of hubris and carelessness: In truth, he probably blamed himself for losing his beloved pet, realizing that no matter how well-trained the animal was, it was foolhardy to leave it unattended for hours in a woods teeming with crackling noises, hoots, and peeps. Akeley never knew whether the dog had left of its own accord or was stolen. The "stolen" theory was more palatable, and was the one he chose to embrace.

Lewis and Carl had grown up with another dog, a big mongrel named Ned. When Carl was eleven years old, the dog was shot, by either their father or a neighbor, for running with a pack of dogs that were killing sheep. In his adult life, Akeley sometimes equated abandonment with betrayal; that notion could well have been born with the loss of these animals. Though Carl's childhood pain in losing animals that he loved is hardly unique, the incidents were important in a cumulative sense; he felt that he had so little to begin with that his losses hardened him, forcing him to banish sentimentality from his heart.

9

Carl Akeley

The second important incident in Akeley's early life began as a day's adventure with his dad. The boys loved accompanying their father on his errands into Rochester. Once, when Lewis and Carl were small boys, Webb let them entertain themselves unsupervised as he attended to his business. The boys made their way to the Powers Building, part of the "Powers Block," where Mr. Powers, one of Rochester's wealthiest citizens, had established a free exhibit to attract the public. As the boys wandered through the building's upper floors, they were struck by an exhibit featuring about fifty small cases housing mounted birds and mammals. The animals were the first taxidermic specimens that Carl Akeley had ever seen. The silent zoo held him rapt, not only because of the beauty of the mounts, but also for the discrete aspect of the cases themselves. Each case was a world unto its own, each a piece of art. The work had been created by an English painter and interior designer named David Bruce. He would eventually become an important influence in Carl's life.

A dramatic turning point in Carl's young life, and the third noteworthy incident, began with a routine errand that took him to a local Glidden home one winter morning. Carl found Irene Glidden in tears over the death of her canary, which had frozen during the night. Touched by her emotion and wanting to comfort her, Carl offered to "fix" the bird. He brought the bird home, skinned and stuffed it, finishing it by inserting two small glass beads taken from his mother's sewing basket for the eyes. He then mounted the bird on a little branch. Pleased with his work but unsure of his friend's reaction, Carl opted to replace the bird in its cage in her absence. Miss Glidden was astonished by the mount—which, of course, delighted Carl, then twelve years old. He was pleased with himself, and pronounced that it "could almost sing."

This true story has become part of the legend that Akeley invented about himself. As Akeley tells it in his autobiography, *In Brightest Africa*, it reveals his early love for and skill at taxidermy and his own precocity. More important, however, is the fact that the incident showed him that he could be successful at something. At that moment the boy realized that he had discovered in himself a talent—something he was proud of, that brought him pleasure and that impressed others. The bird, which is housed in the American Museum of Natural History's Art and Realia collection, is still remarkably lovely and lifelike after over a hundred years.

The following year, Carl was reading *Youth's Companion* when he saw an ad for a how-to book about taxidermy. Carl wanted the book so that he could hone his skills in the craft, but its one-dollar price tag was expensive. He borrowed the book from an older friend in the neighborhood, and sometimes practiced the techniques with his friends. Though Carl rarely dealt with children other than his brothers, he did gain some companionship as a result of his new-found avocation.

Carl usually worked alone in his room, mounting small creatures on leafy branches. He had total control over the little worlds he created and his hobby became an important creative exercise for him. He took painting lessons from Irene Glidden, a fine artist in the community, so that he could represent the habitats of his mountings realistically by painting backgrounds to his assemblages. Carl was proud of his work and always signed it: One case had his name painted in gold on a shell carefully placed in the foreground with the other bits and pieces of wood, stones, and grass. Eventually, he created seventy different small cases featuring the birds of northwestern New York.

Carl grew more adept at collecting animals for his taxidermic experiments. He worked alone or with Oz Mitchell, and the mounting of his collection soon became the center of his life. As his skills improved and his collection of taxidermy grew, so did his reputation as a boy who kept dead things in his room. "Was he not far more than queer? . . . Shouldn't he be put away, where in confinement he might recover from his apparent madness?" wrote a Glidden relative.[19] To add further insult to the community, Carl worked on his mounts on Sunday, against the accepted custom of the time, when the Lord's Day was reserved for prayer and contemplation. Carl felt confused and angered to encounter criticism for something that brought him such joy and pleasure. He had been considered a perfectly normal boy in Clarendon until then.

It seems strange that Carl fell under such fire for doing something that was advocated in the *Youth's Companion* and was a relatively common practice among boys at the time. But Carl's taxidermic work became obsessive, out of step, unbalanced. (The attitude he had towards work as an adolescent would characterize his life long efforts.) More likely the community's real seething condemnation of Carl was that he was wasting his time. Lewis wrote: "They were puritanic in their belief that a youngster should employ every minute of his life in a puritanically profitable manner, and they made Carl's life a burden to him by their offensive insistence on their view, so much so that it required almost a lifetime for him to overcome his resentment toward them."[20]

This early condemnation of Akeley's taxidermic efforts sowed another seed. He never saw himself as "just a taxidermist." In fact, he rarely called himself a taxidermist; he was a sculptor. This notion that taxidermy was not a worthy enterprise touched him, compelling him to transform it into something of which he could be justly proud.

Carl's mother was pressured to pull her boy into line. Already torn between wanting to see Carl do well, and hating the foul odors emanating from his bedroom, she had to deal with societal pressures as well. Webb encouraged his son and refused to let community opinion rattle him. But it was a difficult time for Carl, during which he must have sought his mother's support and found it tentative or nonexistent. Later on, when Carl found success, his mother was very proud of her son's efforts, which held a place of

11

honor in her sitting room: Her collection included a small piece of Jumbo's skin—a remnant of Carl's earliest major achievement, as we shall later see. And even in his youth, she did allow him to mount a white rabbit on a tree stump in the front yard—surely a statement to her neighbors that she, on some level, supported her son's work.

Carl, however, saw and felt only the sting of their early relationship. Lewis described Carl's relationship with their mother as "dreadful." "But there was with me [Lewis] as with him, something unnatural about our relations. Carl was bitter about it, and rightly so I think . . . It is probably impossible to tell the truth about the Akeleys and keep within the bounds of good taste."[21] (Lewis refers to the airing of the family's "dirty linen;" he is not suggesting anything aberrant or perverse.) Akeley seemed to have blamed his mother for his unhappiness, and carried over negative aspects of this early relationship to his marriages: His mother seems to have been incapable of defending and supporting Carl when he needed it most, and as an adult he was ravenous in his demand for total commitment and unqualified support from his wives.

Mingled in these incidents are triumphs and heartbreak, played out against a background of frustration and grief. Carl Akeley did not have the solid underpinnings he needed in order to grow into a mature, happy man. Lewis later wrote that Carl "is never happy unless he is so full of trouble that nothing less than his remarkable powers of concentration can save him from distraction."[22]

For a few months, when Carl was sixteen, he went to the Brockport Normal School not far from Clarendon. His parents traveled weekly to Brockport, bringing Carl food for the week, as they had done for his brother before him. The boys were too poor to buy store food. Carl, like Lewis, must have lived in a rooming house with kitchen privileges. Each week he carefully measured out the supplies, allocating just enough, no more, for each day. His real joy at Brockport was finding David Bruce, whose beautiful little animal cases had inspired and haunted him when he was a child. Between classes he made a beeline for Bruce's workshop, where he spent countless hours watching Bruce working at his taxidermy bench, tanning this or mounting that. David Bruce enjoyed Akeley; he was impressed with his ability, his creativity, and his wry sense of humor.

Again Carl hated school, and after only six months, returned to the farm, where he labored sunup to sundown. He persevered there for another couple of years, working with Ward, Thomas, and their father. Their parents found the money to send Lewis to the University of Rochester; he was on his way to being a great scholar and teacher. Carl was miserable. During this period back on the farm, he tried with a sort of punctuated equilibrium to do what was expected of him, working hard, and rarely finding time to work on his little cases. It was an especially hard time for Carl after he had seen the

12

possibility of the perfect life in watching Bruce. Yet, with Lewis gone, he had the responsibility of helping his family. He had to grow up and make a life for himself. Nature, however, won out, and Carl went to his father to tell him what he already knew. Carl was determined to see if he, too, like Bruce, could find fulfillment and happiness as a part-time taxidermist. Rather than balking or trying to convince him otherwise, his father blessed his decision. Carl packed his bags and left again for Brockport. He returned to Bruce and asked for a job in his decorating shop, with the understanding that when his day's work was finished, Bruce would allow him to help in the taxidermy studio.

Bruce was a scientist, painter, naturalist, and taxidermist who was born in Kent, England in 1832. He had begun his career collecting birds for their plumes, which he prepared for use in ladies' hats. Soon the more complicated techniques of taxidermy intrigued him. He also developed into a painter of local renown, generally remembered for his tropical murals featuring jungle vegetation and brightly colored birds. Many fine Rochester residents commissioned him to decorate their dining rooms or the walls of winding staircases with his murals. Later, Bruce would receive a government assignment to make a collection of butterflies and moths of the United States, and would travel extensively throughout the west, making Colorado Springs his headquarters. In his Brockport community, David Bruce was remembered as a man of "retiring nature, but extremely gifted, very accurate and fast in the preparation of his work."[23]

David Bruce was pleased to have the nineteen-year-old aboard. Akeley was ecstatic: "It seemed to me," he wrote, "that a glorious future was settled for me then and there. If I was not in the seventh heaven, I was at least in the sixth and going up, and then my prospects became so favorable as to become almost terrifying."[24] Akeley was not encouraged to do much dreaming when he was a boy. The notion that dreams could be realized was a new one for him, and fraught with fear that they would remain just dreams, ephemeral hints at what could be. And the prospect of realizing a dream, only to have it collapse was even more terrifying. But Akeley was brave, and took risks throughout his life. He believed that he could follow in Bruce's footsteps, and applied the full force of his determination to accomplishing the task.

Carl spent his days doing carpentry work, wallpapering, plastering walls, and painting the beautiful old Victorian homes in Brockport and the surrounding towns; he might well have assisted Bruce in painting his murals or other decorative flourishes. It was in Carl's personality to enjoy the precision and the specificity of his tasks, and he loved retiring to the studio when his work was done. Soon he felt confident enough to have business cards printed, announcing to the world that he did "artistic taxidermy in all its branches."

He was only with Bruce a few months when Bruce called for a meeting with him. The man had some serious words for Akeley. He praised his work and felt strongly that Carl had already outgrown the demands of his small shop and that he should move on to where he could develop his skills more completely and broaden his vision. David Bruce generously understood that his student exceeded his own talent, and encouraged him to separate and find a fuller life for himself.

Bruce encouraged Akeley to go to Ward's Natural Science Establishment in Rochester. Ward's was a taxidermy studio-factory that turned out mounted specimens for museums all over the country. It was the most famous studio of its kind. If Akeley found the notion of fulfillment in Bruce's shop terrifying, he must have been genuinely stunned at David Bruce's suggestion that he move into the world of taxidermy as a bona fide professional. Buoyed by Bruce's belief in him, and encouraged by his father, Akeley's terror galvanized him to meet his new life head on.

Young Carl Akeley rose before dawn after a sleepless night. He might well have watched Orion in the night sky through his window—Orion, the famous hunter blinded by an angry parent, exposing his empty eye sockets to the rising sun to recover his sight. He shaved with water warmed in the dark kitchen and dressed in his finest clothing. His parents and brothers saw him off for the last time. With a heart filled with anticipation and hope, he set out for Rochester, twenty miles away, and Mr. Ward's Natural Science Establishment.

WARD'S NATURAL SCIENCE ESTABLISHMENT

Viam inveniam, aut faciam.
(I will either find or make a way.)
　　—Motto of Ward's Natural
　　Science Establishment

A S CARL WALKED from the train station toward Ward's, located on the perimeter of the University of Rochester campus, his satchel grew heavier. He chose a labyrinthine route, hoping that his footsteps would feed his fast-draining courage and warm his cold hands. He plodded on for quite a while, finally stopping before the huge sperm whale jaws suspended above the entrance gate to Ward's Natural Science Establishment. The gaping jaws both repelled and seduced visitors at the gate. "This is not a museum but a working establishment, where all are very busy," read a sign hanging from the mouth. No welcome mat here.

After a time, Carl passed under the toothy mouth and made his way along the path past a gruesome stuffed gorilla clinging to a tree branch. He ignored the dead primate and made his way to Professor Henry Ward's house and rang the bell. He was admitted and escorted into a room reminiscent of the beautifully appointed rooms he'd seen in the homes of his mother's relatives. But he found no consolation in his memories. He was scared. The door seemed to explode open, and in walked a "very busy, very brusque, and very fierce man." Akeley later wrote that "not even when a leopard sprang on me in Africa have I had a worse moment than when this little man snapped

15

out, 'What do you want?' The last vestige of my pride and assurance was centered on my business card, and without a word I handed him this evidence of my skill and art as a taxidermist."[1]

Akeley's strong sense of bravura paid off, and Ward offered him a salary of $3.50 per week. The least expensive boarding house that he could find, however, charged $4.00 per week, so Carl shared a room with his cousin, Willis Matson, who may have helped him out by picking up the financial slack.

When Akeley arrived at Ward's in 1883, the Establishment was the cradle of taxidermy in the United States. A circular advertising Ward's described the institution:

> To the small boy this is a benevolent institution, where cats, turtles, birds' eggs, snakes, and other 'vermin' can be converted into cash. To the naturalist we are a place of terrible temptation, where rare and beautiful specimens of all kinds unite to awaking covetous cravings. To the optician and jeweler we are simply dealers in rough diamonds, gems and the like. The great furriers know us solely as artistic taxidermists, to whom the costliest skins can be entrusted for manufacture into rugs and ornaments. With curators of museums we are builders of systematic collections, perfect in their range and scope; the Egyptologist looks to us for his mummies and coffins, his inscriptions and scarabs; the ethnologist finds here his skulls and weapons, idols and clothing of wild and vanished races; the geologist an assortment of rocks, ores, minerals, crystals, models, relief maps and charts unapproached in America; and the zoologist a more comprehensive group of the animal kingdom than ever Noah shipped, unless that navigator was armed with a compound microscope, a deep-sea dredge, an Arctic sledge and an elephant rifle.

Henry Ward was a renowned collector and traveler, who in 1862 gave his peerless geologic collection to the University of Rochester, and was made professor of geology in the institution. He was not fitted for academia, preferring to vent his passion for travel and collecting. He founded the Establishment while still teaching at the University, building it on the campus, and using the revenue to underwrite his travel/collecting expeditions. Ward felt that American teachers would benefit from having fossil reproductions to illustrate their lectures. He traveled worldwide to find some of the most important specimens, and reproduced them in plaster.

In addition to exploring the museums of sophisticated European cities, Ward had traveled to more remote corners of the earth, including West Africa's Niger River in 1859, when he was twenty-five years old. Gripped with blackwater fever, a type of malaria characterized by passing dark-colored urine, he was put ashore and deserted by the frightened and superstitious river boat crew. As the story goes, a woman rescued and nursed him with marriage in mind. Ward slipped from her grip and somehow, miraculously, made it back to Rochester. Feeling tender and grateful, Ward sent a crate of gifts, to be left by a passing ship, to his generous savior. His exploits were such that at a party in London, David Livingstone himself singled out the professor from more distinguished guests to discuss their African adventures.

As he worked at his new job, Akeley heard the tales of Ward's adventures that buzzed through the shops like a flute harmonic—excited, real but unpalpable. The professor's return from an expedition was eagerly anticipated. He brought back treasures, including skins and bones of exotic creatures with textures, colors, patterns, and forms that Akeley had never even imagined. These experiences gave him his first glimpse of the animals that would become central to his later life.

The Establishment was unique in the history of American science. It not only supplied specimens to scientific societies, hospitals, and museums, but also provided scholarly information and data on the specimens. While an offspring of the institution's work was educational, its primary purpose was strictly commercial.

As noted in the circular, taxidermy was but one of the aspects of Ward's Natural Science Establishment, but it was the most famous. The growing popularity of taxidermy in the late 1880s was a result of a collecting frenzy for natural objects for collector's cabinets—a want for curios that swept the western industrial nations after the publication of Darwin's *Origin of the Species*. During this period, people began examining nature from a different point of view, in terms natural selection and evolution. While the scientific community grappled with, argued about, and probed the Darwinian concepts, "nature" became the rage with the general public. But it was nature arrested in time: animals in alcohol bottles, in drawers, or stuffed and mounted under glass bell jars or in ornamental cases. These treasures appointed the parlors and studies of the enlightened and sensitive. The specimens were still beautiful, but lifeless—reduced to conversation pieces.

From "crystal palaces" to liquor store windows, mounted creatures gazed at humans looking at them. Taxidermy was a booming business. At Ward's one could buy anything from a pig embryo, a giant armadillo, a lyre bird skin, or a fossil to a gorilla or bull giraffe. The demand was great. Little attention was paid to quality output, even though Ward's was producing the best work around.

The profession as a whole was relatively young, less than a century old. (There was one mount, a rhinoceros, at the Royal Museum of Vertebrates in Florence, Italy dating to 1600, but no record exists of how it was mounted.) Already some thoughtful practitioners were trying to redefine it. At Ward's there was a Society of American Taxidermists, a group of young employees who wanted to work toward more artistic appeal. Specifically, they wanted to elevate the quality of museum exhibits. Ward's, however, was not an art school, but a commercial enterprise, and the products had to fulfill both the financial and aesthetic demands of the clients. If the money-spending buyers wanted inexpensive, theatrical, sensational, often grisly stuffed mounts, it hardly mattered what a group of motivated young artisans wanted. The society was short-lived, surviving only three years, but it succeeded in influencing taxidermists to aspire to a higher level of artistic accomplishment.

By the time that Akeley had arrived, Ward's had grown to a complex of about fifteen buildings and sheds, and had a work force of about twenty-two men. It was a polyglot community, including French, German, Italian, and American employees, each an expert in some aspect of preparation or mechanical work in the areas of taxidermy, osteology, carpentry, or blacksmithing. The work was intense, lasting from 7:00 A.M. to 6:00 P.M., with no holidays and no sick leave. The workers had to learn anything new on their own time, and they had to finance their own experiments. Though specialists, the men were expected to solve problems in areas outside their expertise.

In the early 1880s, the Establishment published an illustrated magazine, *Ward's Natural Science Bulletin*, which was a precursor to later popular scientific publications. Created as an advertising circular, it developed into a legitimate science magazine. It revealed the educational work of the Establishment through fine descriptions and classifications of Ward's zoological holdings. The employees were urged to contribute to the *Bulletin* in their spare time, without the advantage of even a typewriter.

As in the college itself, there was a great sense of fellowship at Ward's. Most of the young men were on their own for the first time, which produced feelings of vitality and freedom. Professor Ward was wise enough to understand the need for an environment richer than nonstop work and drudgery. There was a "Shakespeare's Club" in which the men could participate, again in their spare time. The exercises in Shakespeare recitation were meant to teach confidence in public speaking and to foster appreciation for the sheer beauty of the language, a classical respite from the down and dirty work of scraping flesh off of disjointed bones. Many of Ward's employees went on to be leaders in American science, and these early exercises in public speaking gave them a good foundation for the classroom or lecture hall.

Professor Ward was a difficult administrator: tough, judgmental, and prone to favoritism. Nonetheless, the advantages of working for him were vast for a young naturalist, if one had the curiosity and ambition of an Akeley. Akeley's full life at Ward's excited him as he learned and experienced marvelous things. Handling macerating skeletal material scooped up from the sludge at a tub's bottom was an excellent way to learn about anatomy. It was like fitting together a great puzzle. He also enjoyed, for a brief time at least, learning the current methods of taxidermy.

Akeley apprenticed himself to William Critchley, who had the "voice and physique of an Italian opera tenor."[2] Critchley had attained the highest proficiency in the taxidermic methods of his day. The techniques were an improvement on those used a century earlier, when specimens were cooked or baked into hard, mummylike little forms. They were also more advanced than the ones Akeley had employed on his bird and mammal cases, but they were hardly innovative or creative. Akeley quickly grew dissatisfied and restless. He believed that there was yet a better way of mounting animals than that used at Ward's. He was put off by the "upholsterer's" method of mounting animals, in which a skin was sewn up, like a pillow, and stuffed with straw or excelsior until it would hold no more, then "artistically" pulled in with thread here and there to create contour. Later on, the mounted animals often hosted dermestid beetles which ate away at the skin, causing the mount to buckle or sag in a hideously unlifelike way. These mounts appalled Akeley's aesthetic sensibility. "It did not take me long to find out that the profession which I had chosen as the most satisfying and stimulating to a man's soul was neither scientific nor artistic as it was practiced at Ward's. We used a method that was simplicity itself. Needless to say, the creatures resulting were awkward, stilted and unnatural. There was no opportunity whatever to carry out my dream of animals mounted in characteristic attitudes, grouped among leaves and branches before a realistically painted background."[3]

Akeley started fantasizing about how the mounts could be more artistic. He always worked things out in his mind, figuring and refiguring, going through each minute step to an idea's conclusion. If the idea seemed plausible, he would invest materials on it, experimenting further. When a zebra carcass was delivered to the Establishment one day, Akeley asked if he could make plaster casts of it. Granted permission, he carried out his tasks after work, laboring late into the night. The next morning the zebra was taken away from him and mounted in the usual way. His casts were pitched on the garbage heap—business as usual. On another occasion he wanted to experiment with a new method of removing the skin itself, again with a zebra. Again he worked into the early morning hours. He removed the skin by making only a few incisions, located where they would not be seen when resewn. He successfully removed the skin, having made only a few cuts along the belly, along the mane, and just above the hooves in the back. The purpose of the experiment was to see if he could peel the leg skin off of the animal like a stocking, and then roll the leg skins up again on a mount, thus eliminating visible seams when the mount was completed. It worked just as he had imagined it would. Thrilled and exhausted, he went to bed. When he arrived the next morning, he found that an unnamed, malicious saboteur had slit the leg skins from hoof to belly, destroying his skin.

Akeley was an indefatigable perfectionist who never ceased giving full energy and concentration to the task at hand. He was solitary, driven, and often arrogant. He made enemies at Ward's—especially of those who were threatened by his accomplishments and ambitions. But William Critchley was a real friend to Akeley during this period. He respected Akeley's talent and skill, which soon surpassed his own. Easygoing and hard-working, Critchley supported Carl and encouraged him to improve and elevate their chosen profession.

While disheartened by the destruction of his work itself, Akeley had to have felt the human hand in the mean act even more keenly. But he was proficient at pushing emotions aside and moving on with his work. He had a success and that surpassed any petty acts perpetrated by his associates. Akeley continued to plan carefully, staring off into space, figuring and refiguring every detail before beginning the execution of a task.

His desk had a disheveled appearance, cluttered with pictures of the animals he was working on in various positions. Ward was distressed by Akeley's behavior, and discussed the matter with Critchley. "Ward said that he did not like Akeley. He liked to see his men working. Akeley always had the appearance of loafing."[4] Henry Ward, son of the professor, was Akeley's foreman. One day he couldn't find Akeley when he was supposed to be working. A search of the building found Carl sound asleep on a pile of tanned skins in the attic—hardly surprising, given his self-imposed, rigorous schedule. When admonished about his absence, Akeley told Ward it was none of his business. This was not the first time that Akeley was insubordinate to his superiors. He often "talked back to Ward [senior] when the latter took any kind of a domineering attitude toward him . . . [he would not] submit to his overbearing attitudes."[5] Throughout his life, Akeley continued to have a reputation for speaking his mind. He "never minced words, but gave things their right names. His language was sometimes unconventional to put it mildly."[6] On the occasion of Henry Ward's reprimand, Akeley apparently went too far. Ward reported the incident to his father, and Akeley was fired.

Carl was genuinely shocked, and sought out his brother Lewis, still at the University of Rochester. Arriving in Lewis's room frantic and depressed, Carl told Lewis what had happened. Lewis wrote: "It struck me as a tragedy of the first magnitude. I could not think what he could do. It was unthinkable that he would go back to the farm."[7]

Akeley had slammed the door to the only institution that had given him what he wanted. His only visible recourse was a shop (it could not even be called a studio) he knew of in Brooklyn, New York. "He did not know that Wallace would employ him. He just went as a desperate boy entering the only avenue of escape in sight on the blind chance that he would find something."[8]

Akeley left Ward's and traveled to New York. John Wallace was a commercial taxidermist "who stuffed, most literally, more animals than any one man."[9] Akeley rented a room from Doctor Issac Kaufman Funk, a clergyman and publisher. Funk was associated at the time with St. Matthews English Lutheran Church in Brooklyn, and eventually became a founder of the publishing company Funk and Wagnalls.

In Brooklyn, Akeley suffered the full impact of his current life crisis. He was disgusted with taxidermy, his chosen profession. It had not panned out as the heaven he envisioned; it was, in fact, little more than a trade. The only thing that kept Akeley from going mad with misery were his visits to the Metropolitan Museum of Art in Manhattan, where he spent hours looking at its sculpture. Akeley knew that he was an artist and capable of doing fine work. He wanted to be a sculptor, saying later that he had the "fever of sculpturing in his blood."[10] Looking at the bronze and marble pieces at the Metropolitan fed Akeley spiritually, fueling his hopes and dreams for his own artistic fulfillment.

But the visits also fed a growing fear that he would never attain the life to which he aspired. Abruptly, Akeley stopped going to the Metropolitan because he became "depressed" when he thought about wanting to be a sculptor. He was very unhappy in Brooklyn. The taxidermy shop at Wallace's was in the basement of a building under the Brooklyn Bridge. Light rarely penetrated the dank room and the river traffic noises assaulted the ears. The work he was doing was dreadful and unappealing. (The type of mounts produced at Wallace's were stuffed crows selling whiskey, stuffed bears selling furs, and dogs treeing cats.) The sculptures at the Metropolitan were finely executed and inspiring—many were masterpieces. Akeley's morale was low and he found it impossible to believe that he could share in that world. He doubted that he could compete in the artistic discipline of sculpture. Akeley wrote that he had enough sense to understand that his contributions to sculpture could never be as significant as those he could make to taxidermy— an admission critical to his life and career. (On another level, it is important to note that Akeley chose to concentrate his efforts in areas where little or nothing had been done before. He did not compete in arenas populated by other artists. True, he was a visionary, but he chose to excel in fields where he would not or could not be judged in the context of others' accomplishments. Akeley called himself a sculptor in the world of taxidermy.)

Akeley's boss, John Wallace, was "irascible and dominating"—the kind of person that Carl loathed. There was friction between the two: Akeley still would not suffer fools, and mouthed off to his superior. Fortunately for Akeley, before the relationship deteriorated to the point of another dismissal, Ward wrote him that his firing had been a mistake. He had been reviewing financial records and realized that Akeley's work was fetching higher prices than the others'. Akeley wrote back with wile and some humility. He told Ward that Wallace was "very kind," that they "got along very well together,"[11] and that Wallace could keep him in work for several months paying him a much better salary than he had received at Ward's. Akeley also said that he would very much like to return to Ward's as he could only really become a first-rate craftsman at that institution, and that he needed ten dollars a week, even though he was receiving fifteen dollars a week at Wallace's. Finally, Akeley apologized for his behavior: "I know now where I made a mistake and freely admit that it was my fault."[12]

21

Carl Akeley

The requested raise was quite a jump from $3.50, but Ward told him to come back at the old salary and within a month he would be given the new rate. Both egos remained intact, each man getting the other to do what he wanted. Carl had remained in Brooklyn about six months, and it is likely that he had visited the American Museum of Natural History, just across Central Park from the Metropolitan, during this period.

When Akeley returned to Ward's in early 1884, there was a new member of the staff, William Morton Wheeler. Ward himself had invited Wheeler to the institution from Milwaukee, Wisconsin. He would be one of Akeley's closest friends and touch his life on many levels.

Professor Ward had heard that there was to be a large exposition in Milwaukee in 1883. Seizing the opportunity to make a major sale of an Establishment collection, he went to Milwaukee, and convinced the city officials they needed a collection of his artifacts and specimens for their show. Ward suggested to them that if they joined the collection to a small existent museum, they would have the foundation for a free natural history museum for the city.

Natural history museums were beginning to crop up all over the country. This phenomenon grew out of the industrial revolution's gift of leisure time to the American people and the desire for "nature" amidst the nation's growing urbanization. Ward's idea appealed to Milwaukee's desire to fall into step with some of the larger eastern cities. (Milwaukee then outdistanced Chicago as a cultural center.) The city fathers bought the idea and the collection. William Morton Wheeler was Ward's young volunteer at the small museum, assisting him in unpacking specimens. Ward was so impressed with Wheeler that he offered him a job at the Establishment—for nine dollars a week! He also offered him room and board in his own home, for which he charged him six dollars a week. Wheeler moved to Rochester.

Will Wheeler was two years older than Akeley and was made a foreman almost immediately. He was then set to work identifying and arranging collections of invertebrates. Akeley and Wheeler became fast friends and spent much of their off hours together. Wheeler was an extremely bright, heady and cultured young scientist who read Latin classics for recreation. His diaries also reveal a rather tortured soul full of the dramatic angst typical of many twenty year olds. Akeley, more practical and down-to-earth, and less educated, proved to be Wheeler's counterpart in many ways. Wheeler described Akeley as "very strong and healthy, [he] had an inexhaustible capacity for work, a great fund of quiet humor, and a thoroughly manly disposition."[13] Theirs was an odd relationship, which they likened to older and younger brothers. Each found in the other qualities that he found lacking in himself.

Wheeler opened Akeley up to wider cultural and mental landscapes. There was a lot to do in Rochester in the mid-1880s. The city was enjoying an intellectual and cultural renaissance, offering plays, musicals, dances, and other activities. Road companies, featuring such major attractions as Sarah Bernhardt starring as Camille, had played Rochester. In 1884 two theaters opened that provided risque entertainment: girls dressed in flesh-colored unitards posed as nude paintings. These "dime museums," so-called for their ten-cent admission charge, attracted scores of young men. They died out quickly because their proprietors were unable to secure liquor licenses. Wheeler found them disgusting. Akeley probably rather enjoyed them. Both men enjoyed the fact that the dime museums helped drive down the costs of legitimate entertainment.

Rochester was also a center of debate between science and theology. A local Unitarian minister, Dr. Newton M. Mann, was one of the first clerics in America to grasp the implications of Darwin's theories of evolution. He held that if all of life's functions were in the process of evolution, then the soul shared in this process. Wheeler and Akeley heard Mann "give a magnificent sermon."

The two went to Chautauqua lectures together, favoring the talks promoting freethinking not only in religious matters but in general. One of their favorites was Robert G. Ingersoll, a popular Republican/Agnostic lawyer whom Wheeler described as a real he-man. Ingersoll made a deep impression on Akeley, who quoted him for decades. Akeley and Wheeler enjoyed the stimulating evenings, rife with lively discussion, debate, and repartee.

Akeley impressed Wheeler with his endless capacity for creativity, invention, and his manual dexterity—"the greatest range of innate ability," Wheeler said, that he had ever witnessed in any person. Wheeler was restless, "unsettled mentally" and often irritable, but the two men never quarreled, owing to "Akeley's self-restraint and sympathetic tolerance."[14] Not many friends and acquaintances of Akeley's would agree with Wheeler's description of him. Love and respect bonded the friends. Akeley would bend only for people who held his respect. Both Wheeler and Akeley were careful never to cross the other's line. It is also possible that Akeley had learned something in the dismissal from Ward's. He checked his impatient and outspoken inclinations. Later in his life he would suppress great wells of fury, allowing them to seethe and "boil inside" only to explode in temper when others would not or could not accept his way of doing things. While quite different, Wheeler and Akeley shared elemental qualities. They were both gifted with humor and childlike exuberance. They also suffered from sporadic bouts with melancholia (both would have nervous breakdowns later in their lives). And finally, they shared the excitement and thrill that only nature can provide, and celebrated it in the microcosm and macrocosm. The two men were joined in a great adventure—trying to discover the mystery of life itself.

By June 1885, both friends felt that they had exhausted the possibilities at Ward's and decided to move on. Wheeler wrote many years later:

Of active, industrious young men there are two types. One of them accepts a given environment and is not only satisfied with its routine and constantly recurring human contacts but prefers it to any change. These young men are apt to marry early and become the conservative and contented *fond* of our society. Those of the other type, probably endowed with a more unstable if not more vivid imagination and with a peculiar defense reaction, or subconscious dread of being owned by people or things, soon exhaust the possibilities of their medium, like fungi that burn out their substratum, and become dissatisfied and restless till they can implant themselves in fresh conditions of growth. Akeley and I were of this latter type.[15]

In the summer of 1885, Wheeler left for Milwaukee. He had been tutoring Lewis Akeley in German during Lewis's attendance at the University, and both Wheeler and Lewis had encouraged Carl to seek a higher education himself. To this end Wheeler tried to persuade Carl to follow him to Milwaukee that fall. He promised Akeley that he would tutor him for entrance into Sheffield Scientific School at Yale. Akeley did not follow. A major career opportunity had presented itself in a macabre locomotive accident in St. Thomas, Canada. P.T. Barnum's famous circus elephant, Jumbo, collided with a locomotive and was killed.

Jumbo was an international star. He had been purchased in England over the cries and castigations of British children, including the Prince of Wales, and even Queen Victoria herself. They were furious to have Jumbo reduced to a cash sale to the Americans, and there was a huge national outcry for Jumbo's owner, the Zoological Society, to cancel the deal. But the money (ten thousand dollars) had already been accepted. Barnum would not budge, and was more determined than ever to take the animal to America, grateful for all the free publicity. (Jumbo was sold partly because of his intractable behavior. With Barnum, the animal became docile and good-natured. The irony is that Jumbo was probably in a bad temper because he was cutting his twenty-eight-year molars; elephants have five sets in their lifetime. As soon as the teeth were in and no longer causing him discomfort, the animal returned to his easygoing ways. He probably would not have been a problem again until he teethed his last set of molars during his forties.[16])

Jumbo, who had led circus parades, enthralled millions of American children for three years. He was gigantic (ten feet, nine inches tall), good humored and remarkably intelligent. He was born in Abyssinia (now Ethiopia), and had been bought and sold several times before Barnum employed him to move railroad cars and lead parades.

Two years before the accident, P.T. Barnum had arranged with Ward that if the animal died, his workers were to be telegraphed immediately and sent to save the skin and skeleton. They were to mount the animal on a moving float so that the star attraction could lead the parades in death as he had in life. Jumbo's sudden death set the wheels in motion quickly. William Critchley and his assistant, Carl Akeley, were assigned the task.

Even though Critchley and Akeley left for Canada as soon as possible, the carcass had already started to putrefy by the time that they arrived. It seemed an exercise in folly to remove the already rotting flesh, but Akeley felt certain that the skin could be saved. Critchley ended up assisting Akeley in the disgusting work, both gagging and retching as they cut away the skin with the finesse of surgeons. The stench was atrocious; it was enough to "gag a maggot," Akeley would comment later. The men hired some local butchers to assist them because time was so dear. The salted skins were taken back to Ward's, where the real efforts began.

Barnum wrote to Ward asking him to make the mount of Jumbo even larger than the living animal had been. They set about to accomplish the task, finding little precedent for mounting large animals to guide them. Earlier in the century, a few such mounts had been created in Europe. In 1817, an elephant was mounted for the Jardin du Roi—later the Musée d'Histoire Naturelle—in France. The crude method consisted of building a large wooden manikin, then shaving down the alum-soaked skin to varied thicknesses and nailing it to the wood. The method would result in the skin cracking as it expanded and contracted according to weather conditions. Jumbo was mounted in much the same way, but Akeley added something new to the process. Over the wooden armature he nailed small thin strips of basswood, steam-treated to curve and bend, giving the impression of musculature. The tanned skin was then sewn in sections and attached to the armature. Paint and putty were added to the exterior and—voilà—the mount looked very much like the live Jumbo.

Barnum was very pleased, and Akeley received his first major recognition. The mount was unveiled on February 26, 1886 at the Powers Hotel in Rochester. The site was adjacent to the Powers Building, where Akeley had been inspired by David Bruce's work several years before. The unveiling was a major public relations event for Barnum. The press was given a lavish banquet and, it is said, were served a jelly made from part of Jumbo's powdered tusks.[17] Jumbo's noble forty-pound heart was offered for sale for forty dollars. The circus traveled with both the skin and the articulated skeleton of Jumbo for several years before the skin was given to Tufts University. (In 1975 a fire destroyed the mount.) The skeleton was given to the American Museum of Natural History, where it stands as a silent sentry next to the mammalogy freezer on the third floor, sadly inaccessible for such an historic piece.

For Akeley, the whole "Jumbo experience" was exceedingly important. Wheeler wrote: "His superb neuromuscular organization seemed to have been specially designed to give plastic expression to the refractory hide of the huge quadruped, and the successful accomplishment of the task furnished the inspiration for his later work in Africa, the Field Museum and the American Museum."[18] Akeley learned first hand about the physiology and anatomy of elephants by working with the bone, muscle, and sinew of the animal. The species caught his imagination by way of the tales and anecdotes surrounding Jumbo, and later on, elephants would become an obsession and a constant theme in his work. Lastly, through this experience Akeley received wonderful recognition for his accomplishment.

During the five months that it took to mount Jumbo, Carl met Harrison B. Webster, a professor of Biology at the University of Rochester. Many students and teachers from the university would visit Ward's studios to watch Jumbo being mounted. Webster met Akeley during one of these visits, and was impressed with him. He told Akeley that "he did not have to scrape bones all his life and that he should take a university course and get the equipment necessary to be a naturalist."[19] The idea had already been implanted by Wheeler, but the encouragement of a prestigious professor must have added further weight to the notion. Akeley took Latin and geometry and started to dress like a college student. For a while he fancied himself a scholar, but he gave it up in short order. "Carl had sense enough to see that college would be the death of all his dreams."[20] Webster understood and encouraged him to follow his heart.

Wheeler, in the meantime, had accepted a teaching position in Milwaukee. He was very involved in the growth of the Milwaukee Public Museum, which had been established along Professor Ward's suggested guidelines. Wheeler saw an opportunity for Akeley to create mounted specimens for the museum. He continued his campaign to encourage Akeley to go to the Sheffield Scientific School, and persuaded him to come to Milwaukee and live so that he could tutor him for his entrance exams. Akeley's opportunities at Ward's were played out.

The time that Akeley spent at Ward's, from ages eighteen to twenty-two, was like a time of incubation under a warm light. He learned a good deal about what he wanted, how to get it, and what his personal limitations were. His curiosity was nourished and encouraged by men very different from those who had impressed him earlier in his life. Akeley's world widened and his confidence grew. He left for Milwaukee with anticipation and excitement, but without the old terror that had gripped his heart on his earlier move. Carl was growing up.

YOUTH IN MILWAUKEE

A fine wind is blowing the new direction of Time.
If only I let it bear me, carry me, if only it carry me!
If only, most lovely of all, I yield myself and am borrowed
By the fine, fine wind that takes its course through the chaos of the world
Like a fine, an exquisite chisel, a wedge-blade inserted;
If only I am keen and hard like the sheer tip of a wedge
Driven by invisible blows,
The rock will split, we shall come at the wonder, we shall find the
*   Hesperides.*
—D.H. LAWRENCE, "Song of a Man Who Has Come Through"

THERE IS A PHOTOGRAPH of Carl Akeley taken when he was twenty-four years old and living in Milwaukee. It is the most sensitive extant photograph of him. He has the faraway look in his eyes that Wheeler often teased him about ("Are you really thinking, Carl, or are you just thinking that you're thinking?"[1]), but the child's sense of wonder that fed and challenged him until his death is strangely lacking in his face. Though he is still handsome, with a touch of residual sweetness in his countenance, his eyes and the corners of his nose are already strained; his jaw is set. He does not smile—the camera rarely caught him smiling. His white skin looks remarkably soft and smooth, hairless, almost feminine. His lips, which seem to have disappeared in thin tight lines by the end of his life, are still beautifully shaped and full—sensual. He looks silly in his too-small jacket, straining at the button, sleeve seams starting up over the tops of his shoulders giving his body a pinched, confined look, undignified—he seems not to notice or to care. Actually he

27

probably does care, as he spent effort to look fine in this studio portrait. One senses a broad strong back and powerful shoulders restrained and hidden from view. A scarf tied carefully around his neck conceals the fact that he wears only an undershirt under the jacket.

Carl Akeley detrained in Milwaukee on November 8, 1886, his step jaunty and secure, his heart vigorous and happy. Wheeler met him at the train. After dropping off Carl's bags at Wheeler's mother's home, the two headed immediately to the Milwaukee Public Museum to meet the "custodian," Carl Doerflinger, Akeley's new boss. Carl was first promised contract work, then a part-time position in taxidermy for fifty cents an hour. He was thrilled to be considered a "museum man."

The old friends were glad to see each other, and Wheeler was excited to show Akeley his haunts and to introduce him to friends. Wheeler was also anxious to begin Akeley's tutorial lessons for his admittance into the Sheffield Scientific School at Yale. He looked forward to the sessions more than Akeley did. Akeley felt the external pressure to produce on an intellectual level that did not quite fit with his personal aspirations. But he felt very strongly about doing the "right" thing and, at that point in his life, was still open to taking direction from those he loved and respected. Akeley plunged into Wheeler's world.

Milwaukee was exploding with energy and prosperity from industry and shipping on the Great Lakes and railroads. The desire to promote Milwaukee's industrial accomplishments had resulted in the Milwaukee Industrial Exposition of 1883. The city was a hotbed of German intellectual thought. The Milwaukee German community had been founded by emigrés fleeing from an unsuccessful revolution against the German monarchies in 1848. The Germans brought with them an intellectual and cultural ferment, particularly manifest in liberal social thought and a desire for education. In fact, education was a top priority for these highly educated Europeans, and they were determined to establish a school for their children that would educate them in German philosophy and thought.

The German-English Academy was established, and acquired a natural history collection. The school founders felt strongly that the study of natural objects was as important as book learning. As the collection grew, so did the responsibility for curating it, and eventually a small museum was established at the academy. It was to this collection that Professor Ward joined his own for the exposition. He had convinced the city fathers to invest twelve thousand dollars for his specimens, and to use the collections as the basis for the Public Museum. The museum held 1,575 specimens purchased from Ward's, including some large, showy items.

Will Wheeler, though not of German descent himself, had grown up in this German enclave of natural history and philosophy. He later described it as "a superheated atmosphere of German Kulture."[2] He had been educated in the German-English Academy. Even as a boy, Wheeler had helped out in whatever way he could with the natural history collection, eventually becoming one of its curators.

When Wheeler returned to Milwaukee after Ward's, he taught classes both in a public school and at the academy. He also participated enthusiastically in the Wisconsin Natural History Society, which met twice a month to hear papers presented and discussed by members. Wheeler's first paper was on beetles. Following his presentation, he was approached by a scientist named Charles Otis Whitman, who directed Allis Lake Laboratory, a research laboratory on Lake Michigan. Whitman was impressed by Wheeler, and encouraged him to spend time in his off hours on a research project at the laboratory.

Whitman was dedicated to enlarging the scientist's scope beyond specialization. Instead of greeting a fellow student with, "What is your special field?" Whitman urged them to ask, "What is your beast?"[3] It was a new notion of research. He admonished students not to overlook or ignore even a seemingly insignificant aspect of behavior. Whitman touched Wheeler's life for decades to come; his influence helped Wheeler become one of the prime movers in the world of biological ecology. And since Wheeler was a born teacher, Akeley, too, would be influenced by Whitman's philosophy of science, which would eventually find full expression in the field of ethology—animal behavior.

Initially Carl concentrated on adjusting to the new environment and preparing his studio. Wheeler's mother offered him a building on her property, which Akeley and Wheeler converted into a work space. Akeley started mounting a "trial" piece for the Public Museum to demonstrate his ability in taxidermy. The administration was pleased, and commissioned Akeley to do more mounts for exhibition.

Akeley often worked twelve to fourteen hours a day to make enough money to cover his expenses and save for the Sheffield Scientific School. As Akeley worked in his studio, Wheeler would visit him and do his own work in the company of his friend. Often repeating a habit from Ward's, Wheeler read aloud to Carl. He once read *Alice in Wonderland* in one sitting.

Wheeler was impressed with the philosophy of Arthur Schopenhauer, the renowned German philosopher who influenced existentialist thought and Freudian psychology. Schopenhauer's thought swerved away from spirit and reason, rushing headlong into the irrational, creativity, and the powers of intuition. The philosophy was vital, if tinged with pessimism, and excited Wheeler, who would prattle to Akeley about Schopenhauer's ideas as Akeley scraped skins or worked on his mounts. Akeley also listened to Aeschylus and to Max Nordau, a German physician-author, as he worked, bits and pieces of thoughts and ideas entering his subconscious. Occasionally, though rarely,

Akeley would enter into discussions, favoring history and politics over philosophy.

In one case, Akeley was thoroughly absorbed in Wheeler's reading. In the middle of Tolstoy's *Anna Karenina*, Wheeler abruptly stopped reading in order to complete an assignment of his own. Akeley, caught up in the novel, grabbed the book himself and began reading aloud to Wheeler.

They went to the theater and opera together. Essentially Wheeler gave Akeley a liberal education, reading an entire library of philosophy and the classics to him. To have been in Wheeler's brilliant company (Harvard philosopher, Alfred North Whitehead, said that Wheeler was the only man he ever knew "who would have been both worthy and able to sustain a conversation with Aristotle."[4]) on a daily basis, to have experienced the thrill of mystery-probing, to have consistently shared insights with him, undoubtedly made the Milwaukee period one of the most intellectually stimulating in Akeley's life. Soon, however, Akeley was exhausted from the grueling schedule of work and study. It did not take him long to again decide that schooling was not his cup of tea.

About one year into his Milwaukee era, Akeley received another letter from Professor Ward requesting his return to the Establishment. Akeley asked for fifteen dollars a week this time, but his heart was not in it; he liked being in Milwaukee, he liked the independence, he liked the praise he received for his work, and he liked the people that surrounded him. There is no record of Ward's response. Whether he refused outright or offered to negotiate, Akeley decided to stay in Milwaukee.

As soon as he was able to afford it, Carl moved to his own apartment, in the Norman building on Seventh Street and Grand Avenue (now Wisconsin Avenue). He began to make his own life. Akeley enjoyed being on his own for the first time, and made some friends of his own, though he continued to be part of Wheeler's extended family.

One of his new friends was a dentist who lived in his building, Charles G. Junkermann. Even though their professions were different, they found enough common ground for hours of discussion. Mechanical devices intrigued them both and they loved to explore ideas with each other, often leading to inventive flights of fancy. Appliances in particular fascinated them, and led them to collaborate on a new type of headrest for dental and surgical chairs. The blueprints for this rest are beautiful in their simplicity and economy of design. They attempted to patent their headrest in 1896, making it Akeley's first invention on record. But they failed because virtually the same design had been submitted to the U.S. Patent Office by another inventor in a different state only three weeks before.

Most of Akeley's creative efforts, however, were directed towards improving taxidermy techniques. He rented a bigger space than Mrs. Wheeler's barn, right across the street from the Norman. Some nights he was so tired that he did not even make it home, collapsing in a chair until morning. His studio was the corner of the world where he was happiest, giving full vent to his work and experiments. He allowed himself to explore the silly and whimsical as well: He created a costume for his landlady's twelve-year-old daughter for her school performance of *White Things That Never Grow Weary*. It was a costume made of real swan wings and was "very effective."[5]

The studio had many rooms. In one room there was only a tiny window and an enormous macerating tub which held huge skins. The lack of light and the strange shapes floating in the tub gave the room a weird, otherworldly quality. The next room was empty save for a mound of hay, home to an opossum mother and her young. The animals were semi-pets and quite tame. Akeley always tried to study the animals he would later mount, so that he could preserve in death their true vitality. The third and largest room of the studio had abundant light and space. Here Akeley had his work bench. He usually kept a live caged animal in this room as well. At this time many of the animals he worked on were small mammals and birds, easy to keep around. Occasionally, there were larger mounted animals standing in silent attention as Wheeler sat in his chair and read aloud for all to hear. At one point, Akeley mounted a gorilla in this space, but there is no evidence of its provenance. It seems that this gorilla was a butt of some humor or practical joke between the two men. (Joking about gorillas would later get Akeley into some trouble.) The studio also had a showroom built into what had been a porch, where mounts and designs for mounts were displayed. It was here that Akeley brought prospective buyers, both museum people and hunters.

Akeley invited many visitors to his studio, a pleasure he enjoyed throughout his life. He was at his best when demonstrating and discussing his work with a small group of friends on his own turf, surrounded by his artistry. Here he smoked and laughed in easy camaraderie. He was proud of the work he was doing. While his first business cards as a boy advertised "artistic taxidermy in all its branches," he now announced a more sophisticated technique on his letterhead: "scientific and decorative taxidermy," with a "specialty of fine group work."[6] This "fine group work" was where he was headed: Family units, animals in struggle, animals at peace—little scenes, little dramas. Actually his first "group work" consisted of an animal and a human trudging over the arctic snow.

One of the trustees of the Milwaukee Museum secured for the institution a sled, reindeer skins, and traditional clothing from Lapland. The whole package was given to Akeley, and he was assigned the task of preparing it for display. Rather than mounting the deer in a case, putting the sled in another case, and consigning the costume to an anthropological display by pinning it flat to a wall, Akeley created a little tableau. He mounted the deer skin over skeletonlike armature covered with plaster that he had sculpted to resemble the animal's anatomy. He harnessed the deer to the sled; seated within the sled holding the deer's taut rein was a costume-clad manikin. All were positioned on simulated snow. The group was a big success with the public and the administration. "It was the beginning of the Museum's tradition of innovative exhibit work that would eventually be called 'the Milwaukee style,' "[7] by historians of American natural history museums.

Wheeler was made custodian of the Milwaukee Museum in September of 1888, and saw to it that Akeley received many contracts. It was a real coup for the twenty-two-year-old Wheeler to snag this prestigious position. As an administrator, he wrote: "The Museum ought not to appear, as it doubtless does to many people, as a depository for cold and lifeless specimens intermingled with cards full of Latin and Greek names, nor as a place to which one can resort to spend an hour idly looking at what is merely marvelous or beautiful, but the Museum should be a place where everyone can feel at home in learning something about the material objects of the wonderful planet on which we live."[8] He closely examined the exhibits, which he felt were too crowded and inconsistently displayed; he began changing things, but wisely, only after he had studied the situation carefully for one year. Akeley and his splendid vision were part of Wheeler's plan.

In 1889 Wheeler saw to it that Akeley was elevated from the position of a part-time employee to a full staff member. He was given the title "taxidermist." Akeley's move had paid off. For the first time, he was a museum taxidermist, and his artistic methods were not only tolerated but encouraged—to a point.

The *Milwaukee Public Museum Annual Reports* are full of Akeley's accomplishments, citing the mounting of ostriches, bears, and a large variety of birds. Because Akeley received some kudos for his work, he felt confident enough to approach the museum's administration. He had an idea to create a series of exhibits featuring the fur-bearing animals of Wisconsin—a concept that extended far beyond adding a leaf here or some snow there. The trustees found it difficult to comprehend the value of such an exhibit. But Wheeler was in his corner, and Akeley succeeded in acquiring the necessary permission and funds to create a demonstration model.

To obtain the animals he needed, Akeley went on a series of small collecting expeditions to northern Wisconsin. He was probably accompanied by his friends, Delia and Arthur Reiss. Reiss was a barber, and Delia his beautiful young wife.

Akeley was impressed by Delia Reiss's charming, quiet aspect, belying an undercurrent of power that manifested itself in her fits of temper. Like himself, she had grown up on a farm under strapped circumstances, and, like himself, she had been desperate to leave it. She had run away from her home in Beaver Dam, Wisconsin, at thirteen and arrived in Milwaukee a scared but determined survivor. Akeley met her when she was fourteen or fifteen years old.

32

Delia, a.k.a. "Mickie" for her bellicose ways, was forever getting into scrapes. Her sharp temper and determination to have her way earned her a reputation in the community as "a little devil." Two vengeful acts reveal much about this side of her. The first was her manner of dealing with boys who teased her. She lay in wait to ambush them as they carried heavy buckets of water home from the well, rushing at them with sand or garbage to dump in their pails and spoil the water. The boys had to return to the well for a fresh supply, as she raced off triumphant. The other act of revenge was even meaner. A group of men who worked in a neighboring brick-making yard were fond of taunting and teasing Delia. She got even with them by stealing into the yard one night and systematically stepping on every new brick manufactured that day. She wore her father's shoes so that her identity would remain a mystery, but gloated over the fact that she had ruined a full day's work.[9] Delia was always sensitive to teasing and kept her shanty–Irish Catholic background a secret until she was an old woman.

The premeditated and determined nature of these acts reveal something of Mickie's struggle to make the world feel her presence. As the ninth child born to poor parents, she was more of a heartache than a blessing, and learned early on to fight for her place. Her father was sixty-one years old when she was born. He was an overbearing, domineering man whom she both revered and resented. Her relationship with him was the basis for her later attraction to the same type of man.

One day her father ordered her to bring water to the farmhands. She disobeyed him. A terrible fight ensued, and she walked out on her family and never looked back. Many years later she wrote that "washing dishes and making beds for a family that did not hesitate to criticize my efforts was to my mind a waste of precious time."[10] Like Akeley, she had a disastrous relationship with her mother, and her attitude toward her did not soften until well after her mother's death. Once on her own, Delia made her way to Milwaukee. There she met Reiss, who helped her get a job washing dishes. Later he decided to marry her; she was fourteen, he, much older.

Akeley and the Reisses became friends, sharing a love of hunting and the wilderness. An attraction grew between Akeley and Mickie on these outings. She became more and more fascinated with him and his work. Akeley was charming, funny, and very attractive, and the brooding, intense side of his nature and his needy childish quality could be seductive.

In spite of the constant presence of Mickie in Akeley's life—or perhaps because of it—Akeley went about his work with a greater fervor. He created his demonstration model—the muskrat group. It was his greatest accomplishment at the museum and still exists today. Wheeler wrote:

This group represents a fragment of marshland from one of our Wisconsin lakes on the approach of winter. The dome-shaped mass of vegetable matter accumulated by the muskrat is given in section so as to show the manner in which the chambers inhabited by the animals are connected in the water. The muskrats, five in number, are variously engaged in and about the water. The great difficulties in accurately imitating the boggy earth, the half dead vegetation and the stagnant water have been very successfully overcome by Mr. Akeley. The case containing the group was planned by Mr. Akeley and presents great advantages over the cases commonly used for such purposes.[11]

The importance of this first diorama cannot be overstated. In this small exhibit, the future of Akeley's brilliant work was promised. Akeley believed that an animal had to be mounted artistically to be able to communicate its inner spirit. But the life of the animal could not really be understood unless the animal was seen in the context of its environment. Instead of being mounted in glass cases, he felt that an animal should be shown in its domestic environ, surrounded by its family. In addition to the foreground accessories, he achieved this impression by using a curved and painted background executed perfectly in terms of perspective. The foreground seamlessly blended into this background.

An artist who does not use what he knows is a fool. A sentence from Lewis Carroll, a department store window, a label on a bottle of beer—everything goes into the mill and is grist for artistic expression. Akeley was no fool. A major art movement popular in Milwaukee at the time Akeley was there must have inspired him, even though no direct link exists. A group of German artists, two of whom were employed at the museum, worked in a Milwaukee studio that was producing cycloramas. These enormous pieces, circular pictures about fifty feet high and four hundred feet around, took a small army of artists half a year to complete. The accuracy of detail and scale remind contemporary gallery visitors of the photorealism movement. The themes were often epic, depicting famous battles and historical events. The audience stood at the center of the piece and pivoted slowly to take in the scene. Akeley loved such dramatic little worlds, and he no doubt loved the Milwaukee cycloramas.

Dioramas, too, had been around since the early 1800s. The word itself stems from the Greek dio "through" and horama "to see" hence "to see through." The word was coined by Louis J. M. Daguerre—inventor of the daguerreotype—and Charles-Marie Bouton to describe a theatrical entertainment that they developed for French audiences. These first dioramas consisted of an enormous painted translucent cloth which hung as a backdrop for houses, trees, boulders, etc. These scenes usually depicted European landscapes and less often, lavishly appointed interiors. Lighting effects used from behind created movement in the otherwise static piece. Eventually people were added to the scenes. In fact, the dime museums of Akeley's Rochester years developed from this original form of entertainment.

An artist uses what he knows. Akeley's ideas were not exclusively his own; he took ideas and made them his own. Akeley thought of himself as the originator of painted backgrounds: "So far as I know, that [referring to his bird cases in Clarendon] was the first experiment of painted backgrounds used for mounted birds or animals."[12] This notion is part of Akeley's self-manufactured legend. Either he was lying or he was simply unaware of the truth.

In fact, in the 1850s there was already much attention being paid to creating appealing backgrounds for animal mountings in Europe. E. T. Booth, of Brighton, England, is actually credited with first mounting bird groups using accessories and backgrounds. He stipulated that the backgrounds should reflect the animal's habitats. Even Charles Wilson Peale, fifty years before Booth, called for sketches of backgrounds representing the homes of mounted animals. The mounting of large mammals was also undergoing a conceptual transformation in the nineteenth century. Group work was nothing new. Groups were often arranged in highly dramatic poses, often in fighting stances such as lion vs. tiger or "Arab Courier Attacked by Lions." At Ward's, after his completion of Jumbo, Akeley himself had executed a mounting of an Indian elephant with its trunk coiled around a lion, holding it aloft the moment before hurling it to its death. These mounts were not considered valid for scientific purposes because they rarely represented the true behaviors of the animals.

In 1884, Professor George Brown Goode at the National Museum in Washington had twelve bird groups mounted in a natural way. Goode revolutionized the concept of exhibit for American museums. Early on he "recognized the educational possibilities of museums and the importance of making them interesting and attractive to the general public. One of his favorite maxims was to keep ever in mind the human interest in any exhibit, to show how it touched man directly . . . Few have possessed greater powers of analysis and classification as applied to exhibits and exhibitions than did Dr. Goode."[13]

While these ideas were in the wind, few museums had either the talent or the financial resources to execute the new notions of museum exhibition. Wheeler and Akeley were both visionaries. Since Wheeler was in power, monies were made available to Akeley for the time-consuming work. When we visit a museum today it is hard for us to comprehend that exhibition once was so primitive, or that it took such a Herculean effort to change it. Today we live in an era of state-of-the-art, scientific, Disneyland (in the best sense of that word) exhibition in museums and in our zoological parks as well.

Akeley's muskrat group was America's first complete habitat display to unfold the life of a creature scientifically and artistically. It was the first diorama to reveal the diversity and complexity of the ecosystem in which an animal lived. It was also the first museum exhibit to give enough information to the viewer to stimulate his imagination and to challenge him to probe deeper into the life of a muskrat and the world surrounding him. Akeley used what he knew and added intuition, imagination, and a touch of grace. He began where his predecessors left off. His genius was showing.

Akeley was pleased with his accomplishment. Its success gave him the impetus to delve even deeper into the problems and solutions of refining museum exhibits. And his obsession for transforming his craft into an art form grew stronger by the day.

The muskrat group was completed in 1890. The joy of triumph, however, was dampened by Wheeler's resignation. Wheeler was restless and wanted to continue his own research. His main interest, even during his museum directorship, had been entomology vis-à-vis taxonomy and embryology. C. O. Whitman at the Allis Laboratory was his mentor, encouraging him to pursue research in embryology. Whitman had just accepted a professorship at the new Clark University in Worcester, Massachusetts, and offered Wheeler a fellowship there. At that time, Clark represented the hope of the scientific future of the United States. Solely a graduate institution, Clark recruited young, brilliant scientists from around the country and encouraged them to work intensively in their fields of research. Wheeler thrashed about trying to decide whether to leave the Milwaukee Museum and his comfortable life, but soon realized that he had again "burned out his substratum" and needed a new place to grow. He was further encouraged to make the move by a friend and colleague of his who was already a Ph.D. candidate at Clark, H.C. Bumpus. (Bumpus would play a critical role in Akeley's life later on.) Wheeler accepted the fellowship and gave notice to the museum effective August 31, 1890.

The parting of Wheeler and Akeley in October was a terribly painful one. Akeley was losing not only a very close and beloved friend, but a champion and supporter of his work as well.

The focus of the museum's new administration shifted from internal concentration on exhibition philosophy and technique to external development. Fully ensconced as part of the cultural capital of the Midwest, the museum now needed to expand. Space was a major issue, and a capital campaign to raise money for a new facility was top priority. Somehow Akeley and his ambition for new exhibits fell through the cracks during this period. The remaining Wisconsin fur-bearing animal groups were never created. Actually, Akeley may not have cared that much because he was still concentrating his efforts on devising a method of mounting agile, lifelike large mammal specimens.

Akeley dragged on for two more years at the museum as he tried to find ways in which he, too, could resign from the institution. The creative highlight of this unhappy time was the mounting of a group of orangutans, his first primate grouping and the beginning of a lifetime involvement with the great apes. Soon after, he succeeded in finding a group of backers to finance him in setting up his own business, and opened a studio in DeKalb, Illinois, not very far from Milwaukee. He left the museum September 20, 1892, but continued to do commission work for the institution for many years, and maintained a good relationship with the people there.

While Akeley was in Milwaukee he seems to have strengthened his relationships with his brothers, Lewis and Thomas. Lewis had gone to the University of South Dakota in Vermillion as a professor of natural science in 1887, teaching physics and chemistry. Carl went to visit Lewis at the university in 1890. Wheeler was just leaving the museum, and Carl probably needed the kind of care, sympathy and support his brother had given him the day Ward had fired him. Of course, Carl realized that Will had to go, but he was sensitive about people abandoning him, and turned to Lewis as a constant friend and a close older brother.

Thomas had come out to the Midwest to work in the American Steel and Wire Company in DeKalb, founded by the uncle, Joseph Glidden, who had invented barbed wire. While Thomas was in DeKalb he met one of Glidden's other nephews, Chase Glidden, who was a traveling salesman for the steel company and a successful real estate investor. Thomas later fell in love with Chase Glidden's daughter, and the whole clan moved to Saskatchewan, Canada. While in DeKalb, Thomas may have stayed with Carl and helped him in his new studio.

Besides Thomas, Akeley had another assistant in his studio—Delia Reiss. At some point Delia had decided that marriage to Arthur Reiss was not for her, and divorced him. She was an extraordinary woman—runaway at thirteen, married at fourteen, and divorced before she was nineteen—all at a time when women were still treated as second-class citizens, relegated to the kitchen and bedroom. Delia was infatuated with Akeley and awe-struck by his enormous talent. She recognized in him a captivating dreamer who had great visions and great needs. At first Mickie began working in his studio just to be near him. Later she began to invest her energies seriously in his career. She wrote many years later that "his invincible spirit which was always my inspiration carried us through the early years of hard work and sacrifice while developing his talents."[14] It would be many years before Mickie would respect her own resources.

There is no way of knowing how intimate their relationship was at this time. Given Mickie's disregard for social taboos and the apparent sensuality in her writings, they were most likely lovers during this period. Mickie was a passionate, loving woman. Carl, on the other hand, always focused more on his work than his relationships. One senses in him a low libido, occasionally surfacing ravenously, but once satisfied, put safely to rest for a time. They would not marry for several years.

In 1892, Akeley received his biggest commission to date. Though it is unclear whether he received it before or after opening his studio, it might well have been the contract that he presented to his investors as the promise of a lucrative future. He was asked to mount a mustang supporting an American Indian warrior for the World's Columbian Exposition in Chicago, scheduled to open in 1893. The museum community was a tiny, interconnected world at the time. Dr. W.H. Holmes, curator in the Bureau of Ethnology of the United States National Museum in Washington, D.C. (now known as the Smithsonian Institution), selected Akeley to prepare the mount that would represent that museum at the exposition. He may well have heard of Akeley's work from Professor Goode, who had his finger on the pulse of who and what was worth noting in American science institutions. Or it might have been good old Professor Ward, who had made another big sale of specimens to the Chicago exposition. But regardless of who suggested Akeley for the job, it was a major opportunity.

The request came in December of 1892. The fair was to open in mid-1893. Akeley was already working on a large number of animals for the agricultural exhibit. Nonetheless, he felt he could deliver the mount on time. Akeley sent a photograph of the horse model to the curators of the National Museum. Excited by what they saw, they wrote back requesting two more mounts. If possible, Akeley moved into an even more rigorous schedule to complete the job. The museum desired the three broncos in representative colors: white, bay, and spotted. Akeley was delayed because he was at first unable to secure a spotted pony. He was given an extension and cut some time by sending the horses directly to Chicago instead of to Washington. Akeley sent skeleton forms of the horses' backs so that the museum preparators could complete the warriors that would ride the mounts, as well as photographs of the completed animals. The spotted pony arrived in Chicago still damp, with Akeley's admonishment to take great care in its unpacking and placement. Akeley was paid $115 for his work and was given an additional $75 for each horse he had to purchase.[15] Wasting nothing, Akeley served up some of the horse meat to his friends for dinner, insisting that it was venison until after dinner when they sat down to coffee and smokes.

The horses were brilliantly executed—seamless and alert as in life; veritable pieces of sculpture. Akeley had succeeded, after years of effort, in creating a mount that was strong without being heavy and unwieldy, and charged with energy and vitality. Akeley was an animal sculptor first and foremost. While the world called him taxidermist, and indeed that was his craft, Akeley ultimately wanted to be called an artist. In fact, on his passport for Africa, he would list his profession as sculptor, not taxidermist.

"Taxidermist": it is not a particularly fascinating title. The name has caused problems for many proponents of the craft/art over the years. The word's etymology is from the Greek *taxis* and *derma*, meaning to arrange or reorganize skin. Unfortunately, the name is conferred on anyone who skins a study specimen, tans a crocodile hide for a belt—or achieves magnificent, truly lifelike mounted specimens. From factory preparators or artists, all grades of ability and product are covered by the one word. There should be a more elevated title for work of Akeley's stature, but there is not. There have been various other titles proposed that might better address the finished product, including "animal sculptor" or "animator," but none has taken hold. Taxidermist will have to do. Yet Akeley left the old concepts of taxidermy far behind, and used animal mounts as part of an artistic vision.

Joseph Cornell's boxes spring to mind as Akeley's counterpoint in contemporary art. Cornell created three-dimensional assemblages in small boxes—little worlds—often using images of mounted birds and small mammals as references for his visions of flight, fancy, dreams, etc., portraying abstract ideas and emotions. Akeley also used mounted animals to reference his inner workings, as well as contemporary philosophy—they represented a return to an idealized nature after the industrial revolution. Akeley's mounts were noble, peaceful, grand, and in harmony with life around them. In fact, they were perfect, in many ways a projection of what he hoped for his own internal landscape. As time went on, he would grow obsessed with delivering these perfect little worlds.

Akeley's mounts revolutionized not only the world of taxidermy but the world of museum exhibits as well. Beginning in Milwaukee, after years of experimentation, Akeley lifted taxidermy out of the realm of "stuffing" into the realm of "art," imbuing his creatures with what Scholastics call "integrity, proportion and splendor of form."

A few words on the process itself: Akeley would take extensive measurements of the animal in death, allowing for the fact that its musculature was more relaxed than in life. He would often make death masks in plaster of the animal's face and other parts of the body, as he was committed to creating an exact portrait of the individual animal, rather than generic renderings. The animal was skinned and the hide tanned and poisoned to prevent insect infestation. The leg bones, skull, and occasionally other bones were fitted together and combined with iron rods to build an armature or basic skeleton. Akeley used modeling clay to sculpt the anatomically perfect, skinless body of the animal over the armature, complete with muscles flexed in the desired stance. During the molding he referred constantly to his measurements and pictures and to a small plaster model of the finished mount he had produced during the designing stage.

When the model was perfect it was covered with plaster. After the plaster hardened it was removed from the model, usually in two pieces to match the bilateral sides of mammals. This plaster form was used as a cast for the finished manikin. A thin layer of water-soluble glue was painted on the inside of the plaster cast. Then a layer of wet papier-mâché and muslin was fitted into every nook, cranny, and crack of the cast and, if needed, reinforced with wire screening.

After the papier-mâché manikin dried and hardened, the cast was lightly soaked, the glue yielding to the water, releasing the manikin. The manikin pieces were then fastened together and swathed with glue. Akeley would stretch the skin over the manikin, working wrinkles and veins into the skin over the wet glue. When the process was completed, he would touch up the skin with paint and brush it. Akeley's animal mounts were and are uncannily lifelike. The Akeley method, with only slight variations (the use of fiberglass instead of papier-mâché) is still used today.

The basic method seems simple, but it grew out of endless hours of experimentation and a passion for perfection. Akeley wrote: "A combination of glue and muslin was the key to the whole problem. The manikin so made is an absolute accurate reproduction of the clay model, even more accurate than a bronze casting, for there is no shrinkage. The manikin of a deer so constructed weighs less than thirty pounds, but is strong enough to hold a man's weight . . . Of the animal itself, only the shells of hooves and horns and the skin is used, and the skin is more carefully cleaned and tanned than those of women's furs. An animal prepared in this way will last indefinitely."[16]

The horses, when they were uncrated for the Chicago Exposition, sent a shock wave through the museum community. They were *perfect*. Akeley had done it. He had fixed his reputation as an extraordinary technician and innovator in the world of museums. His success allowed him a more vivid dream, one that had been haunting him for some time. Why not take everything that he learned from the muskrat group and apply the information to the large mammal mounts? He wanted to create not one, but four groupings that worked together as one major piece. The notion was staggering in its concept and ambition. Another exposition was planned in Paris in 1895, and it could be unveiled there. It seemed like a good idea, and Akeley was feeling very confident.

The idea, groups of Virginia deer during the four seasons, was simple and simply brilliant, but the work would cost a fortune. Mickie encouraged Akeley's dream of being a sculptor and had tried to convince him that he should study sculpture in Paris. Akeley, in turn, convinced Mickie that if they both worked on the deer groups, they could not only revolutionize museum exhibits, but also earn enough money to support themselves in Paris. The deer group could, in fact, allow them the financial security to get married. Mickie accepted his notion and threw herself headlong into the project, merging herself completely with Akeley and his career. Her dream of France had to wait. The deer groups would take years to complete, as they had to continue working on the museum and sportsmen's commissions that were paying the rent.

While working on the deer groups, Akeley experimented on a head mount of a Virginia stag. The power and vitality of the piece is extraordinary. Akeley called it *The Challenge*. The deer's silent bellow is caught in time; he appears as a furious opponent in the game of deer-seduction. The animal's eyes are wild and the piece sustains a feeling of frenzy. Akeley entered it in the Sportsman Show in New York in 1895. It was the show's main attraction and Akeley was awarded a prize for the mount. The judge was none other than Theodore Roosevelt, then police commissioner for New York. (Their paths would cross again.)

Will Wheeler saw Akeley only on holidays, when Wheeler was home from Clark University. In 1893, Wheeler was invited to work in a laboratory in Wurzburg, Germany, and on his way there he stopped at the British Museum to see what was happening in England. His tour guide was the renowned Sir William Flower, England's counterpart to Goode at the National Museum. Will was apparently already much admired as a scientist and as a museologist to warrant such attention. Wheeler was outspoken about the British Museum's shabby animal exhibits, and told Flower about Akeley's work.

Flower wrote to Akeley asking him to come to the British Museum to work in the preparation and taxidermy department. Mickie, thrilled at the prospect of traveling to Europe, encouraged him to make the move. The business was not doing well—both Akeley and his investors had taken a financial beating. Akeley had been reduced to refurbishing ladies' fur capes to pay the rent. He needed the job and decided to leave for the continent.

The deer mounts, however, were not yet complete. To execute the four seasons concept, each season had to be rendered perfectly through the dramatic and subtle changes in the deer habitat. Vegetation, stones, and earth each created their own set of difficulties in reproduction. Every leaf, branch, twig, stone, and spring flower had to be handmade and detailed. No two leaves are exactly alike, and Akeley would allow no short cuts in the manufacture of the deer accessories. So Mickie remained at home to work on these accessories, and they arranged that she would follow Akeley to England as soon as he could make enough money to send for her. The two were bound in a relationship finding its expression not only in love but in work.

Akeley left for London in 1895, traveling via Chicago to connect with a New York train. From there he would embark on a ship bound for the continent. When he arrived in Chicago, he went to the new Columbia Field Museum, which had grown out of the World's Fair. It was a busman's holiday for Akeley.

Akeley's reputation, heightened by the stunning broncos, preceded him. One of the curators, Daniel Giraud Elliot, met with Akeley to give him a tour. Akeley listened with great interest about the goals of the new museum. By the end of the visit, Elliot had convinced Akeley to do contract work in Chicago and to abandon his plans for taking Yankee talent to the English.

INVITATION TO CHICAGO

Fierce as a dog with tongue lapping for action, cunning as a savage pitted against the wilderness, . . .

—CARL SANDBURG, "The Windy City"

WINTERS IN CHICAGO are terribly raw. Freezing winds whip up Lake Michigan, and its icy waters seem to seep into the very marrow of one's bones. The shoreline is dramatic and savage, demanding attention. The city itself was a hothouse of commercial activity when Akeley arrived in 1895. It had grown more rapidly than any other American city, but not in a healthy way—more like an unchecked weed, out of control. Five years earlier, lacking the culture and refinement of either New York or Milwaukee, it was a city of a few wealthy, brash industrialists. As industry grew, so did the immigrant population brought in to work the assembly lines. As the city expanded, so did its needs to accommodate the swelling population and its corruption; franchises could be bought by whomever was willing to grease the palm of a city official.

The year 1892 had marked the four-hundredth anniversary of Christopher Columbus's famous expedition, and the United States wanted to throw a big party to celebrate the event. Congress considered many cities as hosts to the event, and Chicago prevailed almost by pure bravura. Chicago craved the limelight; Congress gave her the chance to shine.

The world's fair, called the Columbian Exposition, was held in a mini-town built on the shores of Lake Michigan, about five miles south of downtown. The White City, as it was called because of its gleaming white and gold painted stucco facade, exuded vulgarity and ostentation. In contrast, squalor

42

surrounded it for miles; typhoid-ridden slums housed the poor, as the pol-
luted lake washed against the shoreline. The White City was a tinsel town
built on the hot air of an undeserved reputation. The rich were thrilled with it,
and the poor were stunned by this dreamlike urban vision in their midst.

Most visitors to the world's fair averted their eyes from the mess surrounding them, keeping them glued to the spectacle of industry's finest.
Before the fair officially opened its doors on May 1, 1893, Will Wheeler
visited the various exhibits, especially the natural history offerings. He was so
excited by what he saw that he brought Akeley to the fair to see them. The
exposition offered a bizarre assortment of exhibitions—from nine thousand
paintings to a map of the United States made of pickles; from beautiful
porcelains and tapestries to livestock; from grapefruit (new to the U.S. at that
time) to telescopes and long-distance telephones. And there, in the midst of
art and technology were those beautiful Akeley broncos. Akeley and Wheeler
stood in front of those striking horses and shared the pride of fulfilled dreams.
President Grover Cleveland, in his opening speech for the fair, praised the
"stupendous results of American enterprise . . . proud national destiny . . .
exalted mission."

Enlightened individuals rising above the muck of corruption and com-
mercialism asked, "What exalted mission?" They called it as they saw it; and
more, they attempted to do something about the moral wasteland. They
acknowledged the need for reform and revitalization. Men like Clarence
Darrow in law, Louis Sullivan and Frank Lloyd Wright in architecture,
Theodore Dreiser in literature, Jane Addams in social reform, and John
Dewey in education attempted to touch the hearts and minds of the people.
They saw that Chicago had lagged behind as a cultural center, giving little to
its population in the way of spiritual nourishment and art. To fully revitalize
Chicago these men and women saw the need for permanent cultural institu-
tions, rather than the eccentric assembly exhibited in the White City.

In 1891, when the fair was in its planning stages, Professor G. Brown
Goode had been brought in from Washington, D.C., to discuss the National
Museum exhibits to be included in the fair. At that time he suggested that the
organizers of the fair look beyond the immediate exposition and develop a
museum for Chicago from the exhibits being purchased for the White City.
The committee heeded his advice; foreign and domestic exhibits were bought
with an eye on the future, including a large natural history collection from
Professor Ward. Further, financial backers of the fair were urged to donate
their stock to the city for the great museum that would outlive the exposition.
Chicago, eager to quiet the protests of the social reformers, was a city
begging for refinement, and a new museum seemed like just the thing.
However, the city needed an endowment to ensure not only the exhibits, but
their permanency. And so the museum committee searched for a benefactor.

One of the major capitalists in Chicago at that time was Marshall Field, who had made a vast fortune selling dry goods. He was infamous for his spendthrift ways; he shelled out forty-seven thousand dollars for his son's birthday party at a time when women in his store made less than a living wage. He was outspoken about the city's cultural needs and so seemed an apt candidate to put up money. The committee solicited a donation and walked away with one million dollars for the museum. A competitive outpouring of major gifts—a sort of Chicago-style potlatch—followed, involving both financial and material donations.

The city now had the Ward's collection of natural history objects; a Tiffany collection of gems; Asian, African, and South American anthropological collections; and agricultural exhibits. The exposition's Palace of Fine Arts was selected as the perfect museum building to house the diverse collections. The building had been constructed as a temporary summer palace, and thus had neither heat nor the artificial light necessary for winter work. Time and money were spent to remodel the facility. For the administration of the museum, experts were brought in from the east, including the American Museum of Natural History's Daniel Giraud Elliot. Elliot was offered a job as curator of the Department of Zoology.

Elliot was a remarkable character. A widely traveled, brilliant naturalist, he had started his career as an ornithologist. When the American Museum of Natural History was founded in 1869, it hired Elliot to secure important avian collections for the institution. He also participated in the museum's first collecting expedition, which sought bison in the western part of the United States. Elliot was preparing systematic papers on certain bird groups when he received the offer of a position at the new Chicago museum. The museum officials hoped that Elliot would be the guiding spirit in laying the foundation of the zoological department, much as what he had done at the AMNH. It was an exciting proposition to lay down the framework for the workings of a new institution, like the challenge blank canvas holds for an artist. And the new museum was giving him all the brushes and paint he wanted or needed to accomplish his task.

Elliot was a visionary, like most of the people who influenced Akeley. He had to have seen those horses, those exciting broncos with Indian warriors on their backs, like a Wild West show—exuberant, vivid, and exciting. Even before he met him, Elliot wanted Akeley to help him realize his own dreams for the new zoological exhibits that would mark his tenure at the new Chicago museum, the Columbian Field Museum—"the Field." Akeley's fateful visit to the Field enroute to London might be considered a "setup." Elliot was very persuasive, and Akeley, feeling wanted and needed, unhesitantly agreed to work in Chicago.

Akeley arrived in Chicago in 1895, settled into this museum world, and started working with his characteristic intensity. He and Mickie had packed up the contents of the DeKalb studio and moved the *Four Seasons* to Chicago. Mickie herself followed soon thereafter.

Their new studio was on a lot rented from a building contractor, S.M. Hunter, who, among other things, manufactured turntables (one of which was patented by Hunter and Akeley in 1909) and road rollers. These inventions fascinated Akeley, who was only beginning his career as an inventor. Hunter rented them the space on Harper Avenue in Hyde Park. On a section of the lot there was a corrugated iron shed where they housed a deer to study. (Just as he had in Milwaukee, Akeley kept live animals around to watch and study while he was preparing his mounts.) The rest of the lot was covered with a roof supported by the neighboring buildings, and they finished off the shed with an inexpensive front wall. There was no floor.

While Akeley was busy doing work for the Field Museum, Mickie would go to the northern woods of Michigan to collect accessories for their deer groups. She wrote that "with my help [Akeley] felt sure that he could . . . make a tremendous contribution to the advancement of museums . . . I made photographs of the forest, made plaster casts of leaves, flowers, and grasses. I garnered samples of bushes and plants and quantities of moss and lichens, and then packing them carefully carried them on my back to the railroad station, where I shipped them to Chicago."

"Mr. Akeley," she continued, "invented the process for reproducing [artificial leaves] in wax, and I spent four years doing the manual labor. Each group is an exact reproduction of what I found on a given spot. There is variety in each leaf. No detail, no matter how minute, was omitted. Even the tiny bud which can be found at the base of the stem on each leaf is there."[1]

Mickie and Akeley worked side by side in the studio. The shack was unspeakably cold in winter, even with the small coal-burning stove. Hunter wrote that the shed's interior was often colder than the outdoors. Mickie and Akeley would work on the deer groups until midnight almost every day, even holidays. On winter evenings their fingers would freeze—they would have to stop often to breathe on them or warm them by the stove. The cold wreaked havoc on the wax leaves, which would often crack or break completely. They had to sustain a moderate temperature to keep the wax pliable, so if it grew too cold, Mickie would end up taking the leaves back to her room while Carl stayed in the studio to work on the mounts. Originally Akeley and Mickie had intended to take the deer groups to Paris. Now they decided to finish them and sell them to the Field. Akeley was, of course, working overtime.

Carl Akeley did not do contract work for the Field Museum for very long. He was offered a position in the taxidermy department on January 1, 1896 at a starting salary of $166.66 per month. The museum was also interested in his process of making leaves and other accessories. Under this process, a plaster cast was made of both sides of a leaf. These casts were hinged at the end to create a "press." Warm wax impregnated with cotton fibers was poured into the mold and pressed. The leaf was then trimmed and painted, and the result was a perfect replica of the original.

Akeley patented the process and sold the rights to the museum for one

45

dollar. Akeley, in fact, never wished to make a lot of money from his art. Someone once said that the world is divided into two groups of people: those who wish to live in palaces and those who wish to live in cabins. Akeley always lived in cabins, and liked it that way. Uninterested in wealth, what he wanted most was to see his work and discoveries used to make museum exhibition more scientific and beautiful. He did not hate money, of course; he saw it simply as a means to further his work. Over and over again in his career he would advance his art and techniques, and then essentially give the results of his labor away. Other times he would be so distracted that he would not notice when they were taken from him.

At the same time that the city of Chicago was giving birth to the Field Museum, another institution was being born—the University of Chicago. The founders of the new university also wanted the best that the east could offer to assist in developing the young institution. Dr. C.O. Whitman, Will Wheeler's mentor, was asked to leave his post at Clark University and come to Chicago to organize a biology department. Like Elliot, he seized the opportunity, bringing his best student along. Akeley and Wheeler found themselves in what appeared an ideal situation—old friends together again as they both furthered their parallel careers. However, there was a major hitch in the reunion. Elliot apparently forbade Akeley from associating with Wheeler.[2] Wheeler wrote that it was because Elliot, the zoologist, disagreed with the scientific theories expounded by the upstarts at the university. But this seems a little trite, considering the depth and perception of the principals involved, and too intellectual for such an emotional edict. Elliot's friend and colleague, Frank Chapman, later wrote of Elliot that "even when his views differed radically from those held by others, I do not recall ever hearing him use a harsh or unjust word of criticism."[3]

Wheeler says Elliot's edict might have come from some possessive jealousy on Elliot's part. Elliot knew he had a good thing in Akeley and wanted to hold on to him, and Elliot must have known what an enormous influence Wheeler had over his friend. After all, it was Wheeler who had presented Akeley to Flower in London. Akeley never mentions any of this. The young friends rarely saw one another and drifted off into their own worlds in the next few years. Occasionally they corresponded, and they continued to respect and love each other until their deaths.

One day, Professor Elliot came into Akeley's museum studio and nonchalantly asked him if he would like to go to Africa with him. Akeley was stunned. A wave of exhilaration passed over him. Africa! He could hardly contain his joy. The Africa of Professor Ward, Stanley and Livingstone, Burton and Speke! The Africa of exploration, magic, discovery, and animals—more animals than even he had ever dreamed of. He would at last be able to observe the unusual African species in the wild, in their natural home. He would have the chance to skin and study the warm musculature of freshly

46

killed specimens, to better understand their anatomy. He would be able to test his own theories about hunting and animal behavior. Akeley had definitely escalated beyond "sixth heaven." Africa, the land of mystery and destiny, was calling him. But it was a literal Africa, a place—an exciting, remote place. Though thrilled, Akeley had no inkling of the power the continent would wield over him for the rest of his life. He had yet to know Africa as a concept, a need, an obsession.

As with every museum in this country, the Columbian Field Museum clearly reflected the personalities and interests of its founders and backers. Founded by a gang of ostentatious industrialists interested in outdoing other institutions, the Field took shape in the ambiance of a Wild West show: exuberant, energetic, and daring. So when Elliot appealed to the trustees with a brash and innovative idea, they listened. Elliot wanted to go to Africa to make a zoological collecting expedition. Never before had an American institution sent an expedition into Africa. (In fact, only one European institution, a museum in Leiden, Holland, had undertaken such an endeavor.) Elliot convinced the executive committee that the only way to secure collections for the museum was to dispatch such an expedition. "For the time is near at hand when in certain lines of zoology, especially in the large mammals of the world, it will be forever impossible to procure examples to exhibit to those that come after us. They are certain, most of them, to become extinct as the Mastodon or Dodo are today. Of all the existing wild creatures, those of the African continent are disappearing most rapidly . . . At present in most cases it is merely a question of money; in the future, money will be of no avail."[4]

The expedition appealed to the committee and they gave Elliot the go-ahead. It was a great day when Elliot walked into Akeley's studio and invited him to be his companion on the adventure. Elliot was sixty-two years old at the time—nothing in his distinguished, charming and congenial but reserved personality suggested to Akeley that he would be as great a companion in Africa as he turned out to be. Elliot, the "courtly gentleman," as "fun-loving as a boy," and his young companion, thirty years his junior, began preparing themselves for their first African adventure.

IN AFRICA'S JAWS

A heap of broken images, where the sun beats,
And the dead tree gives no shelter, the cricket no relief,
And the dry stone no sound of water.
　　　　　　—T.S. ELIOT, "The Waste Land"

INCREDIBLY, when Elliot and Akeley set out on their glorious adventure, they were not certain of their destination. They were leaving some of their travel plans to fate, hedging their bets by hoping to obtain en route recent and reliable information on prospective locations. Originally Elliot intended to collect in Mashonaland, entering the territory from Port Veira (now Mozambique). However, he was warned in both New York and London by hunters and military personnel that human settlement and hunting had reduced the big herds there. There was also a nasty uprising in the wind, which eventually came to pass in Matabele.

When Elliot decided that southern Africa was a bad idea, he turned his eyes to the area around Mt. Kilimanjaro, planning to enter the continent at either Mombasa or Zanzibar. Unfortunately, the Maasai, a pastoral East African people, were in the midst of tribal rebellions and the desired game had been decreased by an epidemic of rinderpest, a measle-like bovine virus. There are several theories about the source of this disease in Africa, the most common of which is that infected cattle were brought in to feed the Italian troops that invaded Abyssinia (now Ethiopia) in 1889. The situations were connected as it was because of the epidemic that the Maasai had to keep their own cattle constantly moving, encroaching on territory to which they had no right, and causing intertribal feuding.

In New York, Elliot sought the advice of an explorer who had just returned from Africa. Arthur Donaldson Smith had recently come home from an expedition to Lake Rudolf (now Lake Turkana in northern Kenya). He offered many welcome suggestions. He had traversed a large part of British Somaliland, and told Elliot of sighting significant herds of game. Elliot listened to all the advice and speculation concerning possible destinations, but had still not decided on their destination when he and Akeley boarded their steamer, the *New York*, on March 4, 1896. Smith also had some bad news for Elliot, not the least of which was that his headman would require a salary of $120 a month. During the crossing, Elliot became obsessed with the fact that the expedition was grossly underfinanced. He began refiguring expenses and realized that they would need about $1000 a month. He also made up his mind that he and Akeley would go to British Somaliland. By the time they reached London his mind was set.

One of the first things that Elliot did was to hire Edward Dodson, a young taxidermist at the British Museum, who had accompanied Smith. He felt that the workload would be too heavy for Akeley and he wanted Dodson to assist him. He also felt that they could rely on Dodson's experience in the area in other ways. It must have been peculiar for Akeley to visit the British Museum and see the taxidermy department where Dodson worked. He might have seen himself in the studio and wondered at the odd twist of fate that kept him in the United States and allowed him to be part of the country's first zoological collecting expedition to Africa, instead of mounting animals for the British Museum.

The logistical details of preparing for an expedition into Africa's interior filled their days in London. They needed supplies, weapons, ammunition, and proper clothing. They also had to obtain permission from the India Office to enter the territory. The office tried to dissuade them from going because of tribal unrest, and warned of its own inability to offer protection or assistance in case of trouble. Elliot convinced them that there was no turning back, and the office sent the necessary word for the expedition's welcome to Aden (the Arabian seaport, now capital of Yemen). Elliot also wired Smith's headman, offering him the job of running the expedition. The headman wired back that he was not available, much to Elliot's disappointment—a good headman was hard to come by. Two more wires were sent. The first went to Conasgi Dinshaw & Co. at Aden, instructing them to buy camels, mules and horses; the other to Director Skiff at the Field, requesting more money. If the money was forthcoming, Skiff was to wire Elliot at Aden with the simple message, "MOVE." If the executive committee voted against him, the message should say, "STOP."

The three men sailed for Aden aboard the P & O Steamer *Britannia* on March 27. Their voyage was no pleasure cruise. Gales from the northwest were so intense that the ship rolled almost continuously and "nobody could stay in the same place even lying on the floor."[1] Akeley was extremely seasick—"He is a new man or ought to be," Elliot wrote, "for there's not much left of him but his outside skin. Neptune has the rest."[2] In spite of seasickness, Akeley was thoroughly enchanted by the foreign ports of Gibraltar and Brindisi, and the extraordinary passage through the Suez Canal, down into the blisteringly hot Red Sea.

Aden was a shock to the system. A crowded seaport that Sir Richard Burton described as "a hot bed of scurvy and ulcer . . . the first arising from brackish water, the want of vegetables, and lastly the cachexia induced by an utter absence of change, diversion and excitement. The ulcer is a disease endemic in Southern Arabia; it is frequently fatal, especially to the poorer classes . . . when worn out by privation, hardship and fatigue."[3]

Elliot and his men immediately reported to Colonel Ferris, the political agent for the Somali coast, who graciously welcomed them with the wire from Skiff that said, "MOVE." Another piece of good news awaited them: Smith's headman, Qualla Idris, wanted to meet them. Idris had the luxury of picking and choosing among travelers he wished to work with. Elliot must have been aware of Idris's unusual past, but does not mention it in any of his writings. One of the reasons that Qualla Idris could fetch such high fees ($120 a month in 1896 in a country where the per capita income in 1989 is $250) was that he "had been to America as a boy and later, was for six years one of Stanley's truist and most faithful followers in the Congo, going eventually with him to Europe."[4] Idris was a well-known figure in African exploration. He served both Henry Morton Stanley and the James brothers in their explorations of Somaliland, and Count Teleki as well as Arthur Donaldson Smith in their explorations of the Lake Rudolf region (now Lake Turkana in Kenya).

Clearly, Idris wanted to meet the men before committing himself to heading their expedition. All went well with the interview and Idris agreed to join them. Smith had experienced some trouble with Idris, who at some point threatened to desert him. We have no way of knowing what caused the argument, but regardless of who was in the right, it was the height of irresponsibility to threaten to abandon an expedition in the desert. In spite of the incident, Smith obviously still felt that Idris was the best man for the job when he suggested him to Elliot. Elliot weighed the pros and cons and was happy to have him accept the contract. Idris swore that the expedition into the interior would be his last. Ironically, he died at sea soon after it was over.

Qualla Idris spoke English, Kiswahili, Arabic, and Hindustani fluently. Elliot held him in high regard. Idris took the controls of the expedition with a firm hand, supplementing the goods from London with items that could be bartered in the interior for supplies along the way: cloth, beads, and foodstuffs. Three horses and three mules were bought for riding.

Elliot was a whirlwind of activity. He had received "dazzlers" (letters of introduction embellished with ribbons, stamps, gold, etc.) from institutions in the U.S. and London, and had to make the social rounds. He needed permission to hunt in Somaliland in an area located between the coast and the Golis Mountains. The area was set aside as a private hunting reserve for the garrison of Britain's Indian Army stationed at Aden. Permission was granted. Again the authorities warned the expedition about the dangers in the interior, urging them to take an armed escort of fifty rifles with them. Elliot planned to follow in Smith's footsteps all the way to Lake Rudolf. He understood the dangers involved, but opted not to take hired guns with them. After a week, Elliot and his men were anxious to get on with it.

They left Aden on April 20, 1896 for Berbera, another seaport on the Gulf of Aden, in "as vile a craft as floats."[5] The vessel had been condemned by the government and was barely seaworthy. The passing, which was mercifully short, was horrid, rank with the odors of horses, mules, and men jammed together. Akeley, Elliot, and Dodson spent the night with the captain on the bridge.

About noon the next day, they entered the harbor of Berbera. Even before the ship cast anchor, a crowd of Somalis ran along the shore shouting. Some jumped into the water and swam to the ship. In a cacophony of jumbled languages, entangled arms and hands grabbed at them trying to bless their heads. Nothing noble or religious here, just Somalis trying to establish territory over the visitors and pronounce themselves their protectors. It was an overwhelming welcome, uncomfortable and claustrophobic.

The Arabs called Berbera "Mother of the Poor" because it seemed such a wretched clump of humanity, surrounded by desert and sparsely covered low hills. The town was a tower of Babel, a confusing combination of peoples and languages. The port was an ancient one, having served Pharaonic Egypt and India through trade for centuries. Tribal people from all corners of the interior still arrived to trade hides, ivory, ostrich feathers, rhinoceros and antelope horns, prayer skins, honey, coffee, ghee (clarified butter), and gums like frankincense and myrrh. Not long before, it had also been a center for slave trade. Strings of camels came and went constantly, their owners trading their goods for beads, dates, rice, cotton, and other merchandise brought in to Berbera by dhow from nearby ports. Any blood feuds were put aside in Berbera in the name of peaceful commerce. The beaches were peopled with traders working out of temporary camps. Piles of camel and sheep bones gave testament to splendid feasts. Berbera had been an important port for centuries, and rival tribes constantly jockeyed for position. The English laid claim to the port because of its strategic importance to the Suez Canal, turning it over to their Indian Office for administration.

Elliot described the city as being two distinct towns, two quarters: native and European. The European section housed two miserably lonely Europeans, an Army officer and his young wife. The other town was occupied by thirty-five thousand people "dwelling in mat huts, thickly clustered together and looking from a distance like a big bed of black mushrooms."[6] A handful of mosques and minarets rose above them, by contrast white and lovely.

The British officer, Captain Merriweather, offered the men hospitality in his gracious house, formerly occupied by the Egyptian governor. The Europeans were happy to have company.

Even though Elliot had wired ahead for camels, they had a terrible time procuring them. The beasts were in high demand for the Italian war in Abyssinia, and as a result, the prices were greatly inflated. The expedition needed eighty animals and they had secured only thirteen. Pack animals in good health were of prime importance to an expedition because their ill health or death could ruin the journey and perhaps even result in fatalities among its human members.

To add insult to injury, camels are annoying animals. They have to be fed four hours a day, or else they cannot march. They die from changes in diet and their backs seem excessively sensitive to galls, or open sores. Elliot had much to say about the beasts:

> The creature has so many talents and so many ways of exhibiting them. To begin with, it can kick worse than a Virginia mule and with all four feet . . . I cannot pay it a higher compliment. Then it can bite worse than a horse, and buck in a way to make a bronco ashamed of its efforts. No cowboy that lived could stay on that perch seven feet from the ground during a camel's exhibition of gymnastics. Then he can run away whenever he feels like it and his rider experiences a sensation between being blown up with dynamite or struggling against the throes of an earthquake until all his joints are dislocated and he drops in a limp inert mass to the ground. Then this sweet creature has a way of evidencing his displeasure that is at least effective and convincing. He twists his snake-like neck into a circle, thrusting his ugly nose into the rider's face, opens his cavernous mouth and bellows a roar of disgust in such a fetid breath, that the human biped is fairly blown into the middle of next month with his appetite lost for an interminable period. And yet with all these recommendations, which to some people may appear objectionable, these are the dear animals I am yearning for.[7]

Additional camels were not forthcoming, and Elliot was becoming increasingly anxious about finances. Waiting around for the animals was costing them money that could be used more productively. To help defray the cost of the expedition, Elliot hit on a plan of buying ivory tusks in the interior and reselling them for a profit at Berbera on their return. He wanted to spend eight months in the field, but needed to know in advance whether, should they find a particularly fertile field, they would have the additional money to remain until the work was completed.

They were miserable in Berbera. The heat was extreme; the men awoke to sopping pools of sweat, their pajamas, sheets, and mattresses as wet as if they had slept in the sea. They had to escape Berbera, even without the needed camels.

Elliot, Akeley, and Dodson decided to leave Idris in town to find the additional animals. They journeyed to the country about twelve miles away in search of wild asses to begin their collection for the museum. At last they were on their way. They were at their first campsite by day's end. For the first time, Akeley was on safari, and filled with adventurous spirit, he grew a beard. This 1896 safari was simple and rugged compared with Akeley's future expeditions—and certainly less organized!

An introduction to safari life, even in its bare bones, should prove useful at this time. The word "*safari*" is Kiswahili for journey, and "*msafiri*," or safarist, means the person going on the journey. The traditional safari was comprised of the safarists and their staff of indigenous people, who served the safari in several capacities. The most important position was that of the headman. His duty was to supervise all aspects of the safari. Not only the pleasure but the success of an expedition fell squarely on his shoulders. If he was weak or indecisive, the discipline of the camp would disintegrate, making life miserable for everyone. If he was strong and just, everything ran smoothly. After the headman, personal gun bearers were the most important staff members, and among gun bearers, the Somalis were reputedly the best because of the fierce courage and loyalty they manifested. It was the gun bearer's duty to be ever at the side of a hunter, to carry his gun, to ensure its constant availability for instantaneous action. Often there were second gun bearers taken from the ranks of porters who carried second weapons, cameras, and canteens. When a hunter faced a charging beast, the gun bearer crouched next to his right elbow with the second rifle pressed against the right leg of the hunter to signal its readiness. The gun bearer was strictly forbidden to shoot, except under extraordinary circumstances when it was clear that the hunter was disarmed and in grave danger. The chronicles of early white hunters in Africa are replete with tales of gun bearers saving the lives of hunters. It was also the bearer's responsibility to skin the animal and bring it back to camp.

Next in the pecking order came the askaris, armed guards who guarded the camp at night against intruders, both animal and human, and who prevented the desertion of porters. Next came the cook, that marvelous magician who was capable of creating exquisite meals out of so little and under such primitive conditions—a makeshift oven of tin pieces placed on hot ashes or stones. Porters followed; their responsibility was not only to carry supplies, but also to set up camp and collect firewood. Lowest on the social scale were the saises or syncs, men assigned to groom the animals, one sync to each horse, mule, or camel. In addition to these staff positions, each safarist had a "tent boy."

The literature on safaris is rife with the word "boy." There is no doubt that it is a condescending term, offensive to most of us and to most contemporary Africans as well, and much of the historical East African literature has racist overtones. There is also no doubt that many of the hunters that we read about had genuine love and respect for the men with whom they worked, whom they called "boys." It was a different time, a time when ethnocentrism prevailed. We live in an age of the global community brought on by technology that can connect us with anyone anywhere on earth in seconds. We are perhaps less apt to try to enlighten the "savage" or bring "civilization" to indigenous peoples who live much differently than we do. Quite the opposite, we have so clearly endangered our planet that we often envy the man who can live in a little closer harmony with the earth. The early explorers mistook the native Africans' simplicity and astonishment at the unfamiliar for childishness. These men were never boys, but equal companions and colleagues in the field, working alongside the scientists, often doing the same work. Today, hopefully, we are not so likely to interpret behavior different than ours as simple or childish, nor are we as likely to consider ourselves superior. But in that earlier time, the word "boy" became part of safari nomenclature. (This topic will be taken up again in a later chapter.)

Life in camp started before dawn. The Somalis, followers of Islam, began their softly chanted prayers when the first hints of light appeared in the sky. Their prayers were steadily joined by the avian songsters in the bush as all life greeted the sun and the new day. Sound built on sound: human voices, then more human voices, sounds of spitting and crackling fire, water sloshing, and camels grunting and bellowing, their bells metallic, jarring. The safarist was greeted by his tent boy with hot tea or coffee as steaming wood-scented water was poured into a canvas basin for morning ablutions. The earth was still cool from the night; the savage blast of the sun would arrive later.

In addition to attending every need, the tent boy laid out all necessary clothing from underwear to hat. Akeley did not know how to dress. His field uniform became more appropriate on subsequent safaris, but in 1896 he was very new to the safari game. It was a wonderful adventure but not without its mistakes. Forget elegance—Akeley looked downright foolish on the back of his mule wearing a scottish golf hat in the middle of the Somalian desert. After they dressed, the men sat down to a breakfast of oatmeal, meat, eggs, bread, and marmalade to brace them for the day's work.

At the end of the day, everyone traditionally relaxed around the campfire in a sweet communion under the star-shot sky. Akeley lay on the ground, leaning on his elbow, with the Somalis. These were times of great camaraderie for everyone.

The Somalis could be divided into four different groups of people: the nomad pastoralists, the settled Somalis who lived in or near the towns, the hunter-gatherers, and the traders or caravan Somalis. They were part of a strong oral tradition—the same semitic tradition that gave us Solomon's Song of Songs—and they had literally thousands of songs in their repertoire. They sang of camels, elephant hunting, life-giving water, friendship, and women. The Somalis would also sing and muse among themselves about the events of the day. "There is a gazelle in your garden," a Somali would point out to a friend who had a grain of rice in his beard. "We will hunt her with the five,"[8] was the response, meaning "I'll remove it with my fingers." They were a decidedly poetic, romantic, intelligent group of people, whom Akeley found very warm and friendly. The Somalis have been called a melancholy race, enjoying the rhythm of the night, gazing at and singing to the moon in solitude. Sir Richard Burton called them "soft, merry and affectionate souls [but] they pass without any apparent transition into a state of fury, when they are capable of terrible atrocities." He said they were courageous, yet possessing the "wily valor of wild men . . . and when the passion of rival tribes are violently excited they will use with asperity the dagger and spear."[9]

It was probably around the campfire, listening to Qualla Idris's tales of his adventure with Stanley in the Congo, that Akeley first felt the driving desire to visit Africa's heart. The Somalis loved a mild narcotic called khat, a drug imported from the interior. The leaves of the *Càtha edulis* were chewed during times of repose to produce a "great hilarity of spirits and an agreeable state of wakefulness."[10] The stimulant was also used on long caravan marches to stave off hunger and fatigue. Akeley smoked his pipe as he watched his friends.

Even though Akeley loved these campfire reveries, he would usually cut short his relaxation time and return to work. After a full day in the field, he developed the photographs he had taken. When the expedition had been in London, Elliot had spent so much money that he had felt unable to purchase a camera to record the work in the field, even though he thought it important to have one. Akeley had bought the camera himself for forty pounds. Elliot wrote: "I feel that the museum is indebted solely to him for the views of people, scenes and animals, over 300 in number, obtained by the expedition, and made by himself, often sitting up the greater part of the night to develop the exposed plates which he had accumulated on his hands when he greatly needed rest."[11] Akeley's excessive work habits had been evidenced for years. Now they were witnessed for the first time in Africa, his seedling muse/nemesis. He always worked to capacity and just a bit more, pressing himself just beyond the limit, testing it.

Most of the information we have about this expedition comes from Elliot's letters to the Field's director. Because they were friends, there were often two letters written at once—one official, the other personal. There are no extant letters from Akeley. We see his experiences only through Elliot's eyes, with the exception of Akeley's hunting narratives. In these recountings

Akeley's own voice is heard. In the story of how he collected wild asses, for example, we hear how shabby he felt when he shot them—not from a sentimental point of view, but because the experience lacked the elegance and finesse of a good hunt. Akeley cared a great deal about good sportsmanship.

Akeley and Dodson set out after a small herd of asses and were frustrated by the lack of vegetation to hide behind. They stalked the animals slowly and were surprised to see that they could close to within two hundred yards, and still the animals would not bolt. Not willing to risk their luck further, Akeley shot one of the animals, who after being hit, turned to look at his killer with curiosity. "The animal was hit hard, apparently," wrote Akeley, "but he recovered and stood facing us. We approached closer, and not taking any chances, fired again. Then he merely walked about a little, making no apparent effort to go away. We approached carefully. He showed no sign of fear and, although hard hit, stood solidly until at last I put one hand on his withers and tripping him, pushed him over. I began to feel that if this was sport I should never be a sportsman."

He had another experience with the wild asses, this one equally disturbing. He shot another, and as the hunters approached, "he turned and faced us with great gentle eyes. Without the least sign of fear or anger, he seemed to wonder why we harmed him. His only wound was from a small bullet high in the neck. It was merely a flesh wound which would have caused him no serious trouble had he continued with the herd. We walked around him within six feet and I believe we almost could have put a halter on him. We reached the camp about midnight and I announced that if any more wild asses were wanted, someone else would have to shoot them. I had had quite enough."[12]

"Collecting" is a scientific euphemism for killing; but the collectors for science are just as sensitive about good sportsmanship as trophy hunters, at least the good ones in both categories. Akeley genuinely enjoyed a good hunt, reveling in his prowess like any white hunter boasting over a glass of beer, but he felt sick at heart about the wild ass incidents—humbled, uncomfortable, out-of-joint.

The safarists and their staff were in this first camp, only twelve miles from Berbera, for ten days. Akeley became ill with "an ailment of the kidneys," caused by long hours in the saddle and unrelenting sun. He suffered from heat prostration several times during the expedition. Dehydration was a real problem; water was scarce, and when it was available, Akeley was probably too preoccupied to remember to drink it. Under such conditions, the body starts to dry up from within, and because of the friction, it becomes difficult and scratchy to even open and close the eyes. Lips are suddenly blistered and the body wants to hold all its precious moisture, even the toxic liquid. The kidneys are affected. The sun and heat seem to bypass the flesh and penetrate directly into the vital organs, cooking them.

Besides affecting his health, the lack of water created a potentially disastrous incident for Akeley. He and Dodson had been hunting asses since morning. Even though the sun was rising higher in the sky, they chose to continue the hunt. They ran out of water, a foolish thing to do in the desert, but Akeley was a true greenhorn. (Dodson's excuse remains unknown.) Their guide kept promising them water just around the bend. No water. Just a little further on . . . no water. After several hours of this, Akeley and Dodson practically fell from their saddles, and sent their men on to find water. They lay down in a semicomatose state, resting their heads on their saddles and shielding their faces from the sun with their saddle blankets. The guide and some of the men returned empty-handed. Just then, like a mirage in a shimmering heat haze, a caravan emerged from around the bend, giving hope to all for a precious drink. Akeley breathed easier as the Somalis approached their brothers to ask for help. The caravan moved on unconcerned with the needs of the white men. Akeley realized, in a bit of a stupor, what was going on. New energy, born of rage, shot through him; he grabbed his rifle and drew a bead on one of the passing men. The Somali guide realized that Akeley would kill the parting Somali and started yelling at him to stop. The caravan Somalis had a change of heart after realizing the extent of Akeley's desperate and reckless threat and graciously offered some curdled milk to the men. It was delicious and refreshing—a drink that fended off potential disaster.

The expedition returned to Berbera with a number of wild ass and gazelle skins safely packed for their journey onward to Chicago. It had been a very profitable ten days. On their arrival in Berbera, Idris met them with the news that they were still short the needed camels, but that they were now up to at least forty. Elliot wasted no time. They deposited the specimens, re-stocked the store, and left again immediately for another area just outside of Berbera. It was another false start. After a few days, they again returned to Berbera to wait for more camels. Dodson was down with fever, and Elliot was disgusted. Akeley celebrated his thirty-second birthday.

Idris had succeeded in rounding up fifty-six animals, and while the number fell considerably short of the desired eighty, the small group was fed up with the constant delays, and left for the interior. Their goal was Ogaden, southwest of Berbera through a corner of the Haud, a dreaded stretch of desert plateau, a no man's land. They pushed the caravan out of Berbera late in the afternoon on May 26th, hoping to cover a lot of ground by traveling at night. Nevertheless, the heat and sun had a cumulative effect; the days were more difficult than they had been on the short collecting jaunts, even though they were traveling through the same territory.

"Nothing short of Dante's description of the inferno could do it justice," Elliot wrote of the area. "Hell on earth, barren rocks and hills covered with lava, the plain a dreary waste of sand and low thorn bushes scattered over it tearing everything that comes near them into pieces with the blazing sun that fairly scorches and not a drop of water save at long intervals." He added that "surely nothing but an ass would stay" there. There were scorpions "built like lobsters," venomous snakes, and "all the hideous things no other land would have," and there was the sun, the "malignant African sun."[13]

The expedition camped several times where they knew an abundance of game lived. Kudu was high on their list of desired specimens, and they spent days hunting these exquisite antelope. The kudus, grand and very clever animals, were a quarry more to Akeley's liking. A kudu is about the size of an elk and has been called the most beautiful of antelope for its subtle grey and white markings and its magnificent spiral horns. Nature gave it perfect camouflage, allowing it to stand stark still in the open and remain unnoticed. Akeley discovered this phenomenon when he was hunting the kudus. He stalked a female into the bush and was about to shoot her when he realized that an enormous bull was standing in the rocks nearby, blending perfectly with his habitat. Akeley saw the animal only after it bolted. He tracked another kudu, and, having lost its trail, succeeded in pursuing it by feel or instinct. Akeley grew more confident in his abilities as observer, hunter, and marksman on this first expedition. Even though he was in a totally foreign land, and was hunting unfamiliar quarry, he trusted more and more his uncanny ability to get inside the skin of a creature and second-guess its behavior.

While hunting oryx in another location, Akeley had his first encounter with a lion. He was preparing to mount his pony to move on when, about a hundred yards ahead of him, a lioness and two males ambled across a sandy patch in open view. Akeley said that they "looked as big as oxen." He felt he had to have them, and sent his gun bearers to encircle the animals from the other side. He was alone, and started advancing on them slowly, into a large clump of bush. Akeley was poised at the edge of the vegetation when suddenly the lioness roared and flew out of the bush on a diagonal line away from him. Seeing Akeley clearly from mid-air, she twisted her body to land squarely facing him only a few feet away. As he shot her, a male came flying out and over her back in a terrible jumble of noise and chaos. Akeley had only grazed the lioness, but uncharacteristically, instead of giving full vent to her rage and attacking Akeley, the lioness raced after the male, who had beat a hasty retreat. Though shaken, Akeley gave orders for the bush to be burned to drive the animals out. The two males escaped from behind, the flames presenting no other choice. The female was never seen again. Akeley had had his first violent experience in the field—one that would soon be eclipsed by one even more dramatic.

While Akeley and Dodson were concentrating their efforts on hunting and preserving the skins of their specimens, Elliot had to deal with the logistical problems of the expedition. He wrote about the difficulties of the life they were leading—the illnesses, the constant search for water—and about the remarkable people they met along the way.

Early in the journey, Elliot had a siege of fever and found it almost impossible to stay in the saddle. He established a camp in the Togo Plains so that he could recuperate. The location was used as a base from which short expeditions would be dispatched, especially in search of hartebeests. At this base camp the expedition was visited by Sultan Nuir, king of the Habr Yunis (a sub-tribe of the Habr Gerhajis, one of the Somali peoples living in the valley between the Juba and the Shebelle Rivers). It was a marvelous event.

On June 12, 1896, as Elliot rested in front of his tent, a horseman approached with the news that the Sultan and his royal family wished to visit him. The Habr Yunis had a fierce reputation. The announcement certainly elicited fear as well as excitement on Elliot's part. Elliot did not move from his spot under "the only tree in Togo." "Pretty soon," he wrote, "a body of horsemen were seen coming over the plains in a stately march, the heads of their spears and gaily-decked bridles and saddles flashing in the sun. The herald dashed up to them and probably informed his Majesty that I was waiting for him, for immediately the pace of the horses quickened and the whole band dashed up at full speed and halted in front of my chair. They were a fine body of men, warriors every one, and I envied them the splendid ponies they were riding."[14] The sultan, "a very tall spare man" was celebrated as a brilliant warrior, having fought in many battles. He sat on his horse in the center of the line looking at Elliot and making no motion to dismount. Everyone looked at everyone else in an odd moment of tension and anticipation. Akeley and Dodson had moved behind Elliot's chair.

> Then one of the escorts, probably the court poet, began a chant expressing the King's delight at my coming to his country, that as soon as he learned who I was, he had hastened to see me and that the European and his people must be firm friends and then they would be invincible and fear no one . . . During the delivery of this effusion, each man sat on his horse like a statue, never moving a muscle and I had a fine chance to run my eyes over themselves and their equipment. Each man carried two spears, one to throw and one to stab with, a short two-edged sword and a shield, a small round one on the left arm made of rhino's hide. Their bridles were decorated with bright worsteds and bright metals, and altogether they made a brave show. Evidently a tough crowd to fight.

The sultan dismounted and Elliot rose from his chair. After the two men shook hands, Elliot offered the chair to the sultan. "He was a man verging on sixty," Elliot continues, "of very pleasant expression and dignified and gentle in his bearing and manner. Indeed I have seen many a so-called swell among the stylish circle in a drawing room show to much less advantage and credit to himself than did this man and savage throughout the entire interview. He never lost his self-possession and dignity and behaved like a thoroughbred gentleman."[15] Elliot ordered coffee, and the sultan's men put on a stunning equestrian show, each of them putting his steed through its paces. The ceremony, known as a *dibaltig*, climaxed with the horsemen turning to gallop away and, en masse, reining up and shouting *"Mot"* (Hail to Thee).

Following the horse show, the men divided into ranks and staged a mock battle. When the ceremonies ended, Elliot and the sultan settled into conversation. The sultan told him of great battles staged only recently:

> Of course Sultan Nuir was in the thick of it and got some hard knocks, one on his right leg above his ankle was a real dusey. It had been fired with a red hot spear or iron out of the same principle, I suppose, one fires a horse for a splinter and the leg looked like a gigantic pepper box, the holes being in the places where the iron had burned. He was in a bad way in sundry parts of his body and would like me to do something for him. I told him he must recollect that he was not as young as he once was and he could not go around getting hard knocks and recovering from them as he once could at which he laughed and said that it was quite true.[16]

Elliot gave the sultan medicine, and apologized for the lack of gifts in the camp. He explained that most of the supplies were with Idris and the caravan and that as soon as he could lay hands on them, presents would be brought to the sultan's camp.

When the sultan had approached the expedition campsite, he had seen Akeley working on the skin of a hartebeest. He inquired about it and Elliot explained that it would be mounted to appear as it had in life for one of the great institutions of the world. The sultan was very impressed with the scientific work of the expedition and departed happily after a visit of several hours.

It seems astonishing that Akeley never mentioned this dramatic encounter in later years—not even when he had a "ghost writer" in his secretary, Dorothy Greene Ross, who wrote down, in his name, the stories that he would sit around and tell to her. Akeley suppressed much of the personal, even in the journals that he wrote only for himself. The very fact that the Somalis were such a wild group, capable of exploding in blood feuds at a moment's notice, must have put some kind of pressure on Akeley and Dodson as they hunted in the field. They never knew whether they might be innocent bystanders caught in the cross fire of violence. For the most part, Akeley's thoughts and actions are filtered through the sensibilities of Elliot who, older and wiser, had a much different perspective on things.

A case in point was the way that Elliot handled the discipline of troublemakers in camp. He dealt with two potentially volatile situations deftly and prudently. One was an incident in which a madman tried to kill Elliot's horse, stabbing it in the flank. The whinnying of the horse and shouting of the men brought Elliot to the scene, where he found his horse covered with blood. The offender was bound and taken off to the proper authorities, and his own horse claimed by Elliot as replacement.

The other incident was even more violent. A feud broke out suddenly, and Elliot's tent boy was attacked from behind; his head bludgeoned by a rival tribe member. Elliot had the Somali bound and tied to a tree. All watched to see whether the sentence would be for murder or attempted murder. The tent boy regained consciousness, and the offender was taken off to the authorities at Berbera. Thus Elliot was able to maintain his position with the Somalis, showing that he would not suffer insubordination, yet excusing himself from the potentially corporal disciplinary measures. Akeley, on the other hand, had been ready to kill the caravan Somali for a glass of milk, which would have been utterly disastrous for the white men in the field. Akeley learned a great deal from simply observing Elliot on this expedition. Their temperaments and rhythms were very different. Akeley had a mentor in Elliot, and Elliot had a great respect for Akeley, the hunter and the worker.

They left the Togo Plains and moved east-southeast into the territory of the Dolbohanta, another Somali tribe known at the time for its intense hatred of white men. The expedition skirted the region as quickly as it could, moving on to a beautiful fertile area, almost parklike in its topography. Water was still scarce, creating fierce competition for the available water, not only for the humans but for their livestock. The land was home to their friends, the Habr Yunis, who were making preparations to raid the Ogaden people. The expedition spent ten days securing a lovely gazelle called the Clark's antelope. They planned to create a group exhibiting the growth of the species from infancy to adulthood.

At this camp, the expedition was again entertained by a tribal people—the Midgan, descendents of the original inhabitants of the area. They were despised by the Somali for their weird and barbaric ways. The word "midgan" means one hand, which connotes the tribe's skill at archery. The Midgan were also known as cannibals. Elliot's wife, on his safe return home, was appalled that the expedition received them so graciously, not that Elliot had much of an alternative.

Elliot had sent Qualla Idris and the caravan to Berbera to replenish supplies for a new four-month trip even deeper into the interior. They had lost six camels and needed to replace them. Idris had also taken specimens to Berbera for shipment to the museum. It was now time for the expedition to circle back on trail northwestward to reunite with the caravan. They marched to the edge of the Haud, setting up camp at its base, which rose in a solid rock wall, not far from Hargeisa. Here they were to meet Qualla Idris and company, but due to infuriating delays, they were stuck in the spot for three weeks. The museum had wired money to the wrong location, and no one seemed to know its whereabouts. No money meant no supplies. And they *still* could not buy enough camels. Elliot must have cursed the Italians and their war, which was still wreaking havoc on his expedition. When Idris finally arrived, the camels were already tired. Their loads were too heavy since they had to carry an additional twelve hundred pounds of salt, necessary to preserve skins, into the interior. The new specimens collected on the expedition were loaded into huge sealed barrels on some of the camels for immediate return to Berbera. No less than ten camels were used for carrying the expedition's water up to and across the dreaded Haud.

Elliot, Akeley, and Dodson braced themselves for the excruciating march across the vast, waterless, sandy plateau on August 4, as they broke camp and began their hundred-mile march across the plateau. Just as they were beginning to penetrate the Haud, violent thunder and lightning storms dumped gallons of rain on the expedition. The mats that were fitted on the backs of the camels under the packs became so sodden and heavy that the animals could not move. Again the expedition had to be halted, to allow for the mats to dry. Starting up again, they traveled on an ancient caravan route to Milmil, leading them deeper into the desiccated wasteland. It took four and a half days to cross the Haud. During this time they hunted only for food. There was no time to stop and prepare specimens.

New camel problems arose. Water and vegetation were very rare, and with nothing to eat the animals became exhausted. One of them "gave out" and had to be shot to save it from hyena attack. But the expedition had to push on. At a somnambulistic pace, they inched their way through Midgan territory. Unlike their earlier visitors, this particular group had recently been attacking caravans, eating the camels and murdering the people. Still they pressed on. Only the promise of water, food, and a fertile game-rich valley motivated them.

Reaching the edge of the Haud and looking out over the valley was a magical moment for all. This region is the upper extension of the Great Rift Valley, dramatic with its contrasting sharp escarpments, arid ridges and expansive valley floors. The valley, 1,500 feet below, held the promise of elephants, rhinoceroses, and giraffes. Elliot intended to continue moving on the southwest course and to cross the Shebelle River, camp on the other side, and collect these larger mammals. They were in Ogaden, Abyssinia (now Ethiopia), moving from tug to tug in search of water. Tugs are dry river beds that can usually provide water if one is willing to dig deep into the earth's surface. Many of the tugs were dry or yielded a liquid thick as pea soup.

The expedition finally found water at a Galla "singing well." These wells, which can still be seen today, are marvelous places where desert pastoralists like the Galla, Rendile, and Boran have dug wells very deep into the sand and stone. There, long lines of men, women, and children position themselves at intervals and pass gourds of water, in relay fashion, from the bottom of the well up to the earth's surface, where they are poured into troughs for consumption. The people sing or chatter away while passing the water from hand to hand, creating a joyous melody almost as pleasing as the sound of sloshing water for the thirsty men. The water-gatherers at this well had never seen white men before. They were treated kindly and given plenty of water for themselves and their animals. Refreshed, the expedition moved ever onward, stopping to collect game at Hersi Barri. The site was chosen for its water supply, accessible by minimal digging. Rhino tracks in camp gave proof of the ample existence of game. The expedition intended to stay only a few days. After a macabre series of events Hersi Barri became the last stop on the trail.

Elliot came down with terrible malaria. As he battled fever for ten days, Akeley had a staggering experience. He had been hunting ostriches in the morning but had killed a wart hog which he put aside to collect later in the day. Late in the afternoon, he and his sync set out with tools to skin the animal. Akeley wrote in *In Brightest Africa*:★

We had no difficulty in finding the place where I had shot the wart hog but there was nothing to be seen. The place was strewn with vulture feathers, but surely, I thought, vultures could not make away with the head. A crash in the bushes at one side led me to hurry in that direction and a little later I saw my pig's head in the mouth of a hyena traveling up the slope of a ridge out of range. That meant that my wart hog specimen was lost, and having got no ostriches, I felt it was a pretty poor day.

The sun was setting. With nothing to console us, my pony boy and I started for camp. As we came to the place where I had shot the diseased hyena in the morning, it occurred to me that perhaps there might be another hyena about the carcass. Feeling a bit "sore" at the tribe for stealing my wart hog, I thought I might pay off the score by getting a good hyena specimen for the collections. The pony boy led me to the spot, but the dead hyena was nowhere in sight. There was blood where he had fallen, and in the dusk we could make out a trail in the sand where he had been dragged away.

As I advanced a few steps, a slight sound attracted my attention. Glancing to one side, I got a glimpse of a shadowy form going behind a bush. Then I did a very foolish thing. Without a sight of what I was aiming at, I shot hastily into the bush. The snarl of a leopard told me what kind of a customer I was taking chances with. A leopard is a cat and has all the qualities that gave rise to the "nine lives" legend. To kill him you have got to kill him clear to the tip of his tail. Added to that, unlike a lion, the leopard is vindictive. A wounded leopard will fight to the finish almost every time, no matter how many chances it has to escape. Once aroused, its determination is fixed on fight, and if a leopard ever gets hold, it claws and bites until its victim is in shreds. All this was on my mind, and I began looking for the best way out of it. I had no desire to come to a conclusion with a leopard—least of all a wounded leopard—when it was so late in the day that I could not find the sights of my rifle. My intention was to leave the leopard until morning. If it had been wounded, there might then be a chance of finding it. I turned to the left and crossed to the opposite bank of a deep narrow "tug"—

★ This excerpt has been included it in its entirety so that the reader can hear both Akeley's voice and his interpreter's. The story is there, and it is a good one, but the arch rendition is that of his ghost writer.

channel of dry sand. When there, I found that I was on an island of sand where the tug forked. By going along a short distance to the point in the island I would be in a position to see behind the bush where the leopard had stopped. But what I had started, the leopard was intent on finishing. While peering about I detected the beast crossing the tug about twenty yards ahead of me. Again I began shooting, although I could not see to aim. However I could see where the bullets struck as the sand spurted up beyond the leopard. My first two shots went above her, but my third scored. The leopard stopped and I thought that she was killed. The pony boy broke into a song of triumph which was promptly cut short by another song such as only a thoroughly angry leopard is capable of making as it charges. For just a flash I was paralyzed with fear. Then came power for action. I worked the bolt of my rifle and became conscious that the magazine was empty. At the same instant I realized that a solid point cartridge rested in the palm of my left hand. It was the one that I had intended, as I came up on the dead hyena, to replace the soft nose. If I could but escape the leopard until I got the cartridge into the chamber!

As the leopard came up the bank on one side of the point of the island, I dropped down the other side and ran about to the place from which she had charged. By this time the cartridge was in place, and I wheeled to face the leopard in mid-air. The rifle was knocked flying and in its place was eighty pounds of frantic cat. Her intention was to sink her teeth into my throat and, with this grip and with her forepaws, to hang to me while with her hind claws she dug out my abdomen; for this pleasant practice is the way of leopards.

However, happily for me, she missed her aim. Instead of getting my throat she hit to one side. She struck me high in the chest and caught my upper arm in her mouth. This not only saved my throat but left her hind legs hanging clear where they could not reach my body. With my left hand I caught her throat and tried to wrench my right arm free, but I couldn't do it except little by little. When I got grip enough on her throat to loosen her hold just a little, she would catch my arm again an inch or two lower down. In this way I drew the full length of my arm through her mouth inch by inch.

I was conscious of no pain, only of the sound of the crushing of tense muscles and the choking, snarling grunts of the beast. As I pushed her farther and farther down my arm, I bent over. Finally, when my arm was almost freed, I fell to the ground with the leopard underneath me. My right hand was in her mouth, my left hand clutching her throat, my knees on her lungs, my elbows in her armpits spreading her front legs so that her frantic clawing did nothing more than tear my shirt. Her body was twisted in an effort to get hold of the ground to turn herself, but the loose sand offered no hold.

For a moment there was no change in our position, and then for the first time I began to think and hope I had a chance to win this curious fight. Up to that time it had been simply a good fight in which I expected to lose, but now if I could keep my advantage perhaps the pony boy would come with a knife. I called, but to no effect. I still held the leopard and continued to shove my hand down her throat so hard she could not close her mouth and with the other hand I gripped her throat in a strangle hold. Then I surged on her with my knees. To my surprise I felt a rib go,

I did it again. I felt her relax, a sort of letting go, although she was still struggling. At the same time, I felt myself weakening similarly, and then it became a question as to which of us would give up first. Little by little her struggling ceased. My strength had outlasted hers.

After what seemed an interminable passage of time, I let go and tried to stand. I called the pony boy that it was finished. He now screwed up his courage sufficiently to approach. Then the leopard began to gasp, and I saw she might recover; so I asked the boy for his knife. He had thrown it away in his fear, but quickly found it, and at last I made certain that the beast was dead.

As I looked at the leopard later I came to the conclusion that what had saved me was the first shot I had fired when she went into the bush. It had hit her right hind foot. I think it was this broken foot which threw out the aim of her spring and made her get my arm instead of my throat. With the excitement of the battle still on me, I did not realize how badly used up I was. I tried to shoulder the leopard to carry her to camp, but I was very soon satisfied to confine my efforts to get myself to camp. When I came inside the zareba [compound], my companions were sitting at dinner in front of one of the tents. They had heard the shots and speculated on the probabilities. They had decided that I was in a mix-up with a lion or with natives, but that I would either have the enemy or the enemy would have me before they could get to me. So they continued their dinner. The fatalistic spirit of the country had prevailed.

When I came within their range of vision, however, my appearance was enough to arrest their attention. My clothes were all ripped, my arm was chewed into an unpleasant sight, and there was blood and dirt all over me. Moreover, my demands for all the antiseptics in camp gave them something to do, for nothing was keener in my mind than that the leopard was feeding on the diseased hyena that I had shot that morning. To the practical certainty of blood poisoning from any leopard bite was added the established fact that this leopard's mouth was particularly foul with disease.

While my companions were getting surgical appliances ready, my boys were stripping me and dousing me with cold water. That done, the antiseptic was pumped into every one of the innumerable tooth wounds until my arm was so full of the liquid that an injection in one drove it out of another. During this process I nearly regretted that the leopard had not won. But the antiseptic was applied so quickly and so thoroughly that it was completely successful.

Later in the evening my gun boy brought the leopard in and laid her beside my cot. Her right hind foot showed where the first shot had hit her. The other bullet that struck her was the last one before she charged, and that had creased her just under the skin on the back of the neck, from the shock of which she instantly recovered.

In spite of their fighting qualities I have never respected leopards. This is not because of my misadventure, but because the leopard has always seemed to me a sneaking kind of animal and perhaps, also, that he will eat carrion, even down to a dead and diseased hyena. I have seen a lot of leopards since that memorable day and I have occasionally killed one, but I have taken pains never again to attempt it at such close quarters. [17]

It is a great story. And through this episode, Akeley learned a lot about himself and about Africa, too. He called her "fatalistic," and indeed she is fatalistic and impersonal, like a great god of indifferent and savage power, administering life on the edge. Akeley had never felt as alive as in the battle fought astride the furious and murderous cat, and he imploded with—to borrow Michael Herr's words—"the reserves of adrenaline you could make available to yourself, pumping it up and putting it out until you were lost floating in it, not afraid, almost open to clear orgasmic death-by-drowning in it, actually relaxed."[18]

The leopard event proved consummately seductive. It is the kind of experience that one plays over and over again in one's mind, trying to revive a memory of it. It is an experience so powerful that it can change the course of one's life. Carl Akeley was never the same again. He lay on his cot, trying to calm his bitten and battered body, with the dead leopard stretched out next to him on the ground. He watched her as she slept in death, flies accumulating on her body. He smelled the scent of blood mingle with his own medicinal smells, and let the astounding spirit of the continent wash over him as he slipped into sleep.

Nearby, a very ill Elliot also slept. After ten days of high fever, he called Akeley and Dodson to his cot to talk about their future. They felt that Elliot needed medical assistance and advised leaving for the coast the next day. It is ironic that malaria-bearing mosquitoes, nasty but tiny little bugs, halted the expedition, rather than a leopard with a poisoned mouth. Akeley could have gone on after resting and healing for a few days. Elliot took his colleagues' words to heart and decided to return northward to Dagabur (now Dagahabur) to recuperate. Meanwhile Akeley and Dodson would return to the area to finish collecting.

Akeley and Dodson fashioned a platform, attached to the back of a camel, on which Elliot could be transported, as he was too weak to sit upright in a saddle. Akeley, too, remained in a weakened state during the two day trip to Dagabur. The trip for Elliot was excruciating; the awkward lunging and sliding and tilting of his body, caused by the camel's movements, exacerbated the pain already racking his body. After a week in the village, Elliot was worse. It was sadly clear to all that the expedition would have to be aborted.

Elliot gave the order to return to Berbera. They packed up the camels and started off once again for the horrible Haud. Elliot could not face the camel ride again and requested a hammock stretched between two mules. It is hard to believe that the ride was any better that way. It took them one very strenuous month, from the end of August to the end of September, to travel the 250 miles to Berbera.

Completely depleted, they took time in Berbera to rest. Qualla and Elliot disposed of their livestock, making a nifty profit on the Italian war themselves. They sent the collections on to Chicago. Akeley and Dodson themselves came down with fever, and Elliot administered the admittedly unorthodox treatment to them: "I was told," he wrote, "that champagne was the only thing that cleaned the mouth in fever and so I took a small supply merely as a medicine. In such a hot climate, without ice and drunk from tin cups, champagne is a very mean beverage anyway."[19]

After almost six months in Africa, the small expedition sailed from Aden to England on October 1, 1896. Akeley and Dodson were still ill during the crossing. Akeley's pulse fell to fifty every afternoon and Dodson showed signs of typhoid. Back in England, Elliot's physician congratulated him on being alive at all. Elliot noted, "Another month in Africa would have I think, closed out the white men of this expedition and it was fortunate I turned back when I did."[20]

In spite of the myriad problems of human and animal sickness, attacks by beasts great and small, financial anxiety, enervation and dehydration from a hostile sun, and misery from a hostile earth, the expedition was a huge success. Africa gave up some treasure to the small band willing to probe her secrets. The Somaliland expedition yielded almost two hundred mammal skins, three hundred bird skins, numerous reptiles, about half a barrel of fish, skeletons, plaster casts of animal heads and body parts, and three hundred photographic negatives of people, scenery, and animals, as well as a collection of ethnographic specimens for the Field Museum.

Elliot was very pleased with himself and his companions. He wrote that "We will make the Field Columbian Museum lick all creation as a scientific museum and a Mecca for all naturalists to visit."[21] They were all very proud of themselves; there was a good deal of backslapping when they were all well enough to appreciate their accomplishments. After all, they were the very first American institution to embark on such a noteworthy venture. The only regret that they had was that they failed to collect any larger game, like rhinos, elephants, and buffalos. Nonetheless, they fully realized the success of their expedition, in spite of this shortcoming.

Elliot wrote to the trustees about Akeley, "who throughout the entire expedition devoted himself exclusively to its service, and strove to insure its success. He worked day and night totally unmindful of himself, and accomplished results that would have been praiseworthy if attained by the labor of half-a-dozen men, and much of the credit for the successful outcome of the expedition is largely due to his untiring efforts."[22]

Akeley fell in love with Africa on this first expedition. He would grapple with his passion for the continent for the rest of his life. The scientific side of the experience was very clear to him. He became thoroughly determined that collecting for museum exhibition could only be properly executed in the way of that first venture: being there in the field with the animals, watching them, studying their habits, observing how they related to their mates and offspring, watching them negotiate their environment. He would be back; he knew that for certain. It was just a matter of time. And he would bring Mickie with him the next time.

THE FOUR SEASONS

What had been lost was the sense of being part of a miracle; . . . of being shut in a cellar after living in the sky.
— EVELYN AMES, *A Glimpse of Eden*

. . . These most brisk and giddy-paced times.
— WILLIAM SHAKESPEARE, *Twelfth Night*

CARL AKELEY CAME HOME from Africa alone, leaving Elliot in London to do his own research at the British Museum. Elliot had sent strict instructions that none of the specimens were to be opened prior to Akeley's arrival because "Africa supplies a breed of insects that will eat anything from dough to cast iron, there should be no opportunity for them to escape, and Mr. Akeley best understands how to deal with them."[1] There was a great deal of work for Akeley to do at the museum. He also had to pick up the pieces of his life.

Carl returned a changed man. Even his face had changed: it was more solid, more rugged, more set. Weight had fallen from his nearly six-foot frame which had supported 190 pounds. His shoulders were more rounded. Akeley was different in ways that were impossible for Mickie to understand or explain. She felt uncomfortable and alienated, and jealousy scarred the corners of their relationship. She envied the experiences and the wild stories that he brought back, and examined the streaked scars and punctures on his arms with laserlike concentration, tracing them with excited fingers as he told her slowly and in great detail the story of the leopard fight.

Long trips, especially trips that turn into pilgrimages of a sort, can separate couples that do not share the adventure. The one who has taken the journey is fuller, sometimes feeling guilty for his or her exuberance, often irritated with the mate's lack of comprehension, always clearer and more resolved. The one left behind feels distrustful, anxious that the rules have changed, when confronted with a different mate. When the added ingredient of an experience as staggering as facing mortality in a violent dead-on encounter is thrown into the mix, it takes a powerful bond to survive. Carl and Mickie had to find a new path that they could travel together as equals—the *Four Seasons* provided that path, and they worked on the groups of deer with a new fervor.

At the museum, Akeley also set to work immediately mounting the skins they had collected in Africa—kudus by day, and Virginia deer by night. Elliot's return from England and tour of the African work underway in Akeley's studio provided a cause for celebration. He also visited Akeley's and Mickie's shop and had a sneak preview of the *Four Seasons*. Elliot definitely wanted it for the Field Museum. It was probably the deer groups that sparked Elliot's interest in a new and spectacular hall that Akeley was envisioning for the museum. In Milwaukee, Akeley had wanted to create an exhibition featuring the fur-bearing mammals. Now he wanted to create a great hall dedicated to the North American ruminants and fur bearers. But unlike the Milwaukee hall, Akeley wanted to feature the larger game—elk, wapiti, moose, and others—in groupings similar to the "Four Seasons."

Akeley had not yet conceived a grand plan for African mammals. He mounted them in lovely, exquisitely designed groups, but they stood alone as pieces of sculpture not yet integrated into an overall habitat. All of his creative efforts were being poured into the deer groups. Elliot was so excited by the prospective hall of ruminants that he planned a new expedition for Akeley and himself to the more civilized area of the Olympic Mountain range in the northwestern United States.

The expedition could hardly have differed more from the Somaliland trip. Elliot, Akeley, and companions left Chicago on July 16, 1898, traveling via Seattle to Port Angeles, Washington, on the Juan de Fuca Strait. There they assembled a pack train consisting of nine horses conducted by six men, and proceeded into the interior of the mountains, which according to Elliot, "loomed grand and massive before us, their rugged sides and towering peaks, many of them covered with snow, shadowed in the clear waters of the sea that washed the shore at their feet."[2] Almost immediately, the expedition suffered a mishap. A horse lost its footing on the slippery trail and fell about fifty feet into the valley below, sending up a crashing noise that echoed throughout the canyons and yawning chasms of the mountains.

Rushing down to the horse, the men expected to find a mangled body. Instead they found the animal yawning deeply, as if awakening from a sound sleep. He had landed squarely on his back, heavily padded with bedding for the expedition members, which had cushioned his fall. He had been blinded in one eye from hitting a root on impact, but was otherwise unhurt. In general, the trails were treacherous as they moved deeper into the primeval forest. The mountains were exceedingly difficult to negotiate for their steep slopes, sudden ravines, and abrupt landslides.

It was cold, crystal clear, and brilliantly colorful with a profusion of summer wildflowers blanketing the meadows. Spectacular cedars, often bald and straight as needles piercing the heavens, surrounded them. They were after elk, camping for weeks at a stretch while they looked for signs of the animals. For all the treasures that Mother Nature had bestowed upon the region, the expedition had a hard time finding animals. Elliot wrote: "I do not think I was ever before in a country that was so devoid of animal life. One could walk for days and see nothing save a squirrel, chipmunk, or blue jay."[3]

They decided to change their course from southward to westward, hoping to have better luck. Elliot wanted to proceed to the headwaters of the Solduck River, which emptied into the Pacific Ocean, but he did not know if it was possible to get there from their camp. It was difficult to chart a course without some reconnaissance.

Akeley and an assistant left the expedition on foot, traveling deeper into elk territory, to find an available trail. They found themselves trapped in a ravine, unable to proceed, and backtracked to tell Elliot. Finally the expedition discovered a way to penetrate the range, but not without new difficulties. This broken and rough country along the snow line proved almost impossible for men to traverse, and absolutely impossible for pack animals. The horses were left behind, and the expedition proceeded on foot, carrying all that they needed on their backs. The rainy season set in. Out of thirty days, it poured in torrents for twenty-eight. In spite of the hardships, they managed to collect five elk and over five hundred mammal specimens, which represented almost every species indigenous to the Olympic Mountain range.

The expedition, which lasted only three months, was very successful. The participants not only returned with ample game for the hall, but discovered five new lakes, one of which was named after Elliot. They also discovered a new species of mouse which Elliot named after Akeley: *Peromyseus akeleyi*.[4]

Akeley returned to the Field Museum with new resolve. He plunged himself into the vast workload entailed in mounting the African and North American mammals recently collected. He also had to complete the deer groups once and for all so that he could proceed to other personal projects.

Akeley worked on the deer groups constantly, if not physically, then mentally. One of the problems that he had in mounting the deer themselves was in holding the velvet onto the male antlers. One night when he, Mickie, and Thomas were at the theater, Akeley suddenly blurted out in the middle of the performance, much to the chagrin of his companions, "I've got it!" He had cracked the problem and found a solution: pouring melted paraffin into the hollow antlers would make the velvet adhere to them. Though a seemingly trivial incident in the scheme of things, it showed the incessant and acute attention to detail that consistently made Akeley's work so brilliant.

In 1900, the Field decided to buy the *Four Seasons*, though the completed work would not be on exhibit until 1902. When the groups were finished, it was estimated that over seventeen thousand leaves alone had been produced. Mickie had executed most of them herself, though Akeley's brother, Thomas, helped complete the project. Akeley and Mickie invested much of their future on those deer groups.

Having sold the *Four Seasons* to the Field Museum, and feeling secure about his financial future, Akeley bought himself an Oldsmobile, then a new car on the market. He and Mickie made a pittance on the deer groups ($5,500),[5] barely covering their expenses, much less the value of their time or design. But the sale of the groups to the Field Museum held great promise for the financial stability of their lives and for Akeley's professional future. They got married quietly two days before Christmas, 1902. Their love affair would last almost a quarter of a century, from their meeting until their divorce. Mickie attached herself to Akeley for her own fulfillment as much as for love. They married at a time when women could only live the lives they wanted for themselves through their spouses. Akeley was a reflection of Mickie's own aspirations—a type of spirit, redolent with creativity and accomplishments, that she was unable to see in herself. When they married, he was thirty-eight, Mickie was twenty-seven. We might guess that two close friends, Dr. Warren and Olive Howe, were with them at their wedding. Dr. Howe and Akeley were good friends, who enjoyed working on their automobiles together. (Through an odd twist of fate, Mickie would someday find herself married to Warren Howe as her second husband.) Akeley promised Mickie a postponed honeymoon in Africa.

Between the African and North American mammals, Akeley needed assistance. The deer groups brought him great notoriety and admiration from his colleagues, many of whom offered their help. The letters from friends and colleagues alike are quite touching, telling him how marvelous his accomplishment was. They offer, almost for the first time, a sense of how dear Akeley was to his friends: "[you are a] Star in the taxidermy sky," says one.[6] "[w]hen you pass out of this world you had better donate your own hide to the museum and get some expert to put you up among your own work—I never enjoyed anything of its kind so much as I did the mounted animals in Chicago," raves another.[7] One of his admirers was C. L. Dewey; Akeley asked the Field Museum to hire Dewey as his assistant. Another museum preparator for whom Akeley interceded was Richard Raddatz. (Over twenty years later, Raddatz would be with him when he died.)

Akeley's worlds were converging in a pleasant way in 1902. His work was going very well at the museum, he was happy with Mickie, and he was held in great regard by his colleagues. Akeley received a letter from Wheeler asking his advice on whether he should accept a position at the American Museum of Natural History. By then Will was teaching at the University of Texas. He was put off by the internal politics of academia, but he also feared the politics of big scientific institutions like the AMNH. He feared that he would be moving from "the frying pan into the fire."[8] He relied on Akeley, who was himself comfortable in a museum setting, to advise him honestly about the AMNH position. Akeley had also visited the museum that same year, and had met some of the staff.

Wheeler's old friend, H. C. Bumpus was the new director of the American Museum of Natural History. He wanted Wheeler to come aboard and reorganize the museum's invertebrate collection. Wheeler found the offer tempting. At that time, Akeley was happy at the Field. He had a friend and champion in Daniel Giraud Elliot, and he had no way of knowing then that the museum's internal politics would restrict him when Elliot later resigned. Since Akeley was then content at his job and removed from museum politics, he advised Wheeler to make the move. Wheeler accepted the job.

Dr. Bumpus had been hired by the AMNH in 1900 because of his commitment to educating the public about natural history. In particular, he was very outspoken about conservation issues. He campaigned actively against the killing of birds for ladies' hats, ultimately urging legislators to do something about the slaughter. Bumpus was brought on as an assistant to the museum's president, Morris Ketchen Jesup, and was promoted to director in 1903.

Besides his administrative duties, Bumpus dealt directly with the public education aspects of the museum, including exhibition practices. This particular bailiwick provided Akeley's first connection with the AMNH. Bumpus had traveled to Europe to visit museums there so that he would be better able to make informed decisions about needed changes at the AMNH. He recognized a need to improve the natural history exhibits to provide "innocent amusement and instruction."[9] He was committed to the concept that exhibition be pleasing and artistic. To achieve this, he brought in James Lippitt Clark, a young sculptor who was a student at the Rhode Island School of Design.

When Akeley visited the AMNH, he was impressed with Clark's work. He asked Bumpus to send Clark to the Field Museum to work with him for a while; he said he would be happy to teach Clark his new taxidermy techniques. Bumpus and Akeley had a friendship dating back to Milwaukee, where Bumpus had visited Will. And Bumpus had continued to closely observe Akeley's progress for years. He seized the opportunity to have Akeley instruct Clark, whom he sent to Chicago later that year.

Akeley taught Clark the new methods while they worked together for two months, producing a mount of a beautiful Virginia doe. Clark was a bit awe-struck by Akeley and his work, but was even more overwhelmed by his generosity of spirit. Clark's observation of Akeley provides a moving portrait of the man:

> With a very sympathetic nature, he was always kind and considerate and a staunch and loyal friend, but an unyielding enemy when one broke faith or was not up and above-board with others. His face and features were strong but kindly. With a rather broad skull, a fine high forehead ran back under thin lightest hair, which was slightly wavy and seldom well groomed.
> There were always clouds of smoke about his head from a pipe or cigarette as he worked or talked, and he was always at his best when reclined in his big chair, thinking out loud, rambling his dreams and plans, which were always quite idealistic, while his listener sat spellbound under the ease and charm of a strong but mellow voice . . .
> Indifferent to dress, he went busily about his affairs in an intent and preoccupied manner. Full of rare humor, he was astutely original and direct in his remarks. If he did not like a person, he could very well tell you why in a few cutting and appropriate words, and when he swore he did so with much ease and an equally appropriate vocabulary. Generous to the extreme, he would share his time and money to help any friend and ask little or no return.[10]

The Chicago period of Akeley's relationship with Clark reveals an often misunderstood aspect of Akeley's character. After his death, there was a good deal of talk in the press that Akeley was stingy with his inventions and in particular with the taxidermy techniques he developed. This was untrue. He was quiet about his developments through a sense of modesty, a genuine lack of interest in promoting himself, and an incessant reluctance to finish anything absolutely. He was always perfecting his designs and putting off their "publication" until they were finally in their finished and ultimate form. There never was a last word on anything. Akeley even joked about this shortcoming himself: "I have a reputation for having no terminal facilities."[11] He was always fiddling with alterations and improvements, so he rarely "published." However, his work in-progress was available to anyone who wanted it.

William Alanson Bryan, a colleague and friend from the Field Museum, worried that Akeley's work was undervalued. Bryan visited Clark at the AMNH after his Field Museum sojourn with Akeley, and was appalled at the lack of credit given to Akeley by either Clark or his colleagues. Later in life, according to Clark's colleagues, there seemed a tinge of jealousy coloring the Clark/Akeley friendship. But in defense of Clark, at this particular point, he had come back to the AMNH fired up with enthusiasm over the new Akeley method and was told by the administration that the process was too slow and costly and that he had to find a way to modify it for the museum. Clark was, therefore, disgruntled, and his frustration probably carried over into his attitude about Akeley to Bryan.

In any event, Bryan felt that the AMNH was not giving Akeley due credit, and that the museum community at large would take Akeley's ideas without crediting him. Bryan wrote to Akeley, in a letter full of the passion of a protective friend:

> Now Carl, since I have seen you I have seen the hole for the new Carnegie museum, the new Washington museum, the proposed new Brooklyn museum and I want to say that if you don't publish those methods for constructing your groups before the snow flies, they will have those ideas away from you in some unknown way and will be using them in these museums. Now publish them at once—add to them later if you can—but publish them. I believe that if your notion was in print today that tomorrow the whole drove of them would be on the train going to see you. And Akeley, that idea as you have shown it to me is in the atmosphere . . . I hold my breath for you for fear some one will tumble on to it either accidently or through cross talk among architects and scientists . . . and beat you out of the "Akeley idea" in museum construction. There is nothing like it in the world today, but I see it coming, in fact it has haunted me ever since my delightful visit with you and your dear wife . . . Think of all this and now if I have said too much forgive it as being a heartfelt desire to have you get your just desserts, and be as you should be, acknowledged as the greatest museum man that has ever lived. [12]

William Alanson Bryan was the assistant curator in Ornithology at the Field Museum when he and Akeley met. At the time of this letter he was the curator of Ethnology and Natural History at the Bishop Museum in Honolulu. He had traveled extensively and was very interested in the growth and development of American museums. His credentials added weight to his words; Bryan was not merely a loving friend. But it was not until May 1908 that Akeley presented publicly his revolutionary new techniques in taxidermy. At the Chicago meeting of the American Association of Museums, Akeley propounded his ideas to the world, thereby "publishing" them.

One of Akeley's ideas was to paint the diorama backgrounds on curved glass, taking the cyclorama concept another step by adding a translucence to the background. He hoped to incorporate this new idea in another new hall for the Field Museum that would feature the birds of Illinois. The bird hall's design should be noted as it was this unrealized concept that developed into the AMNH's Hall of African Mammals. The bird hall was to be an enormous, open, darkened space with a series of bird dioramas, individually illuminated, around the perimeter of the room. There were also to be four more spacious corner groves that would feature the larger bird species. The idea of painted backgrounds on glass soon evolved into the notion of photographic transparencies. The Field Museum found the idea interesting, but not interesting enough to spend the necessary money; they needed the money for more basic and less artistic endeavors—like survival and expansion. Akeley took one of the bird groups in-progress and tried to sell it to the AMNH. When the crate arrived in New York, the photo transparency background was smashed into a million pieces. But the idea was there. Significantly, when the AMNH opened its 1910 Africa Ethnography Hall, there were large glass transparencies of indigenous people figuring directly in the design.

The Field Columbian Museum began to expand. It dispatched anthropological, paleontological, and archeological expeditions to the western United States and Mexico. At the close of the Louisiana Purchase Exposition in St. Louis, the museum bought some major collections of anthropological and archeological materials, including a large collection of African ethnographic artifacts. The museum was turning its head toward the "dark continent" once more. At the urging of Elliot and Akeley, and based on the glorious success of the previous expedition, the executive committee voted to support another expedition to Africa.

Elliot chose not to repeat his life-threatening experience. He was seventy years old by then, and chose to turn over the leadership of the expedition to Carl Akeley and some younger colleagues. The goal was to supplement the earlier collections and, specifically, to bring back the larger African mammals, especially elephants.

Ward's Natural Science Establishment. Whale jaw bones gate can be seen at right.

An illustration of a Ward's Natural Science Establishment preparation studio drawn by F. A. Lucas.

The house where Akeley was born in Clarendon, New York. (COURTESY AMNH NEG. #2A 13666)

Above left: Daniel Webster Akeley, Carl's father. (COURTESY AKELEY FAMILY)

Above: Julia Glidden Akeley, Carl's mother. (COURTESY AKELEY FAMILY)

Canary mounted by the twelve-year-old Carl Akeley.

The magnificent "Four Seasons."
(COURTESY FIELD MUSEUM PHOTO COLLECTION)

Carl Akeley and J. William Critchley in 1885, the year they mounted Jumbo for P. T. Barnum.

A photo of a young Akeley just after he arrived in Milwaukee.

The articulated skeleton and mounted skin of Jumbo in 1888, both of which traveled with Barnum's circus after the elephant was tragically killed by a locomotive. Akeley mounted the skin for Ward's. (COURTESY CIRCUS WORLD MUSEUM, BARABOO, WISCONSIN)

*Carl Akeley's muskrat diorama at the Milwaukee Public Museum which held the promise of all his later brilliant work. This diorama was the first of its kind anywhere and celebrated, in 1990, its one hundredth birthday. (*COURTESY MILWAUKEE PUBLIC MUSEUM NEG. #7623*)*

A bearded Akeley on his first African expedition, Somaliland, 1896. (COURTESY FIELD MUSEUM PHOTO COLLECTION)

Akeley with a greater kudu collected on his Somaliland expedition with Daniel Giraud Elliot. (COURTESY FIELD MUSEUM PHOTO COLLECTION)

Akeley with the leopard he killed barehanded. He signed his own copy of this image "First and second money." (COURTESY FIELD MUSEUM PHOTO COLLECTION)

Opposite: A horse mounted by Akeley for Washington D.C.'s National Museum (Smithsonian) exhibit at the Columbian Exposition in Chicago, 1893. (COURTESY SMITHSONIAN INSTITUTION)

The Akeley cement gun is used at the Panama Canal for the purpose of preventing rock slides.

Nairobi's Norfolk Hotel in 1909. Akeley was a guest there many times.

Akeley sculpting his big bull elephant. Ironically this method proved too unwieldy for such large animals and this model was dissembled. Akeley refined his taxidermy processes for the AMNH elephant group. (COURTESY AMNH NEG. #330591)

Mickie, the huntress, atop one of the elephants she collected for the Field Museum.
(COURTESY AMNH NEG. #46355)

Cunninghame ritually "bloods" Delia, according to the Abyssinian hunting tradition, with the tusk nerve of her first elephant in 1905. (COURTESY AMNH NEG. #211527)

TEMBO CIRCUS:
Bibi and Bwana
in Africa

*We carry within us the wonders we seek without us: There is all Africa and
her prodigies in us.*

—SIR THOMAS BROWNE, *Religio Medici*

MICKIE WAS SHAKING so violently that she could hardly conceal her
terror. Speech could not come from her dry, tightly clenched mouth.
Elephants were everywhere, their grey, saggy skins appearing in flashes and
shadows through the variegated vegetation. Only bits and pieces of the beasts
could be seen; they looked like one enormous monster with a million parts
that one can only vaguely sense, more frightening in its eerie indiscernibility.
Branches cracked and bark was being stripped from the trees like zippers. A
little one practiced with his trunk, happily swinging it around like a snake,
not certain yet that it was anything but a plaything as it wove a path through a
forest of grey leg-trunks. Mickie was usually amused and engaged watching
animal young. Not today. Her sweat was acrid; nervous sweat. Elephant
rumblings—low infrasonic vibrations that hunters used to think were merely
stomach noises made when the animals were at peace—throbbed in the dense
air. (We know now these sounds are part of a highly complicated communication network.) Mickie guessed they were communicating, but what were
they telling each other? There were terrible stories about angry rogue elephants with human blood ground into their knees and feet from punishing

84

their predators. Still, the peace of the elephant scene prevailed—eating, talking elephants. But the movie that played on in her head was a violent one. She was on dangerous ground and she knew it. Mickie had to kill one of the animals, a large one with great tusks. She gripped her Mannlicher as she crept forward on the path. Suddenly her nerve endings exploded. She bolted, turned, and ran. Akeley, a few feet behind her, grabbed her arm and bullied, then cajoled her into holding steady. The elephants had not heard; there was still a chance of bagging one. Mickie fought for self-control; she was excited, terrified, resolved, and eager to please this hard taskmaster, her husband.

She returned to her spot as R. J. Cuninghame, their elephant hunter, coached her in quiet tones. She aimed her rifle carefully, breathed through her heightened anxiety, and fired. Trumpeting, screaming, and bedlam detonated the forest as mighty elephants crashed through forest walls as if they were cobwebs. Two more shots for good measure and the great bull was down. The humans held very still until the forest quieted. Mickie could hardly contain herself for the rapture and relief flooding her, soaking her. Finally Cuninghame approached the elephant corpse, a stilled and looming spirit permeating the glen. He called Akeley and Mickie to see the great thing she had done. Her nerves were still frayed, and the photographs of her look as if she is in a state of semi-shock.

The men were very proud of her, and in fact, she was very proud of herself. They all touched the warm, tough hide of the fallen monarch, fingering the bullet holes, as hunters always did—examining, probing, in an almost sensual manner. Akeley took photos of Mickie and R.J. sitting on the corpse, relaxed, R.J. leaning on his elbow and Mickie comfortable with legs crossed—they could be on a picnic in the south of France.

After the butchering, R.J. went through the elephant christening ritual with the seriousness of a priest saying mass. In an old Ethiopian custom reserved for young brave hunters, the cone of jellylike pulp in the nerve base of the elephant ivory tusk was drawn out, its tip cut off, and a cross of blood marked on the forehead of the killer—much like the ritual of Ash Wednesday, with its annual remembrance of death and decay. The blood got into Mickie's hair.

They were on Mt. Kenya—Kirinyaga—the holy mountain of the Kikuyu people in British East Africa (now Kenya). Mickie had killed an elephant two days before, but it had been easier—beginner's luck, really. Akeley had exhausted the quota designated on his license and needed Mickie to collect the elephants for which they had journeyed so far. Mickie was a brave soul, though she had little choice in the matter with Akeley pushing her. In her downing of two elephants on Mt. Kenya, Mickie had bagged the biggest ivory and surpassed the records of all hunters who came before her. Akeley was extremely proud of her and eventually wrote an article about Bibi's (the Kiswahili word for "Mrs."—the native staff called Mickie "Bibi") great hunt. Her accomplishment, however, never made it to the pages of the *East African Standard*, British East Africa's newspaper. A woman holding the record? They let that one slip by as unnewsworthy. Alice Roosevelt's exotic wedding dress was more important for the ladies to read about. It is also noteworthy that Mickie herself never bragged about this accomplishment.

The Akeleys had left Chicago on August 13, 1905, for Africa. They travelled via London to outfit themselves, much as Akeley had done in 1896. British East Africa was then still a primitive paradise, a land bursting with great herds of animals. It would not be so for long. There was a big advertising campaign in progress to sell BEA as a great place to live—a white man's country. And when men who are not in harmony with the land arrive, the animals are pushed aside or out.

In brief, during the scramble for African territory in the late 1800s, the British had grabbed the area around Lake Victoria to prevent another power from gaining control over the source of the Nile. If hostile forces succeeded in holding the White Nile's headwaters, they could conceivably redirect them, causing the river to dry up in Egypt. Desolation, native uprisings, and revolts would follow, which would jeopardize the Suez Canal. The Suez was access to the "Jewel" of the British Empire, India, and many felt that without it, disaster would strike England as well. While the notion was convoluted, it created a chain of events and a British policy in Africa that would prevail for over a half-century.

Once the British possessed what is now Uganda, they realized it was of little use if it remained inaccessible. The British hit on the great idea of building a railroad from the coast to Lake Victoria. Work commenced in 1895 and was completed in 1901. The Uganda railroad, nicknamed the "Lunatic Express," cost a fortune, and many imported Indian laborers lost their lives. Now the British had to make it pay for itself, and so urged settlement in the region. BEA became a protectorate in 1895, and adventurous settlers began to inhabit the land.

Akeley had done his homework and knew that the great herds had been demolished in South Africa as soon as settlers arrived. He realized that they needed to go to BEA in search of large game for the museum before it was too late. Not only was he going to Africa again, but now he was taking Mickie with him as his assistant. The Field requested that she collect butterflies and "native curios." This arrangement was perfectly satisfactory to Mickie, certain that this was to be a great romantic adventure with Akeley in paradise.

Another member of the expedition team was Edmund Heller, who was a collector in the Field's Department of Zoology. He had been recalled from field work in Central America to join Akeley's expedition. Heller was a slouchy, deliberate character with an enormous capacity for dry humor. He and Akeley were very similar, and they were both veterans of the field. Heller joined Akeley and Mickie in London, where they also joined Vernon Shaw-Kennedy, who had been sent ahead to make arrangements.

Tembo Circus

They left for Mombasa from Dover on board the SS *President*. The trip thrilled Mickie, the unsophisticated farm girl. She was learning quickly, though: In London she ordered herself a beautiful, fashionable wardrobe for Africa's bushland (including peach silk underwear which became essential to her later on—it helped her feel lovely and feminine amidst the harsh and rigorous expedition life). After arriving in Mombasa, where they spent six days checking supplies, procuring hunting licenses, and adjusting to the exotic, but hot, African coast, they boarded the Uganda railway on October 14, arriving in Nairobi the next day.

In 1905, Nairobi was merely a handful of buildings on mile 327 of the railway line. It had grown out of a railhead established by the dictates of topography: Just beyond it, the plains gave way to a sudden bulging up of the earth's surface into the lush central highlands of Kenya. Railroad supplies and men were regrouped and reorganized there to begin the ascent to the higher western landscape. The first photographs of Nairobi are simply of railway sheds. The location was a pleasant one, at almost six thousand feet above sea level, and was named Nairobi, meaning a "place of cold water." The Kikuyu from the highlands met the Maasai from the plains at this junction, to trade goods as the Maasai watered their cattle.

In no time, Asian-run shops cropped up to supply the railway workers, and with the arrival of the settlers, government houses and hotels were added. The Stanley and Norfolk Hotels were already established by 1905. Akeley's expedition camped at the location where the Kenya National Archives now stands, in the middle of Nairobi. Akeley and Mickie stayed at the Norfolk, established less than a year before by a big game hunter, Major Ringer. It was a principal meeting place in town for men leaving for or returning from the bush.

While at the Norfolk, some unknown American hunter brought to Mickie a nine-year-old Kikuyu boy who wanted to go on safari. African boys wanted to go on safari the way American boys wanted to join the circus. His name was Gikungu Mbiru—nicknamed "Bill" by the Europeans. Mickie immediately took to the child and wanted to bring him along. Her companions complained that he was much too young, and would only cause problems in the bush. But the Irishwoman was determined: "in a flash I was overwhelmed with a desire to possess that child."[1] Bill went along. (In fact, he would be with Akeley for more than twenty years, and claim a place of great importance in his life.)

The 1905 stay in Nairobi brought another lifelong friendship to Akeley. He was wandering around some corrugated tin warehouses near the railroad station, looking for a specimen storehouse, when he ran into Leslie J. Tarlton. They soon struck up a fast friendship. Tarlton, a redheaded Australian, and his partner, V. M. Newland, had served in the Boer War, and then come to East Africa in search of fortune. They had applied for a large tract of land near Naivasha. The Land Office had tentatively granted it, but when they arrived, they discovered that the land had been set aside as a reserve for the Maasai. They were offered alternative sites, one of which was a thousand-acre farm in Kiambu, Kikuyu territory. They soon became bankrupt, sold the land, and set their sights on Nairobi. There they worked as auctioneers and estate agents.

When Akeley returned from the bush with specimens to store in Tarlton's warehouse, Tarlton suggested that he and Newland might do the logistical business for Akeley. "His proposal," Akeley recalled, "was that he act as my agent, sending food and other supplies to us in the field as they were required and thus obviating the necessity of my coming in whenever a consignment of skins was made. As time is precious in the field and one does not often happen upon a helper of such ingenuity and diligence, we soon came to terms. Newland, Tarlton, and Company had acquired their first safari client."[2] Whether Akeley was really the very first client of this company, which later became one of the biggest and most successful of all, is unclear. Certainly he was one of the first.

Africa had not yet been established as a big hunting capital, and "white hunter" was not yet a common term in safari nomenclature. While today some shame hovers around the word because of depleted and endangered wildlife, then the name was acceptable, even romantic, and worn like a badge. Carl Akeley was one of the first to be given this name. Among the ranks of white hunters, Americans were rare. He fascinated the British settlers as a white hunter making a scientific collection for a rich American's museum in Chicago. They followed his adventures and accomplishments in the *East African Standard*.

Akeley led the expedition first into the Athi Plains, only a few miles outside of Nairobi. There were enormous herds of game meandering over the plains. From a distance, they looked like sluggish rivers flowing haphazardly over the burnished gold grasses. The expedition stayed in the Athi Plains about ten weeks, making a number of collections. In fact, the expedition had its greatest success during that first stretch. Initially, Mickie stayed in camp, content to keep the books and occasionally venture out to collect insects with a net. She soon graduated to collecting small birds. Then one day, while she and her guide were out together in the bush, they heard a lion growl at them. Mickie became terrified. She knew that if she told the men about the incident they would not let her go into the bush alone again. She decided to keep silent. The next day she announced that she was going hunting even though she had shot little more than a target and a few birds. The men were amused by her bravado, and their laughter made her even more resolved. As always, Mickie remained extremely sensitive about being teased. Where Akeley enjoyed a good laugh at his own expense, his wife took herself very seriously. "So the next day," she wrote, "I went out, first asking Mr. Akeley what I might shoot. Highly amused, he assured me that I might shoot anything but an ostrich. An hour later, I came across an eland and brought it down with my first shot. When Mr. Akeley saw it he grinned rather wryly and said that I would have to pay a fine of $25, for eland were protected by the government.

"From then on I hunted and learned how to preserve their skins. I learned from my gunbearer the names of the different species, how to stalk and trace them on the veldt and in the forest."[3] Akeley and Mickie spent Christmas in this camp, decorating a small acacia tree for the occasion. It must have been a wistful holiday for Carl, as he received word that his father had died at the end of October.

On December 30, they moved by rail to Kijabe, about forty-four miles northwest of Nairobi. There, for the first time, the Akeleys saw the spectacle of the Great Rift Valley. Gouged out of the earth, the Rift is like an enormous zipper ready to rend the earth from the Afar triangle, at Africa's horn, down to Mozambique. Created millions of years ago, the Rift is a classroom in geology, as layers of strata are clearly visible. The valley is an immensely dramatic place. Perched on the edge, watching a fast sunset burning out in the western sky, an individual at last feels that the scale is right. Rather than feeling tiny and insignificant, the human heart and spirit fill up and expand— liberated, ecstatic. In fact, seeing the Great Rift Valley for the first time is akin to déjà vu, to sensing something we have known for thousands of years— man on the brink of timelessness. It is one of the most evocative places on earth, regardless of how many times one sees it or from which direction it is approached.

Kijabe is located on the edge of the valley, still in the highlands at about six thousand feet above sea level, nestled equidistant from the foothills of the Aberdare (now Nyandarua) Mountains to the east and the Mau Escarpment to the west. It seems the last outpost before the full drama of the Great Rift takes over. The expedition intended to make a collection of African buffalos here. In a month's time they succeeded in obtaining only one buffalo specimen, as well as a series of colobus monkeys and their first rhinoceros.

In Kijabe, Akeley received a letter from home that demanded his attention to some family problems. The letter also contained cause for rejoicing. His brother Thomas had a baby girl, Vernette. This was welcome news following, as it did so closely, the sad news of his father's death. The birth touched him, particularly as babies seemed to be on his mind. He wrote: "Mickie is thinking of adopting one here, they are certainly plentiful and easily inspected as they are not wearing any clothes."[4] It was no joking matter for Mickie, who thought about adopting a child more than once.

More urgent, however, was the need to deal with Carl's mother. She had moved in with Thomas after their father's death, and was causing havoc in the household. Akeley felt that she was mentally unbalanced, and suggested that Thomas treat her like a child and not allow her to be so disruptive. He had already written a stern letter to his mother. Carl continued to be intolerant of his mother's behavior throughout his life, never acknowledging the depth of her disappointment and pain. He chose to see her as a spoiled child and refused to recognize that she was miserable and ill after the death of her husband. Ironically, on Akeley's next expedition to Africa in 1910, he would receive word from strangers that his mother, too, had died. We know nothing of his reaction.

Mickie was very successful in obtaining various ethnographic specimens. She became a major attraction to the indigenous Africans wherever she went, not only because she was a beautiful white woman, but because her hair was prematurely grey. The African women she met inevitably asked her to let down her magical hair and shake it out. When the sun hit it she would look like a gossamer angel. For the performance, Mickie demanded payment in native ornaments: "A priceless ivory bracelet, an armlet carved from a rhino horn, barbaric weapons, cowrie shells, beads and girdles were the bounty I exacted, and my audience always seemed to consider the entertainment worth the price!"[5] Several years later, Mickie's hair appears darker in photographs. Bothered by her older appearance, particularly when her marriage began to get rocky, she probably rinsed it.

February was spent at Lake Elementeita, about fifty miles northwest of Kijabe. Elementeita is one of six lakes dotting the floor of the Great Rift Valley. One of the shallow soda lakes, it attracted numerous avian species. Flamingos on its surface, reflected by the water, sent up a glorious fiery haze that mingled with the undulating heat waves. Papyrus and other grasses surrounded the lake, and tracks of animals coming in to drink were crunched into the brittle sand. The "sleeping old man," a small hill so-called for its appearance, watches over the lake in his dreamy slumber. This beautiful lake today is on Lord Delamere's ranch in Soysambu. In 1905 Lord Hugh Delamere, one of Kenya's most famous settlers, was only beginning to buy up huge tracts of land in the lake area. The Akeleys were enchanted by the beauty of Elementeita. Their month was a profitable one, as they collected various antelopes and waterbirds.

About March 8, the expedition again moved by rail to Molo, about 484 miles from the coast on the western edge of the Mau Escarpment, two thousand feet above the valley's floor. There they encountered incessant cold rains. In spite of the miserable weather, they gathered an excellent collection of topis and a series of Jackson's hartebeests. The expedition also brought back a black-maned lion, reputedly the first reported in British East Africa. Akeley had been hunting topi on the slopes of the Mau Escarpment when he realized that the topi seemed distracted and anxious. He kept a watchful eye on the side of the small valley opposite from where they were grazing. Akeley realized that there was an old, but grand, lion langorously watching the topi, though a dead zebra nearby gave evidence of his momentary lack of appetite. Akeley was almost out of ammunition and had to return to camp. The next morning, Akeley and Shaw-Kennedy went after the lion, assuming that he was still in the vicinity. They also drew lots to see which of them could have the lion. Shaw-Kennedy won and was given the preferred position for shooting the animal. They pursued their unseen quarry with native beaters, trying to flush the animal out of hiding. Akeley recalled:

> The first patch of bush that the beaters tackled was about 100 yards long and 50 yards wide. As they set up their usual racket before entering I thought I heard a lion's grunt, but as nothing more developed I concluded that it had been one of the boys. This patch of bush was a mass of nettles, brier, and thorns, and made exceedingly disagreeable going. The porters were making very slow progress so I went in to encourage them. However by the time we were halfway through I was so scratched and torn that I quit and went out toward the bottom of the ravine. The briers had somewhat cooled my faith in the theory that the lion was in the ravine. I sat down on an ant-hill where I had a fair view. Kennedy fired and I looked up quickly. The lion which had come out in front of Kennedy had turned and was running across down the ravine and up the other side. I had a good shot at him and the bullet knocked him over. However, he got up again and went into a clump of bush. The clump just filled a kind of pothole about fifty feet in diameter. Kennedy watched one side and I watched the other so that we had every avenue of escape covered. The beaters then began throwing stones and sticks into the bush. The lion made no move. He might be dead or lying close. We wanted to know, but no one wanted to know sufficiently to crawl in and see.[6]

They all stood there by the pothole, wondering what to do next. Akeley's gun bearer, Dudo, suggested starting a fire to burn him out. They threw firebrands at the animal's location, then more sticks and stones. Finally they started shooting again, above the animal but in his general direction. Nothing could entice the lion to bolt. "Finally the old fellow was so close to the edge of the brush that while we couldn't see him he undoubtedly could see us. He stood looking out on thirty black men and two white men in front of a great fire—a crowd of enemies. The path was not blocked in any other direction. He looked us over carefully for fully five minutes and then of his own volition, with a great roar, he charged out of the brush and up from the pothole. Halfway up the slope the fatal bullet hit him. He was killed charging his enemies and without thought of retreat."[7] Akeley was always impressed with lions; he thought they were true "gentlemen."

The expedition had set aside Voi, about one hundred miles inland from Mombasa, as the last collecting site because of its extremely unhealthy atmosphere. Malaria was endemic, and two of the whites and several of the black staff came down with the disease. Consequently, the expedition was not very successful in this location. (Today Voi is still a very unhealthy place, and not just because of its mosquitoes. Voi is near Tsavo National Park, where a full-scale war is in progress against poachers, who have been decimating both the rhino and elephant populations. Extinction hangs over the rhino in particular, like Damocles' sword. This issue will be discussed in the treatment of Akeley's next African expedition.)

The expedition broke camp at Voi and returned to Nairobi to pack the specimens for shipment to Chicago. Vernon Shaw-Kennedy decided to continue hunting in Uganda. Heller had to return to the States, leaving Akeley and Mickie to do most of the packing. They had ordered barrels from England, which proved to be terrible packing containers. Akeley and Mickie had to adapt railway oil drums to secure and ship the specimens. It was painstaking, tedious work, and took five full weeks to accomplish.

During these days in Nairobi, the Akeleys received instructions from the Field Museum to prolong their African sojourn until they succeeded in collecting more buffalos. They secured the necessary permission to hunt buffalos in the Tana River area. However, they were restricted to a specific time in July, which meant they had some time to kill. Akeley and Mickie decided to collect accessories for the groups and began to retrace their steps, leaving for the Athi plains, then moving on to Kijabe at a more relaxed pace. The Akeleys moved on to Lake Naivasha, where they requested permission to make a collection of birds as well as accessories. They were shocked to receive news that their request was denied.

Bibi and Bwana were stuck. Time and money were running out. It was already the middle of July and they were still not allowed to proceed to the Trans-Tana region because of native uprisings. The British government had its hands full with angry indigenous Africans who were not pleased to have their land taken from them and to be told what to do. As these upheavals impacted on Akeley's movements, it is worthwhile to take a closer look at them.

Three main tribal groups, in different parts of the country, were causing the most trouble. Two of these groups were warlike nomadic pastoralists: the Maasai in the plains south of Nairobi and in the Great Rift Valley, and the Nandi in the west above the valley along the Elgeyo Escarpment and the Uasin Gishu Plateau. The third tribe was the Kikuyu, an agricultural people who lived in the central highlands and on Mt. Kenya. None of these people got along with one another.

The Nandi, a Kalenjin-speaking tribe, succeeded in causing the British the most heartache, their revolt surviving the government's attempts to suppress them from 1890 to 1906. The saga of their guerrilla campaign and resistance is fascinating, and was well known to Akeley. He was especially taken with the Nandi, and immortalized their valor and courage in one of his sculptures. The word "Nandi" comes from the Kiswahili "*mnandi*," the name for a cormorant known for its greedy and rapacious fishing habits. The Nandi were so-named by the Arabs who traveled in caravans raided by the Kalenjin-speaking people as they passed through their lands. Like so many of the names pinned on African peoples by other races, "Nandi" was derogatory and is not in preferred usage today. These Kalenjins were fierce, determined warriors who sought to protect their land and families as the British penetrated deeper into Nandi territory to create trade routes to central Africa.

The Maasai were broken by the British relatively early. Their herds were decimated by rinderpest, resulting in a scattering of the tribal people. Thus the Maasai could create no united front, as could the Nandi. The Maasai *laibon* (spiritual leader), Lenana, befriended the British, who were then able to rule by indirect power: they ruled Lenana; Lenana ruled his people. The Maasai fought the British in ineffectual spurts. Usually the problems were centered around the Maasai proclivity for cattle-raiding. Settlers were never pleased about having their livestock stolen. But the Maasai were subdued. Karen Blixen (a.k.a. Isak Dinesen) wrote that they were "fighters who had been stopped from fighting, a dying lion with its claws clipped, a castrated nation. Their weapons have been taken from them, their big shields even, and in the Game reserve the lions follow their cattle." The Maasai were pushed onto reservations in Laikipia, north of Lake Nakuru, and Kajiado, southeast of Nairobi.

For a couple of centuries the Maasai engaged in war with the Kikuyu, raiding their animals and stealing their women. The Kikuyu were agricultural people establishing their *shambas* (farms) in the highlands or on Mt. Kenya. They were protected from the Maasai by the forest cover. As the Maasai became less of a threat, the Kikuyu began to descend to lower altitudes to build their farms. These lower areas were precisely the lands most coveted by the settlers, for their rich earth and ideal growing conditions. The British did not bother to find out that the land was ancestral Kikuyu territory and therefore thought nothing about taking it. The Kikuyu have a saying: *Gicigo kia mugunda gitinyihaga*, which means, "A piece of land is no little thing." Thus, a little land well tilled is great wealth. Sometimes it seems that earth grows in the bones of the Kikuyu, so important is land to them. Land is to the Kikuyu what cattle are to the Maasai. This is not only because of land's productive power, but because land is the home of the ancestors. A Kikuyu with no land loses his connection with his past. In addition to the land itself, the settlers needed the Kikuyu to work the farms, and could only succeed in forcing them to do so by creating a need on the part of the Kikuyu. They accomplished this by imposing a hut tax on the Africans. To earn the money for taxes, the Kikuyu worked for the settlers. The Kikuyu are a proud, intelligent, industrious and family-oriented, loving people. Except for periodic scrapes, they did not vent their whole tribal resentment of the British until the Mau uprising in the 1950s.

These are very broad strokes and do not cover the nuances of tribal organization, which most settlers found impossible and tedious. The point is that the British were trying to bring the Africans to heel. Excerpts from the

East African Standard illustrate this: "[The Nandi were] thoroughly thrashed and quelled" (October 21, 1905). "[We have to] show natives in the future how to behave." "Rebellion is in the air." [The Maasai should be] "houseboys and herdsmen for whites" (January 28, 1905). "Main Street in Nairobi should be kept exclusively for whites" (April 14, 1906. This statement was made by Leslie Tarlton's partner, V. M. Newland). Punitive expeditions, great and small, were regularly dispatched to areas where settlers needed assistance.

When it looked as if the government had subdued the "native problem" at the base of Mt. Kenya, the Akeleys felt that they could proceed with their plans. They hired Richard John Cuninghame, one of the finest white hunters in the history of East Africa, to accompany them to hunt elephants and buffalos. A Scot by birth, and educated at Cambridge, Cuninghame dabbled in a number of professions. He was an Arctic whaler, a hunter-naturalist in Lapland, and a collector for the British Museum in various corners of the world, ending up in South Africa. There he shot buffalos and traded their hides before running a mail coach between Kimberly and Johannesburg. At the end of the 1800s, Cuninghame had come to Naivasha, where he began his career as an elephant hunter. Considered the best in his field, Cuninghame was hired to teach Akeley everything he knew about hunting. Actually the word "hired" is not appropriate. Cuninghame wanted no money to assist in making a scientific collection, but Akeley insisted on negotiating a fee mutually acceptable to both of them.

En route to Mt. Kenya, the small expedition stopped in the Aberdare Mountains to hunt elephants. We know very little about this hunting foray except that Akeley collected a single-tusked elephant. This fact alone is very interesting. Akeley in later years became obsessed with hunting only "perfect" specimens and would never have killed an animal with only one tusk. In fact, on his next expedition he killed an elephant only to find that one of the tusks was mutilated and abandoned the carcass, taking only the ivory, which he sold to help finance the expedition. The taking of this first single-tusked elephant demonstrates his excitement at hunting the animal at last. The fact that he even mounted it for exhibit at the Field Museum is equally noteworthy. Akeley would not have done this later, wanting only the finest species representations to be offered to the public.

At Fort Hall (now Muranga) near Mt. Kenya, the expedition was met by Her Majesty's Commissioner for BEA, Sir James Hayes-Sadler. His commission would be short-lived due to his unpopular reputation with the settlers. Essentially, they considered Hayes-Sadler indecisive and weak. But as far as the Akeleys were concerned, he was a welcome sight. He not only gave them the necessary permission to hunt on Mt. Kenya, but later invited them to join him and his party on a journey to the Trans-Tana region. They jumped at the opportunity and spent several days in Hayes-Sadler's company before leaving him at the base of Mt. Kenya.

Kirinyaga—Mt. Kenya—is the holy mountain of the Kikuyu people because they believe that "*Ngai*" (God) lives on the mountain. The name "Kenya" is a corruption of the original Kikuyu "*Kere Nyaga*" meaning "the white mountain"—this magnificent snowcapped beauty situated on the Equator. To this day, the Kikuyu build their houses so that the front door opens to Mt. Kenya. When one witnesses the early morning sun rising over the snow-clad peak of Kirinyaga, bathing the valley in a brightness and magical translucence that appoints every animate and inanimate thing; when one is seized by the stillness, the jewel-like dampness covering the vegetation, by the tinkling song of the bell bird; one is convinced, in this sacred moment, that God does indeed live on the mountain.

Bibi and Bwana and their bearded companion, R.J., were anxious about the recently quelled uprising and were informed that there were still hostile elements on the mountain. Hayes-Sadler must have alerted them to the continuing danger. The expedition did not venture into the vicinity of the hostile villages, but chose, rather, to build camp not far from friendly Kikuyu on the lower slopes of the mountain. Akeley worried especially about Mickie, who remained in camp to continue her own collecting efforts when the men hunted elephants.

Elephants ranged over the entire mountain in 1906. Akeley and R.J. traveled over elephant trails which snaked through the forest in an immense maze. The indigenous Dorobo dug pits along these trails to trap the elephants for easy killing. At the bottom of the pits, planted in their floors, were spiked barbs covered over loosely with leaves and branches for concealment. The elephants, very intelligent creatures, changed their paths constantly, creating a network of interwoven, crisscrossing paths. The trails were astonishingly narrow, passing through walls of thickly tangled vegetation. Traveling these trails could be terrifying, as one never knew if elephants were in front or behind. The first week, Mickie described the forest as the most "glorious in Africa." Later on, when anxiety set in because of the nerve-wracking work of stalking the animals, she called the forest "gloom-filled" and felt that "the odds were all in favor of the elephant."[8]

No white woman had been seen on Mt. Kenya before; thus Mickie became a major attraction of the expedition. She used the opportunity to make collections of Kikuyu artifacts. Bill, her "adopted" Kikuyu boy, must have been an enormous help to her during this period. Later on he would introduce her to his mother, who lived not far from Fort Hall. Bill helped Mickie exclusively on this first expedition; later Akeley would want Bill for more difficult assignments than collecting bugs and curios.

Akeley and R.J. were off in search of elephants. They spent many days trying to locate the feeding grounds. They finally found them in the forest and bamboo belt higher up the mountain. Akeley was entranced by elephants, and was disappointed that Cuninghame knew and understood the animals only as quarry. He felt that when R.J. looked at a herd, he saw only ivory. The Akeleys learned a great deal from Cuninghame, but they were more interested than he was in the daily habits of elephants. Akeley grew to think of the elephant as "the first animal of them all," in spite of a few serious run-ins. On the first expedition to hunt elephants, Akeley lacked not only selectivity but patience. He shot the full allowance of his license almost immediately. One elephant charged him and he had no choice but to kill it. Another was inadequate as a museum exhibit. As a result, Akeley needed Mickie to shoot her allotment of elephants.

Akeley and R.J. sent for Mickie. Akeley wrote that Bibi came "with the keenness of an old campaigner."[9] Together they went in search of elephants. The expedition would often leave camp at dawn, stalking the great beasts until nightfall. In a state of total fatigue, they told their exhausted staff not to bother clearing bush and setting up camp. Rather, they would turn in around the campfire with their native staff, wrapped only in blankets for protection from the elements. In the morning they broke out of their icy chrysalises to begin the hunt again.

Often, the Akeleys, traveling together through the great mysterious forest, would forget the object of their search, "lost in admiration of the weird and sombre vistas, brightened here and there by festoons of flowering vines or the crimson flash of a plantain-eater's wings . . . in harmony with our surroundings."[10] They watched the white-tailed colobus monkey, looking down at them like old sad men from high in the canopy. These were blissful treks on the soft, springy floor of a great cathedral. Then they would find elephant spoor, which jerked them back to reality.

R.J. discovered a place where a big bull had laid down on the soft earth, his body and trunk clearly outlined. They meandered endlessly on the labyrinthine paths until they finally found the bull they were after. Mickie was given the choice shooting position; it was her responsibility to take down the animal. Akeley recalled: "Breathlessly we waited until, as he moved slowly forward, there came into view a splendid pair of tusks followed by the massive head and great flapping ears of the best elephant we had ever seen. What a monster he looked as Bibi raised her rifle and with a steady aim, placed a bullet in just the right place."[11]

Akeley was thrilled with the specimen and immediately set to preserving the skin for mounting. This was no small job. A series of photographs, sketches, and measurements were made of the fallen creature. They began the task at twelve noon and it took until four the next morning to remove the two-thousand-pound skin. During their work, porters were dispatched to bring camp equipment and great amounts of salt and knives to pare down the removed skin. Everyone was busy through the night as word traveled over the mountain that an elephant had been killed. The surrounding Dorobo came in to butcher the remaining carcass for meat, much of which they smoked for later use. The Akeley's too, ate elephant (the flesh has been described as having a gelatinous, almost gluelike texture, rather bland in taste). After they had their fill, the scavengers of the forest took over.

The staff worked for six long days to pare down the skins to half of their original thickness, inundating them with salt to remove the moisture. The cured skins were rolled and sewn up in canvas, then lashed to poles, along with bundles of the skull and bones for conveyance down the mountain. The Akeleys called this campsite "Tembo Circus." *Tembo* is Kiswahili for elephant.

Mickie was entitled to another elephant and Akeley wanted her to have it. We do not know how keen Mickie was to go after the next elephant. One might think that her new Artemis self-image might have both inflated and terrified her. But whatever the emotional cost to her, she ended up capturing the record for the largest elephant tusks ever acquired on Mt. Kenya.

It may make some readers uncomfortable to think of a beautiful woman enjoying the hunting and killing of big game. The idea may seem especially unpleasant today, when humanity has had to resort to a triage system of determining which species to fight for and which others—perhaps less beautiful, cunning, or, to our mind, worthwhile—we have had to let fall into the black hole of extinction. In fact, Mickie was more proud of her work with tribal people and ethology than she was of killing these elephants. She shot for food and science and never "became hardened to killing." She saw no pleasure in killing to "satisfy the lust for excitement."[12] Nevertheless, Mickie, in particular, was attacked in a letter sent to them when they returned home: "Who gave you . . . the right to mistreat my brothers whom, with us, the great Spirit of Life has created? . . . And a *woman*, who is supposed to typify gentleness and compassion, to be a leader in such work! Bloodsport is one of the basest relics of a barbarous past; and even when it is given the background of a nominal 'scientific' purpose, it poorly excuses the blunting of the mind's higher instinct."[13] The letter is not a crank note, nor is it irrational, and it must have stung Mickie to the core. Akeley, on the other hand, did harden to killing; at one point he even contemplated breaking an elephant's legs as an experiment. Hamstringing or tendon-slashing had been one of the oldest and most successful ways of hunting the animal, as it became totally immobilized and easily killed. But it was unsportsmanlike, causing the animal extreme pain. Akeley did not do it, but he admits to changing his mind out of a loss of nerve, not a change of heart. One does harden when one kills; it is part of a reality focused in man's darker side. This presented a conflict for Akeley, who wrote, "while I have found but little enjoyment in shooting any kind of animal, I confess that in hunting elephants and lions under certain conditions I have always felt that the animal had sufficient chance in the game to make it something like a sporting proposition."[14] Akeley usually lived by a "good sportsman" code, which made his digressions from it so obvious and abrasive. The most interesting thing about the letter protesting their animal-killing is that the Akeleys saved it.

After the dramatic sojourn on Mt. Kenya, the Akeleys proceeded to the Tana River for their buffalos. The buffalos of the region at first showed absolutely no fear of man. However, after Akeley began shooting them, the animals quickly learned that man was an enemy. Buffalos are considered more dangerous than any other African mammal. This stems from their volatile, unpredictable, and vindictive nature. Buffalos hold a "grudge," and have been known to kill a lion, any lion, after one of their herd has been taken by the big cat. Akeley was rightfully nervous hunting the formidable and protective buffalo. Mickie again took the biggest bull. And again Akeley gave her the credit—a significant act on his part. He was proud of his wife, and he felt confident enough to celebrate her prowess in the field. They spent six difficult weeks in the region, especially in the *tinga-tinga* (swamp) between the Theba and Tana Rivers where the mosquitoes, "for their size and tormenting power . . . are unsurpassed in the world." Sickness ravaged the expedition staff; still the work continued, and the Akeleys succeeded in collecting six buffalos.

They returned to Fort Hall on November 22, where they hired 175 porters to carry the collections to Nairobi for shipment home. Ultimately eighty-four packages weighing about seventeen tons were shipped to the Field Museum—first by rail to Mombasa, then on the S.S. *Admira* bound for Naples, and then on another ship to New York. The collections arrived in New York on January 28, 1907, in perfect condition, and continued the journey to Chicago. (It is interesting that we know more about how the specimens traveled than we do about how the Akeleys got home!)

The Akeleys received a joyous welcome in Chicago. Their exploits and accomplishments were celebrated by the press. Yet for all the brouhaha surrounding the triumphant duo, all was not well for Akeley at the Field Columbian Museum.

FINAL YEARS
IN CHICAGO

Chewing the food of sweet and bitter fancy.
　　—WILLIAM SHAKESPEARE,
　　As You Like It

REENTRY INTO the museum world was a shock for Akeley after Africa. Marshall Field had died in January, 1906, and the Field Columbian Museum was renamed the Field Museum of Natural History. The scientific scope of the museum was now more focused, limited to the four great natural sciences—anthropology, zoology, geology, and botany. Along with the refocusing came a plan for a new museum building. The Fine Arts Building of the old exposition was rapidly deteriorating, and seemed beyond restoration. Field had left $4 million to build a new museum building that was to be constructed along the same architectural design as the Fine Arts structure.

　　Important things had happened while Akeley was away and they had happened quickly. Changes in administration, an altered institutional mission, and plans to relocate the entire museum, with its hundreds of thousands of specimens, can shake up staff members at every level. Add to this chaos and muddled aspect the contrasting shock of returning from a land that allows for elemental understanding and focus, and at best, one's vision gets clouded by the onslaught. Then add to all of these elements the awful resignation of Akeley's friend and champion, Daniel Giraud Elliot, and finally, add the ultimate injury of a new boss, Elliot's replacement, Charles Barney Cory,

99

who was predisposed to dislike Akeley. All in all, it was quite a homecoming for Bibi and Bwana in early 1907.

Akeley was warned in a letter from a colleague that he was returning to a highly charged political situation. Since Elliot's replacement as chairman of the Zoology department was at the center of the controversy, it is important to take a look at the man who was given the job, Charles Barney Cory.

Cory was one of the founders of the American Ornithologists' Union and had an extremely full and accomplished life. He was a millionaire whose family fortune was reaped through imported goods, especially silks, fine wines, and other luxuries. He was educated at Harvard and Boston Law School. He never had to make a living and spent his time pursuing his avid interests, hunting and traveling. Cory's main passion was collecting birds, and the ample funds available to him allowed for nearly thirty years of hunting and collecting trips.

In 1887, Cory had been given an honorary position as curator of birds in the Boston Society of Natural History. In 1893, when the Field Museum was first being established, many of Cory's friends and associates sat on the Board of Trustees. They knew of his bird collections and wanted them as a nucleus for the new museum's reference collections. Cory was willing to give his collections and his significant library to the museum, but he wished, in return, to be given the position of curator of ornithology, and that he should hold the position for his lifetime.

The original concept of the Field Museum's founders called for the Department of Ornithology to be part of the zoology department. However, to secure Cory's bird collections and to conform to his wishes, the museum created an independent Department of Ornithology. All the other aspects of zoology were to be placed under the administration of Daniel Giraud Elliot. Cory thus became Elliot's equal. Cory was, in effect, given an honorary curatorship without the resident responsibilities. It enabled him to continue his collecting "without being burdened with petty details of its care, and offered no serious interference with the almost nomadic life he was leading."[1] His assistant in 1898, who of course carried on the work, was the aforementioned William A. Bryan. Cory was delighted with the agreement, which gave him liberty to work as much or as little as he pleased. His only real responsibility was to direct the general care of the bird collection.

In 1906 calamity struck Cory: he lost his entire fortune because of heavy speculating in "securities" of shipping and sugar trusts. He had received bad advice from men far wealthier than he. Somehow he had believed that if he ran into financial trouble, they would bail him out. They did not. He felt shocked, bitter, and dispirited when he realized that he had lost everything. A middle-aged man who had never had to earn a dollar in his life, Cory now needed a job.

The Field Museum had to find a salaried position for Cory; they offered him Elliot's job. The president, as spokesman of the Executive Committee, advised Elliot that they would "dis-continue" his services as soon as he had concluded his work at hand. Elliot was "surprised," and requested an explanation for the committee's actions. The official response was that the department needed a "younger man with larger powers of endurance."[2] The whole affair was painful for everyone, especially Elliot, who never seems to have lost his composure in the midst of the bureaucratic turmoil. Cory, on the other hand, was a very angry, depressed man when he took over the governance of the Department of Zoology.

Akeley was apprised by a friend that the staff was split into two camps—Cory's and his own (Akeley's): "Cory sailed into position with all his rags unfurled and expected to take the entire cargo on board. I doubt that he was fully aware of all that had occurred in recent years. He probably knew enough to make him wobbly. I imagine he bumped into a rock or two early in the rush. Also it became known through yours truly that you were a dangerous mine liable to explode if jammed roughly, and blow up a few plans."[3]

The main source of contention seems to have been the Illinois Bird Hall that Akeley had envisioned before he went to Africa. On his arrival, Cory immediately set to work on the preparation of a book, *The Birds of Illinois and Wisconsin*. He, no doubt, also had strong feelings about the new bird hall. Akeley tended to be arrogant about his designs and needed total control over all aspects of their production. Akeley's colleague suggested that he "stand pat" that "the Museum simply cannot afford to lose you at any price."[4] We do not know very much about this feud surrounding the hall. What we do know is that the exhibit never materialized, and that Akeley took his trial bluebird group with a photographic transparency background and sent it to the American Museum of Natural History to see if they were interested in buying it. This was the same background, previously mentioned, which arrived smashed into a thousand pieces, like Akeley's dream of the bird hall. Another source of contention was a grand scheme that Akeley brought back from Africa: He wanted to expand his elephant group into a larger exhibit but Skiff, the Field's director, "showed no enthusiasm whatever for the idea of having five elephants in his main hall."[5]

Again, we have the advantage of seeing these events in perspective and understanding the motives of the different parties involved. Cory was a broken man trying to pull together the pieces of his life. He wanted to do something positive and fine. His steps were not sure-footed and confident, but he had the full force of the museum administration behind him. Akeley was extremely confident and arrogant, and felt that his vision superseded everyone else's. He "always conceived things on an universal and perfect scale which took great vision and courage. Others would not dare to strive for so much, fearing it would not be possible," Jimmy Clark wrote. He continued:

101

But Akeley never let his fear stop him; he shot for the stars, and often paid dearly for it in self-sacrifice to accomplish the ends which he believed should have been appreciated and made financially possible by others who could well afford it . . . he was bitter when his plans and expectations were not fulfilled by those he thought should have had vision enough to go along with him . . . When things did not come to pass as he has so enthusiastically hoped, his spirit would sink in discouragement and despair and he would suffer considerably under such disappointment.[6]

When Akeley failed to get backing for his bird hall, he retreated and concentrated solely on mounting the elephants that he and Mickie had collected. He also started looking around quietly for another job.

A strange opportunity knocked on his door one day as he and his colleague C. L. Dewey were working in the studio. Director Skiff made his routine rounds and chatted with Akeley, who was completing one of the mounts. As they spoke, Skiff watched Dewey spray some artificial rocks with plaster of Paris shot from a large handmade atomizer operated by compressed air. The Field Museum administration had just received another complaint about the shabby appearance of the building and Skiff was hard pressed to repair it with the available funds. He asked Akeley if he could develop a squirt gun large enough to repair the crumbling stucco facade on the badly deteriorating museum building.

The challenge brought out the inventor in Akeley and gave him something to ponder while he worked in his studio. He and Dewey set to work to create such a machine. Within days, they had fashioned an apparatus that could spray liquid plaster. But the plaster hardened in the hose, clogging the works. They made adjustments, and within two weeks, they had built a crude machine that could accomplish the task of spraying liquid concrete on the facade. It was not a very sophisticated piece of equipment. However, the mechanism sparked enough enthusiasm in their friends that soon Akeley and Dewey were offered enough money to perfect, manufacture, and sell the device.

Its development took two strenuous years of work during Akeley's off hours, before and after his normal workday. Dewey tells a story about the effort involved:

Akeley could work more hours at a stretch without being mentally and physically tired than any man I have ever known. Only once did I hear him suggest a temporary let-up and that was shortly before his departure for Africa in 1909 when it was our custom to work on the cement gun in a shop near the Field Museum for about two hours each morning before breakfast. Then we would snatch a bite and walk to the Museum. On this particular occasion I happened to be about one step ahead of Akeley when he grabbed me by the coattail and said in his dry joking manner: "Slow up a bit, Dewey. This is the only time these days that we get a chance to rest—when we are walking from one job to another."[7]

There were many obstacles facing them in the development of the cement gun. Water and solid material needed to be blended, but in unequal measures, as a fifty/fifty mixture would be too thin and watery to adhere to a vertical surface or to build up to the necessary thickness. Chemical reactions between the materials made the substance set prematurely, again clogging the machine. To solve the problem they invented a substance they named "gunite." While it had the same constituents as concrete—water, sand, and cement—it was materially different in its proportions and consistency.

The machine itself was a tank on two wheels. The tank held two chambers divided by a "feed wheel." The dry sand and cement were held in the upper chamber. The feed wheel allowed small amounts to drop into the lower chamber, from which the mixture was shot in short bursts through a rubber hose. Water was introduced at the nozzle, thereby "spraying" the substance onto the desired surface.

The concept was simple and effective. In 1910, the machine was introduced to the public in New York at the Cement Show. It has been put to endless uses since then. A great economic reason for the cement gun's success was that it eliminated the need for lumber forms; instead, wire lath or screening could be positioned about one quarter of an inch away from the surface to be coated, and sprayed. The machine's uses included refurbishing old houses and building new ones; reinforcing the interior of mines; lining furnaces, kilns, and cupola domes; and constructing piers, pilings, and seawalls and lining canals and basins in marine engineering. The cement gun was used in the construction of the Panama Canal and of the Hayden Planetarium dome at the American Museum of Natural History. One of its most unusual uses was in the building of concrete ships, and it was also used during World War I to line the trenches in Europe. Today, a more sophisticated version of the apparatus is employed to construct swimming pools.

In 1916, the Franklin Institute for the Promotion of the Mechanical Arts awarded its John Scott Legacy Medal to Akeley for the cement gun. When he opened the letter announcing his award, he told his friend Roy Chapman Andrews, "This gives me more satisfaction than getting a check for fifty thousand dollars."[8] The Cement Gun Company, in Allentown, Pennsylvania, lined the pockets of his backers quite nicely, but never made Akeley a rich man; he had given up all financial interest in the company soon after its founding, characteristically moving on to other work. While Akeley's link with the invention has long been forgotten by the cement industry, his word "gunite" has remained in use.

Although Akeley and Dewey worked assiduously on the cement gun in off hours, Akeley's main passion continued to be mounting the elephants that he and Mickie had brought back from Africa. He further experimented with his taxidermic techniques, refining them for the large animals. In his small study model, he created a grouping that was quite beautiful and demonstrated elephant interaction. To mount an animal as large as an elephant and make it appear buoyant and agile was no easy task. The single tusker in his group is seen to attack the larger elephant, which stands on only three feet, the fourth raised slightly off the ground. He posed them in a fighting stance, even though in *In Brightest Africa*, he wrote that "I think, too, of the extraordinary fact that I have never seen or heard African elephants fighting each other. They have no enemy but man and are at peace amongst themselves." He had seen young elephants in mock fight, but noted in his diary that afterwards, they would "stand there, wiping each others heads with their trunks in an affectionate way." Akeley felt, nonetheless, that the public would rather think of elephants fighting than playing, and decided to name the piece "Fighting Bulls."

His work now took a new, more advanced turn in taxidermic efforts. Again Akeley used the full scope of his experience and the fruit of his experiments to fashion the animals in a fascinating way that was more complicated than the method, described earlier, that he used for smaller mammals.

Under this new technique, Akeley chalked out the perimeter of the elephant skin on the floor, creating a diagram for steel armature that corresponded to the animal's backbone and belly. The two steel channels were connected by vertically positioned two-by-four pieces of lumber. Separately, he modeled the head in clay over the immense skull with its tusks attached, casting it in plaster as he had done before. Using the plaster cast, he fabricated a light steel framework, attaching this head frame to the torso armature.

The shell of the body was filled out with one-inch wire, loosely woven so that it was capable of bending without buckling. Wire mesh over a light steel frame was used to form the ears and trunk, the trunk further reinforced by two pipes to support its raised position. A combination of plaster of Paris and tow (hemp fibers) was modeled over the frame. This plaster manikin looked like an elephant without his skin; over it was stretched its tanned hide, with all its sparse, stiff hairs, wrinkles, warts, tick-holes, etc. Through tiny slits, a mixture of glue and plaster of Paris was shot under the skin, and the skin was modeled into shape with the wrinkled folds the animal wore in life. After the sections and slits were sewn or joined, they were filled with colored beeswax so that even the most critical eye could not detect them. One rural visitor to the Field Museum was quoted as saying, with some astonishment, "That old bull looks just like he growed into his hide."[9]

The work was fabulous for its time—far more progressive than what the rest of the museum world was doing in exhibition. The mounts still dominate the central hall of the Field Museum—Mickie's elephant is the larger animal. While they are grand, they lack the finesse of Akeley's later group of elephants at the American Museum of Natural History in New York. Nonetheless, they attracted the attention of the world's museum community, including that of the AMNH.

Henry Fairfield Osborn, president of the AMNH, had corresponded with Akeley regarding "growth rings" on the tusks of African elephants. Osborn, a paleontologist by discipline, was working on a monograph concerning the ancestors of elephants, *proboscidea*-mammoths. Both he and Bumpus, the museum's director, were keeping an eye on Akeley's work at the Field Museum. At the same time, Akeley continued looking around for another place to work.

The Field Museum was under new leadership by 1908; Stanley Field, nephew of Marshall, had assumed the position of president. He and Akeley had enormous respect for one another and a friendship grew up between them over the next few years. Although things could have been different for Akeley under Field's administration, Akeley had no way of knowing that, and he had already set the wheels in motion to move on. He would, however, continue doing contract work for the Field Museum for many years.

Akeley thought about the AMNH, but must have mulled over his friends' thoughts and comments about the Museum—Wheeler's anxiety over politics and Bryan's warnings that he, Akeley, was not given proper credit for his accomplishments. He must have felt a little ambivalent about approaching the institution. But he no longer felt on terra firma at the Field Museum, whose administrators now thought him a dreamer with extravagant methods. Also, Akeley had visited Bumpus at the AMNH in 1902, at which point he met Jimmy Clark and "sized him up" as someone whose work and enthusiasm he appreciated. The AMNH, after all, had sent Clark to Chicago to learn Akeley's new methods. Akeley weighed these things in his mind. He finally communicated to Bumpus in 1907 that he would like to collect and mount some elephants for the AMNH. Bumpus was thrilled. His sentiments were echoed by Osborn who, as the obvious heir to the AMNH presidency after Morris Ketchen Jesup's (the president who originally hired Bumpus for the AMNH) death, could see a special hall of elephants realized. Osborn was elected in 1908 and presented the ideas to the AMNH trustees—who, however, were less than enthusiastic about the Osborn-Akeley plan. Although they were impressed with Akeley's work and appreciated the revolutionary aspects of his exhibits, it was difficult to convince them of the hall's value. One trustee, J. P. Morgan, wrote that "a hall full of elephants was too many elephants."[10] Osborn rethought the idea and proposed that an elephant grouping be placed in the anthropology hall. He was ultimately able to convince the trustees that "an elephant group would not fail to interest a wide public,"[11] and by 1909 had managed to secure a twenty-five-thousand-dollar contract for Akeley to collect and mount a small herd of elephants.

The *Fighting Bulls* was still not finished in early 1909, and Akeley had to complete it before he could move on. The museum world greatly anticipated the group based on the brilliant success of the *Four Seasons*. The *Four Seasons* was still creating a stir and had attracted the attention of a very prestigious visitor to the Field Museum—President Theodore Roosevelt. He was so impressed with the exhibit that he asked Chicago Congressman Mann to bring Akeley and Mickie to the White House for dinner. It was a thrilling invitation, and Akeley had to go out and get a new "store bought" suit.

At dinner, the president told Akeley about his desire to hunt in Alaska when his term of office was completed. During that fateful dinner Akeley captured TR's imagination and turned his mind toward Africa instead. One of the stories that Akeley told the assembled guests was about a pride of sixteen lions that emerged from a cave on McMillan's Juja farm near Nairobi. TR was having trouble with the Senate at the time and said to Congressman Mann: "I'd like to have those lions right here in Washington today." Mann asked, "What would you do with them, Mr. President?" "I'd turn them loose in the Senate," TR replied. "But aren't you afraid that they'd make some mistake?" Mann said. "Not if they stayed long enough,"[12] TR retorted. The badinage was repeated often in Washington circles. When Roosevelt left for Africa the Senate retaliated with the slogan "America expects every lion to do its duty."

Teddy Roosevelt made extensive arrangements to lead a spectacular safari into British East Africa for the Smithsonian Institution, and asked Akeley to join him. He also sought Akeley's advice on safari logistics. TR must have heeded Akeley's suggestions: It turned out that TR used Newland & Tarlton as his safari outfitters, took Edmund Heller along as a preparator, and hired R.J. Cuninghame as a hunter—all principals in Akeley's 1905 expedition. Akeley, however, could not accompany the Roosevelt party as he had just committed himself to the AMNH and was leading his own safari into British East Africa. Akeley suggested that his and TR's expeditions at least meet in Africa, if their itineraries crisscrossed, so that TR could bag a couple of elephants for the AMNH. Akeley fully realized that this would bring not only additional animals but prestige to his own mission.

It all happened rather quickly. The machinery was set in motion, and within a few months, Akeley and Mickie were on their way to New York and preparing for their new expedition to BEA, this time for the American Museum of Natural History.

TEMBO PIGA BWANA:
The AMNH British East African Expedition

I have been here ever since I began to be, my appearances elsewhere having been put in by other parties.

—SAMUEL BECKETT, *The Unnamable*

AKELEY STRAINED through a film of ants and blood to see the flickering light of the campfire. He couldn't think; he couldn't feel. There was no pain; he was in shock. He could make out the spectre-like forms of his staff, spread out and gesticulating around the fire, laughing and boisterous. In semiconsciousness, he slipped back into oblivion only to wake again, his mind drifting in and out of memory and the present, finally aware that he was shivering and freezing. A moan alerted his Kikuyu and Swahili porters that it was not a corpse that they were guarding. He was lying on the cold, sodden earth of Mt. Kenya. His staff was spooked by the presence of the "dead" man, and while it was taboo to touch him, they dared not leave him to mountain predators and scavengers. He lay there certain that his back was broken because he could feel nothing but the intense cold searing his wet flesh.

The porters, finally realizing that Akeley was alive, carried him closer to the fire and under some shelter from the drizzle. They had already sent for Mickie, and now tried to make Akeley as comfortable as possible. The cold kicked off a sense memory for him, and slowly he remembered the morning's events.

107

Carl Akeley

He had been freezing despite the fact that he was virtually on the equator. He had left base camp with fifteen men for a three-to-four—day excursion to make photographic studies of the upper region of elephant habitat on Mt. Kenya. He had encountered fresh elephant spoor and decided to hunt them. Akeley had been stalking a particular big bull through the dawn mists of the bamboo belt, at an altitude of nine thousand feet. His hands were so numb from the cold that he stopped momentarily to warm them. He leaned his elephant gun, a Jeffery .475, against his stomach while he massaged blood and feeling back into his fingers. A sudden cold sweat on his back alerted him to danger from behind. Akeley swung around in time to confront an angry bull elephant crashing at him through the thicket of bamboo. He grabbed for his gun but the safety catch was either jammed, or just seemed that way in the panic. But Akeley had fantasized this moment many times, whether through prophecy or a sense of the inevitable and he was ready. With a mentally well-rehearsed movement he tossed aside his gun and faced the charge head-on. He grabbed one tusk, maneuvered his body between it and the other, and remained in this great ivory cage. He wasn't certain of the next move, but he knew if he could just hold on, goring wasn't a possibility. The enraged bull plunged his tusks into the earth to smash the body dangling before him. Akeley saw his "merciless little eye gleaming revenge" close to his own as the animal pushed harder at his chest with his curled trunk to crush him deeper into the earth. But something was preventing the tusk's complete penetration—a root, a stone, something. Akeley heard a "wheezy grunt" and felt a cracking in his chest under the impact, and then an excruciating pain made him "go to sleep." His lungs had been stabbed by his broken ribs. The bull pulled back, thinking his task complete—in the process whacking Akeley's face, breaking his nose, rending a gash in his forehead, and tearing away part of his cheek to lay bare a few molars. When the elephant disengaged from his victim, he tore out after the attendant Africans who scattered into the bush. Often elephants return to their victims and further maul the corpses. But this one was either distracted or didn't bother, much to Akeley's good fortune. The Africans returned to Akeley and presumed that he was dead. Nonetheless, they set up some shelter to guard the body and dispatched two porters to Mickie at base camp, over three thousand feet down the mountain.

When Akeley became conscious he asked for his wife and some whisky, in that order. He ordered the men to fire location shots at regular intervals. The two porters who had been sent to Mickie casually wandered into the base camp at about six P.M.—close to ten hours after the incident. They didn't even report to her but went to the cook's tent. A delegation led by Bill finally came to her tent to relate Akeley's ordeal. The Africans registered no alarm when Bill announced calmly that "*tembo piga Bwana*"—"an elephant has beaten the mister." Mickie felt an internal jolt of shock compounded by the

Africans' evident lack of compassion. It was not as though the Africans felt nothing for the tragedy—quite the contrary—but it was always exasperating to encounter their apparent indifference and lack of emotion when someone or something is wounded. It may come from their stoic acceptance of everyday hardship, pain and death. But Mickie was stunned.

Regaining her equilibrium quickly, she shot into action. She chose twenty men on the spot who would accompany her into the jungle on the rescue mission. She also offered a reward to the man or men who could get word to Dr. Phillips, the Scottish medical missionary on the mountain, by daybreak. Mickie dismissed the men, telling them to rest for a few hours while she prepared for the journey. As they left her, she started assembling tents, supplies, and medicine. She then laid out lengths of striped Americani, cotton cloth used for trading, to begin sewing together a crude stretcher. She sewed on the floor of her tent, indifferent to the chilly, driving rain pelting down on the canvas above her. Hyenas prowled outside as she sewed in those lonely hours, her mind jarred by disparate and frightening images and thoughts.

By midnight she had finished fashioning the stretcher and sent the camp askari for the men. Bill alone reported and told Mickie that the men were in an "ugly mood" and that they threatened to kill her and leave her body to the hyenas if she forced them to go into the jungle before morning. Mickie's thoughtful, almost maudlin mood gave way to anger, an emotion that never failed to focus her actions. She snapped at Bill that he would be better off staying in camp and babysitting J.T. Jr., her pet monkey, while she took the men into the forest without him. Bill was humiliated and angry; his mood darkened. In the meantime, the two porters who were to guide Mickie to Akeley had deserted. Mickie panicked at the news. She struggled for self-control and fetched her small, but effective, .256 Mannlicher Schoenhauer rifle to meet the mutinous staff. She could hardly speak for the fear gripping her throat like an icy hand. She announced resolutely that it was time to go. "Twenty primitive, superstitious men with murder in their hearts and the cold, black night against me," she wrote.[2] They stood there at an impasse: one white woman and twenty black men, locked in a war of wills and control. The hairsplitting shriek of a hyena shattered the silence and again Mickie almost buckled. Instead the moment allowed her to reconnoiter her broken nerves and try a new tactic. She pranced around the men, a sudden dust devil of energy, released from her stony and deadly snare with the Africans, which would have come to nothing but ill. She whined like a baby, calling, "mommy, mommy," and accused them of being like women—the consummate insult. Her wild theatrics made someone laugh and for the moment the tension slackened as others started laughing, too. Mickie shoved one of the porters toward the loads. How this feisty woman's antics prevailed is a mystery; we can only suppose that her resolve and energy level were so spectacular that the Africans were both astounded and confused by her behavior. They might have even thought her mad and wanted to give her a wide berth. No matter—they actually fell into line to begin what for them was a treacherous, terrifying journey into a forest haunted with unkind spirits.

The first thing they had to do was to find the recalcitrant Kikuyu guides. It was pitch black, and even though Bill called out that the search party meant no harm, the Kikuyu villagers thought they were being raided and fled from their huts. Mickie and Bill finally found the wife of one of the guides and threatened to take her into the forest if she didn't forfeit her husband. She feared her husband's wrath less than that of the forest gods and relinquished him without too much argument. When Mickie and Bill found the guides they tied them together. Meanwhile the twenty porters had had time to think the whole thing over, and some of them had deserted. It was the stuff of a dreadful black comedy. Now Mickie had to backtrack to find them. She later wrote:

> When about halfway, a hand suddenly grabbed my coat. Panic-stricken, I struggled frantically, exerting every nerve and muscle to free myself from this new danger which threatened me. Suddenly under the strain of the old worn buttonholes, my coat opened and caused us both to lose our balance, but this hold on my rain soaked garment did not relax. In that awful moment which I realized meant life or death not only to me but perhaps to Mr. Akeley, I was the first to regain my equilibrium. With the strength born of fear, I struck out wildly with the stock of my gun. As he released me and fell, I ran back to the waiting men. To my dying day I shall feel the shock of that blow and hear, above the roar of rain and wind, the awful thud of a body striking the sodden earth.[3]

The worst part of the incident was that she had no idea of who her enemies were.

It was two A.M. before they were finally on their way. The opaque blackness, the stumbling and falling, the ropelike tendrils hanging from the trees like so many indifferent grabbing arms, the incessant and palpable fear, and the frantic, nerve-racking sounds of suddenly awakened beasts, created a hellish night journey for all of them. Just before dawn they realized that they were surrounded by elephants and huddled together in terror until the animals passed. The nocturnal forest sounds slowly gave way to the colobus monkeys' dawn chorus, and the entire band thanked God for the new day. But their relief was short-lived when, at eight A.M., they realized that they were lost. Mickie's nerves finally split and, losing control, she threw herself on the ground, crawling around on all fours looking for a trail, any trail. Even if she had found one she couldn't have seen it for the tears burning her eyes. The Africans watched the strange scene—Bibi was unique in their experience. Just then Mickie remembered her gun. Its report rang through the jungle and soon they heard its answer. The shot directed them to Akeley's camp, only a half-hour away.

Anticipation banished her fatigue as Mickie approached Akeley. Her husband was unconscious but he was still alive. She set about the gruesome task of cleaning his wounds. Akeley wrote: "Altogether I was an unlovely subject and hardly worth saving."[4] Mickie described the condition to a mutual friend, Roy Chapman Andrews: "Carl was a dreadful sight. The elephant's trunk had scalped his forehead, closed one eye, smashed his nose and torn open one cheek so that it hung down and exposed the teeth in a horrible grin. Many of his ribs were broken. Several had punctured his lung and blood was running out the corners of his mouth.[5] Her realization that there were internal injuries frightened her the most, as Dr. Phillips wouldn't arrive for another twenty-four hours. Mickie was totally exhausted but kept constant vigil, slipping out of the tent only to commend the men for their bravery during their nocturnal ordeal. Phillips did arrive the next day. A newcomer to Africa, he had hurried to Akeley's aid—a more seasoned physician would have taken his time, knowing that elephant maulings were almost always fatal. It took three days to bring Akeley down the mountain, as trails had to be slashed through the jungle to permit passage for the covered stretcher. But at long last, Mickie bathed and changed her clothes for the first time in a week while Akeley slept.

The details of these events differ slightly in Akeley's and Mickie's accounts, but given Akeley's semi-conscious state, one is more prone to believe Mickie, despite the emotional overtones of her rendition. The *Leader*, dated July 23, 1910 (the mauling happened June 24), presents other subtle differences—for instance, that Akeley crawled into camp and sent for Dr. Phillips and Mickie himself. But whatever the specific chain of events were, the overriding reality was that Akeley survived a horrible ordeal, and that Mickie helped him do it.

Carl and Mickie had left New York in August for their voyage to London. After examining their equipment (ordered several months before) they purchased additional supplies and clothing at Silver and Edgington and moved on to Paris. Their fellow safarists, John T. McCutcheon and Fred Stephenson, arrived later in London. Stephenson was a big game hunter from Minnesota and had hunted extensively in the United States, Canada, and Mexico. J.T. McCutcheon was a cartoonist for the *Chicago Tribune*. He had attended a lecture given by Akeley, and was so thrilled by the African vision presented that he approached Akeley and asked if he could join him on his next safari. The way that J.T. describes it in his book, *In Africa*, one would think that anyone could just approach Akeley and end up in Africa with him. This was far from the case. Akeley was extremely calculating. He did few things without a great deal of deliberation. Even then, safaris were very expensive, estimated at one thousand dollars per month per safarist, and Akeley was always scrambling for financial backing. Throughout his career he led wealthy men into the field in search of private trophies, while they in turn helped defray his expenses. In addition to providing money, J.T. was an attractive companion because of the attendant publicity the expedition would receive in the *Tribune*.

Where Stephenson was overly serious, McCutcheon was full of good humor and seductive charm, and the two men balanced each other well. Mickie enjoyed them both, often teasing Fred, who became very fond of her. Given the hardships of expedition life and the perpetual closeness of it, companions had to be carefully chosen.

J.T. and Fred spent a longer period of time in London than the Akeleys. Besides purchasing personal safari clothing and firearms, Fred taught J.T. to hunt. Using the mounted animals at the British Museum and the live ones at South Kensington Zoo, he showed him how to pick out, from every angle, the vital spots that would bring down a beast quickly. Fred and J.T. met the Akeleys in Paris, the four traveling together to Naples by train for their voyage to Africa.

They embarked on August 31, 1909, aboard a German vessel, *Adolph Woermann*, in the company of about sixty first class passengers. Professional and private hunters, government workers, and some military personnel comprised the passenger list. Of particular note on the roster was the new governor of British East Africa, Sir Percy Girouard. The Akeley party found him a terrific companion and would see more of him in Africa. Another group they befriended was one led by W.D. Boyce, a Chicago millionaire, publisher (*Woman's World*), and newspaper proprietor (the *Chicago Blade* and the *Chicago Ledger*). The groups had much in common: Akeley and Boyce were both going to make movies in Africa and J.T. was recording the trip's events for a rival newspaper. Boyce was also taking balloons to East Africa to have a look at the plains from a bird's-eye view. As a result of this voyage, Akeley and Boyce would plan their own expedition.

An article in the *Leader*, dated November 27, 1909 states that Boyce commissioned Akeley and hunter R.J. Cuninghame "to discover the remote and obscure habits of the gorilla. He has commissioned [them] to traverse central Africa from coast to coast in this endeavor defraying the cost of the expedition."[6] Akeley wrote later that he had intended to make a gorilla trek that year but never mentioned his backer. Akeley's friend Tarlton tried to dissuade him from dealing with Boyce, as he thought that Akeley had "made a pact with the devil."[7] This point became moot with the mauling on Mt. Kenya. Akeley would not go on the expedition until 1921.

The passage from Naples to Mombasa, which took seventeen days, was a pleasant and relaxing one, affording the Akeley party ample opportunity to get better acquainted in close quarters. While Akeley himself wasn't much of a game player, he must have enjoyed watching the varied and silly deck games that the British passengers indulged in. Among others, there was the "cock-fight," in which two men with arms and legs trussed tried to push each other out of a circle with their heads or trunks. The British found these games hilarious.

The expedition members had a wonderful voyage, full of anticipation and excitement about being the first scientific institution to collect an entire elephant family for public exhibition. Mickie wrote, "We sailed on our dangerous mission . . . little dreaming that the penalty for trying to unravel some of the mystery which surrounds the giants of the animal kingdom would be so severe." No dark presentiment clouded their glorious arrival in Mombasa.

They arrived in Kilindini, Mombasa, on September 16, amidst a festive air, as the town—indeed, the whole protectorate—was welcoming its new governor. They were in Mombasa for only a couple of days to complete forms and financial arrangements; Mr. Newland of their safari outfitters met them to expedite matters. They then graciously accepted an invitation from Sir Percy to travel with him to Nairobi aboard a private train.

During the ride, J.T. was especially overwhelmed with the magnificent wide views as they passed through the Yatta Plateau and Chyulu Hills as Mt. Kilimanjaro peeked over them from the south. Mickie and Carl surely reveled in the joy of sharing the lyrical beauty and clean clear light of the countryside with newcomers to Africa. They intrigued them with the tales that clung to the station names of Tsavo and Simba, haunted by the man-eating lions that all-too-recently wreaked havoc on the workers building the railroad to Uganda.

The train ride was magnificent. The group wrapped themselves in blankets in the cold night, taking turns on the observation bench (or cow-catcher) attached to the locomotive's engine to watch the dawn break and see the silhouetted nocturnal predators return home after a full night. The plains were alive with giraffes, zebras and antelopes, and the morning pure and perfect. Akeley, too, was thrilled with these vistas, which never failed to touch him, but he also felt a growing alarm as he witnessed far less game than he had seen only three years before.

The train arrived in Nairobi to great fanfare which, while in honor of Sir Percy, made the Akeleys feel most welcome and happy to be back. Mickie's tent boy, Bill, was the first to greet them as they got off the train. Bill was still very young—only thirteen years old—but there was a new maturity in his bearing. Lord Hugh Delamere gave a welcoming speech to the assembled crowd.

Nairobi had grown since the Akeleys had last been there. More pony and bullock carts, bicycles, rickshaws, motorcycles, horses, and even a couple of automobiles threw up dust along the streets. The city center was still one main thoroughfare (first 3rd Avenue, then Delamere Avenue, today Kenyatta Avenue), but *dukas* (small stores) and tin sheds had started radiating out from the main road. Off in the hills about a mile away were Governor's House (today State House) and the new European Hospital (now State House Road Girl's School). The hospital would later play an important part in Akeley's life. A mere hour's walk from city center brought one to the spectacular, sun-bleached Athi Plains, where antelopes numbered in the thousands. But even in town there were zebras that disrupted one's bicycle ride, an occasional leopard on one's veranda, or a lost hippo clogging up the Nairobi River.

During the four short days they were in Nairobi, the safarists attended to endless details, including buying their hunting licenses for fifty pounds each. This license allowed them to kill: 2 buffalos, 2 rhinos, 2 hippos, 1 eland, 2 zebras (Grevy), 20 zebras (Grant's), 6 oryxes, 4 waterbucks, 1 greater kudu, 4 lesser kudus, 10 Topis, 26 hartebeests, another 229 assorted antelopes, 6 of each species of colobus monkey (there are 14 species), and as many lions and leopards as they wished, as they were considered vermin. In addition, special licenses could be purchased for giraffes and elephants at ten pounds each.[8]

It is all rather astounding to us today, this liberal permission to kill, but we have to bear in mind that it was a different time, and that the country was very young and in need of revenue. One of the ways that British East Africa promoted itself was as a hunter's paradise, and so it had to make the journey to prospective visitors very attractive. Then, too, the supply of game seemed limitless, even though some professional hunters were already promulgating conservation measures, having done their math and been alarmed at the calculations.

Akeley wrote caustically about so-called sportsmen who felt that they had to kill the full compliment of animals that their license allowed. He had heard many stories about unethical hunters from his friends at Newland & Tarlton Safaris Inc. He was using them again on this trip, and they felt very loyal to Akeley, one of their first safari clients. The business had grown considerably since 1905. To buoy their budding safari enterprise, Newland and Tarlton had been auctioning off to the settlers the cattle and other live-stock seized by the government during the Nandi punitive expeditions. Their warehouse, a stone's throw from the railroad, bustled with activity.

If a safarist wished, he could arrive in Nairobi with little more than a toothbrush and Newland & Tarlton would have everything prepared for him to leave for the bush the next day. But Akeley always dealt with even the smallest details on his expeditions, and used the safari company mainly for hiring staff (there were 118 men on this expedition), securing pack animals, and taking care of last minute odds and ends.

A letter from Theodore Roosevelt awaited them in Nairobi. He wanted to set up a rendezvous with the expedition in the Uasin Gishu Plateau and needed to firm up his schedule. Supplies and ammunition had to be reviewed and organized and Akeley spent most of his time with Newland & Tarlton attending to last minute details. He still managed to make some time for his companions, however.

The Akeley party explored Nairobi and its environs. They visited a research center where researchers studied sleeping sickness through experiments on small primates. The disease is caused by trypanosomes—blood parasites—transmitted by the bite of an infected tsetse fly. The center's monkeys were restrained and bitten by flies imprisoned in small screen cages held to their stomachs. It was crucial to discover a vaccine for the illness if BEA was ever to become a "white man's country." Tragically, a vaccine has yet to be developed, for all our sophisticated medical technology, and the center's experiments, in which hundreds of monkeys were sacrificed, proved nothing because it could not be determined whether the monkeys were dying from sleeping sickness or another killer, tick fever. Akeley was a realist and never sentimental about animals, but he loathed wasted life. Mickie, on the other hand, had begun to study monkeys on her previous expedition and had a growing emotional investment in them. The visit to the station was fascinating and disturbing.

They adjourned in late afternoons to the Norfolk Hotel for drinks at the bar, joining the outrageous assortment of professional guides and safarists. Where Mickie went is uncertain, as women were not welcome at the bar (perhaps for tea in the garden). They had stayed at the Norfolk before, but it, like everything else in Nairobi, had expanded as the volume of safarists grew. The Norfolk was still the primary meeting place in town for men leaving for or returning from the bush. The men stood around or leaned on the bar, affecting an array of individualized costumes. One of the most popular outfits was a Buffalo Bill get-up with a wide, soft-brimmed hat, spurs, neckerchief, and a big knife in its sheath hanging from the belt. The vintage photographs of these hunters almost always reveal men with wiry little physiques, looking top-heavy in their big hats. Others appeared like Lords of the Empire, impeccably dressed in sartorial elegance with beautifully crisp khakis and pith helmets, while still others arrived straight from the field, filthy and shabby before their "hot or cold baths," as advertised by the hotel.

One of the highlights of the Nairobi sojourn was the balloon ride given them by Boyce. His African Balloonograph Expedition was heading for Kijabe but sent up the Akeley party, without Akeley, on a hill overlooking Nairobi just as a lark. The basket was very small, only three feet deep and three feet in diameter, so only one person could go up at a time. Each went up in turn, thrilled and terrified, and Mickie had the honor of being the first woman to rise above the plains of BEA.

The expedition left Nairobi for the Athi Plains September 23, and spent the next five weeks hunting as they moved northeastward toward the Tana

River. Early on they spent time at the ranch, called Juja, of Sir Northrup McMillan, an important figure in colonial BEA. A wealthy American who had made his fortune in Malaysian rubber, McMillan had a vast estate of almost twenty-six thousand acres near Thika at the base of Ol Doinyo Sabuk. The name Juja itself came from the names of two West African gods, Ju and Ja. McMillan had brought carved images of the gods to his estate, in spite of the alleged curse visited on anyone who owned them. Ironically, the curse called for death by drowning and McMillan died at sea in 1928. The Juja house itself was imported in parts from England and reconstituted on the estate in 1905.

McMillan was a bon vivant with a capacity for generosity equal to his enormous bulk; he tipped the scales at over four hundred pounds. Juja house was used as a hospital for British officers from 1914 to 1918; McMillan picked up the entire tab and was rewarded for his altruism with knighthood. He kept a pet lioness chained by day to iron rings embedded in cement near the front door. An oft repeated story tells of McMillan's delight in watching his lioness in heat, in rut with a wild male; he sat chuckling away in his chair as his staff watched from behind locked doors.

Theodore Roosevelt had been a visitor at Juja a few months before the Akeley party arrived. He writes, in *African Game Trails*, about his lovely week of hunting at Juja, but fails to mention one of the shenanigans that he and McMillan were involved in during his stay. They had a party in Nairobi and at its conclusion, feeling that the night was still young, set out on a sophomoric prank: They took two stone idols from the gates at the Khoja Mosque and installed them by the fireplace at McMillan's Nairobi town house, Chiromo. The Muslims were outraged by the theft, and a few days later, while calling on other business, the district officer spotted the idols and advised McMillan to dispose of them quickly and quietly so as not to taint the reputation of TR.[9] McMillan seems to have been preoccupied with idols that caused him trouble.

The Akeley party camped on a site at Juja reserved for visiting safaris. McMillan was probably away at the time as there is no evidence of them meeting him for dinner or otherwise. The farm abounded in game and the expedition successfully collected antelopes for the museum during their days at Juja.

While Akeley's main goal on the safari was to collect elephants, both Fred and J. T. were more interested in lions, which were plentiful at Juja. Once one had been spotted nearby, a lion drive was organized in which thirty to forty porters beat the bush in an effort to flush out the animal for shooting. In spite of the effort and time involved, they never even spotted lion. That it was so difficult to find and hunt lions at a time when they were so numerous must seem incredible to anyone who has visited one of Kenya's game parks where the lions appear ubiquitous. Actually, it is easier to see all game today because they are habituated, if not to humans, at least to their vehicles, and wander or lounge around practically under the noses of safarists. Still, the lions' mere existence testifies to the admirable conservation efforts in Kenya.

After passing through Thika, Punda Milia (Zebra in Kiswahili), and Fort Hall, the party finally reached the Tana River where they remained for about two weeks. They chose a magnificent parklike setting along the river with spacious, grassy areas spotted with umbrella acacias, near where they had stayed before. The Tana River area was, and still is, notorious for breeding enormous and lethal mosquitoes. Most of the indigenous Africans had left the malaria-ridden area and as a result the game proliferated. For some reason the expedition party had no problem with *dudus* (Kiswahili for bugs), and the time spent there was not only productive but terribly enjoyable.

The rhinoceroses were a particular treat. The party saw hundreds of them. Akeley wanted to film them charging, so a good deal of time was spent inciting rhinos to charge for the camera. Fred and J. T. flanked Akeley with their guns readied in case there was a mishap. The rhino's eyesight is notoriously bad, but his nose and ears are excellent, so he charges in nonspecific spurts in the direction of a smell or sound. Therefore if a hunter can approach him from upwind he can easily kill the beast—which is one of the reasons this species dangles in the balance today. The animals raging charge could usually be averted by whistles or yells. The sportsmen's writings at the time all addressed the fierce and deadly charge of the animal, and indeed it can be so, but Akeley felt that they were more stupid than vicious: "He is the stupidest fellow in Africa . . . It is true that as soon as he smells a man he is likely to start charging around in the most terrifying manner, but the rhino is never cunning like the elephant, nor is his charge accurate like the lion, nor is the rhino vindictive like the leopard or the buffalo."[10]

One day near the Tana, a rhino came charging full blast towards Akeley, only to stop abruptly and take a nap as Akeley stood there amazed, adrenalin pumping through his body. There is a Bantu myth that explains the behavior of the rhino: Ngai (God) gave each animal a needle with which to sew on its own skin. The rhino took the needle in his mouth and ran off into the bush, searching for a place to sit down while he sewed. En route something scared him, and as he gasped, he gulped down the needle. The tale explains why the animals seem so ill-tempered, why their skin fits so poorly, and why they have the odd habit of scattering and examining their manure—they are still looking for that damn needle!

Akeley had constructed a special rhino "dummy," or blind, to get closer to the animals to make photographs. It looked like one of the horses used in vaudeville, in which two men are concealed in the body, while their legs, clothed in color-coordinated fabric, were exposed and free to move around. What is clever on the stage is outrageous in the bush; the blind was cumbersome, uncomfortable, and hot, and even worse, didn't fool the rhinos. They also had an ostrich blind, equally hilarious. But no one can fault Akeley's wild imagination and resolve to realize his fantasies.

During the filming, in spite of the constant harassment of rhinos to incite them to charge, only one animal was killed, and that killing was admittedly

117

done for the benefit of the camera. Another rhino was killed by Fred Stephenson. He tried to avert a charge by shooting his gun into the air, yelling, and waving his arms, but she just kept coming at him. After he shot her, frantic squealing filled the air and a young rhino dynamo charged. They realized that the charging female had been defending her youngster. The expedition party made a baby rhino carrier of soft zebra skin suspended from two long poles. Holes for the *toto's* (Kiswahili for child) legs were cut into the leather and they transported the baby to camp, feeding it milk for about ten days before it died.

Today we understand how difficult and time-consuming it is to raise a young rhino or elephant—they need constant companionship and attention for several years. The poaching of rhinos has become so severe today that we will invest vast amounts of time, labor, and money into saving even one rhino. In 1968 there were 65,000 rhinos in Africa, 1,000 in Meru National Park alone, the area near the Tana where Akeley and company camped. Today there are 3,500 rhinos left in all of Africa, and less than 400 in Kenya. There are absolutely none in Trans-Tana. In 1988, the five remaining animals, semi-domesticated white rhinos that had been introduced to Meru, were savagely cut down by automatic weapons and left hideously butchered by poachers who wanted only their horns.

A single horn can now bring $5,000 to $15,000 on the Asian retail market. The poacher may only see $40 for his effort, but in a country where the average yearly income is $320, it seems a fortune. The horn is keratinous material, like matted hair, and for centuries has been ground up in the Orient and used as medicine to treat a variety of ailments, from fever to insanity to impotence. But today the largest market is in Yemen, where the horns are carved into dagger handles, connoting virility and wealth for the wearers. The market exploded with the need for oil in the West, which created many more wealthy Yemenites than there used to be. With wealth came the demand for the accoutrements of affluence. And the poachers murderous weapons are killing off not only the animals, but the men who are assigned to guard them as well.

Carl Akeley would have been bereft to see what we see today; even in 1909 he was acutely and painfully aware of the world to which we have had to grow accustomed. We are seeing the sad realization of Akeley's prophecy: "The coming of the white man with a rifle upset all this [the natural balance of wildlife], but the rhino has learned less about protecting himself than the other animals."[11]

They hunted lions in Trans-Tana. Most good hunters understood the nature of the animals they hunted. They respected them on a more profound level than the sentimentalists, and spent hours discussing the nuances of a particular stalk or kill. In addition, Akeley possessed the curiosity of a scientist and an ethologist, probing even deeper into the nature of living things. He had that enviable quality of being a man of both thought and action, and could sit for hours in quiet observation of animals without feeling fidgety or restless. Lions fascinated him.

There has been so much written about the lions for so many hundreds of years that it is clear that the creature fascinates nearly everyone. Even today safarists would rather stay and watch a pride of lions from a vehicle's window than anything else. Karen Blixen wrote in a letter home about her first experience with lions: "I shall never forget it. In their build, carriage, and movements lions possess a greatness, a majesty, which positively instills terror . . . and makes one feel later that everything else is trivial—thousands of generations of unrestricted supreme authority, and one is oneself set back 6,000 generations—suddenly comes to feel the mighty power of nature, when one looks it right in the eyes."

Akeley too felt deeply about lions and their noble natures. He observed that they would rather avoid fighting if possible, but when their fury was roused nothing could stop their charge. In the Trans-Tana area, Akeley made movies of lions as well as rhinos. He carried his camera while the others carried their guns and the porters beat the grass to scare out a hiding lioness. As the grass was very high, they had to push it down with their guns as they proceeded. At one point the grass was thrown back violently, almost throwing them over. They had pressed the grass down on a lioness's back. Despite this intrusion, she made off and did not attack them. They, however, went after her, pursuing her and trying her patience. After a bit of this she got fed up and charged; Fred shot her, making her even angrier, and she made straight for him. A second hit brought her down. Akeley was impressed with this behavior on the part of the lion and discussed it many times. In a way, the behavior was like his own; he would walk away from trouble but if provoked, he could be very mean and aggressive.

One evening after dinner, as they all sat around the campfire, conversation turned from the day's hunting events to capturing animals for American zoos. There was a hot communion about how deplorable zoo conditions were and the pity of caging in the splendid wild animals that surrounded them at their Tana camp. The discussion soon centered on primates, and on the filth and squalor in which they preferred to live, evidenced by their universally dirty zoo cages. Mickie took great exception to this and defended monkeys in particular, citing her observations on her previous expedition and addressing their fastidious habits in nature.

To prove her point, the next morning she and Bill baited a basket cage with corn to capture one. A young vervet monkey took the bait and was outraged and terrified when the cage closed around her. Mickie intended to release the animal a few days later after her companions could see firsthand that she was correct in her argument. But she made the mistake of naming her. The naming of animals usually implies a psychological and emotional

119

investment and almost immediately alters the pact between man and beast. The monkey was named after John McCutcheon—J.T. Jr.—and Mickie couldn't give her up. As unlikely as it sounds, Mickie's relationship with the animal would dramatically influence the next nine years of her life.

It started simply and innocently as a study in animal behavior. Mickie's sharp, intuitive observations and her assiduous attention to detail gave weight to her primate studies, which she wrote about many years later. They were popular if not scientific in tone, but her work long predated the famous female primatologists of our time. With her own little monkey, however, she suspended any objective observation and became involved with J.T. Jr. very quickly and very intensely. In her book about the animal, *J.T. Jr.: The Biography of an African Monkey*, she constantly refers to her in terms of a human child. Mickie was childless herself and at least twice refers to wanting to adopt children. We do not know whether the Akeleys had no children out of choice or physiological problems. They both enjoyed the company of children and it is hard to imagine that they would have consciously decided not to have any. Regardless, Mickie centered her maternal energies on the monkey. J.T. Jr. was just a needy youngster and much of her behavior coincided with early and adolescent human development. If she had been an adult when she was caught, Mickie might well have proved her point and released her. But J.T. Jr. was a child, and Mickie behaved accordingly. She and J.T. Jr. went on picnics together and climbed trees to watch sunsets together, and J.T. Jr. slept every night in Mickie's tent and bed. Mickie justified this fact (it is interesting that she thought she had to) by writing that she needed to see how the animal dealt with night noises. But J.T. Jr. would become wild if anyone interfered with their sleep. This new phenomenon had an adverse affect on Akeley and his relationship with his wife, sexual and otherwise.

The monkey brought great joy to Mickie. It is clear from photographs of her with the animal how much she doted on it, often gazing at it with an easy comfort born of intimacy and communion as it sits in her lap. But the relationship started to slip into something unhealthy. The Africans were astounded by her behavior towards the animal. Anyone who has spent any time in Africa has witnessed firsthand how badly even domestic pets and beasts of burden are treated. (In fact, there is at present a campaign launched by the Kenya SPCA to raise the consciousness of the public and rectify the abusive behavior.) But early in this century, Mickie's dotage on J.T. Jr. must have really confounded the Africans.

J.T. Jr. had her own valet, Ali, a young Swahili boy outfitted in a khaki suit and a red fez. Ali held an umbrella over the sun-sensitive animal during long marches and collected flowers for her to keep her preoccupied and distracted. She wore a silver collar engraved with her name and always traveled in the same train compartment as her mistress—on a child's ticket. No one was allowed to discipline the animal, not even Akeley, who felt it necessary on a number of occasions when the animal bit either Mickie or others. Akeley grew jealous of J. T. Jr. and Mickie's affection for her. The whole sad mess would spiral downward over the next several years. But J. T. Jr. was a charming, if spoiled, animal, and she had many human friends.

Mickie soon gave something of herself over to the animal—some type of control. It was as if the monkey were a magnet, a projection of something in her; she elevated the animal and, in a way, became subservient to it. Even when she was in the field she would often return before the others because she would be haunted by J. T. Jr.'s "pouting lips and the wistful look in her sad brown eyes,"[12] as if she were being summoned. Was this a projection of her own sad brown eyes? Was there something so elemental and essential missing in her own life, creating a void so difficult to deal with that she externalized the pain and let the monkey carry it for her? She seemed to get a perverse delight in J. T. Jr.'s destructive antics—tearing apart the kitchen tent, terrorizing the staff. Even though she dutifully tied up the animal, she was amused and seemed to act in collusion with her. (The destructive rampages would be less amusing in a New York apartment.) Mickie might have craved anarchy and J. T. Jr.'s outrageous behavior exorcised some muted knot of self-control for her. Perhaps Mickie always had to be the sober one, to allow for her husband's wild excursions into fantasy, creativity, and scrapes with death. They had to get tiresome after a while, and maybe J. T. Jr.'s behavior— explosive, wild, unpredictable, and sometimes violent—was just the therapy Mickie needed. She could not and did not behave badly; she kept playing the dutiful wife as her monkey spun farther and farther out of control.

The time on the Tana was enjoyable and fulfilling but the expedition needed to move on to Mt. Kenya and the elephants. Mt. Kenya, where they had collected one of the *Fighting Bulls* for the Field Museum in 1906, held the promise of success. Akeley was excited to return to the mountain and led the group to one of the sites where he and Mickie had pitched their camp before. It was a beautiful spot, just on the edge of dense bush and looking out over the orderly Kikuyu *shambas* on the side of the mountain below. Kikuyu and Dorobo guides, some of whom had been with Bibi and Bwana in 1906, walked into camp only hours after the Akeley's arrival, offering their tracking skills.

Elephants had been sighted the day before and Akeley was pleased not to have to travel far for them. The party set out the next day on what turned out to be a miserable adventure. They followed the crisscrossing trails of elephants through the bush, and the vegetation was so densely matted on both sides of the path that they felt walled in and anxious for lack of an escape route. The forest walls seemed alive as they reached out with thorns and grabbing "monkey ropes"—aerial roots. When they did reach an opening in the bush, they had to beware of elephant pits created by the Dorobo. The forest was magnificent with its vaulted canopy and variegated greens mottled by thin streams of sunlight piercing through the vegetation, but few noticed the beauty of the scene. The trails led them in circuitous routes, and as the trail lengthened so did their fear and the penetrating chill from the altitude.

Finally the Dorobo guide, masterfully reading the nuances of the trail, led the group along a fresh spoor–strewn path that took them into forest so dark that they couldn't see more than twenty-five feet in front of them. If an elephant realized that they were there and decided to turn on them, there was absolutely no egress for escape. The realization exacerbated the tension seizing the group, yet still no one vocalized the terror felt by all, and they just kept moving on toward the animals they knew were before them. The silence was broken by a sudden, sharp crash of a tusk taking down a tree. The group couldn't determine its location, and froze, not knowing whether to proceed or retreat for safety. An elephant squeal sounded from another direction, setting off yet another from behind them. J.T. wrote: "We waited for several years of intense apprehension. There was absolute silence. The elephants also were evidently awaiting further developments."[13] After a few traumatic minutes, they began inching their way ahead, surrounded by elephant crashings yet still not able to see anything. After what seemed an eternity they reached a small clearing where everyone tried to relax the cramps in their trigger fingers. Each of them had concentrated the tension he or she felt in the hand and arm carrying the gun, but they were all pleased they hadn't needed to use the weapons. The clearing was essentially an intersection of elephant trails with a tree at its center.

"All immediate danger seemed to have passed," wrote J.T. "It seemed to but it hadn't. Like a sudden explosion of a thirteen–inch gun there was a thundering crash in the bushes behind the porters, then a perfect avalanche of terrified porters, a dropping of bundles, a wild dash for the protection of the tree, and a bunch of the most startled white men ever seen on Mount Kenia [sic] . . . I don't think I was ever so frightened in my life. But I had company. I didn't monopolize all the fright that was used in those few seconds of terror."[14] Finally a porter was sent up a tree to spot the elephants' location, and the group shot off their guns to frighten the animals away. The elephants seemed as frightened as the humans, and instead of scattering or stampeding, merely rustled a little at the guns' report. Akeley and company beat a retreat, resolved never to commit that mistake again; in the future they would hunt only where they could see the animals.

The next day, and the next, they hunted elephants but killed nothing, even though they found and approached one closely enough to have done so. Akeley was searching for perfect specimens and was not interested in killing an animal that didn't measure up. The group knew they had to move to the protectorate's western regions, so they left Mt. Kenya and her elephants for Nairobi. Akeley planned to return to the mountain within the year.

The Akeley expedition left by rail from Nairobi's station for Londiani around November 1. Once there they would detrain and move northwestward by foot to the Uasin Gishu Plateau, where they hoped to meet Theodore Roosevelt. The safari to the west was planned for ten weeks. Akeley must have felt very excited on the journey: Not only would he again see TR, whom he loved and respected, but he would also be able to hunt in an area that had been forbidden to him in the past. The territory had only recently been opened up after the problems with the Nandi tribe that had prevented Bibi and Bwana's trip there in 1905.

Londiani is located just above the equator and about eighty miles from Lake Victoria. Meeting the party were one hundred porters and two transport wagons, each with a span of thirty oxen and some horses for riding down lions. The country in western Kenya is magnificent—vast, green, clean, and ordered like an enormous garden. The forested areas, covering several miles, exist in neat clumps, the edges of which border huge meadows appointed with wildflowers. The skies are wildly dramatic, dense clouds whipped up by Lake Victoria against a field of vivid blue, and truly immense. Every aspect of the earth and sky is big and expansive. Nothing about it feels raw or savage, like parts of the east and north. The altitude is about seventy-five hundred feet above sea level, making trekking comfortable, though a bit nippy at night. The roan antelopes had calved in early November and mothers with young were everywhere. The hills and plains throbbed with life, and hartebeests were so prolific that barely a termite mound was safe, as it is their custom to stand sentry astride the the small hills to show dominance and to get a better look at what is coming along. Occasionally Akeley's party would see a Boer farm off in the distance. It was quite surprising to see anything related to civilization in country so untouched.

The open, undulating hills allowed oxen and transport wagons to pass easily. The group marched for several days, passing through Eldama Ravine, crossing and recrossing the equator, and traversing miles of varied habitat to the edge of the Uasin Gishu Plateau. There the trees ended abruptly and they were suddenly faced with a glorious flat expanse of grassland with Mt. Elgon a rolling hump in the northwest corner of the vista. They headed for Elgon, their next destination.

Their arrival at Sergoi Hill on November 10 was highlighted by a letter from TR with information on his location. Even with this more or less specific information on his whereabouts there was no guarantee that they would find him on the plateau, and TR's expedition was not alone in the field because the recent quelling of the Nandi resistance had made the area accessible to hunters.

TR was about a three-day march west on the Nzoia River. The Akeley party had no idea whether he would still be there when they arrived, but they hastened towards their destination, setting up camp near a swampy area that held the promise of lions. An African runner arrived with a message for TR, but instead of moving on to find him, settled in to enjoy the hospitality of the expedition. A morning march the next day brought them closer to the Nzoia and they sent out runners of their own to locate TR. Akeley and Roosevelt learned of each other about the same time and each in turn set out to find the other, meeting en route.

Akeley was extremely glad to see TR and the ex-president was happy to see old friends. TR accompanied Akeley to his camp to see Mickie, Fred, and John. While they were standing around, exhilarated to see each other, the African runner casually gave TR his message. TR laughed and read the message to the group: "Reported here you have been killed. Mrs. Roosevelt worried. Cable denial American Embassy, Rome."[15] TR would respond saying that the report was premature. An article in the *Leader* on December 11 suggested that the rumor of TR's death was started on Wall Street to influence the Stock Exchange.

They had a wonderful lunch together, full of badinage addressing everything going on back home, from the Cook-Peary controversy, to dramatist George Ade—a good friend of John's, to Chicago politics. John wrote that TR "talked with the freedom of one who was glad to see some American friends in the wilderness."[16] The Akeley safari was the only one, American or otherwise, that TR had met in the field, and he was starved for conversation.

While it was fun to see friends in the bush so very far from home, the meeting was not strictly social. Their joint mission was to collect some elephants for the American Museum of Natural History, as had been discussed at that White House dinner when TR first decided to come to Africa. TR had already collected hundreds of animals for the Smithsonian but had agreed to shoot two cows and a calf for the AMNH. He had seen a herd only hours before, and after lunch Akeley returned with TR to his camp, from which they would depart in the morning.

By noon the next day TR had killed three cows in a frenzy of shooting and his son, Kermit, had shot a calf. Roosevelt was not a crack shot and had less-than-perfect eyesight. Akeley later complained that the cows were too small. Two of the cows and the calf were to be shipped back to the museum; the other skin was to be cut up and shared by all as souvenirs.

TR and Akeley ended up sitting alone together under an acacia tree as they guarded the corpses until the porters brought salt and assistance to preserve the skins. Those hours with TR were one of the highlights of Akeley's life. TR discussed intimate subjects with Akeley, including his wife and children. He was traveling with his son, with all the attendant difficulties of parent-child relationships. Kermit's son, Kermit, in his book *Sentimental Safari*, wrote that "Leslie Tarlton had been hired, according to Percival [a renowned white hunter and friend of TR's and Akeley's, who is discussed on a later expedition] and others familiar with the expedition, to ride herd on KR. This was no slight task, for the twenty-one-year-old Harvard sophomore was fast afoot . . . [and] full of ideas."[17] Kermit could be exasperating and TR might have been airing dirty linen with Akeley, the way two strangers on a bus will reveal terribly personal things about themselves—facts that bind people together in an unspoken oath of silence and trust.

Akeley, in a lecture at Albany's Assembly Chamber to the committee studying memorials for TR after his death, spoke about that afternoon saying "I got a new vision and a new view of Theodore Roosevelt; it was then that I learned to love him, and it was then that I realized that Roosevelt—well, that I would follow him anywhere; even if I doubted, I would follow him, because I knew of his sincerity, his integrity, and the real bigness of the man . . . those Christlike qualities, if you like, which made Theodore Roosevelt what he was."[18]

TR doesn't even mention the incident, nor is he overly generous to Akeley in his book. This hero worship on Akeley's part speaks to an important side of his nature.

Theodore Roosevelt was not just the president of the United States; he was the consummation of every enviable male quality to which a boy or man could aspire. This "great man" had deigned to befriend and respect Akeley, which flattered Carl immensely. To strip away formality and sit alone as two equal men under a tree in Africa must have been a dear event. But add to this an intimate conversation that revealed TR's vulnerability as well—a crack in the facade. TR was human, with many of the same doubts and insecurities as anyone else, and Akeley felt a little awe-struck at being the one with whom TR chose to share these personal fears. The exposé bonded Akeley to TR in a new way and he forever treasured their relationship. For TR, the afternoon's conversation was hardly serious; he just needed to get a few things off his chest. He probably never gave it another thought.

One might describe the "Christlike qualities" Akeley speaks of as simply the highest attributes of humanness. One of the virtues ever near to Akeley's heart was courage. And for Akeley, the act of hunting embodied both courage and honor. While this may sound like an antiquated or "macho" attitude, in some respects Akeley was enlightened for his time. He did not consider courage or hunting as a virtue and privilege restricted solely to men. In fact, as he demonstrated on the 1905 expedition, Akeley was extremely proud of Mickie's hunting prowess, even celebrating it in print. "Fear is the very essence of pleasure or sport; the real sport begins when there is the excuse to feel afraid," wrote Sir Alfred Pease in his book on lions. Hunting and the battleground are two areas where one can prove his or her mettle—the courage of holding steady in face of terrible, though exhilarating fear, against an animal or human charge. It is a moment of self-realization. Few of us ever experience that moment in the pure sense hunting offers, and consequently have no idea how we would behave.

Akeley had some trouble with such moments, and on a couple of occasions found that he was incapable of meeting his own expectations. He watched TR hunt, with not so much as a flicker of indecision or fear in his stance, and must have envied him. Of course, in today's conservation-minded society we might view TR's hunting as excessive and obscene. In fact, one of his friends, the famous American naturalist and conservationist John Muir, later asked him, "Mr. Roosevelt, when are you going to get beyond the boyishness of killing things . . . are you not getting far enough along to leave that off?"[19] But what matters here is the way Akeley looked to the man for inspiration, and how he was overwhelmed by TR's great courage. Bwana Tumbo, "Mister stomach"—TR's Kiswahili name—was undoubtedly also afraid, but that hardly matters as he covered it so well.

The hunting was over in an astonishingly short time. Kermit returned to Akeley's camp to direct James L. Clark to bring more salt. Clark had just arrived from his own expedition in Tanganyika (now Tanzania), led by photographer A. Radclyffe Dugmore. Clark also assisted photographer Cherrie Kearton in making the extant movies of Roosevelt on this safari. Now, Clark came north to the Uasin Gishu to help Akeley with the elephants.

Kermit accompanied Clark to TR's camp, gave him a guide and directions, and promptly went to bed. Clark set out to find Akeley and the elephants but ended up lost, meandering around the bush for hours with his salt-bearing porters. In the middle of the night they stopped their frightful journey, built a fire, and slept until daybreak. TR and Tarlton left their elephant camp at the same time, heading for base camp, and the two groups met en route. As a result, Akeley had only a few African assistants to help him, and he removed the one and a quarter–ton skins of three adult cows and one calf almost single-handedly. This monumental and exhausting job was exacerbated by a brush fire that came close to claiming the valuable elephant skins—and their lives. As assistants fought back the flames, Akeley worked frantically in the intense heat. The smoke burned his eyes, obscuring his vision. When the bush fire was no longer a threat, the sun's intensity intensified the gases of decomposition, causing the skins to rot. Akeley ordered a tarpaulin erected over the carcass he was skinning as assistants splashed saltwater over its surface. It was grueling work for Akeley, who removed the skins in four sections.

When Clark finally arrived, the two men began the arduous task of paring the skins down so that they could absorb the salt, which would preserve them until they arrived at the museum. Because the salt absorbed moisture, Akeley had to find a way to make the skins moisture-proof. They were too large to be folded and sealed in the usual chop boxes. Akeley dispatched helpers into the surrounding countryside to collect beeswax, which was melted and poured over cotton cloth, used to wrap the elephant skins into enormous bundles for shipment home.

Meanwhile, Mickie, Fred, and John were also destined for the temporary elephant camp, guided by the rested Kermit. They too met TR en route. TR excitedly told them about a bizarre hyena incident that had occurred the night before. One of the creatures ate his way into an elephant carcass. When he tried to eat his way out again, the flesh of the dead animal closed like an elastic band around the engorged scavenger's throat, imprisoning it, making it an easy target for TR's gun. TR feared that no one would believe the story unless he found witnesses and photographed it. The Roosevelts, Akeley, and J.T. recorded the odd head protruding from the side of the elephant, looking like some macabre medical experiment.

While Akeley and Clark worked on the elephant skins, the rest of the party had a lovely lunch with TR. After the meal they examined his famous "pigskin library," sitting around on the floor and trunks of his tent, reading. The library was a collection of classic literature published in small volumes and covered in pigskin, the whole thing designed to fit into a trunk and weighing sixty pounds, equivalent to one porter's load. TR always had a volume in his saddlebag so that he could read whenever the opportunity presented itself; this time he had taken Macaulay's essays on the elephant hunt. The light in the tent, which doubled as Kermit's darkroom, was tinged with pink; its rosy glow added to everyone's sense of well-being. The afternoon's stimulating conversation skipped like stones on the water, touching on Longfellow, natural history, alcohol abuse, and vaudeville. Akeley missed the afternoon, as he seems to have missed so many of the good times on the periphery of his life. Again he was working. He was always working. The Akeley party spent only three days with TR and company, but this time was a personal highlight for each member.

The AMNH British East Africa Expedition, hoping to complete their mission to secure two large bull elephants and one young one for the museum, crossed the Nzoia River and moved on to Mt. Elgon, the 14,178-foot mountain on the Uganda-Kenya border. They were also trying for a black-maned lion.

If Akeley couldn't get his bulls on Elgon he would have to travel into Uganda, draining not only his time in Africa but also his limited funds. They were trying for the herds on the southwestern slopes of the mountain, as the Arabs, Swahilis, and European sportsmen had already decimated many of the elephants in the northern area.

They hunted for days in the Trans-Nzoia area without seeing a single elephant. The plains animals, however, were plentiful. And in the midst of the immense sky and earth, the party celebrated Mickie's thirty-fourth birthday on December 5, sitting around on chop boxes in camp, no doubt noting the day with a swig of scotch, and Bibi enjoying a cigarette or two.

The troupe pushed on to the mountain and spent twelve days there searching for *tembo*. Food supplies were running low, as was their morale. John and Akeley peeled off from the others for a few days to make a hard, fast march in pursuit of a herd they had begun tracking, hoping for a speedy success. One of their Maasai syncs spotted some shifting dots on the horizon and they realized that they had finally encountered a herd of elephant. With a sense of relief, the small group moved toward the animals, a herd of forty to fifty with a number of *totos*. Since elephant society is matriarchical and the herd is organized around the "grand dame" female and her sisters, plus two generations of young, a herd rarely contains mature males (unless a visiting bull is in consort with a female in estrus). Akeley and John sighted a couple of young bulls in this herd, and decided to move in on it. *Kongoni* (hartebeests) were standing sentry for the herd but seemed not to have noticed Akeley and John. *Kongoni* are like the old women who sit outside on the street, minding everyone's business but at the same time, guarding against mishap—a peculiar mixed blessing. Even though the *kongoni* sounded no alarm and the men were upwind, the herd became agitated. These animals possess amazing intelligence and sensitivity to their surroundings; their trunks went up to feel the air for a sensed threat. Through a network of communication still known only to elephants, the herd moved off rear-guarded by the dominant female and three or four other adults.

Akeley and John pursued the herd with only their gun bearers. They crouched down in the grass and crawled around the herd, no longer able to locate the young bulls they were after. For five tension-filled hours they circled and recircled the animals, never certain of their aim and therefore never shooting. Elephants have a sense that it is their ivory that is the cause of their danger, and countless naturalists over the years have recorded incidents where elephants clump together to hide the larger tusks from view. No elephants were killed that day and Akeley's frustration escalated.

On Christmas Eve, Fred and John succeeded in bagging two young bull elephants, but Akeley's Christmas would consist only of the hard task of securing the skins, and a growing anxiety that he was not even going to see his perfect bull, much less collect it.

The party ranged over Mt. Elgon, turning to the indigenous people for assistance. The Ketosh, today known as Bakusu, were a Bantu-speaking tribe belonging to a larger group of people called the Luhya, who still inhabit the area today. They were agriculturalists who were often raided by the southern Maasai and Nandi, and who found shelter and protection by moving their villages into the enormous caves of the mountain, one of which is seventy feet high and two hundred feet wide. This is Kitum cave, now famous for its salt-mining elephants.

The expedition became enchanted with the cave people and the other tribes living on the mountain. However, the safarists often frightened the Africans, most of whom had never seen whites before. A fascinating episode occurred when the Akeley party startled a Dorobo family group so badly that they abandoned their baby, so that its wails would not attract the *wazungu* (more than one muzungu-European or white person) to their hiding place. Ali, J.T. Jr.'s keeper, found the baby naked, freezing, and screaming, and brought it to Mickie, who "lost her heart to the helpless child and announced that [she] was going to adopt it."[20] She and J.T. Jr. took turns holding and hugging the two-month-old, wrapped in nothing but a bath towel. Mickie decided on the name Elgon.

Mickie's immediate and powerful reaction to the baby sent the rest of them into a state of panic. The native staff was dispatched into the forest to call out that gifts would be offered in peace if the parents would come and reclaim the child. The parents did come, much to Akeley's relief, just as Mickie was "wondering how [she] could share [her] cot with a monkey and a baby."[21]

Fred and John had to return to Nairobi. From there they would travel to India and Java before returning to the States. The Akeleys were continuing on to Uganda in search of what would be Akeley's "Moby Dick." Incredibly, John McCutcheon would complete his travels in the Orient, return home, write and publish his book about the expedition, and actually send it to the Akeleys, who would still be in Africa, searching for the perfect elephant.

In Uganda, the Akeleys hired a fresh team of porters to continue their search. Marching along the Hoima Road down to the Kafu River, navigating the Kafu in dugout canoes, they finally reached the Masindi-Kampala Road and proceeded to Masindi. They traveled for two weeks and did not see a single tusker. The area between Masindi and Foweira was famous for enormous old bulls carrying tusks of two hundred pounds each; the Akeleys hunted there for one month.

Carl became obsessed with the notion of his big bull and the anxiety, coupled with the months of pressure and strain of expedition life plus the odd, mysterious ailments born in Africa, made him a candidate for serious illness. Akeley came down with blackwater fever, spirillum, and meningitis, which often accompanies malaria. Mickie fell ill also, but her bouts were neither as long nor as violent as Akeley's. It fell to her, alone but for their native staff, to nurse him back to health. Her endless nights of vigil over Akeley's fever-riddled form and the dark, gloomy forests conspired to destroy Mickie's confidence and stamina. She heard elephants foraging for food in their vicinity almost every night. Even by day, guides were coming and going with news of the great animals in various locations, but the herds were basically female in composition and therefore not appropriate to Akeley's needs. Mickie had terrifying nightmares about being stampeded by elephants and her "nerves rebelled." She felt that only J.T. Jr. seemed to comprehend her fearful jumpiness, and was there to comfort her.

During the days in the forest, while Akeley was recovering, she sometimes sat up in the trees with her monkey and watched elephants "making love," which brought her peace of a sort. (This very unscientific nomenclature tells us a great deal about how Mickie viewed elephants, sex, and herself. We must bear in mind the time during which she wrote—an era of suppressed puritanic sexuality, making her own sensuality all the more obvious when she spoke of animals "making love" rather than copulating or in rut.) Often,

Akeley would hastily leave his bed when one of the porters brought news of a bull elephant sighting, only to collapse from the exertion, and Mickie would "begin the stubborn fight for his life all over again." She wrote, "Although repeated attacks of fever had poisoned his blood and dysentery wasted his strength to such an alarming extent that I often feared for his life, he refused to give up. Even when the impoverished condition of his blood caused ugly ulcers to appear on his hands and feet he would not heed my pleadings to return to civilization where he could obtain skilled medical treatment."[22]

Their depression deepened when they found they were running out of money and the AMNH decided not to send them any more (after all, Akeley was not a known quantity to the museum and the whole contract was speculative). Akeley decided to sell some New York property to finance the remainder of the expedition, but as he was required to personally sign the closing documents, the deal fell through. Newland and Tarlton came through for him, offering him credit, writing to him that he was "an ass . . . we are your friends not only your agents."[23]

The rainy season descended upon them and as the forests grew more dank and oppressive, so did Akeley's mood and health. The couple's nerves were shot, and they began bristling at one another. Mickie knew that she had to get Akeley out of Uganda before things worsened, and convinced him that they should take a vacation and rest in a more healthful location than the deep forests which could claim their lives and hearts. They would return to the Uasin Gishu Plateau for a working holiday in the temperate climate and make movies of the Nandi spearing lions.

On the way out of Uganda, en route to the Uasin Gishu, they encountered a charging elephant that was almost the end of both of them. Akeley wrote about it:

I had thought best to hunt alone in the beginning but after four or five weeks of rather intimate association with hundreds of elephants I became less respectful and just at the last I consented to take M. [Mickie] out. It was the morning of the third day out that we came into the spoor of a herd of seven or eight bulls and were following hard for perhaps two hours when the first alarm came. One of the boys heard them across the little valley into which they were descending. Porters and all unnecessary followers were "deposited" with instructions to remain quiet till sent for and we began the stalk. But it was not until an hour later that our tracker pointed out patches of elephant skin visible through the trees 100 yards ahead of us. It was high bush and grass country—good cover—conditions reasonably favorable. We made a stalk to within thirty yards of where they stood beneath a big tree milling about somewhat uneasily, fanning themselves with their great ears. The wind was uncertain so we did not delay longer than necessary in choosing an intended victim, an enormous fellow with very wide-spread tusks. He stood at the moment quarterface to us and I told M. to shoot two inches below the eye, which she did to within one-quarter inch. I followed

130

with a shot in the neck as he fell. There was a crash and roar as the rest of the herd stampeded. According to all rules and regulations, the proper thing at this time would have been to rush in and finish our beast off before he should have time to recover from a possible nerve shock. But when one is accompanied by his wife in such a situation he may be forgiven for ignoring "rules." At any rate we did not rush in promptly.

I waited a bit to make certain that the coast was clear or rather that there was no foxy old tusker quietly awaiting our appearance as sometimes happens. It was not more than a minute but it was too long, for the old fellow suddenly got onto his feet and got away in spite of six shots rained into his shoulders and neck as he went. We took up the spoor and followed cautiously . . .

Ten minutes later we had him in view again and as we swung to the left in order to get the wind right for a close stalk—at the time it was blowing from us to him—we saw him head around facing us. He had winded us and in an instant he started, ears spreading and closing, trunk thrashing the bush right and left, screaming with rage.

Twenty yards away I fired a .475 and he stopped, then I threw more of the same as quickly as possible at the vulnerable spot which I should know so well and all the time M. sending in those little swift ones of hers as fast as she could work her gun and the result! He took them as a sand bank might—just a little spurt of dust and that was all. [Akeley wanted to quit, saying that the elephant had more than enough shot in it, but Mickie insisted that he finish the job. Akeley reloaded.]

It was not more than a minute when he made a third charge. As he came out from behind a clump of trees swinging aloft in his trunk an enormous branch which he had torn off in passing, I fired midway between eye and ear, just above the zygomatic arch and pierced his brain. I was never so thankful to see an animal go down . . . As I stood by the carcass I felt very small indeed. Mrs. Akeley sat down and drew a long breath before she spoke. "I want to go home," she said at last, "and keep house for the rest of my life."[24]

As dramatic and dangerous as this episode was, there is more to the story. Ali and J.T. Jr. arrived on the scene after the second charge. The elephant changed direction and went after them. Mickie panicked when she saw Ali and the monkey, and raced to divert the wounded elephant's attack. After the animal finally went down on the last charge, Akeley humiliated her in front of the staff by asking, "What the hell did you run away for?"[25] She was stung by the accusation of cowardice and spat out some cursed retort, as the Africans rushed to her defense by explaining to Akeley what had happened. The couple's nerves were frayed. They started fighting more often. Akeley wanted to appease her at one point by killing a lion and giving her the skin because "they had not parted the best of friends that morning." Many years after their divorce, Mickie said that she, herself a crack shot, was so angry with Akeley that she shot an elephant to only wound it so that it would charge and kill him. Whether or not this was hubris or the exaggerated

Carl Akeley

memories of an old woman, it was clear that vengeance, temper, and ill will existed between them at times.

Soon Akeley and Mickie were in the Uasin Gishu again, enjoying the relative warmth of the western Kenyan sun and the plain's vast expanses of earth and sky, a relief after the claustrophobic density of the Ugandan forests. Akeley hired about one hundred Nandi warriors to stage the stunning lion-spearing ritual for him so that he could film it. It is ironic that the Nandi, only recently subdued and pacified, were willing to be hired out to whites to perform one of their most valued rituals. Shortly before the Akeleys arrival, TR had also paid to watch the spectacle.

At the onset of this adventure, which would last three weeks, a leopard was mistakenly put upon in some scrubby bush, and succeeded in scalping the young *moran*, a young warrior, who was annoying it. While other *moran* rushed in to kill the cat, Akeley immediately began sewing the man's scalp back onto his head. During the surgery, the African asked, "What is the white man doing to me?" "They are sewing you back up," he was told. "Oh, I thought that it was something like that," the African said as he took a pinch of snuff.[26] His only concern was whether the white men would let him participate in the lion hunt. He was allowed to continue and was given a steer for his trouble. Akeley commented, with characteristic Akeley humor, that the Nandi surgery was one of his more lifelike works to date.

Three days into the journey in lion country, they finally had an opportunity to film. *Simba* (Kiswahili for lion) bolted from the bush, crashing through the Nandi *moran* line. The young warriors gave chase, whooping and hollering as the animal ran a hundred yards over the open plains and stopped abruptly, sinking down into the high grass. The lion was exhausted from the long morning chase. The tired but exuberant warriors pressed on. Splitting their line, they surrounded the animal, now running again. The first spear thrown sailed high, catching the sun on its blade, then found its mark, plunging high in *simba*'s flank. Akeley, unnerved, wasn't getting his pictures—the action was too fast.

The Nandi screams muffled the lion's furious roars as he, hit time and again, turned and bit the spears in his agony. The field exploded with heat and violence as the *moran* barked and retched, like their Maasai cousins, while the bloodshed and excitement climaxed. *Simba*, dead, lay there as if still alive, twitching with reflexive jerks.

Akeley recorded only part of the astonishing event and stood there in the field shaken by his failure. Frustration and anger knotted hard in his stomach. Here was one of the most dramatic events East Africa had to offer, and he was having trouble recording it on film. When adrenaline subsided all around, Akeley calmly shot the rest of the ritual. His Urban bioscope camera was perfectly adequate for a bunch of posed Africans and a dead lion.

The jubilant *moran* pulled out their bent spears and circled the bloody corpse with shields and spears held high, chanting as they danced. It was still a thrilling spectacle. As custom allowed, the first warrior to spear *simba* claimed his mane for a headdress.

Akeley tried again and again to film the ritual, capturing bits and pieces of the action. The warriors ultimately killed fourteen lions and five leopards over the course of the three weeks. The Nandi were finally trying so hard to help Akeley get his film that by the end of the period they were actually holding a lion at bay to give Akeley time to set up his camera, after which they would finish the spearing. The waste in lion life was extreme—and absurd—all to get some decent footage! Akeley was wild, swearing at the camera equipment, because it simply was not manageable or fast enough for field work. Akeley decided that if such a camera did not exist, then he would invent one for just such an event. He resolved to create an instrument that would be light and easily set up and negotiated. With his customary vision, Akeley began designing a camera in his mind.

The sojourn in the Uasin Gishu had been relaxing and healthful, if not totally successful. Akeley and Mickie decided not to return to Uganda for elephants, but to push on to Mt. Kenya instead, where they hoped to find their bull. They stopped at Lake Hannington (now Lake Bogoria) and stayed for a few days, celebrating Carl's forty-sixth birthday on May 19. Akeley had fever.

By June the Akeleys were on Mt. Kenya, confident that the mythical great bull was just before them, and that once they collected it they could go home. The elephant mauling changed all of that. Their lives would never be the same after the June 24 "smash-up"—Akeley's name for the mauling incident described at the start of this chapter.

Akeley spent three long months recuperating after the mauling. He looks excruciatingly fragile in the photographs taken during his recovery. Almost more painful was the horrible period following the incident, when he had lost his "morale"—his word for courage. He was terrified, but would push himself to go after elephants in spite of the fear he felt when one of the staff sounded the alarm. More often than not, he collapsed in the bush. Then the Africans would bring him back in a blanket and Mickie would have to nurse him back to health. Once Mickie ran after him into the forest, in "fog so thick that they couldn't see one another . . . a strange dark prison,"[27] only to find a sad old man sitting on the ground incapable of moving. One day Akeley and Bill went out after elephants together, along with a porter who carried a chair so that Akeley could sit down when he felt weak. That day, he actually was able to shoot an elephant, but he didn't kill it, and committed the inexcusable sin of not going after it.

The most positive event of this period happened when Akeley was in bed, not in the field. While he lay on his camp cot for those three months, his forced stillness allowed him the luxury of serious daydreaming. Perhaps his inventive fantasizing helped him cope with his constant pain and maintain his sanity. But in his dreams, he built a monument to his "brightest Africa," eulogizing a dying continent as he knew her—vital, charming, mysterious, and violent. In his mind he expanded the idea of the elephant exhibit into a grand palace unfolding the whole picture of life in Africa. Akeley built the hall in his mind brick by brick; he mounted every animal, painted every background, directed every scene, and sculpted every bas-relief decoration. Over and over again he built his hall, each time sweeping it clean of any excess or untruth, honing it down to essential simplicity. And when he recovered, he had a very specific visionary plan. The dream became his obsession for the rest of his life.

J. T. Jr. visited Akeley daily to entertain him in his bed while Mickie was out hunting for food or running the camp. Akeley read *Ivanhoe* during his recovery, slowly gaining strength to take short walks and to sit up at table so that Mickie could cut his hair. When he felt well enough to travel, the Akeleys decided to return to Uganda for the big bull—Mt. Kenya must have seemed too emotionally loaded for real success. They traveled southward through Trans-Tana with the intention of returning J. T. Jr. to her home, en route to Nairobi. Another extravagant and explosive situation awaited them there.

The Tana River abounded in crocodiles, creating terror in the men and beasts who had to ford its waters. An entire expedition crossing a river created a great stir and the reptiles descended in the hundreds looking for an easy meal. Akeley and Mickie shot volleys into the waters and onto the shoreline to force the crocs away. When the path seemed clear, a small group of porters would enter the waters, yelling and beating the river's surface with sticks. They formed an open column and continued making noise as the rest of the porters, bearing packs, marched between them, singing loudly. They were nerve-wracking crossings, as one never knew if one of the vicious reptiles was submerged and waiting, in spite of all the precautions.

Akeley was still in a weakened state, and no doubt feeling delicate and angry about his "morale" problem. He shot a crocodile basking in the sun on the opposite bank of the river. There was no real reason for shooting the animal, and undoubtedly he came to regret it very much. Two young porters dived into the croc-infested waters to fetch the dead animal. The other porters immediately began making bets on which boy would retrieve the corpse first. Akeley and Mickie were horrified and, grabbing their guns, ran to the river and began shooting at the swiftly moving waters to fend off crocodile attacks.

One of the boys triumphantly reached the other side and straddled the dead croc. The other boy was swept downstream by the current, away from the volley-protected waters, and in to the greedy jaws of a waiting crocodile. The Akeleys watched him "throw up his hands, clutch wildly at the air, and with a haunting, blood-curdling shriek that ended in a gurgle, disappear beneath the water," leaving nothing but a memory of the death scream "echoing weirdly on the air."[28]

Allowing no time for the shock to paralyze them, the Akeleys moved to get the other boy back across the waters, made even more deadly by the spilled blood. Mickie sent for her canvas bathtub, thinking that it would make a good boat, but even before the porters fetched it, the boy had hurled the croc carcass into the water and was diving in after it. He grabbed hold of the floating carcass and swam leisurely and safely to the shore where a wild Akeley awaited him.

Akeley grabbed the boy, cursing at him and shaking him violently. The boy's stupid grinning and pointing gestures to his magic fetishes enraged Akeley even more. The African was unhurt, but Akeley collapsed from the emotion and exertion. Overwhelmed by the tragedy, he suffered a relapse of black water fever that night.

Mickie nursed him through his chills and fever, then sat outside the tent to calm her own nerves. As she sat there, exhausted, she listened to the porters reenact the dramatic episode of the afternoon. They found it hilarious, guessing at which body part was eaten first, guessing at how much money the Akeleys would give the dead boy's parents. They laughed as they mimicked the dead boy's face receding under the waters. Their vaudeville act grew to a frantic crescendo, shattering Mickie's nerves until she exploded with "*basi kelele*" (shut up), and went back into the tent with Akeley, falling asleep near his bed, listening to the mutterings of his "fever-tortured" brain.

It seems that what held Mickie together during these long bouts of Akeley's illnesses was her assiduous interest in primate behavior. She concentrated on this study with a new fervor, going into the bush at night with a flashlight to watch nocturnal baboon behavior whenever she could not sleep. Even watching baboons, however, added to her nightmares when she witnessed a troupe kill and tear apart a leopard who had taken one of their young. Everything seemed to exacerbate the darkening mood of the safari. She studied Taoism and karmic law with a vengeance. Her concentration on these studies helped her counteract the "morbid country [that] clutters up one's mind and life."[29] Mickie had brought booklets about Taoism into the field, including *A Collection of Pearls* by Lao-tse, attempting to find an alternative to the Catholic philosophy taught by her religious parents.

The Akeleys moved on to Nairobi (with J.T. Jr. still in tow as Mickie could not give her up to her Tana River home) and Mickie put Carl in the European Hospital, where his fellow patient was Leslie Tarlton, also down with a bout of malaria. The two men were moved to the Tarlton home for further recovery, and the wives shared responsibility for nursing them back to health. On October 15, Akeley finally seemed well enough to proceed to Uganda to finish the expedition's work of finding the perfect bull.

Even in Uganda, Akeley was chronically ill. In addition to his usual ailments he suffered from jigger-infected feet so painful that he could not even walk. Female jiggers lay tiny egg sacs under the toenails, which are very painful, necessitating daily examinations and removal with a sterilized needle. Even Mickie, feverish, "collapsed through the long strain through which she had held up through sheer will power,"[30] Akeley wrote in his second Uganda diary. He also wrote after one of his scrapes with death that "once more Mickie pulled me back just as I was slipping over to the other side." It is quite staggering to think of the endless drain on this woman, having the responsibility of pulling Akeley back from the dead over and over again. The wonder is that she did not buckle more often. It is clear why J. T. Jr. was such a joy: she cost so little energy—then, at least. We can also understand why Akeley grew jealous of the creature: Mickie was giving to the animal that which Akeley wanted—needed, in fact—for himself. He needed all of her energy, all of her attention, whatever the cost to Mickie. Once, when they were separated, Mickie at base camp and Akeley in the field, he wrote, "My own Mickie: I love you XXX, I want you with me darling. So much separation is hell for me. I'm jealous of your thoughts. Yes, I'm even jealous of the monkey. Oh Mickie, can't you feel how much I need you, how much I worship you? Your letters are full of everything but yourself. I want to know about you."[31]

Other setbacks in Uganda, besides illnesses, included the porters, whom Akeley called *shenzies*, or wild men. Their drunkenness, marijuana smoking, and women "collaring" caused endless troubles. Akeley had secured a license to kill an additional four elephants and he fully intended to kill all the animals he was allowed. To accomplish this he needed a good staff in addition to Bill, and the unreliable porters definitely added to his problems. His journal reveals a pathetic report of stalking endless herds of elephant and going down constantly with fever, spirillum, jigger-toe and even temporary blindness when he caught his eye on a thorn.

Mickie was in charge of moving base camp around the Uganda jungles as Akeley went out with Bill and his gun bearers on short forays into the bush when elephants were sighted. Akeley continued his obsessive search for his elephant, and Mickie turned to colonial companions for relief.

Their friends the Tegerts, missionaries at Masindi, not only offered them hospitality, but nursed them back to health with good food, good companionship, and tennis matches on their court, built behind the church. The Akeleys spent Christmas with the Tegerts and some of their friends. One of them "entertained" everyone at dinner with the gruesome story of an old African friend of his, converted and preaching in his church, who had to prove his manhood as a youth by "eating a [bound] man alive—first a hand, the elbow, the shoulder, both arms; then the feet, knees and thighs when the man was dead."[32] The Akeleys' Uganda trip was beginning to smack of Joseph Conrad's *Heart of Darkness* rather than the joyful safari they had shared a year before with J. T. and Fred.

136

Tembo Piga Bwana

When Mickie and Akeley heard about *tembo* nearby, they rode their bicycles along the Ugandan roads until they were in proximity to the herds. More often than not, they found females, which they left untouched.

There is a fascinating dichotomy in Akeley's behavior in Uganda. When he finally regained his courage in facing elephants in the field, his passion for killing seemed excessive, emotional, and unmeasured. He called himself "elephant mad," and wrote in his journal on the anniversary of his mauling that "I must kill a tembo today." (He didn't.) But he was still frightened of the animals, the anxiety of hunting elephants repeatedly ending in bouts of illness. Mickie wrote to Akeley's brother, "I am beginning to get desperate, I don't know what to do for him next . . . I don't think we'll ever see America again . . . I think the sun and the nervous strain he is under when he comes up with elephants effects his [old] injuries in some way—even old elephant hunters cannot stand the strain more than a few days at a time."[33] Yet they were in the Ugandan forests for weeks at a stretch.

Yet, as violent as Akeley felt about elephants, he once traveled eight hours, round trip, after a bull with fantastic tusks, only to refuse to kill the animal because it was not perfect, having a tumor on its face. He encountered this animal several times, referring to it affectionately in his journal. He also refused, at times, to kill animals whose tusks were not large enough. Most importantly, however, he became even more enchanted with the ethology of the elephant, and grew to love and respect the animals more profoundly than he had before, which ultimately added an exquisite elegance and passion to his later sculptures of the animals.

This sequence of events quoted from Akeley's field diary gives a fuller picture of his feelings about his elephant encounters in Uganda:

[a]fter two days of most tiresome and discouraging work in the elephant grass and dense bush whose outer edge lies forty minutes from the banana grove in which we are camped, not seeing or hearing an elephant, we were sitting down to dinner when we heard distant trumpetings of elephants and an hour later we could hear not only continual trumpetings, but so close had they come that we could hear them blow and break the limbs of trees as they fed. From 11:00 P.M. to 2:00 A.M., Mickie sat by the camp fire listening to the din. I think that she was a bit nervous, though she didn't confess; for some of them were within two hundred yards of camp and on three sides of it. [Mickie was terrified, according to her own rendition of the events.] When I was ready to start at daybreak, they were still well within hearing though they had drifted down to the edge of the forest. Five hundred yards from the edge of the forest, but just before crossing a bush filled "nullah" I climbed onto an ant hill where the first thing I saw was the back of a cow just showing above the grass. We had gone almost *too* fast. She soon got our wind and made off. I could see nothing from the nullah, but I felt that there were elephants there so I decided to go to the top of a rocky kopje some three hundred yards to the left. When I reached the top, it was to find two cows at the base on the forest side and a fine bull at the edge of the wood three hundred

yards away. There was practically no wind just little gusts and eddys, and the elephants soon smelled us and made for cover in the forest. I waited on the kopje till at least twenty-five elephants had boiled out of that little nullah into which I was so near to plunging recklessly. The last of them, a band of seven or eight got wind of us as they came out and instead of making direct for the forest as the others had done, got confused and swung around beneath our feet where their panic increased. They made off at double quick. What a picture of animation and power. It is a sorry idea of a real elephant that we get from the zoo specimen. By this time, practically all were in the forest. As I stood on that rocky grass smothered kopje, it was to receive an impression which somehow seems to make all other African experiences fade away. I have become so accustomed to herds of fifty to three hundred elephants—sometimes all under my nose at once. Here there was not an elephant in sight but the forest sloping down from the higher land beyond almost to our feet and from right to left for a mile in each direction seemed to boil with them. [Akeley later estimated that there were some seven hundred elephants in this herd.] From my position, the view was over the top of the forest. There was scarcely a breath of wind. From all directions came the constant crash of breaking trees, the squeals and screams and roars of hundreds of elephants. Added to this, the hoarse leopard like call of angry Colobus and the chatter of smaller monkeys, the bark of dog-faced baboons and last but not least, the almost human shrieks and yells of chimpanzees. Monkeydom was disturbed and monkey-like, was not slow to show resentment. I've no doubt, however, that they were well up in the tree-tops out of reach of tembo's trunk. The forest is as dry as tender, the ground covered with dead leaves and even the leaves on the trees are dry and parched. There was some sort of general alarm sounded. All monkey chatter ceased, as the elephants apparently all moved off in one direction and there was no sound except the scuffling of dead leaves, the swish of branches against their sides. The sound was like that of a mighty wind storm in the forest. The whole thing was indescribably impressive. Then I went into the forest with the gun bearers . . . a band of ten or twelve [elephants] got our wind and rushed past us nearby but the bush was so dense that only glimpses of them could be had. I tried to follow them but the maze of trails made it impossible to hold to my individuals; so we followed in a general way. We came to a break in the forest where a point of timber extended out into burned grass land. In this point, we heard elephants. At the base of the point, I got up to a young bull that was not worthwhile. I backed off to head the herd off at the end. We were in time, for just as we neared the end I got a glimpse of elephant legs going back. They had got our wind and decided to stay in the bush. I went quickly, but not in time, to get a view through the opening where I first saw them. I followed a short distance, and as I craned my neck to get a view of the tusks of a bull forty yards ahead of me, I suddenly became aware of a big cow midway between me and the bull. The big cow had a tiny calf concerning whose welfare she was very solicitous. When she wheeled and faced my way, I felt very uncomfortable and was mighty relieved when she turned with her trunk about the baby's body and followed the bull who was moving off. I went out of the bush and came to a point in time to see them rounded up on burned ground at the opposite side of the bush. There were perhaps twenty-five of them, and for a bit I could see nothing good among them but just as I was about to leave them and look for another lot, a good pair of tusks emerged from the wall of grey on the forest side. There was a convenient bush within twenty yards of them and behind cover of this I was able to get very close. It was rapid action. When I got to the bush they began to move and as the bull put his front foot forward, I got a couple of .475s in his heart. I immediately lost sight of him in the jumble of screaming elephants and the cloud of dust and as there was no immediate charge to deal with, I made a hasty if not graceful retreat of almost fifty yards to a place where I could see the doings. The bull had gone about twenty-five yards and fallen. The other bulls made off at once. Half a dozen cows were around their fallen chief trying to lift him to his feet with their trunks. I had heard of this thing but had my doubts. Now I have seen it . . . [I] waited for the mourners to depart—which they did when he was pronounced dead.[34]

Akeley not only finally got his bull, but a powerful lesson as well. This story encompasses a great many poignant aspects of elephant natural history and behavior. The very idea of seven hundred elephants massing together is almost incomprehensible today, when their numbers have been so drastically depleted by poachers. The Ugandan elephants were used as target practice by Idi Amin's troops as well, during that frightful and bloody period in the country's history. The big tuskers are gone. In Akeley's day there were still two hundred-pound tusks; today the average weight is only thirteen pounds, which means that more animals need to be killed to make up for the lost weight. Cows, young bulls, anything with a touch of ivory are being murdered by renegades, leaving small groups of confused animals without leadership, starving to death and too traumatized to reproduce.

Elephants are atricial, like humans, taking many years to mature. Scientists are only beginning to comprehend the extreme depth and complexity of elephant behavior and what we do understand about them is staggering. In spite of the Mt. Kenya incident, Akeley respected the elephant (and the gorilla) as the most remarkable animals he ever encountered. He immortalized their love and compassion for each other in a brilliant piece of sculpture called the *Wounded Comrade*, based on his experience that day when he witnessed firsthand the cows trying to assist their fallen companion. (We will examine this and his other sculptures in chapter eleven.)

In spite of the monumental hardships experienced on this expedition, it was an extremely successful one. Akeley and Mickie—Bwana and Bibi—returned home triumphant, their exploits celebrated by the press. They had captured the imagination of the country and were honored at a banquet at the Blackstone Hotel in Manhattan, around Thanksgiving, 1911. They had a great deal to be thankful for. Akeley had bagged his perfect bull, Mickie had her surrogate child, they had hunted with the ex-president, they still had their lives, they were even more experienced than ever, and their love for Africa had exploded into a full-grown passion to honestly and perfectly represent her in the world's greatest natural history museum. It was a glorious homecoming.

AKELEY'S AFRICAN VISION

Africa Hall will tell the story of jungle peace; a story that is sincere and faithful to the Africa beasts as I have known them, and it will, I hope tell the story so convincingly that the traditions of jungle horrors and impenetrable forests would be obliterated.

—CARL AKELEY, *In Brightest Africa*

WHEN AKELEY RETURNED to the American Museum of Natural History, his focus and vision were absolute. He had gone to Africa for elephants and had returned with something more spectacular than he had hoped for—a full-blown dream of what he wanted. He would stay on course for the rest of his life, and the price of his dream would be astronomical. He took the ideas that had surfaced in delirium and pain on Mt. Kenya to Henry Fairfield Osborn.

Osborn had founded the museum's Department of Vertebrate Paleontology in 1891. By 1899 he was involved with the administration of the AMNH through his close association with the museum's president, Morris Jesup. The museum came close to losing Osborn in 1906 when he was offered the secretaryship of the Smithsonian Institution, then the most influential position in the American scientific world. His maternal uncle, J.P. Morgan, advised Osborn to stay in New York because he was the heir apparent to the AMNH presidency after Jesup's death. Fully cognizant of the brilliant opportunity that lay before him, H.F. Osborn remained at the museum, and was elected its president in 1908.

Osborn revealed the depth of his vision for the AMNH early on, and the museum grew physically and intellectually throughout his administration.

140

One constant theme that surfaced during his tenure at the AMNH was the potential for marrying artistic values to science to create beautiful, compelling exhibits. These exhibits could communicate the order and splendor of the natural world while at the same time disseminating information about it.

Osborn had accomplished this in his own field when he hired the great artist Charles R. Knight to make drawings and paintings of restorations of prehistoric animals. He also hired artisans to articulate the bones of fossil animals as they had been in life. These innovations departed greatly from the conventional modus operandi of museum exhibition, where fossil remains were stored in drawers or on shelves. Osborn, committed to creating high quality exhibitions in his museum, was eager to hear what Akeley had to offer.

The AMNH African hall in 1910 consisted of an ethnology exhibit with some representation of African mammals. It was a well-ordered, beautifully designed space, but it was more like a trophy room than a museum exhibition, with mammal heads and various tribal weapons hanging on the walls and other enthnographic specimens arranged in cases, which were positioned in the hall to correspond geographically with the continent of Africa. The AMNH was pleased with its novel display of large, illuminated photographic glass transparencies featuring Africans, which appointed the side walls of the hall. This use of photo transparencies as a background reference was one of the ideas Akeley had presented to the AMNH before he even left the Field Museum.

Originally, both Osborn and Bumpus had hoped that Akeley could include human figures in the elephant mounting that they had hired him to complete—perhaps Africans hunting the behemoths with primitive weapons, played out before a painted backdrop representing the environment in which they lived. Akeley had come back with a far greater scheme.

Rather than a hall of elephants, or a dramatic group of them in the ethnology hall, Akeley believed that the AMNH should create an entire African Hall that would be a monument to the whole continent's "fast vanishing wildlife." Akeley sketched out the plan for Osborn: an enormous open hall with a balcony and over forty animal groupings positioned before painted dioramas. The groups, or scenes, would also be appointed with artificial vegetation that would characterize the animals' natural environment. A visitor, as "he passes from group to group, may have the illusion, at the worst, of passing a series of pictures of primeval Africa, and at the best, may think for a moment that he has stepped five thousand miles across the sea into Africa itself."[1]

Osborn loved the idea and took the proposal to the trustees, who strongly preferred it to a hall of elephants. The younger trustees, in particular, were impressed with the plan. Many of them were sportsmen who fully realized that the earth's resources were dwindling. They saw the hall as a

141

means of "preserving forever" the "fresh mountain mornings" of Kenya and the "great plateau of Tanganyika" long after "the progress of society cuts down the trees and ploughs the meadows."[2]

The trustees' openness to the idea delighted Osborn, who envisioned the hall as the start "of a great new era in nature education at the Museum." He wrote, "We have been searching for years for a means of teaching the lessons of nature to the people of the city." Instead of bringing small nature cabinets to the city schools, "after the African Hall was built, the Museum could take these people to Africa."[3] And, of course, he knew that "the building of the African Hall would put the American Museum first among all the natural history museums in the world."[4]

The married concepts of nature education and vanishing African wildlife proved irresistible to the younger trustees. They organized an African Big Game Club and offered membership to wealthy sportsmen nationwide, urging them to contribute to the creation of a monumental hall of African wildlife. The hall would also be "monumentally expensive," and these sportsmen were asked to guarantee a subscription of five hundred or a thousand dollars a year for five years.

Akeley was swept away by the speed with which Osborn and the trustees embraced his plan. They approved the African Hall in 1912 and Akeley assumed that the work would begin immediately. First he needed to settle into a New York living situation and organize his life to accommodate its many facets. He and Mickie moved into a hotel and, soon after, a sunlight-filled, spacious, three-bedroom apartment on Central Park West, just a few blocks from the museum. J.T. Jr. was given her own room and they all settled into a comfortable life style, the three of them living like a family, taking meals together in the sunny dining room overlooking the park.

While Akeley wanted to begin work on the elephants immediately at the AMNH, the museum was not prepared for him to do so. The authorities needed to find monies from outside the institution to honor the contract with Akeley. But he was very impatient to get started, and rented a loft nearby where he could work on his mechanical inventions. Akeley also contracted with James L. Clark, who had not yet rejoined the museum staff after his own African expeditions, to share his studio in the Bronx so that he could work on taxidermy contracts commissioned by individuals and other museums. He had accepted a contract offered him by the Field Museum to mount some African buffalos and elands. Akeley began a period of intense work in which he moved from the museum to the loft to the studio, working on a variety of projects.

One of the first things that Akeley did was begin work on a motion picture camera that would be appropriate for field work. Even before the blunders in Africa during the Nandi lion-spearing, Akeley had thought about and made drawings for motion picture cameras and tripods. With the new insights into the problems fresh in his mind, Akeley attacked the project with an urgency and a clarity not possible before. He needed a financial backer for the project and found one through his colleague and friend, Roy Chapman Andrews.

Andrews had come to the AMNH from Beloit, Wisconsin in 1906. The twenty-two-year-old asked Director Bumpus for a job, and when told that money was tight and no jobs were available, Andrews offered to scrub floors. Bumpus accepted the offer and paid Andrews forty dollars a month. To help make ends meet, Andrews shared an apartment with Jimmy Clark. Andrews's scientific discipline was mammalogy with a specialty in whales. He would go on to national fame as the explorer who penetrated the Gobi desert in Outer Mongolia in search of paleontological discoveries (an expedition to be addressed later in the text). Akeley was twenty years older than Andrews and Clark, but they remained fast friends until Akeley's death.

Andrews was charming, affable, passionate, and extremely good at raising funds to back his own adventures. He introduced Akeley to his friend M.S. Slocum, heir to a considerable fortune, who had recently graduated from Princeton with an engineering degree. Over dinner, Akeley impressed Slocum with his ideas and enthusiasm for his new camera, and Slocum decided to back its development. Jimmy Clark was to help Akeley on the camera, and became vice-president of the company that manufactured it.

Within months Akeley had designed a camera that was better than anything else on the market; yet during production he refined it with countless improvements. When the original camera was finished, he immediately threw it away and started on a second model; but again during production, even more refinements occurred to him. Akeley's passion for perfection drove everyone around him mad, especially his backer, who was "in a swivet,"[5] exasperated by the vast expenditures of money which seemed to result only in discarded cameras. Slocum finally stopped the seemingly endless flow of money into Akeley's work. Both Akeley's and Slocum's friends had invested heavily in the Akeley Camera Company, and Akeley felt backed up against a wall. After all his labor, he finally saw the end in sight—the ultimate instrument that he had hoped for in Africa. He had to find more money to complete it.

Some wealthy Cleveland businessmen saw the camera's financial possibilities and formed a syndicate to refinance the instrument. "The stock in the original company was not worth a plugged nickel," wrote Andrews. Akeley was a terrible businessman. But the camera was patented in 1916, and went on to win for Akeley another Franklin Institute award—the John Wetherill Medal.

The camera was a brilliant invention that revolutionized movie-making both in the field and in Hollywood. Akeley wrote, "There was no movie director to tell my untutored animal actors where to move in order to keep

143

within the field of my camera lens, so they were apt to, very often, jump clear out of the picture at its most interesting moment. If one of my carrier-boys stumbled and dropped it into a river, or on a rock, it came to more or less grief, or the contained film did."[6] These were the problems; Akeley set out to solve them. His main goal was to create an instrument that could satisfy his needs in the field.

The final version of the camera weighed forty pounds (including the tripod)—half the weight of existing cameras—and it could be removed from the tripod and set up quickly on any sturdy surface—a rock, a tree stump, etc. Equipped with a head that could move in any direction the camera allowed the operator to follow vertical and horizontal movement evenly and easily. The pan and tilt functions were accomplished by a system of gears and flywheels in the head itself, which could be maneuvered by a lever projecting from the camera case. But if the operator needed to swing the lens around quickly, there was a release which removed the camera case from the gear mechanism.

The camera held two-hundred-foot film magazines which could be changed within seconds in broad daylight. A coupled viewfinder enabled the operator to follow the action while holding his head steady, and to change the focus as he was filming. The shutter admitted 30 percent more light than previous cameras. The all-metal, elegantly shaped camera was also virtually indestructible, watertight, and moisture-proof. An Akeley camera later proved its unbreakability by surviving an airplane crash; in fact, recovered by the operator, it was used to film the wreck.

One man could operate the camera, a critical advantage in field work, which is so often carried out in isolation. Akeley had made out a wish list for himself, enumerating all the ideal characteristics that a motion picture camera should possess. Then he had systematically integrated every feature on that list, inventing a state-of-the-art instrument.

Just as he was nearing completion on the camera, the United States entered the First World War. Akeley wrote that "One had to serve to be happy in those days,"[7] and he realized that the requirements of the war photographer were the same as his own: the need to set up equipment anywhere, easily and quickly, and be able to follow fast, unpredictable action. Patriotism took him to Washington, D.C., where he placed his invention at the disposal of the newly created Photographic Division of the U.S. Signal Corps.

Major Barnes, Chief of the Division, was quick to see the possibilities of the revolutionary camera. The corps did tests with it from on top of the Washington Monument. The images created by the camera showed very clearly people a full mile away. The U.S. government, impressed by the Akeley, which outclassed all other motion picture cameras under consideration, adopted it as the corps' official instrument, and bought the entire output of the Akeley Camera Company factory for use in aerial reconnaissance.

Akeley wrote that the Akeley camera "lost heavily on war contracts," but with typical Akeley humor added that he had "the satisfaction of escaping governmental investigations on the score of excess profits."[8] Carl, proud that the camera was used in the war effort, fondly told an amusing story about the camera's unexpected value in the field. It seems that in France, while the camera was being set up to make some movies of a still-burning village, the young American lieutenant operating it was confronted suddenly by a group of Germans. They mistook the Akeley camera for a new type of machine gun and threw up their hands in surrender. The story appeared in the January 1919 issue of *Photoplay*.

In 1919, as the country was settling down after the war, industry embraced the camera. Both Pathé News and Fox Movietone News adopted it for their "weeklies," newsreels shown in movie theatres and changed often. The first of these pictures to make a splash was a film of the 1919 Sheepshead Bay auto races, followed by a "remarkable" series of football pictures of the Dartmouth-Cornell game. Fox filmed the Brooklyn-Cleveland World Series and bicycle races at the Newark Velodrome. The public started paying attention to these interesting pictures, which culminated in the newsreels of the famous Man'O'War-Sir Barton Kentucky Derby race. Only the Akeley filmed the entire race and captured the movement of the champion. Speculations about how the "mystery film" was made rivaled the excitement of the race itself. Was it shot from a plane? A fast moving car on the track itself? The film was actually shot by two Akeley camera specialists positioned at opposite ends of the field. One of these specialists, J.B. Shackelford, would later become involved in an important Akeley scheme.

The Akeley camera's unique abilities were celebrated in the contemporary trade journals and its popularity spread to Hollywood. The fast action of silent serials, westerns, and airplane melodramas were filmed by cinematographers who bought their own Akeleys and, as specialists, made themselves available to the studios. Nearer to Akeley's heart, the lone movie makers and explorers, men of courage and patience, also adopted the versatile camera. They used it in the field to create "true" films of beauty and interest. Robert Flaherty used an Akeley when he filmed the epic *Nanook of the North* in the frozen Hudson Bay area. Ernest Schoedsack, a Mack Sennett cameraman, had made movies in the U.S. Signal Corps during World War I, and took his Akeley expertise into the field with Merian Cooper, creating the film classics *Grass* and *Chang*—documentaries about the hardships experienced by the Baktyari people of Persia and native people of Siam, respectively—and the famous gorilla classic *King Kong*. Ubiquitous Akeleys were airborne for combat in *Hell's Angels* and *Sky Devils*, documenting buffalo stampedes in Montana, shooting *Trader Horn* in Africa, exploring the frozen North for *The Viking* and the frozen South with Admiral Byrd, and recording almost every other wild, unexplored region on the earth.

While Akeley was working hard on the camera, he was also trying to move the plans for the African Hall along at the American Museum of Natural History. He gave lectures at the AMNH, including speaking to a group of 344 crippled children about his exploits in Africa.

The Annual Reports of the Museum during this period, between the time that the hall was approved in 1912 and when work actually began in 1914, are interesting in their lack of attention to Akeley and his work. The AMNH, at that time, did not even consider Akeley's expedition to Africa as one of their own, mentioning it as "the elephant group expedition," and not including it with its other three expeditions into Africa. While the AMNH had sent the Tjader expedition into East Africa in 1906 to collect specimens, and the Rainsford Expedition in 1912 to do the same, the museum's greatest African expedition of all time was the Lang-Chapin Expedition to Central Africa, which lasted from 1909 to 1915.

This was an extremely important expedition for Akeley as well as for the museum, not only because he used some of the animals secured by the expedition for the African Hall, but because it created an entree for his own future relationship with the Belgian Congo.

The fascinating chain of events leading up to the Lang-Chapin Expedition began for the museum in 1904 with a visit by director Bumpus to the St. Louis Exposition. On display there was an exhibit of "live Congo Pygmies" that piqued his curiosity about central Africa. The exhibit's popularity suggested to Bumpus that the AMNH might be well-served by an exhibition of Congolese artifacts.

Around 1906, the Museum began planning an African expedition focusing on the Belgian Congo (now Zaire). During the same period, the American public grew more aware of the atrocities being leveled at Congolese Africans by the agents of King Leopold. An organization called the Congo Reform Association, originally formed in Britain, disseminated the publicity against Leopold's Congo Free State. Essentially, Leopold had grabbed an enormous tract of land in central Africa as his own personal estate when he discovered, through the exploratory efforts of Henry Morton Stanley, that there were valuable resources to be gleaned from the region.

His actions were part of a European "feeding frenzy" on the African continent. To set perimeters for behavior and trade resulting from European involvement, the Berlin Conference of 1884–85 was convened. Leopold's state was recognized, but it did not take long for his agents to slip from grace, violating the trade agreements and making Leopold's name synonymous with horror, suffering, and greed. The king installed unscrupulous and vicious agents, according to Joseph Conrad, "recruited amongst the pimps, non-coms, bullies and failures of all sorts on the pavement of Brussels" to work on his behalf in the Congo. They tortured and killed thousands of indigenous people, shooting them and/or cutting off their hands when they did not fulfill

146

the commands and quotas imposed upon them for harvesting the natural resources, mostly rubber and ivory.

Accounts and photographs of the sordid deeds were leaked to the press on both sides of the Atlantic. International outrage precipitated negotiations between Leopold and his country, and he was forced to hand over the territory to Belgium. In 1908, the Congo Free State became the Belgian Congo. The atrocities ended (and another whole set of problems began, but that is another fascinating story).

While the debate raged as to whether the U.S. should take action against Leopold's government, his lobbyists in Washington, D.C., were giving major trade concessions to American businessmen. One of Leopold's financial advisors was none other than AMNH trustee J.P. Morgan. The museum was pressed to back Leopold's Congo Free State and, incidently, given an extraordinary ethnographic collection of artifacts originating in the Congo. The collection caused some embarrassment to the museum when the gift was interpreted by the press as a ploy by Leopold to garnish museum support. The AMNH walked a tight line between both sides of the issue, maintaining the collection behind-the-scenes until a time when their exhibition would prove less controversial.

Another lure of the Congo for the museum, besides the richness of its ethnography, was the "discovery" (the Africans, of course, knew of its existence), at the turn of the century, of a forest-dwelling creature related to the giraffe, called the okapi. The museum wanted some specimens of the animal for exhibition. The AMNH set about to raise money for an expedition which would travel to the Congo to secure not only the rare animal, but other animals and artifacts as well—the AMNH Congo Expedition.

The expedition was led by Herbert Lang, a German mammalogist hired by the museum. With him went a young ornithologist, James Chapin. The men were in the field for six years and brought back fifty-four tons of material, some of which was given to the Belgian Museum. The AMNH maintained a close relationship with Belgium. In fact, Leopold's successor, King Albert, visited the AMNH with his Queen in 1919. These events laid the valuable groundwork for Akeley's own work in the Congo.

Akeley suffered financial strain during his wait to begin his work on the elephants, and sold the movies he had made in Africa to a wealthy American hunter, Paul Rainey, to help make ends meet. Rainey was the first hunter to bring dogs, a valuable pack of hounds, into Africa to hunt big game. He took along a film maker and his series of images of animals drinking at water holes were the first popular movies of Africa to be shown commercially in the United States. Rainey bought Kikuyu footage from Akeley. Osborn was interested in seeing Akeley hunt with Rainey, who was an African Hall benefactor, but Akeley refused, put off by the "commercial influence and notoriety" of Rainey's African expeditions. He also did not approve of animals being hunted by trained dogs, he felt it was unsportsmanlike because the animals were driven to the point of exhaustion and treed by the dogs, allowing the hunter to arrive and simply shoot the bayed quarry. (Some of the footage that Akeley shot still exists today in the Library of Congress's Paper Print collection. Many of the early filmmakers copyrighted their movies by making prints on rolls of paper rather than film stock. The Library of Congress transferred this original paper print collection back onto film stock.)

Akeley also sold his own collection of elephant skulls to the museum for additional capital. He offered George Kunz, President of Tiffany & Co., the tanned hide of an elephant cow shot by Roosevelt for one thousand dollars to be used for fashion accessories. Osborn had also grown anxious about money for Akeley because the museum had already made a substantial investment in the elephant group. Akeley was discouraged that the plans for the African Hall seemed to go so slowly, and assumed that the museum was losing interest. One of the trustees, anxious that the museum would lose Akeley, urged Osborn to act quickly in advancing money to Akeley against future contracts.

Osborn kept assuring Carl of his "undiminished interest" in the African Hall, but by the summer of 1914, Akeley wrote to the president: "My seeming impatience is because I feel the urgency of getting the work started . . . I do not intend to accept half-hearted support. I need enthusiastic support of the museum authorities to insure the doing of a big thing in a big way. I shall withdraw my proposals only when I am convinced that the apparent indifference is real and not caused by unfortunate conditions in the business world."[9]

Osborn sent copies of the letter to some of the trustees in an effort to move things along financially. One of them felt that Akeley was pressuring them with a type of blackmail: "Mr. Akeley might take a somewhat different tone . . . which [now] reads . . . a little like a hold-up."[10] The museum had raised money for Akeley to supervise work on a model of the African Hall which was presented to a joint meeting of the Architectural League of New York, the National Sculptural Society, and the MacDowell Club. Blueprints were presented as well, and the specificity of the plans was extraordinary, encompassing electrical layouts, elevator placement, exact measurements of canvas backgrounds, foregrounds, the base for the elephant group, etc. He also designed bronze bas-relief panels to be placed in friezes above the mammal groups, depicting the relationship between African man and his environment. Akeley even presented ideas about the conservation of the dioramas themselves, which he knew would be subject to temperature fluctuations, dirt, light, and simple aging. An article about Akeley and his hall was published in the *American Museum Journal*, precursor to *Natural History* magazine, in May 1914. This "press release," published the same month he turned fifty years old, exacerbated his impatience to get on with the hall.

By the fall of 1914, under the title of Specialist on Zoological Exhibits, Akeley was finally working on the elephant grouping, fully two years after the museum had approved the plans for the African Hall. True to form, Akeley discarded the technique that he had employed on the *Fighting Bulls* exhibit at the Field Museum for the more sophisticated method of mounting pachyderms he had been considering. The museum also gave him full-time assistants to help in the monumental task: Louis Jonas, a brilliant young taxidermist from Denver who would be Akeley's star student, and Ray Potter, the only man for whom Akeley ever wrote a letter of recommendation. Akeley himself was never a full-time salaried employee of the museum because, as Roy Chapman Andrews wrote, "if he'd been on salary he would have felt constrained to abide by the Museum's rules . . . Ake was not a man who could stand being bound."[11] The museum paid him a retaining fee, which increased over the years with his value to the institution. When he died in 1926, he was making ten thousand dollars a year, a lot of money for the AMNH to pay anyone.

Akeley faced a formidable obstacle in finding a large enough space at the museum in which to mount a group of elephants. Osborn had worried about this during Akeley's African sojourn and was determined to have the problem solved by the time that Akeley returned. He had written to Akeley in Africa that he wanted to have built a "special temporary building . . . in the east court, [that would] be amply heated and lighted . . . for the prosecution of your work."[12] By 1915, however, the building remained unbuilt. There was a new director of the museum, Frederic Lucas, a Ward's "graduate," as Bumpus had been fired, essentially because of differences with Osborn, during Akeley's last days in Africa. Lucas, too, was committed to giving Akeley all that he needed to accomplish his dream of the African Hall, but he complained to Osborn that the need for space in which to house and prepare the African collections was as "difficult to fulfill as it would be to make ropes out of sand, and the devil himself failed at that, as any glance at a sandy beach will show."[13]

In the meantime, to mount the elephants, Akeley was given an enormous space on the second floor of the east wing of the museum, where the Hall of Asian Peoples stands today. The museum has grown into a complex of twenty-two buildings, but then it consisted of essentially three buildings, and the need for space has been an issue that has dogged the administration since the Museum's founding in 1869. To allow for Akeley and his assistants to be given the needed room, fishes had to be moved to the bird hall and part of another hall had to be closed to the public. Even given the rearrangement of existent collections, no one knew where the finished pieces could be stored. The impact of the African Hall on the other departments would be severe. At one point, Lucas suggested that the animals be mounted at Jimmy's studio— but then, how could they transport a herd of elephant down the stairs and across the river to the museum?

Carl Akeley

Akeley let Lucas worry about space, and as soon as he had the "elephant studio" on the second floor he and his assistants began work. Jonas and Potter were assigned the tanning of the hides which, when finally unpacked, were stiff and hard—so hard, in fact, that a man could dance on their surface and not cause a dent. Originally the skin had weighed over a ton, but it had been pared down to four hundred pounds in the field. Now they had to take the hide down to a thickness of one-quarter inch and make it as soft as glove leather.

The process entailed weeks of soaking in a saltwater solution. The hides were hoisted daily from their bath by block and tackle so that the men could painstakingly pare them down with small knives, which reduced the danger of cutting through the skin. After weeks of this arduous work, the skins were ready for the tanning bath in which they soaked for three months, turned over frequently. Finally, the rinsed and partially dried skins were rubbed with oil.

While they worked on the skins, Akeley worked on his study model and reviewed the extensive measurements, notes, photographs, and plaster casts that he had made in the field. When he had produced the model in the exact pose that he wanted, he proceeded with the mounting. At the Field, his elephants had been made of plaster because, due to the animals' great bulk and weight, he could not figure out how to cast them in papier-mâché like his smaller mounts. He had been thinking about this problem, and by the time that he mounted the AMNH pachyderms, he had a couple of ideas with which to experiment. Even the trial and error aspects of the work took months of effort.

The solution that he decided on was nothing less than brilliant: On a large slanting platform, Akeley built a wire mesh and plaster armature of one-half of the elephant's body, cut laterally with its rounded side up. When the plaster was dry it was shellacked, and when dry again, a three-inch layer of modeling clay was spread over it. The tanned skin was placed over the clay so that he could work in the numerous folds characteristic of elephant hides, utilizing the depth of clay. The skin had to be kept moist during the modeling stage and was covered with wet blankets overnight. When the modeling was complete, the entire side of the animal was given a light clay wash and then a plaster jacket to hold the modeling in shape during the drying process. The skin was then turned over and the original wire mesh and plaster armature replaced with a new layer of plaster and burlap, so that the skin was sandwiched between two layers of plaster. When the skin was thoroughly dry, the inner plaster was removed and the skin reinforced with layers of wire mesh, papier-mâché and wood. The process was the reverse of the one used earlier by Akeley; the manikin was built within the finished skin, rather than the skin stretched over the finished manikin. Then the outer plaster jacket was scraped off with a wire brush and the other parts of the animal, which were prepared in the same way, were joined together from inside. The men actually spent

150

days inside the elephant, taking a fan inside to help them stay cool, and leaving occasionally to have a smoke.

The result was spectacular, as any visitor to the AMNH can testify. The mounts have a presence that is incredibly lifelike; they are not generic elephant, but individual portraits of specific animals. Akeley mounted four of the elephant group, as called for in his contract; the other four were added later. It took almost six years to mount three of the animals, and Akeley had two, then three assistants. Akeley's aim was always so high and his passion for perfection so outdistanced the world around him that the exasperated museum authorities lost patience with him. But he would not compromise. "To their everlasting credit," Andrews wrote, "be it said that the authorities of the Museum realized that they had discovered an outstanding genius, and did their best to give him a free rein."[14]

The elephant group is magnificent, and it reveals even more about Akeley than his genius as an artist. Akeley publicized, time and again, that he had mounted the cow shot by Teddy Roosevelt as one of the four original elephants—the one posed with Kermit's calf entwining its trunk around its mother's. But even in Africa, Akeley had complained to the museum that TR's cow was too small and that he was looking for bigger animals.[15] The accession catalog in the museum's Mammalogy Department shows that TR's animal was shot at Meru near Mt. Kenya in central Kenya while the calf, Kermit's animal, was killed on the Uasin Gishu in western Kenya. We know that Akeley, TR, and Kermit met to shoot elephants on the Uasin Gishu, not near Mt. Kenya. Either someone made a mistake about the location when making the original entry in the catalog, which is not likely given the rigid scientific discipline of most mammalogists, or Akeley substituted another animal for TR's, which we know he found unacceptable. He wanted perfect individuals to represent their species, but he also wanted the publicity of having an animal in his group that had been collected by Roosevelt. Akeley had a passion for telling the true story of nature, but he was also a pragmatist, and would subvert his scrupulousness to what he saw as the greater good. In this instance, having TR's name attached to the group was more important than really using TR's specimen.

One of the reasons that we can believe in the TR elephant substitution is because of Akeley's handling of the provenance of another animal in the group, even more clouded in mystery. The young bull—the "rear guard," turned facing backward to protect the group from an unseen threat—was an animal shot by Mickie in Uganda. This is documented in at least two letters to the museum. There is no evidence in the accession record of this animal at all. It is customary to alter the accession record with new, important information; for instance, the fact that a skin has been destroyed, or has been traded with another institution, or has been mounted for exhibit purposes, will show up as amended information, often added years after the original entry. For

151

some reason, the records indicate that only three animals were mounted for this group by Akeley.

Again, there could have been an initial mistake in the recording of data, but more likely Akeley let the animal slip through the cracks to prevent any mention of Mickie being part of the permanent record of the elephant group. While he had been so proud of her achievements on Mt. Kenya in 1905, by the time he mounted the "rear guard," circa 1918–19, his marriage lay in ruin and Mickie had left the country. Rather than giving her her due vis-à-vis the elephant on display, he simply ignored its existence completely. It was not beyond Akeley to be as petty and vindictive as a child when he felt wronged.

In his early fifties, Akeley's workload and interests distracted him so much that he seemed oblivious to life around him, often forgetting to put gasoline in the car and stalling out in traffic. Once he even arrived at the museum wearing unmatched shoes. Akeley and Andrews became good friends during the period just before the war. Andrews wrote that "Akeley did not lead a balanced existence. He had no hours of play, as the ordinary man conceives it. The particular problem on which he was working at the moment seemed to occupy his mind so completely that he would relegate it to the subconscious background for only a short time . . . I never knew him to sit down to a hand of cards; he had no small talk. Hostesses who tried to capture him as a star around whom they could build a dinner were doomed to disappointment unless he knew it would include someone whom he might interest in his work."[16]

Something else distracted Akeley; all was not well at home with his wife. He spent more and more time at the museum, entertaining his friends and colleagues in the "little corner of the elephant studio," as he called his office. His office was where he felt most at home. Akeley appointed his surroundings with art and objects that inspired him or that made him comfortable—from his own sculpture to a copy of the *Venus de Milo* to African baskets, he surrounded himself with beautiful pieces. A plaque that read, "Whom the gods love die young does not mean that they die when they are young, but that they are *young* when they die" hung over his desk. He had important visitors, like Orville Wright and the Duke of Connaungt, whom earlier he and Mickie would have entertained at their apartment. But over the years from 1912 to 1918 their social life ebbed, then stopped completely, as indicated by their guest register book during these years.[17] Mickie became more reclusive and ultimately would not leave J. T. Jr. alone, even for important museum functions, let alone for social engagements like the theater or dinner at the homes of friends. She slipped deeper and deeper into an obsession with the little monkey. Her distraction maddened her friends, who seemed not to understand the serious nature of the episode.

Mickie's life revolved around J. T. Jr. She sat around her apartment playing with the monkey and holding her. Mickie did nothing to nourish herself, either spiritually or professionally; she did not even have housework to distract her, as the Akeleys had a maid. Her entire attention was focused on the monkey, and the monkey grew jealous of any time Mickie would spend with anyone or anything else—at least, that was how Mickie perceived J.T. Jr.'s behavior when she tried to destroy all of Mickie's clothing other than those worn at home. At one point, J.T. Jr. tore every bead off of an expensive evening dress, and another time she destroyed a new hat, which had been mistakenly placed on the dining table by a delivery boy. Mickie resorted to hanging a leopard skin—which harkened back to a primal image that awakened terror in the animal—on the closet door to keep the monkey from entering. When J.T. Jr. became upset, as she did when she saw a circus parade marching down Central Park West with a procession of elephants and camels, or when a shipment of cattle escaped into the park and were pursued by armed men, Mickie cradled her and played "Minuet in G" on the harmonium.

The monkey became upset more often, and she became more destructive. Nothing in the apartment was safe. An entire dinner table of dishes and food would suddenly crash to the floor when J.T. Jr. yanked off the tablecloth. She made the bathtub overflow, destroyed furniture, and terrorized visiting guests and staff. Mickie became a slave to the animal, cleaning up after her, placating and soothing her, and making excuses for her chaotic behavior. More than the elephants, camels, and leopard skin were speaking to the monkey's nature. She was a wild animal, domesticated to a point, but once she reached estrus, her internal clock pressed her to reproduce her own kind. While contemporary experiments in interspecies communication are advancing through sign language and electronic devices, and while we are understanding better the ways in which man is similar and dissimilar to monkeys and apes, we cannot expect to change the nature of the animals with whom we work just because we love them or profess to understand them. Primates, more than any other animals, cause us to anthropomorphize. While it was a horrible situation in which Mickie found herself trapped, her partner, J.T. Jr. was caught in the same snare.

One of the ways that Mickie dealt with the situation was to get J.T. Jr. a monkey companion, one that the Akeleys had given to the Bronx Zoo. Delia received "Patch" in a weakened, undernourished, and sickly state and felt she could revive the animal. Mickie and J.T. Jr. doted together on the new monkey, J.T. Jr. pouring her maternal instincts onto the animal to such a degree that she began to lactate. Mickie wrote:

Under the abnormal strain that nature had put upon this little female who had never been a mother, she became quite ill and I had two sick monkeys on my hands instead of one. In spite of all my care of poor little Patch, his life was fated to be short. One night after I had sat up with him for twenty-four hours, keeping a hot-water bottle under his chilly little body, he gave up the struggle. As I reached over to feel his heart, just before he died, my hand touched him. With an effort he closed his icy fingers over mine and pursing his lips gave forth a long drawn-out wail. It seemed to me that all the sorrows of his caged existence were in that pathetic little cry, and I am not ashamed to write that I laid my head down on the table beside the dying animal and wept as the life passed out.[18]

When Mickie writes about nursing Patch or J.T. Jr., her tone is the same as when she writes about nursing Akeley time and time again in Africa. These words reveal much about Mickie. They tell us something about how she saw herself in relation to the world around her. She was meant to serve, never asking nor demanding what she needed for her own well-being. This exhausting vigilance for others combined with self-denial made her sick as well, depleted. She could have been writing about herself.

Mickie fell into a deep depression after Patch died; she even wore mourning clothes and refused to leave the apartment for three weeks. One of Akeley's closest friends, Vilhjalmur Stefansson (an Arctic explorer who will be discussed elsewhere), wrote to Akeley while on expedition in the frozen north that he was sorry to hear about Mickie's grief. Their friends were obviously concerned about Mickie's relationship with her monkey, but no one had any idea of how to deal with it—least of all Akeley.

J.T. Jr. was like a child to Akeley also, who would race around the apartment playing hide and seek with her. He would let J.T. Jr. help him shave in the morning, actually allowing her to put his ivory-handled straight razor to his throat. But when the situation worsened, with Mickie holed up in the apartment for days on end, Akeley simply stopped coming home, which fed a terrible sense of isolation in his wife. She gave up her social life and many of her friends—"to devote myself to the care and study of this interesting little creature," she wrote. But it was not the study that engaged her, it was some need, or the projection of some inner reference—chaos or anarchy—that had to be satisfied.

Akeley's career was moving cometlike, with social and business engagements demanding his attention. He suddenly found that he did not have Mickie at his side—Mickie, who had been a driving force in his career for almost twenty years. He was angry with her for her withdrawal from him and his career. He punished her by withdrawing from her as well, at a time when she most needed help. The once charming, affable Mickie became a depressed, lonely soul—silent and inconsolable at times, at others a screaming banshee who accused her husband of having a love affair with someone. Akeley also felt saddened and frustrated by the deteriorating situation, one he thought outside his control.

Finally, J.T. Jr. bit Mickie severely on the ankle, almost severing one of the tendons. Mickie, shocked and in excruciating pain, made her way to the bed. The next day her leg was swollen to twice its normal size and she couldn't even get out of bed to call the doctor. The maid helped her around and the doctor was called on the third day after the incident. The sight of the wound appalled him and he told Mickie that she needed an immediate operation to save the leg. Mickie refused to leave J.T. Jr. to go to the hospital; the doctor summoned a surgical nurse and the operation was performed there in the apartment. Blood poisoning had set in and Mickie was in bed recuperating for three months—ironically, the same amount of time it took Akeley to recover after the Mt. Kenya incident.

After the operation Akeley reprimanded J.T. Jr., pulling back the bedcovers to show her Mickie's wound. The monkey was furious with Akeley and tried to bite him. Still Mickie defended J.T. Jr., saying that the monkey appeared remorseful about her crime. The animal's temper tantrums became more pronounced. Mickie moved around with a cane and grew nervous that the monkey would bite her again. Her fears were realized; J.T. Jr. did bite her, not once but twice more, the second time on the wrist, cutting through Mickie's nerves and almost hitting a large vein. Mickie at last knew that she had to send the monkey away. She and J.T. Jr. had been together for almost eight years.

Akeley immediately made arrangements for the animal to go to a zoo in Washington. He knew that he needed to move quickly before Mickie changed her mind. Mickie was beside herself with grief, crying for days and feeling "lost" and "empty." Her life seemed a wasteland to her. She had few friends left, her relationship with Carl seemed beyond repair, and she did not have her little monkey. Totally depleted, she found it difficult to go on mending and revitalizing her life. So many harsh words and actions had torn her and her husband apart, and so many lines had been crossed between them that she knew she had to get away from Akeley and New York to find some perspective. Mickie turned to the thing she knew best to help her regain her confidence and vitality; she served. Mickie sold her elephant tusks to the AMNH for funds and in July 1918, she left for Nancy, France to do canteen work for the American Expeditionary Forces. She sailed aboard the *Carmania*, one of the biggest ships at sea and an attractive target to German submarines, resulting in a nerve-wracking crossing. Mickie noted these details in some blank pages in Carl's 1910 African journal, which she took with her to France—a way of staying close to him and reminding herself of the extent of her own bravery and power. In the midst of the German air raids that shook the nights, Mickie began pulling her life back together.

Akeley flew into a rage over Mickie's departure, accusing her of desertion. He would never forgive her for leaving him. He never saw his own role in the breakup of their marriage; he placed all the blame on Mickie. It took enormous strength for Mickie to extricate herself from the miasma of her life in New York and especially from the devouring persona of Akeley. She had "pulled [him] back from slipping over to the other side"[19] so often, but when it was clear that she was in serious trouble, he stayed at the office to drink and smoke with the boys. It took her a year to find strength again to return to New York and face Akeley and her marriage.

In the meantime, Akeley worked in his elephant studio and continued to push the work on the Africa Hall along. But with the involvement of the United States in World War I, all normal work ceased at the AMNH, and Akeley, also, threw himself head on into the war effort. The museum supported Akeley while he worked for the government, continuing to pay him his retainer. Work on the African Hall limped along as Akeley spent more time in Washington, D.C. The ten dollars a day he received for his work with the Army Engineers did not even cover his expenses.

The Army Engineers' Office of Research and Development originally felt that Akeley could make his most valuable contributions in the Camouflage Division, to take advantage of his wide knowledge and experience with animal concealment and the protective coloring schemes of nature. But most of the work in this field was done by Allied forces in France, and the office felt that he was too valuable in other areas to send abroad. The office head, Major O.B. Zimmerman, set him to devising a more reliable tank. Zimmerman and Akeley had been friends for thirty years, since they were boys together at Ward's. Now they were working together to win the war. The existent American tank was considered too vulnerable, and Akeley began work on the "Turtle Tank." Before the design and mechanism of the tank were completed, Akeley, true to form, began making improvements. A snafu arose when drawings for the weapon to be used on the tank were requested from the Ordnance Corps. The drawings were withheld and there was a disagreement over which department Akeley's tank designs belonged to. It was decided by the War Department that the Turtle Tank was to be assigned to the Ordnance Corps, and as Akeley did not want to leave the Engineers, he discontinued his involvement in the tank's development.

The Akeley camera and the cement gun were both employed extensively in the war effort, but his greatest contribution was the development of searchlights and auxiliary equipment. At the time the standard searchlights used by the Navy and the Sea Coast Defense were thirty-six inches and sixty inches in diameter. The sixty-inch light weighed about six thousand pounds, and was extremely unstable, difficult to move from one location to another, and expensive. Its glass mirror and front glass were costly and vulnerable. After only a few seconds of flashing, the enemy could locate the light and easily destroy it, if not by a direct hit, then by exploded shells in its vicinity.

Many engineers had tackled the problem but Akeley succeeded in solving it. In his studio at the museum, Akeley utilized his experience with taxidermy manikins, papier-mâché, wire mesh, and plaster. As with his modeled skinless animals, Akeley made a cast of the glass form of the existent searchlight. After correcting the inside curvature of the cast, which was necessary so that it could fully reflect the center light, he coated it with plaster. A deposit of copper was used to coat the plaster on which silver was later electrolytically deposited, creating a perfectly parabolic reflective surface. This mirror could withstand numerous bullet and shrapnel holes and still serve its purpose. The unit was mounted on Ford wheels, allowing easy mobility, and could be managed by two men.

The result of this development was an instrument that weighed one-eighth as much as its predecessor and cost one-third the price. It was smaller and more efficient, producing a light 10 percent stronger than the former unit for the same expenditure of energy. The searchlight was produced in one-fifth the time and had a range of three miles. Akeley further developed a remote control device to maneuver the light from a considerable distance. These developments were patented by the U.S. government.

Akeley's boss, Major Zimmerman, wrote:

> Many a night Mr. Akeley was at the experimental field at Tenney Park near Washington from 9 P.M. to 2 A.M. He never seemed to tire, yet those of us who worked with him realized fully the intensity of the strain he was under. His patriotism amounted to fanaticism, his loyalty to his associates was passionate— My, how he worked!
>
> Mr. Akeley's genius and ingenuity became well known in Washington. He was called here and there—the Shipping Board, the Bureau of Standards, the Ordnance, the National Research Council, etc. The various divisions of the Engineers often said—"Let's see what Akeley says."[20]

By 1919, Akeley was famous and well-respected professionally, and yet it was the lowest point in his life. The African Hall had ground down to a standstill and his wife had left him. When Mickie returned to New York from France the Akeleys parted once and for all, though they still would not divorce for several years. Mickie stayed in the apartment while Carl took up bachelor quarters with Herbert Spinden and Vilhjalmur Stefansson. Both of Akeley's roommates were fifteen years his junior. Akeley was fifty-five years old.

Herbert Spinden was a curator in the AMNH's Department of Ethnology with an expertise in Mayan archaeology. Vilhjalmur Stefansson was an Arctic explorer and a closer friend to Akeley. Stefansson was a Canadian, born of Icelandic parents, who studied theology and anthropology at Harvard. His main claim to fame was exploration in the polar regions over a period of twenty-four years; he spent five years at one stretch in the Arctic Circle. During the years 1908 through 1913, he lead the Stefansson-Anderson Arctic Expedition for the AMNH, which cost the museum much more money than anticipated, distressing the administration. Added to the expenditure of money, the men neglected to turn in their scientific reports on time, further exacerbating the museum's disapproval. A second expedition was sent out, under the auspices of the Canadian government, during which considerable hostility arose between the men, resulting in charges brought against Stefansson by Anderson.

Anderson tried to discredit Stef—as he was known to Akeley—claiming that he "subordinated the interest of science to his own advantage."[21] Anderson also charged Stefansson with economic extravagance and mismanagement of the expedition. The controversy appeared in international newspapers, humiliating Stefansson, who asked for backing from the museum. Osborn gave Stef an official letter signifying his satisfactory conduct on the AMNH-sponsored expedition, but added a personal letter admitting his disappointment in Stefansson, who had failed to give the museum enough credit for its support. Osborn also refused Stefansson's request to rejoin the museum staff in the light of his vast expenditure of money which had yielded too little in results. Osborn felt that Stef's expedition was a failure due to "lack of character." Nonetheless, Stefansson was respected as an explorer of exceptional ability who performed best while being alone and living off the land.

The controversy surrounding the failed expedition meant that Stef, as well as Akeley, was under emotional pressure in 1919. They found mutual comfort in each other and spent a lot of time at the Explorer's Club and the Century Club in the company of other explorers. Akeley had served as president of the Explorer's Club from 1917 to 1918, a position which added further responsibilities to his already frantic life while providing him an opportunity to concentrate on problems other than his own. But after Mickie and Akeley separated for good, Akeley started looking around for other female companionship. The men had dinner parties at their apartment during this period, and Akeley began to be more socially involved. A friend of his, Frank Seaman, had a farm called YAMA in Ulster County, New York, where Akeley would bring his girlfriends for weekends. Frequent visitors to YAMA also included John Burroughs, Thomas Edison, and Henry Ford. Akeley, at fifty-five, was extremely attractive, manly, charming, witty, and confident of himself professionally—and his split with Mickie had shaken him enough to expose a softer side. His friend "Sammy" Sherwood described this lovely side of Akeley's nature: "[t]he great charm of Akeley's personality was a sweetness of nature, accompanied by a sympathetic understanding which led both old and young to seek his advise and counsel. Never was he too occupied with his own affairs to be interested in yours. There was a subtle indefinable something in Akeley which enabled him unconsciously to impart to those around him something of his enthusiasm, something of his idealism and something of his determination to achieve, which inspired them with new courage, new hope and greater effort."[22]

These qualities were attractive to both men and women. Akeley's guest book during this period is replete with women's names. Akeley swung rapidly between moody depression and elation, depending on the progress of the African Hall. At the museum, he felt pressure to complete the elephants and to push the hall along, but the hall was beginning to feel like Sisyphus' stone, and the mountain before him too steep. Osborn wanted Akeley to create one of the dioramas to demonstrate the final product, and asked that he mount a lion group. Akeley felt ambivalent about the project, writing to Osborn: "Prospects of doing the Africa Hall in my way under conditions that would guarantee its final achievement might perhaps revive my interest; but to do it in the way that these things are usually done in Museums would not interest me in the least. Museums throughout the country or Museum men are willing to steal but not accept ideas, and Museums generally accept nothing new unless forced to. Every decent thing that I have ever had to get across, I had to force."[23]

The AMNH had hired Trowbridge & Livingston to create a new wing for the African Hall which would also serve as a memorial to Theodore Roosevelt. When the New York State Roosevelt Commission and the architects visited the museum in 1920, the African Hall model was in a dilapidated condition and gave a "serious setback" to the museum's plans. Osborn blamed Akeley, who in turn complained that he received no assistance from the museum for even the carpentry work, which he felt he had to do himself. Akeley proposed to make a fresh start with fresh people if they wanted the hall to succeed at all, and to look for a single backer to finance the entire undertaking.

All things considered, it was a good time for Akeley to leave the country, to let things settle down at the museum and with Mickie, who was still very angry, especially in light of the fact that Akeley was by then having a love affair with a female explorer and mountain climber, Mary Lenore Jobe. He was trying to keep the whole thing quiet, as he was still married to Mickie and the potential press exposure would have certainly tarnished his reputation.

Ever since his aborted gorilla expedition in 1910, Akeley had wanted to return to Africa to collect the great primates for the African Hall. It was a splendid time for him to go to the Belgian Congo. Traveling to Africa had never failed to revive his spirits and he had friends in Chicago who were willing not only to back him, but to go with him as well.

AKELEY THE SCULPTOR

. . . I speak of Africa and golden joys.
　　　　　—WILLIAM SHAKESPEARE, *King Henry IV, Part Two*

Sculptor and Biographer of the vanishing wild life Africa—I do not feel that I can adequately and truthfully characterize Carl E. Akeley better than in these words. I have always maintained that he was a sculptor and that sculpture was his real vocation in which taxidermy was an incidental element.
　　　　　—HENRY FAIRFIELD OSBORN, Forward to *In Brightest Africa*

TO BETTER UNDERSTAND the important personal implications of the gorilla expedition for Akeley, it is helpful to take a moment and examine his art, specifically his sculpture. Ever since he was a boy, Akeley had projected his vision, fantasy, and feelings into his animal habitat cases, dioramas, and small sculptures. After the gorilla trip, his art changed dramatically; it began to convey a more directed and defined sense of human emotion than it had before. Two sculptures that grew out of the gorilla expedition reveal this change, and so before returning to Africa, we will look at this evolutionary artistic process in his life.

Carl Akeley had wanted to be a sculptor ever since he haunted the Metropolitan Museum of Art in New York during the dreadful period he spent at Wallace's. Throughout his Milwaukee and Chicago periods he had produced small plaster and clay models as studies for his animal mounts. The "itch in [his] hands and brain to become a sculptor" had become more pronounced as he grew more confident and successful. As observed earlier, Akeley had sublimated the desire to abandon himself to the art because he lacked confidence that he could add anything significant to the field of sculpture. Instead he chose to focus his artist's eye where none had been focused before, on virgin territory where he was free to experiment and excel without the constraints of an established academic or artistic tradition—in taxidermy.

For years, colleagues and friends joined Mickie in an effort to convince Carl to cast his small sketch models in bronze, but it was not until he realized its potential to help him further his dream for the African Hall that he began to seriously consider doing so. Just because Akeley felt that mounting animals was artistic did not mean that potential financial backers for his African Hall felt the same way. "A taxidermist couldn't talk art. Especially he couldn't talk art convincingly to the kind of men who supported great museum ventures," Akeley wrote.[1] He perceived that one of the ways that he could touch potential backers and obtain their support would be to appeal to them culturally and artistically. Through the production of bronze sculptures he could prove himself an artist, and perhaps then his animal mounts would be examined in a different light.

"The fever of sculpting in his blood"[2] allowed him to seize the pragmatic function of his art and begin work on his bronzes with customary Akeley intensity. Akeley turned to African subjects and interrelationships that differed from, yet complimented, his large animal groupings. He celebrated specific moments in the animals' lives rather than on the larger stories he told in his dioramas. In his small bronzes, he told stories of ethology and animal nobility; he augmented the truthful representations of the African jungle and veldt already portrayed in his larger work. Akeley gave free reign to his love for the animals of Africa.

The first and most prominent subject of his sculptures was the elephant. In spite of the collision on Mt. Kenya, the animals remained his favorite and most respected creatures, followed closely by mountain gorillas. This first piece featured three elephants moving through the forest, tightly locked as one enormous creature. The center elephant of the trio has been wounded and is flanked by two more, who buoy him up and assist him in his escape from danger. The piece is not only brilliantly executed but also embodies the intelligence and compassion of the species—a gripping portrayal of sympathy expressed in action. Akeley enjoyed the work and felt that the theme "that always aroused enthusiasm" in him was well portrayed, and that it seemed to take shape on its own. It was easy.

J.P. Morgan arrived at the studio one day to discuss the African Hall, and saw the sculpture Akeley had named *The Wounded Comrade*. He loved it and pledged his support for the Hall based on the piece. Akeley's scheme had worked. Phimister Proctor, a renowned animal artist, saw the sculpture and told Akeley that he wished he himself had created it. The comment was the highest praise that Akeley could have received. Based on Proctor's enthusiasm for the sculpture when speaking to one of his friends, the museum trustee George Pratt, Akeley received his first order, sight unseen, for a bronze of the clay model; other orders followed. Akeley's confidence as a sculptor grew, slowly reversing his earlier apprehension about his ability in the realm of fine arts.

The Wounded Comrade was exhibited at the Winter Exhibition of the National Academy of Design in 1913. By virtue of this beautiful bronze, Akeley was made a member of the National Sculpture Society. Almost immediately, art lovers perceived his great talent and looked with new understanding and appreciation at his taxidermy work. Akeley was made a member of the National Institute of Social Sciences in 1916 for "making taxidermy one of the arts."

His sculpture provided both a new way for Akeley to tell the African stories that he felt compelled to tell, and a relaxing and satisfying pastime. In off moments in the elephant studio, to relieve the stress of his work and his life, he poured his concentration into the small pieces. When we look at the body of work, a magnificent collective tale about African mammals crystallizes, and we get a fuller picture of the artist. Akeley's art expresses his feelings about the events and individuals of Africa and, equally important, transmits to the viewer an understanding of those feelings.

One of the main themes running through the work is the charm and good-tempered nature of animals in their natural home, free from the anxiety of predators—the "golden joys" of Africa. *Jungle Football* depicts a group of four juvenile elephants playing with a piece of termite mound that they have found, rolling it over as a team and having a marvelous time, illustrating the peace and pleasure of the jungle. *Patriarch* is an ancient single-tusked elephant bull who stands still and grand with dignity and self-possession. *Going* is a young bull elephant running from danger, while its companion piece, *Stung* (the two were conceived as bookends), is another young bull who did not have time to escape. Instead, in retaliation for a bite on his sensitive trunk, he has pulled a tree snake from its branch and is trampling it to death while he carefully curls his injured trunk out of harm's way. *Lion and Buffalo* captures a moment of violence as a lion "bulldogs" a buffalo by catching his nose with a front paw and bending his head to the ground in an effort to throw him. The buffalo has braced himself with a front foot, making it obvious that he is set for a murderous fight and will not go down easily. The muscles of both animals strain in combat, and the power of the life struggle emanates from the piece. Another elephant sculpture, *The Charging Herd*, communicates the solidarity of the animals moving in valiant self-defense. One of Akeley's most poignant pieces was a clay model of *At Bay*, which depicts an elephant, exhausted, his foot bound to a log to prevent his escape, fending off the arrows of his attackers. His head and curled trunk are held back and turned aside in an attempt to avoid the arrows. The bronze of this piece was cast without the arrows piercing the elephant's hide.

The *Old Man of Mikeno*, a silverback gorilla, is one of the two pieces directly relating to the gorilla expedition. The piece is a bust of the first gorilla that Akeley killed. In Africa he was haunted by the animal's sweetness and intelligence. The death of the "Old Man" precipitated a journey of transformation for Akeley in which he embraced the species and launched an effort to save it. He was moved by the humanlike qualities of the animals, and the face on this bust expresses timid curiosity. It is a touching depiction of an animal who elicited terror and dread in human beings for centuries.

None of these sculptures is sentimental. They are powerful representations of a unique and private vision. Akeley's talents inspire wonder and admiration, yet the finest aspect of his work is that we recognize precisely what he wants us to know about these animals. On April 22, 1914, Akeley addressed the National Sculpture Society, the Architectural League of New York, and the MacDowell Club about the African Hall at the museum. The event, which included an exhibition of some of Akeley's clay and bronze sculptures, was a momentous one for Akeley, as it presented a holistic view of him as an artist. The audience first heard Akeley lecture on his African exploits and dreams for the African Hall. They then visited the elephant studio, where they saw the enormous clay model of the skinless big bull, the other members of the elephant group in preparation, the model for the African Hall, and a small collection of Akeley's sculptures. The evening was billed "From Jungle to Studio," and was a big success.

Akeley chose Roman Bronze Works, then located in Brooklyn, as his foundry. It was one of the most famous foundries in the world of fine art, having been used by Frederic Remington, Charles Russel, James Earle Fraser, Bessie Potter Vonnoh, Anna Hyatt Huntington, and others. The foundry had a reputation for expertise in the intricate lost wax process of bronze casting executed meticulously by Italian craftsmen. When a clay model was brought to the foundry, it was cast in plaster and used as the image to reproduce the bronzes themselves. These plasters were inspected and approved by the sculptor before the bronze was ever poured.

According to the records at Roman Bronze Works, there were twenty-three castings of the *Wounded Comrade*. It was Akeley's most famous piece. (In December of 1988, several of Akeley's plasters were sold at auction. The *Wounded Comrade* was purchased by the Lyme Academy of Fine Arts in Old Lyme, Connecticut. The Lyme Academy is known for its extensive curriculum in fine arts taught in traditional ways. The administrators intend to cast bronzes of Akeley's sculpture to finance scholarships for young sculptors. Akeley would have appreciated this new pragmatic use of his work.)

The most controversial work that Akeley created was a stirring, evocative piece entitled *The Chrysalis*. This piece expressed the emotions, beliefs, and theories raised during his most important gorilla expedition. In this instance the creature emerging from the chrysalis is man, and his cocoon, a gorilla skin. When Akeley submitted it for exhibition at the National Academy of Design in 1924 it was refused. Society was not open to evolutionary concepts, as evidenced by the famous Scopes trial one year later. The Academy's refusal of the sculpture fueled the public debate between evolutionists and fundamentalists that was already reaching white-heat levels in New York.

On April 20, 1924, the *Philadelphia Ledger* featured a full-page article illustrated with photographs of Akeley, his sculpture, cartoons of chimpanzees and scientists measuring skulls, and a line-up of hominoid and ape skulls. The headline read: "Why is the Ape-Man Hidden in the Cellar?, Akeley's Statue, 'The Chrysalis,' Symbol of Evolution Theory, Rejected by National Academy of Design—Is it Because of Offense to Artistic Taste or Shock to Religious Belief?" Akeley had seen the controversy coming, and half-expected the Academy's refusal of the work. He was interviewed in his studio right after the bruhaha began and asked if he was disturbed by the criticism. He waved his arms around and said: "It makes people think. Whenever we can make people think, for goodness sake, let us not delay!"

The publicity led one of the staunchest supporters of evolutionary thought, the Reverend Charles Francis Potter at the West Side Unitarian Church in New York, to write to Akeley: "I know of no concrete symbol which so well expresses the religious message which I am trying to preach every Sunday . . . If we could have it [the sculpture] on exhibition in our church, even for a brief period, it would afford me great pleasure, and would, I am sure, be helpful to all who view it."[3] Akeley accepted the offer and succeeded in turning the flame into a bonfire. For months the public debate reached hysterical proportions. Akeley was attacked, the museum was attacked, the Unitarian Church was attacked. It was just the sort of fight that Akeley loved; he was accused of being a "jungle-worshipper," unconcerned about his integrity and unabashed by the criticism. "Isn't it singular," his critics asked, "that his worship among the cathedral forests of the African jungle didn't give him one little peep at the Almighty God?"[4] He was even accused of altering the photographs of gorilla feet and hands and falsifying the scientific records that he brought back from Africa in 1922. Akeley's questions about man's relationship to gorilla as a possible "missing link" exploded around the public showing of *The Chrysalis*. The controversy crossed the Atlantic and raged in England and Germany as well. It was, of course, the fact that Akeley's work was exhibited in a church that so exacerbated the already volatile debate and brought it to an emotional peak. It was the ultimate insult to the fundamentalists, and a vivid symbol of the loss of grace in a "sin-cursed, lost world."

Akeley's "favorite" piece was alternately the *Wounded Comrade*, *Jungle Football*, the *Old Man of Mikeno*, and *The Chrysalis*, depending upon his disposition at the time. These four are connected to Akeley's heart. His grandest, most ambitious piece, or group of pieces, was connected to something more ephemeral, more unpalpable—his idealization of valor and courage in man: the *Nandi Lion Spearing*. These life-size pieces are stunningly executed. The first piece depicts three Nandi having just thrown spears at a lion and lioness, who face the Nandi head-on from the second piece. The power and tension between the two groups is astounding—the wounded lions angry and snarling, ready to charge, and the men alert and daring without arrogance or hubris. The third piece in the group is entitled *Requiem*, and represents the ritual of honor performed over the dead body of the lion by the Nandi with their shields held high over their heads.

Akeley designed the pieces to be used in the African Hall. Two museum trustees, George Pratt and Childs Frick, contributed money so that the pieces could be modeled. Akeley used American black men to pose for his African models. When the pieces were completed, there was no money for their expensive casting in bronze. Akeley's friend, Stanley Field, wanted to have the pieces for his own museum, but Akeley insisted that they be part of the African Hall. Field asked if he could have a second casting in consideration of his finding the initial money to have the pieces cast for the AMNH. Akeley agreed to the proposition and felt certain that the AMNH would agree also. Field asked his friend and Field Museum Trustee, Richard T. Crane Jr., for the backing, which Crane readily contributed so that the Field Museum could have a set of the magnificent sculptures. Roman Bronze Works cast the two sets for the sum of $17,500 in May 1925. A third set was requested by the Belgian Ambassador in Washington to decorate the lavish estate of Prince de Ligne, located on an island in the middle of Lake Kivu in the Belgian Congo. Permission was granted in light of the close association that had developed between Akeley and the Belgian government regarding the gorilla sanctuary.

Today the pieces in the Field Museum are positioned as Akeley intended them to be and are highlighted with spotlights; they are given the respect for the artistic achievement they represent not only for Akeley, but also as part of the noble tradition of American sculpture.

As an aside, the *Nandi Lion Spearing* group shows us something else quite important about Akeley: the notion of man vs. boy. Theodore Roosevelt makes a strong point when he calls the Nandi "men" and other tribal people "boys" or "savages" in his book *African Game Trails*. Akeley writes about Africans as "little more than children" yet, as with TR, faced with the "proud, cruel, fearless" faces of the Nandi, Akeley saw the Africans no longer as boys, but as men. TR, though he found the Nandi lion spearing incredibly exciting, lost his stomach for the ritual after one event, but Akeley lived through many over a three-week period. He was fascinated by the courage and almost stoical acceptance of pain and death demonstrated by the men. The Nandi somehow embodied everything noble in man; they encapsulated his highest aspirations of masculinity.

In 1919, when the African Hall was stalled in its tracks, Mickie had left, and he was feeling frustrated and moody, Akeley received word that Theodore Roosevelt had died. "On my return from the funeral at Oyster Bay," he wrote, "I was terribly depressed. For me the bottom had dropped out of everything. I had to find expression. I found it naturally in modeling. I set to work on a lion. I meant to make it symbolic of Roosevelt, of his strength, courage, fearlessness—of his kingly qualities in an old-fashioned sense."[6] Akeley holed himself up in the museum for days working on the lion. He was not sure what he would do with it when it was completed; he thought that perhaps he would cast one bronze for Mrs. Roosevelt and destroy the model.

TR's son Archibald visited Akeley soon after the model's completion and, embracing the pedestal supporting the sculpture, said, "this is Father." The children, unbeknownst to Akeley, had called their father the "Old Lion." Other family members arrived to see the piece. Akeley sculpted model after model, honing and refining the human qualities he wished to express through the real characteristics of the lion in nature. Arthur Page, Akeley's publisher at Doubleday, felt that the sculpture should be executed as a colossus in a huge amphitheatre in Washington, D.C., as a national monument to TR.

Akeley worked hard for two years to promote his lion as the nation's monument to Roosevelt's ideals. The sculpture itself was a semirecumbent lion, grand and at peace, yet alert and ready to spring into action if necessary. Many personal friends of Roosevelt became supporters of Akeley's memorial; however, in the meantime, the Roosevelt Memorial Association had been founded, and had decided to sponsor a national competition for the memorial.

Akeley attempted to modify the design to lend itself to the size and conditions dictated by the Memorial Association. With an architect, James Brite, Akeley reconceived the lion in granite, thirty-eight feet at the base and eighteen feet high and set among the hills on the outskirts of Washington. One of the monument's advocates wrote that it would be: "Enduring as the hills, undisturbed by the changing fortunes of sect or party and their institutions, the massive granite lion in alert repose with a majestic dignity of strength and courage, to stand through the ages as a tribute to a great man and an inspiration to the coming generations."[6] At the lion's base were to be inscribed quotes from TR's writings and a dedication by Herman Hagedorn, secretary of the Roosevelt Memorial Association. The location was to be Rock Creek Park; the creek itself would be widened to a reflecting pool from which would run a grassy causeway twelve hundred feet long and lined with cedars. The lion would be at the center of an enormous circle of granite walls, forty-four feet high and planted with cedars towering above the earth. The approach would be through an opening in the wall at the end of the causeway. The monument was to be "among the chosen of earth's shrines for the lovers of right." Part of the architectural concept was the use of light and shadow; the sun would bathe the lion in light while the cedars would create spectacular shadows at dawn and dusk. The estimated cost of the memorial was $4,732,800.

Akeley encountered resistance from critics who felt that, while he was "a good naturalist . . . he was not the man to produce a lion that [would] symbolize Theodore Roosevelt; nor [was] Mrs. Roosevelt the one to pass judgement on the lion from the standpoint of its proper qualities for such symbolism," and that Akeley had "hypnotized the Roosevelts" to gain their support. Akeley was furious, and the situation was exacerbated by politics and infighting among the memorial committee members themselves. Akeley's intensive work on the piece lasted two years, 1919 and 1920, during which it was given top priority, but by 1925 he withdrew the lion from the competition.

Nine years after Akeley's death the AMNH considered casting the lion model in bronze to display in the Roosevelt memorial at the museum. After bids for the casting were received from various foundries, James Lippitt Clark wrote to the vice-director, William Faunce, urging him to drop the project. He wrote: "It is not a good piece of work, and Akeley never considered it finished, and I believe it would do him and the Trustees who make the decision to put it on exhibition more harm than good."[8]

The saga of Akeley's Roosevelt lion is one of the only failures in Akeley's professional life. It is significant that he created the piece during such a desperate period in his life. His marriage had fallen apart and his dream for the African Hall continued to be just that, a dream. His work on the lion was a frantic attempt to create something positive in the midst of his own negativity, and to gain acceptance from the friends and family of the man who had represented for him everything that a man should be. It was like exorcizing a demon from himself, but what came out was not full of power and vengeance, a brilliant sculpture precisely executed. Rather, when one looks at photographs of the lion, one is struck by its banality—a word never associated with Akeley or his work. Given the fact that Akeley was always able to turn his troubles into creative energy, it is doubly interesting that the lion was a failure. It is as if he could not even see the work's shortcomings, blinded by emotions too intense for him to redirect. One of the saddest outcomes of the lion's failure was that it realized his greatest fear—that in the world of fine art and sculpture, his work would be considered insignificant; that he would be considered "just a taxidermist." As always, he wanted to be appreciated as a sculptor, and it disturbed him when other aspects of his work, such as hunting and taxidermy, were given priority over his art in articles published about him.[9]

Akeley's last sculpture, which was incomplete when he died, was the *Lion Rampant*. It is a moving image of a wounded lion rearing up on his hind legs, trying to extricate with its paw an arrow lodged in its head. The piece, though unfinished, shows remarkable energy, rage, and pain. Akeley had a distinguished mind and aesthetic sensibility. Even in the crude state of this last sculpture, we find enlightenment—not only about a wounded lion, but also about Akeley's efforts to deflect his own negative feelings and to cope with situations he could not control.

A frustrated Akeley filming Nandi warriors after the lion spearing ritual in 1910. The unsuccessful attempt to shoot the ritual itself inspired his invention of the Akeley camera. (COURTESY AMNH NEG. #211912)

Above: Dinner in the bush, 1909. L. to R.: John McCutcheon, James L. Clark, Delia Akeley, J. T. Jr., and Fred Stephenson. (COURTESY AMNH NEG. #212153)

Above right: Akeley recovering in his hospital camp after he was mauled by a bull elephant on Mt. Kenya in 1910. (COURTESY AMNH NEG. #211509)

Right: Kermit and Theodore Roosevelt with one of TR's elephant cows killed on the Uasin Gishu Plateau, 1909. (COURTESY AMNH NEG. #330588)

Delia Akeley on mule (J. T. Jr. on boulder in front of her) before the towering summit of Mt. Kenya, 1909. They were searching for elephants. (COURTESY AMNH NEG. #219019)

Above left: Delia and J. T. Jr. sharing binoculars in the bush, 1910. (COURTESY AMNH NEG. #211788)

Above: J. T. Jr. and "Bill." Akeley found J. T. Jr. "more fun than a barrel full of monkeys." (COURTESY AMNH NEG. #211854)

Left: An ostrich blind or decoy fabricated by Akeley to get nearer to the earthbound birds. They were not fooled. (COURTESY AMNH NEG. #334091)

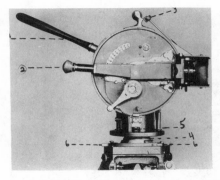

The Akeley camera: 1. the handle, 2. viewfinder, 3. focus screw, 4. ball-and-socket joint allowing quick leveling of instrument, and 5. release buttons for flywheel which was designed to prevent jerky movements under ordinary conditions, but when released allowed camera to swing quickly in any desired direction. (COURTESY AMNH NEG. #337629)

Above left: The "Wounded Comrade," Akeley's first bronze sculpture. (COURTESY AMNH NEG. #311832)

Above right: Akeley's bronze bust of the "Old Man of Mikeno," a private tribute to the gorilla that started his process of conversion. He wrote of the Old Man: "I am really fonder of him than I am of myself."

Left: Akeley's controversial sculpture, the "Chrysalis," which many found offensive because of its evolutionary subject. (COURTESY AMNH NEG. #249306)

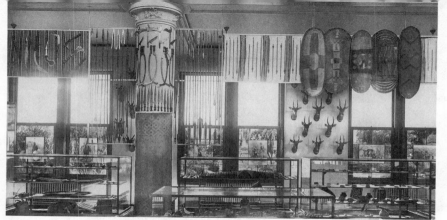

The AMNH African Hall, 1910, as it appeared when Akeley came to the museum. (COURTESY AMNH NEG. #32925)

Sketch and model of the African Hall as Akeley conceived it, much as it appears today. Notice that his Nandi sculpture was part of the original design. (COURTESY AMNH NEG. #310924 AND #34344)

Akeley thinking about gorillas as he holds the death mask of the "Old Man of Mikeno." (COURTESY AMNH NEG. #311654)

Akeley's exquisite mount of the "Old Man of Mikeno." (COURTESY AMNH NEG. #39807)

*Akeley working on the "Roosevelt lion,"
one of his few professional failures.*
(COURTESY AMNH NEG. #239321)

*Above: Akeley's studio in the American
Museum showing his personal African
collections, gorilla death masks, the
plaster and bronze of the "Chrysalis"
and other plasters of various sculptures.*

*Right: Alice Bradley and the White
Fathers who provided hospitality to
Akeley and company at their mission
at the foot of Mt. Mikeno in Zaire.*
(COURTESY AMNH NEG. #258709)

Bull giraffe skin hoisted into tree in the Northern Frontier District, Kenya 192
The bull dominates the Water Hole diorama in the African Hall. (COURTESY
AMNH NEG. #412195)

The predetermined meeting of Martin Johnson, left, and Carl Akeley, right, took
place in the Serengeti, 1926. The men used their Akeley cameras to film the
Kipsigis lion spearing which climaxes Johnson's film, "Simba, King of Beasts, a
saga of the African veldt." (COURTESY AMNH NEG. #412239)

The gorilla diorama: The Old Man of Mikeno knuckle walking to the left,
"Clarence" to the right, and the Lone Male of Karisimbi dominating the center
shown chest beating. Akeley felt that the vista was the most beautiful in the world.
(COURTESY AMNH NEG. #314823)

"Those fabulous Johnsons," Martin and Osa with their movie cameras. Note the Akeley camera to the right. (COURTESY AMNH NEG. #314030)

Carl and Mary in their Lukenia Hills camp on the Eastman-Pomeroy-Akeley Expedition, 1926. Behind Akeley is the model for the klipspringer group. Note Akeley's weary expression. (COURTESY AMNH NEG. #412166)

Group portrait of the Eastman-Pomeroy-Akeley Expedition, 1926. Eastman, center; Pomeroy, left (middle row); Akeley, left of Eastman; Leigh, left of Akeley; Martin Johnson, right, standing; Mary Jobe and Osa Johnson, left and right in the bottom row. (COURTESY AMNH NEG. #412213)

THE OLD MAN
OF MIKENO

I am really fonder of him than I am of myself.
> —CARL AKELEY, referring to the "Old Man of Mikeno"

This journey from the heart of Africa became for me a kind of drama of the birth of light . . . I had wanted to know how Africa would affect me, and I had found out.
> —C. G. JUNG, *Memories, Dreams, Reflections*

AKELEY WROTE to Osborn in early February 1921 that he was planning to go to Africa to begin his work with gorillas, "the object being to secure, first, sufficient first-hand data to justify the killing of gorillas for the group, and then of course the data and materials necessary for the production of the group."[1] Thus began one of the most important and vivid periods in Akeley's life, a period during which his dream for the African Hall led him off on a significant tangent. His mission began as a collecting expedition, but changed into a kind of personal pilgrimage of metanoia (change of mind upon reflection–conversion) or rebirth—of a conversion from hunter to conservationist. Besides collecting the primates, Akeley intended to make photographic studies and motion pictures to be used as reference tools for his work on the African Hall. Akeley wanted his motion pictures to tell a "true story of 'beautiful Africa' rather than the 'horrors of darkest Africa,' " and saw the expedition to gorilla country as a way to tell the story.

176

The expedition, which would last about six months, would cost between twenty thousand and thirty thousand dollars; Akeley requested that the American Museum of Natural History provide some financial support. Osborn was very pleased at the prospect of having a gorilla group, because no other American museum had one, and also because the AMNH scientists were keenly interested in primate and evolutionary studies. Osborn pledged museum support of ten thousand dollars. Akeley would have to raise the rest of the money himself. (He also had to finish mounting his elephant group before starting a new project. Work on the four elephant mounts was moving into its eighth year.)

Akeley needed a backer. For years, he and Mickie had promised to take their Chicago friends, the Bradleys, on a hunting expedition to Africa. Akeley decided to invite them on the gorilla trip, which stung Mickie, as she was to have gone to gorilla country with Akeley in 1910, before the incident on Mt. Kenya killed the opportunity.

In addition to Herbert Bradley, Akeley's lawyer and friend, and Bradley's wife, the writer Mary Hastings Bradley, the group included the Bradley's five-year-old daughter Alice, Alice's nanny Priscilla Hall, and Martha Miller, Akeley's secretary and the daughter of an old friend. Akeley wrote to the Bradleys: "The object of our expedition is gorillas and gorilla country—the last word in Africa adventure. I cannot possibly come back from this expedition as a hero because I am taking ladies and a little baby into a country that is full of beauty and charm, and I shall not be able to tell a tale of hardships and dangers overcome; but it is just as much fun to pull down the pedestals of fake heroes as it is to build the pedestal for yourself."[2]

Akeley was perpetuating a great joke: "The older one grows the more fun one has because soon after fifty one ceases to take anyone else or any thing seriously; and the world considered as a joke must be the funniest thing in the solar system."[3] In spite of his cynical tone, Akeley was genuinely pleased to be taking women, one of whom would "rather dance than anything else," to hunt the large ape. While he had no assurances that his female entourage would be safe, he was confident that his own insight and experience in the bush would be sufficient to guarantee their welfare. He was amused by the idea that the publicity about the expedition would humiliate and undermine fearless hunters going after the "terrifying quarry" called gorilla. On a more personal level, Akeley knew his expedition would needle Mickie—herself a fearless hunter—because he would be traveling with inexperienced, beautiful women whom she considered her own friends as well.

The press covered the expedition plans in a sensational fashion, suggesting that Akeley was taking women into gorilla country to attract the male gorillas so that he could kill them. It was rumored that the apes loved to kidnap human women, dragging them off to their caves and making wives of them—much like the ill-fated King Kong and Fay Wray of Hollywood mythology. Akeley was not at all pleased with the publicity the Bradleys were promulgating, feeling that they were "sacrificing Museum dignity." He was also annoyed that they had advertised the departure date, which Akeley wanted to keep secret, fearing that, in her heightened state of rage, Mickie would try to abort the expedition. He objected most strongly to an announcement that they were going to central Africa to "hunt" gorillas. Akeley wrote: "Say that I am to study gorillas. One of the big objects of the whole expedition is to kill the idea that hunting gorillas is to be considered a sport. Everyone is getting mad to hunt gorillas and I hope that I will be able to influence legislation to prevent the hunting of gorillas except for strictly scientific purposes."[4]

Throughout history, gorillas have been one of the most misunderstood species. This resulted, in part, from their similarity to man; they provided rich material for anthropomorphising. In addition, in 1921 there was scant real information about the animals. Mountain gorillas had only been discovered nineteen years earlier, and hard evidence of the existence of lowland gorillas had only surfaced about seventy-five years prior to that. Until then, there had been only sketchy, sensational accounts about the great primates. The Carthaginian, Hanno, an explorer seeking new regions for colonization on the west coast of Africa, actually named the animal in the fifth century B.C. At that time, "wild women with hairy bodies" were killed, and their skins taken back to Carthage and nailed to the walls of the Temple of Baal and later the Temple of Astarte, where they hung for centuries. They may actually have been baboons, and not gorillas at all. Hanno's story was recounted in a Greek document entitled *Periplus*. Even Pliny, the Roman writer and naturalist of the first century A.D., described an animal with feet and hands like a human, which he called *cephos*; the animal fought with men in the Roman games on at least one occasion.

In 1559, Andrew Battell, an Englishman captured by the Portuguese in what is now Angola, described two kinds of apes: chimpanzees and gorillas. He called gorillas Pongo, which he described as "in all proportion like a man, but that he is more like a giant in stature than a man; for he is very tall and hath a man's face, hollow eyed, with long haire upon his brows. His face and eares are without haire, and his hands also . . . They sleepe in the trees and build shelter for the raine. They feed upon the fruit that they find in the woods, and upon nuts, for they eate no kind of flesh. They cannot speak and have no understanding more than a beast." He described their strength, their habit of living together in groups, and their family orientation, all of which is accurate. He also wrote of them hovering over the smoking fires, abandoned by the Africans, to keep warm, "for they have no understanding to lay the wood together." This anthropomorphic image—a family sitting around a bonfire—is charming, but inaccurate. Battell's account—the first written account of a real gorilla—appeared in Samuel

Purchas's *Purchas His Pilgrimes, A History of the World in Sea Voyages and Land Travell by Englishman and Others* in 1625.

In 1819, when Africa was becoming more accessible to Europeans and explorers were better able to penetrate the interior, Thomas Bowdwich published *Mission from Cape Castle to Ashanti*, which recounted his adventures in Gabon and Ghana. He called the gorillas "Ingena," though he never saw any and simply repeated stories told to him by the indigenous peoples.

It was not until the 1840s that scientists finally laid their hands on hard evidence proving the great ape's existence. The discovery was made not by a hunter or a professional scientist, but by a missionary. The Reverend Mr. Savage visited his friend the Reverend Mr. Wilson near the Gabon River and became fascinated with a large primate skull that Wilson had received from one of the local Africans, who had described the living animal as similar to a monkey but larger and more ferocious. Savage, an anatomist by avocation, collected additional skulls. All the missionaries working in western Africa had heard stories of the great ape from the Africans, but the animal had remained clothed in mystery. The Africans themselves were divided: some believed gorillas were animals, and some thought they were pitiable, alienated wild men who had been ostracized from their communities. Now the missionaries had evidence that the animals really existed. Savage was familiar with chimpanzees, having studied and written about their anatomy and behavior with Jeffries Wyman of Harvard University, so his trained eye recognized that the new skull came from a different species altogether.

In 1847, Savage and Wyman wrote an account of the gorilla in the *Boston Journal of Natural History*. Hard evidence aside, the animal's behavior was still described in sensational and extreme language:

> They are exceedingly ferocious, and always offensive in their habits, never running away from man as does the chimpanzee . . . he approaches the enemy in great fury, pouring out his cries in quick succession . . . If the latter be a man, and armed with a gun, there is a chance for him; just one chance and no more. If he discharge his piece at too great a distance, so that the bullet, however rightly aimed, cannot penetrate the tremendous skull, then is the gorilla only the more terrible for the attempt on his life. If, on the other hand, the hunter wait a little too long, the gorilla is upon him with a terrific spring. In an instant the firelock is wrenched from his hand, and the next moment it is crunched in two between the monstrous teeth, just as easily as a donkey would bite through a carrot.

The work of Savage and Wyman caught the attention of Sir Richard Owen, England's premier anatomist. He, too, became intrigued by the great ape, taking the research one step further and suggesting that the gorilla was the closest animal to man, anatomically speaking. His views reflected the new scientific ambience created by Darwin's *The Origin of Species* (1859). But in his *Memoir on the Gorilla* (1865), even Owen succumbed to reiterating fantastic tales about gorillas:

If the old male be seen alone, or when in quest of food, he is usually armed with a stout stick, which the negroes aver to be the weapon with which he attacks his chief enemy the elephant. When therefore he discerns the elephant pulling down and wrenching off the branches of a favorite tree, the gorilla, stealing along the bough, strikes the sensitive proboscis of the elephant with a violent blow of his club . . .

Sometimes . . . when a company of villagers are moving rapidly through the shades of the forest, they become aware of a presence of a formidable Ape by the sudden disappearance of one of their companions, who is hoisted up into a tree, uttering, perhaps, only a short choking sob. In a few minutes he falls to the ground a strangled corpse, for the animal, watching his opportunity, has let down his hind-hand and seized the passing negro by the neck with a vice-like grip, and has drawn him up into the branches, dropping him when life and struggling have ceased.

Judging from this account, gorillas may well have been blamed for murders that were really the result of tribal infighting.

These gorilla portrayals reflected the biased intellectual climate toward Africa in the western world at the time. Westerners viewed the Africans themselves as little more than wild animals, constantly at war with each other, living in a jungle world fraught with danger and chaos. In a *Harper's Weekly* article published March 5, 1859, an unidentified author further suggested that the gorillas were thought to be men who "would speak if they did not believe that they might be obliged to work—a sulky race of idlers." In the racist perception of white westerners, the animals and the Africans were muddled together, creating terror and fascination in the minds of "civilized" men. And all these stories were based on hearsay and a few dried bones. No European had yet seen a live gorilla.

The story changed in 1855, when a Franco-American explorer named Paul Du Chaillu traveled to Africa with the sole intention of finding gorillas and bringing some back, dead or alive. (Actually, the irrepressible and sexually curious Sir Richard Burton was also searching for gorillas around the Gabon River during the same period. His quest, however, was to kill the animals for their brains, which were reputed to have aphrodisiac powers. He met one gorilla, which he described—more accurately than Du Chaillu did—in *Two Trips to Gorilla Land and the Cataracts of the Congo*, published in 1876. But it was Du Chaillu's work that interested Carl Akeley.)

Du Chaillu promoted himself as a scientist of sorts, but was little more than a traveler—and was later considered a bit of a charlatan. He published two books about his adventures: *Explorations and Adventures in Equatorial Africa* in 1861 and *A Journey to Ashango-Land and Further Penetration into Equatorial Africa* in 1867. Akeley pored over Du Chaillu's books before his own gorilla expedition. Although Du Chaillu's accounts were sensational to the extreme, he was nonetheless able to assemble accurate observational data on gorilla behavior. Still, the books again reveal a fantastic mix-up among Africans, gorillas and chimpanzees. Du Chaillu wrote that *Troglodytes Nschiego*—probably the chimpanzee—with an almost bald head and chest, was the most intelligent ape, and lived with his spouse in "a house he builds himself like any Christian." The husband and wife were seen to cooperate in "building a canopy or umbrella" in the trees, though they actually never slept in the same bed, but in "separate establishments close to each other." The animal Du Chaillu called *Troglodyte Kooloo-Kamba* was probably an imagined hybrid of a gorilla and a chimp. "The most fierce looking of the quadrumana . . . with a terrible expression [and] having wonderfully-stout fingers [like] a large negro hand."

But the passages that most interested Akeley were Du Chaillu's descriptions of gorillas and the hunting of the great ape. Du Chaillu knew that he had stumbled onto the primates when he and his staff found themselves in the midst of a ravished cane field near the mouth of the Ntambounay River in Gabon. He wrote:

> I knew that they were the fresh tracks of the Gorilla and joy filled my heart . . . We followed these traces, and presently came to the footprints of the so-long desired animal. It was the first time I had ever seen these footprints, and my sensations were indescribable. Here was I now, it seemed, on the point of meeting face to face that monster of whose ferocity, strength and cunning, the natives had told so much; an animal scarce known to the civilized world, and which no white man before had hunted. My heart beat till I feared its loud pulsations would alarm the gorilla and my feelings were excited to a painful degree.

After much terrified searching, Du Chaillu finally found a gorilla:

> It stood about a dozen yards from us, and was a sight I shall never forget. Nearly six feet high, with immense body, huge chest, and great muscular arms, with fiercely glaring eyes, large deep gray eyes, and a hellish expression of face, which seemed like some nightmare vision; there stood before us the king of the African forest. He was not afraid of us. He stood there and beat his breast with his huge fists till it resounded like an immense bass drum, which is their mode of offering defense; sometimes giving vent to roar after roar . . . His eyes began to flash fiercely for we stood motionless on the defensive, and the crest- of short hair which stands on his forehead began to twitch rapidly up and down, while his powerful fangs were shown as he again sent forth a tremendous roar. He advanced a few steps, then stopped to utter that hideous roar again; advanced again and finally stopped when at a distance of about six yards from us, and then, just as he began another of his roars, beating his chest with rage, we fired and killed him. With a groan which had something terribly human in it, and yet was full of brutishness, he fell forward on his face.

181

Akeley was fascinated by these words, and read between the lines, eliminating all the spine-chilling aspects of the rendering. There was, within Du Chaillu's tale, an accurate description of gorilla behavior; the first account given to western scientists. Du Chaillu sent the bones and skins of about five animals to England, causing an immediate uproar. Du Chaillu's fame and fortune brought him into the public spotlight, where he could vent his overactive imagination. Soon the sensational renderings outweighed the truth and the gorilla was reduced to "an impossible piece of hideousness . . . One blow, with its bony paw, and the poor hunter's entrails are torn out, his breast bone broken or his skull crushed." The stories enthralled many listeners and helped build Du Chaillu's reputation as a courageous and intrepid hunter.

He basked in this glory until another traveler, following in his footsteps so that he too could share the excitement and mystery of the gorillas, found that Du Chaillu's account had been overblown and melodramatic. The traveler, Winwood Reade, an American, returned with another story about gorillas: that they do not attack men accept in self-defense, and then probably only administer a warning bite before fleeing into the jungle. Reade, who interviewed some of the Africans who had been with Du Chaillu, brought home different versions of the Frenchman's stories. He discounted Du Chaillu's exploits and brought the scientific world a more measured image of the gorilla coloring the reputation of the great ape with a different palette.

While Du Chaillu was harassed and threatened by the lowland gorillas in western Africa, Akeley was interested in the species that had been discovered in central Africa, not far from where he and Mickie had hunted in 1911, in Uganda. In 1902 Captain Oscar von Beringe, a German, and his physician, Dr. England, had encountered two gorillas during their assault on Mt. Sabinyo, one of the Virunga peaks on the border where Zaire, Uganda, and Rwanda meet. They shot the animals and, through the examination and study of their skins, a new species of gorilla was named: *Gorilla gorilla beringei*, commonly known as the mountain gorilla.

After von Beringe killed the first mountain gorillas, thus discovering a new species, the scientific community grew even more fascinated by gorillas and concluded that the animals lived in groups unrelated genetically to each other. Therefore, institutions sending hunters into the Virungas to collect gorillas instructed them to kill two from each mountain. Since there were six peaks in the range that comprised the suspected home of gorillas, a minimum of twelve animals would be killed on each expedition. These numbers could have quickly decimated a population. Prince William of Sweden, leading the Swedish Zoological Expedition to central Africa in 1921, was determined to collect primates from each volcano. He, like Akeley, had intended to hunt gorillas almost a decade before, but his plans had been dashed by World War I. Prince William had arrived in Africa just before Akeley's expedition and had killed fourteen specimens, fueling Akeley's growing anxiety that too many animals were being killed in the Virungas.

From the outset the gorilla expedition was clearly going to be a very different experience for Akeley. Even his preparation was unusual. He focused his thoughts by writing a "gorilla creed," and promised to further illuminate gorilla behavior for the scientific community. Akeley's creed was fascinating because it revealed not only his beliefs about the animals, but also additional aspects of his character and personality. Akeley had always related to his quarry according to the level of respect that the animal "demanded" of him—elephants and lions were worthy partners in the hunting game; wild dogs, which he found filthy and disgusting, were not. He usually followed the rules of good sportsmanship when he respected the quarry. Akeley's gorilla creed illustrates that his approach to hunting these animals differed significantly from any other. Gorillas were going to be a different type of quarry. In Akeley's eyes, a gorilla was tantamount to a human. He would engage in the hunt as if he were the protagonist in Arthur Conan Doyle's story "The Most Dangerous Game"—a hunter after his own species. The creed, written in Akeley's own hand, has emotional overtones as well:

> I believe that the gorilla is normally a perfectly amiable and decent creature. I believe that if he attacks man it is because he is being attacked or thinks he is being attacked. I believe that he will fight in self-defense and probably in defense of his family; that he will keep away from a fight until he is frightened or driven to it. I believe that, although the old male advances when a hunter is approaching a family of gorillas, he will not close in, if the man involved has the courage to stand firm. In other words, his advance will turn out to be what is usually called a bluff.
>
> I believe, however, that the white man who will allow a gorilla to get within ten feet of him without shooting is a plain darn fool, for certainly the average man would have little to show in the clutch of a three or four hundred pound gorilla.
>
> My faith in the general amiability and decency of the gorilla is not based on experience or actual knowledge of any sort, but on deductions from the observation of wild animals in general and more particularly of monkeys. There are few animals that deliberately go into fight with an unknown antagonist or with a known antagonist, for that matter, without what seems to them a good reason. In other words, they are not looking for trouble.
>
> The lion will fight when the maintenance of his dignity demands it. Most animals will fight only when they are driven to it through fear, either for themselves or their young.
>
> The first living gorilla that I ever observed was in the Zoological Park in London many years ago. It was very young and its chief aim in life seemed a desire to be loved. This has seemed to be the chief characteristic of the few gorillas that I have seen in captivity. They appear to have an extremely affectionate disposition and to be passionately fond of the person most closely associated

with them; and I think that there is no doubt that John Daniel, who died in the Ringling Brothers Circus in Madison Square Garden in the spring of 1921, died of a broken heart because he was separated from his mistress. I did not have the pleasure of seeing John Daniel alive; but in death he certainly had the appearance of anything but a savage beast. The above notes are here set down for the purpose of recording the frame of mind with which I am going into the Kivu country to study, photograph and collect gorillas.[5]

In his creed, Akeley established his future emotional involvement with the species. After his gorilla expedition, Akeley would sign letters to close friends with the closing, "the old gorilla." For this cursing, smoking, gun-toting, "macho" hunter to write of the gorilla's need for love is rather astounding, especially considering the repressed climate of the times, when expressing personal feelings and affections in print was distasteful, and when husbands and wives referred to each other as "Mr." and "Mrs."

These accounts of gorilla behavior and his own strong feelings and beliefs about them were all Akeley had to go on as he prepared the expedition. He needed advice about exactly where to find the animals. Akeley's acquaintance, Ewart Grogan, the man who had walked the length of Africa (from the Cape of Good Hope to Cairo) to impress his would-be father-in-law and gain the hand of his beloved, had found a skeleton too large to belong to a chimpanzee in the Virunga volcanoes several years before von Beringe's gun cut down the first specimen; so it was to Grogan that Akeley turned for directions to gorilla country. He wrote to Sir Northrup McMillan, a good friend of Grogan's, asking him to set up a dinner in London for the three of them so that Grogan could advise Akeley on the best routes and logistical aspects of travel in the Congo.

Another peculiar aspect of Akeley's preparation for this trip was his desire to prepare his companions for life in the field. While he found it amusing to take neophytes to Africa, Akeley also knew that they needed some coaching. He went with the Bradleys on a short vacation to Maine to review the responsibilities of each member while in the field. They also discussed weapons, travel logistics, clothing and medical needs and countless other details necessary for a smooth-running safari. Most importantly, the "vacation" provided Akeley with an opportunity to see how they would interact as a group. Every safari has a shakedown period during which all members fall into their respective slots, and relationships are established. Akeley tried to get a head start on this with the Maine vacation. (It was the first vacation he had taken in his fifty-seven-year life.) The problem, of course, was that Maine was not Africa, and lacked its attendant physical and psychological problems. Akeley warned the others: "You must remember that after we have been in the country one month no one of us will be our normal selves. Everything will change. I anticipate that there will be times . . . when the rest of you will congregate in your tent somewhere and vote me the meanest old devil that ever lived, and I may be lonely for weeks at a time; but I am perfectly willing to take my chances because I know in the end you will be grateful to me for the very things that you cursed me out for during the trip; and four to one is about all that I will stand for."[6]

Akeley plotted the expedition in a measured, thoughtful way, and his extensive experience in Africa made him confident that he could negotiate the jungles for a group of greenhorns. The expedition left New York for England aboard the *Baltic* on July 31, 1921, transferring in Southampton, on August 12, to the *Kenilworth Castle* for their eighteen-day voyage to Cape Town, South Africa. It was a new route for Akeley, and the voyage proved both lovely and adventurous, as their vessel had to rescue another, the *Saxon*, which had caught fire just off Sierra Leone.

One of the passengers rescued from the *Saxon* was the famous Boer, General Jan Smuts, then the prime minister of the Union of South Africa, who was returning from a peace conference in Ireland with President Woodrow Wilson and other heads of state. Mary Bradley, in her book about the gorilla expedition, *On the Gorilla Trail*, wrote of their encounter with Smuts. The prime minister felt jaded, philosophical, and talkative in the wake of the conference. He was anxious to share his thoughts and reflections with Americans, and socialized with Akeley's party. He spoke about the extinction of modern man, of him going the way of the Neanderthal. "The problem of life is too much for man," Smuts said. "We are in this frame of earth and God has given us a soul . . . and we strive and fight . . . and the consciousness of the world and the sorrows of it wear us out . . . It is too much for us, and we may go and another race take our place."[7] He was reading Sinclair Lewis's *Main Street*, and identifying strongly with the physician in the story. Smuts impressed Akeley in many of the same ways that Teddy Roosevelt had, and he loved the easy intimacy with which the general spoke to them about the things in his heart. The two remained friends until Akeley's death.

Alice Bradley's sixth birthday celebration provided another important event during the voyage. Alice was like a surrogate child to Akeley. (Mickie, too, was fond of the child.) Akeley loved Alice, often holding her and entertaining her with African tales and "making his feet smoke." He always dusted his feet with powder, which would cloud up through his socks when he wiggled his toes, a remarkable feat often demanded of him by Alice during their voyage. Later, when expedition life did become difficult and the adults were holed up in tents grumbling about the "mean old devil," it was to this child that a lonely Akeley turned for comfort.

Alice Bradley grew up to be a fascinating woman, a writer like her mother. She wrote science fiction novels under the name James Tiptree Jr., and also taught experimental psychology in Washington, D.C. Alice had much to say about Akeley's behavior on the gorilla expedition. She felt that he was an "emotional tyrant" who would act the needy child until the adults acceded to his needs and softened in their attitude toward him. As soon as they approached him in a defenseless way, Akeley would attack again, making life miserable for everyone. To his credit, Akeley knew he was acting monstrously toward his companions, and later attributed it to the state of his nerves on this expedition. Alice loved Akeley and remembered him fondly, but was quick to admit that her parents found him very difficult and moody. He was off in his own little world, a world of work and vision, but little pleasure.

After a few days of socializing and business in Cape Town, the party took a five-day train journey to Victoria Falls. As they traveled north across the Great Karroo, the lack of game became noticeable; Ostriches seemed the only animals to inhabit the veldt; when men move in to work the land the animals disappear. Akeley had predicted the same situation in East Africa, and the apparent accuracy of his prophecies heightened his determination to accomplish his goals for the African Hall before it was too late. The train was luxurious and the journey marked the last such comfort experienced by the Akeley party. As they chugged north, the climate and topography changed dramatically; the weather heated up and the plains gave way to the mountains, lakes, and rivers that formed the heart of Africa's landmass.

They reached the spectacular Victoria Falls, where the Zambezi River rushes, like a madwoman, headlong over the rocks, plummeting into an enormous dent in the earth's surface. The red aloes along the bank appeared like small fires amidst the white foam, creating an almost supernatural picture of fire and water cohabiting. Akeley made some movies of *mosi oa tunya*—"the smoke that thunders." He was able to pan the height and width of the magnificent falls, named after England's Queen by David Livingstone, with his Akeley camera. The stop was a brief but lovely respite. They were impatient to move on to the Virunga mountain range, home of the gorillas, still far away.

After a series of short train rides involving the frustrating logistical problems of connecting, reconnecting, not connecting, or waiting to connect, all in "Africa time"—which means never on time—the group reached the border of the Belgian Congo on September 10. Lost luggage problems detained them in Elizabethville (now Lubumbashi) for a week. Akeley decided to use the time to assemble his core staff. The only help that Akeley could secure were three Africans who had worked as domestics for Belgian employers; none of them had experienced safari life. Martha Miller graciously gave the most destitute of the three a pair of pink pajamas to wear in the name of modesty and warmth, as they were moving ever onward into higher altitudes and lower temperatures. They traveled by rail to Bukama, where again the luggage was missing—but Herbert stepped in and cool-headedly negotiated with the station master, recovering it quickly before Akeley lost his wits again. Bukama was the railway's end and a junction of embarkation for the Lualaba River, a tributary of the infamous Congo River (now Zaire River). It was by the Lualaba that Henry Morton Stanley had discovered the Congo River. (Stanley's exploration of the Congo basin set in motion the rapid political changes that Africa has experienced in the last hundred years.)

The river journey was a strange mixture of small luxuries and inconveniences, homey and exotic pastimes, and hypnotic beauty. They shared cramped quarters and delicious meals; the men took pot shots into the crocodile-infested waters and the women played paper dolls with Alice, all against a stunning backdrop of borassus palms towering along the shores and elephants, hippos, and antelopes going about their business. They disembarked the river steamer at Kabalo and set up a campsite near the river to await a weekly train that would take them on to Albertville (now Kalemie) on Lake Tanganyika. The train eventually arrived and took them to their destination, but they found they had been deceived by the "ville" in Albertville, as there was no real town there. Without the desired comfortable accommodations, they camped on a hill overlooking the glorious lake to await a steamer.

A few days later, the steamer *Baron Dhanis* picked them up. The boat, having ten staterooms, conveyed a variety of interesting characters, mostly bureaucrats and missionaries. The captain was enchanted by Akeley's female companions, and entertained them often at his table. During the five-day journey north, all meals were cut from a pig carcass that hung from the rail. The teatime offering of chocolate became the Akeley party's favorite meal on board.

En route, they tied up for a couple of days at Kigoma, near Ujiji, on the eastern shore of the lake (now in Tanzania). The expedition took the opportunity to visit the tree, in Ujiji, under which the famous meeting of Stanley and Livingstone took place. Burton and Speke had also arrived there in 1858. Akeley the explorer was tracing the steps and meditating on the accomplishments of his predecessors. The whole journey was different from any of his other expeditions. He was seeing and experiencing unknown people and places; even their extensive river and lake journeys were atypical of his African sojourns. It was like a new Africa for him, inspiring and exciting him; yet his mind and heart remained set on the gorilla, not far away.

They disembarked at Usumbura (now Bujumbura in Burundi), on the north end of the lake, and camped for five days until they could secure two hundred porters for the trek north to Lake Kivu. The Bradleys, Martha, and Akeley took the opportunity to go into the bush for elephants, leaving Priscilla Hall and Alice behind. In base camp, a fight broke out among the Africans over an alleged infidelity. The accused woman was beaten savagely until Priscilla, terrified herself, arrived with a pistol to settle the affair. The beaten woman threw herself at Priscilla's feet for protection as the mood in the camp darkened. Priscilla defended and guarded the woman until Akeley's return. By that time, the tension in camp had eased. Priscilla's companions were impressed by her courage and decisive action. A few days later, Martha succeeded in killing an elephant with her first shot fired in Africa. The women were proving themselves to be intrepid and feisty companions.

The expedition members began their eight-day march to Lake Kivu. Actually, the white adults rode bicycles and Alice was carried by two Africans in a long basket fitted to poles. The group traveled along parallel to the Ruzizi River, camping each night.

Another fight broke out among the Africans, this one involving the more serious crime of attempted murder. The offender was beaten by his fellow porters. Akeley's wisdom had grown with his years and he decided to take the man to the proper authorities. He directed the Africans to care for him in a humane way until they arrived at a district office. Akeley developed a fever that night. From his cot he heard the prisoner's blood-curdling screams, but could do nothing. The Bradleys also heard, but were paralyzed with fear. In the morning, the man was gone. One of the core staff members, himself shaken with fear, reported to the expedition members that the man had been murdered and eaten by the porters. Many of the porters had the filed teeth of indigenous cannibal people, but the expedition never knew for sure what had happened.

They finally reached the mountainous backbone of the continent, and stood stunned by the beauty of Lake Kivu nestled below, the grey, gossamer-wrapped peaks of the Virungas still distant on the horizon. A tear fell from Akeley's eye for the astonishing vista that lay before them. Storm clouds over the lake, backlit by shafts of bright sun and rainbows, punctuated the natural beauty, creating a scene of magic and enchantment. Those forested peaks to the north were the gorilla's home. Before long they would encounter the great ape face to face.

It was late October and the expedition still had three days of travel on the Lake and a couple of hard marches before they would encounter gorillas. They made official and social stops at Costermansville (now Bukavu) and Katana, where they dined with the White Fathers (now Missionaries of Africa), the Catholic missionaries working in the region, and heard tales of recent gorilla invasions; the primates raided native *shambas*. At Gisenyi, at the north end of the Lake, Akeley left the expedition behind. On October 31, with thirty porters, he pushed on.

The others spent ten days recovering from fatigue and fever, resting and socializing with the Belgian settlers. Some Africans visited the Bradleys during this time to see Alice. Word had spread that Jesus Christ, as a child, had arrived. Alice, with her long curly locks, looked like the Christ child depicted in the sentimental pictures and holy cards distributed by the missionaries. She was nonplussed when the Africans knelt before her.

Akeley was anxious to proceed alone, as he professed to be worried that the gorillas would elude him with so large a party tramping through the bush. More importantly, however, was his need to be by himself. Akeley had been with the others for three months, and everyone was beginning to get on each other's nerves. Akeley was especially irritable; he later attributed his mood to his anticipation of the gorilla hunt. He was nervous because he felt, "an alternating current of eagerness to go and fear that [he] would find nothing."[8] He had invested so much in this gorilla hunt—in his own long-awaited encounter with the animal. Besides his eagerness and his fear of not finding gorillas, he felt anxiety over finding and killing them. Would he have the courage to face this dangerous opponent, and how would he feel about killing an animal that he felt was so similar to man? The hunt was emotionally charged for him and he had to do it alone.

A three-day march brought him to the White Fathers' mission at Lulenga, which was to be the expedition's base. After a night's rest, he set out on his mission to find gorillas for the museum, alone except for his guides and porters.

He trekked up the side of Mt. Mikeno along elephant and buffalo tracks, astonished by the magnificent vegetation surrounding him. For several hours he saw nothing except the spoor of the large animals left from the night before. Then he came to a small clearing where he found a perfect hand print in the mud—four great knuckles—and, Akeley noted that, like Du Chaillu, "his feeling were really excited to a painful degree." They pursued the animal, but never found it that day, halted by unspeakably difficult slopes, a seasonal downpour, and guides who had little interest in making the climb. Even today there is an expression in the Virungas: "*Les gorilles sont magnifiques, mais ce n'est pas la peine monter*"—"The gorillas are magnificent, but not worth the climb." Akeley returned to the mission exhausted and frustrated.

Disgusted with his first guides, Akeley decided to find new ones the next day. He went to the sultan of Burunga (now Kibumba), about a three-hour march from the mission, and asked for assistance. The sultan gave him splendid guides (one of them, Muguru, would be a close companion to Akeley for years to come). The guides told Akeley to leave everything—porters, camera, and even his scientific kit—behind, as they would be moving through very dense forest. Leading the way up the mountain, the guides hacked rough paths out of the tangled vegetation. Akeley slipped and skidded on the wet earth, cursing the biting siafu ants and the ubiquitous stinging nettles. The nettles, a plant's simple protection, become like projectiles in the neighborhood of a live body. Each individual sting did not last long, but there were so many of them that the cumulative affect was exasperating. The trek was grueling work, exacerbated by a terrible weakness overtaking Akeley's body from the blood poisoning that he had been fighting for weeks. But all this was forgotten when Akeley saw a black, shaggy head pierce a wall of vivid green across the Kanyamagufu canyon. The animal was on an upper slope; Akeley descended into the chasm and up to the other side to the location where he had spotted the gorilla. The guides scrambled up before Akeley, who admonished them to stop so that he could catch his breath. The going was excruciating at an altitude of ten thousand feet.

They heard the gorilla bark and beat his chest up on the slope above them. Everything became exceedingly quiet while Akeley and the gorilla listened to each other, and each tried to determine the other's next move. Akeley braced himself against a tree to give him the leverage he needed on the steep slope. Without it, the kickback of his Jeffery .475 would have knocked him off of the mountain. He waited without breathing for the next move. While Akeley believed in the good nature of gorillas, he also knew full well that no animal would take being shot gracefully. He was happy to have his Jeffery. The gorilla began his marvelous charge, which consists of a beautifully orchestrated series of actions—almost like a ritual. We now know that the charges are usually bluffs full of bravado, and if one has the courage to hold steady, the gorilla's ire usually dissipates. But the energy and power of a charge can be terrifying. A roar, a rush through the vegetation, and Akeley fired. The animal was about thirty feet above Akeley, and below him was a three-hundred-foot drop to the canyon floor. The gorilla crashed down and struck the earth about eight feet away from Akeley, then kept on plunging downward. Akeley's heart sank as he feared he had lost the animal and that the killing had been in vain.[9]

The body of the silverback (a male gorilla, so-called because of the silver saddle that develops on its back at maturity) was lodged against a tree overhanging the canyon floor. Akeley made his way down the slope to where the dead gorilla lay. Because Akeley had left his tools in camp, he had nothing but a jackknife with which to skin and skeletonize the animal. One of the guides assisted him with his own iron knife, as the others held onto the bodies of the gorilla and the skinners alike so that they would not fall into the canyon from their precarious perch. Akeley held his feelings about the killing of this animal in check for some time. There can be no doubt that Akeley enjoyed the hunting and killing of his first gorilla, whom he later named the "Old Man of Mikeno." He recounted the adventure as being "thrilling," "exciting" and "dramatic."

Back at the camp, Akeley set his staff to cleaning the skeleton as he made plaster death masks of the Old Man's head, feet and hands. Akeley, though depleted by the rigorous trek, the excitement of the hunt, and the blood poisoning, felt he needed to push on as "science is a jealous mistress and takes little account of a man's feelings."[10] Measurements had to be made, photographs taken, and the brain and organs properly preserved immediately; yet all he really wanted to do was to go to bed. The next day he continued work on his first specimen, and began to sense the sweetness and openness of the gorilla's face haunting him. Nevertheless, he planned another gorilla hunt for the next day.

At dawn the next morning they left camp for the same spot in Kanya-magufu where they had bagged the silverback. Little did Akeley know that the day's events would prove a turning point in his life. They soon came upon a gorilla family. In his fervor, Akeley did not take the time to shoot accurately, and missfired twice at the large female he wanted for the group. The shots set up a hysterical frenzy in the animals, who beat a hasty retreat from danger. Akeley pursued them, scrambling up the same slopes he had climbed two days before. The group was right above him. There was no sapling to brace Akeley this time, so he tangled himself up into a small bush for added security. The large female was only fifty feet above him, standing in bushes that looked as if they could hold her from falling down onto the canyon floor.

Akeley shot her and was surprised when she came tumbling down the slope straight at him. He lost his balance in those frantic seconds and thought that her body would take his with her on the plummet downward. He hit the dirt just as she passed over him, knocking a welt on his head in the process. As he started to get up, a squealing, screaming ball of black fur rolled past him, touching him; then two more—an "avalanche of gorillas"—raced after the female. Akeley thought that it was a charge, but soon realized that "the others had followed her not in anger but in fear and because they accepted her lead without realizing that it was involuntary." The black ball of fur was the female's four-year-old son, following his mother in her rush down the mountain. Akeley recovered his senses enough to pursue the youngster, only to find him in a clearing, racing about terrified. One of the Africans speared the young gorilla as Akeley approached, but he was still alive as Akeley looked into his face. Akeley wrote: "There was a heartbreaking expression of piteous pleading on his face. He would have come into my arms for comfort."[11] In that moment, as Akeley gazed into the dying youngster's eyes, something happened to him. Here he stood, locked in a moment of profound contact with a living gorilla, and what he saw in the youngster's eyes were emotions of terror and pain—familiar emotions registered in familiar ways. In that face he saw kinship, intelligence, and sensitivity. Akeley had a growing sense of being the "savage," the "aggressor," the "murderer."

Dense fog and nasty, freezing rain moved in on them as they searched for the dead female. The Africans were shivering in their nakedness and Akeley took off his Burberry raincoat and shared it with seven of them using it like an umbrella. When the rain lessened, the search continued on a zigzagging course downward into the canyon. The Africans tried to convince Akeley that it was impossible to find her and wanted to give up, but Akeley was not about to waste the life of the animal by abandoning her corpse. He swung down the slopes on overhanging roots, an effort that would have strained the constitution of a healthy twenty year old, much less a blood poisoned fifty-seven year old. The path he chose took him into the chasm, but nowhere near the fallen animal. He followed along a stream bed winding around the side of Mt. Mikeno, climbing up again, through a small waterfall, to where the animal was lodged in the vegetation. The space was so tight that only Akeley and one African could skin and skeletonize the animal. Akeley was exhausted and she was heavy and difficult to maneuver. He tied the animal and himself to a tree so he could work without both of them tumbling to the canyon floor. He succeeded in getting the skin and skeleton off and organized into bundles for the Africans to take to camp. Akeley was touched by the Africans' dogged efforts as they slid and slipped up the slopes with their valuable packages, but he was also anxious that one would lose his footing and send himself or a bundle crashing down the mountain.

The physical exertion, the anxiety, and the emotional overtones of the day proved almost too much for Akeley, who later said that it was the hardest day of his life. He worked into the night, carefully skinning the four-year-old gorilla, whose skinned body he also preserved intact. Akeley named the youngster "Clarence" after himself. There is irony in Akeley's giving the young one his childhood name (no one in his adult life ever called him Clarence), and it was not his custom to name animals, though he named three of the gorillas collected on this expedition. The look on Clarence's face at death continued to haunt Akeley.

The next morning, the Africans arrived at Akeley's tent to report that they were quitting. The work was too hard. Akeley did not blame them; he certainly would not have endured the ordeal just for money. But he succeeded in convincing the Africans not to quit with higher wages and a day off. Akeley needed the day off also, but continued working on his specimens. He felt that he was weakening, but pushed himself onward to complete his tasks.

The next day, Akeley and the Africans again went after gorillas, but to film them, not hunt them. Akeley filmed a female and a couple of young playing in the crotch of a tree—the first pictures, motion or still, ever made of live gorillas in the wild. He enjoyed watching them and they watched him. The youngsters "performed" for him and the female rose once from her rest to beat her chest, then settled down again, always keeping an eye on Akeley and his machine. The animals bolted only when Akeley began to speak to them.

As if some spell had been broken, Akeley followed the gorillas until he reached the group, picked out an animal that he thought was an immature male, and shot it. The animal turned out to be another female, whose infant was collected by another member of the group and carried off to safety as it cried piteously.

Akeley did not anthropomorphize; he was not sentimental. Yet he used words like "love" and "pity" when speaking or writing about the gorillas. Something was happening to him on this expedition; some internal change. He made an offhand comment to Alice that is revealing about his state of mind. She asked him how he felt when a gorilla "went for him." He said, "I was thankful it wasn't a lady, Alice." When she asked why, he responded,

"Because I'm more afraid of ladies." Alice asked if this was because he couldn't shoot them, to which he replied that it was something like that, "but certainly the gorillas didn't go for you as hard as the ladies did."[12] Clearly, he was referring to his problems with Mickie, and with his mother before Mickie. Even through his jesting, he was beginning to allude to the cracks in his own foundation, his own fears and pain.

While Akeley was moved by the gorillas themselves, they also reflected his inner landscape. The gorilla's manlike appearance, his tremendous power and intelligence, and what George Schaller called his "transcendent quality" enabled Akeley to identify with him. In addition to naming the juvenile after himself, he called himself "the old gorilla," and acted out his identification with animals in other peculiar ways. There are odd, uncharacteristic photographs of Akeley posed with the body of the Old Man of Mikeno. Their heads are next to each other, peering out of a bush—Akeley has put his glasses on the animal's face and his pipe in its mouth. The image is bizarre, almost ghastly; his actions are a vague attempt at humor, but neither amusing nor charming.

Akeley later referred to the Virungas as the place "where the fairies dance." He said it often to people who asked about the region. He saw the mountains as an enchanted place, due in part to the spell he felt himself under while there. But the emotional and physical strain of hunting gorillas, added to his recurrent health problems, made Akeley ill. He sent a message, via an African runner, to the Bradleys—one day's hard march away—telling them to come immediately, that he had "broken something."

The Bradleys, Martha, and Priscilla were pleasantly ensconced at the White Father's mission at Lulenga, in a building constructed years before for some nuns who had been expected but who had never arrived. The fathers did not know quite how to react to the strange party going into the mountains after gorillas, even though they had hosted gorilla-hunters before. The women made wisecracks at the dinner table, sometimes using religious subjects as a source of wit. And as if the beautiful, outspoken women were not enough, Herbert upset the Fathers even more with a bad joke that ended up damaging Akeley's relationship with the holy men. Herbert told them that Akeley wanted to put an African woman in a room with a male gorilla to see if they would mate.[13] (Akeley would later jest that he was looking for a "nice gorilla lady" to take him in.[14]) The fathers were not amused and behaved coolly toward Akeley. Even years later, when Akeley returned to Lulenga looking for hospitality, the fathers were barely cordial.

On receiving Akeley's message, Herbert, Mary, and Martha immediately prepared themselves for the trek up the "greasy mud chutes" of Mt. Mikeno. The climb was arduous, lasting nine hours, during which they often had to pull themselves up the steep slopes by grabbing the vegetation closing in on them over the path. Yet in spite of the extreme exertion, they enjoyed the spectacular beauty of the mountain forests. The quality of light sifting through the bamboo and the pale green, gauzy, bearded lichen was so gorgeous as to appear other-worldly. The silence was broken only by a bird's song and a soft whoosh made by breezes flowing through the ancient trees. The enormous hagenia trees were drenched in mossy tendrils and puffy clouds of tiny orchids. The huge, dense pads of vibrant green moss, sometimes eight feet long, called to them like fairy beds, seductive to the trekkers in their state of fatigue. Wild celery—gorilla food—was everywhere. And the sweet, pungent smells of the vegetation wafted up at every step.

When they reached Akeley, they found a man "looking as if years instead of days had intervened. He was very worn; he had done the work of ten men under particularly trying conditions; he had started with fever, infected by jiggers which he had not been able to extract; he had killed his gorillas in most inaccessible places . . . he had skinned and skeletonized and dissected without rest, and now energy and appetite had deserted him. What was broken, he said, was his vigor. We felt troubled when we first saw him."[15] The Bradleys and Martha saw to it that Akeley had some dinner and they all stayed in camp to rest the next day.

They all felt rested, revived, and excited the next day. On November 15, they set off for Mt. Karisimbi, the highest mountain in the Virunga range, to find at last the gorillas they had come so far to see. They camped at Kabara, the meadow on the saddle between Mt. Mikeno and Mt. Karisimbi, venturing onto the slopes of Karisimbi by day.

They found a silverback, later called the "Lone Male of Karisimbi," their second day out. Herbert shot him because that is what he had traveled so far to accomplish; he wanted to kill a gorilla. Akeley, however, said that if Herbert had not killed the animal, he could not have done it himself. He added that he had lost his stomach for killing gorillas and was feeling like a murderer.

The animal crashed down the slope and lodged against a tree. The animal did not go down easily. After the first shot he looked at his killer with "an expression of wonderment; not a sound did he make; not a scintilla; not an indication of savagery," Akeley recounted. A second shot brought him down and the autopsy proved that he had survived an earlier hunter's bullet. The massive, 360-pound gorilla had the "face of an amiable giant who would do no harm except in self-defense or in defense of his friends."[16]

The vista stretching out above the spot where the gorilla fell was one of ineffable beauty and Akeley, swept away by it claimed: "I envy that chap his funeral pyre."[17] These words exploded with irony: Akeley would die very near the site five years later, to the very day. Akeley described the scene:

Mikeno was at her best; she had thrown aside her veil of cloud; her summit was sharply outlined against the tropical sky. The warm greens and browns of the moss-covered cliffs suggested a drapery of lovely oriental weave. From the summit well down the wonderful line of the western slope the eye was arrested by old Nyamlagira smouldering lazily and sending her column of smoke and steam to join the hovering cloudbank above—then on again the eye swept over a scene of marvelous opalescent color in which were dimly seen distant mountain ranges, suggestions of shimmering lakes, and mysterious forests—then around to Chaninagongo [Nyiragongo], looming dark and massive in the middle ground, smouldering, too, but less demonstrative than her sister, Nyamlagira. Lying almost at the foot of Chaninagongo and to the south, glistened in the tropical sun the loveliest of African inland waters—Lake Kivu . . . It was the high spot of my African experience. It was a scene of the primitive world, the world in the making, and at our feet lay the dead giant, the primitive man.[18]

Akeley had collected two silverbacks, two females, and the youngster. Because he had little actual knowledge of the gorilla's social life, he felt that he or Herbert needed to collect a young male to complete a family unit, and use the other silverback as an intruder. Therefore, the men stayed on the mountain and sent the women back to the fathers' mission. Akeley and Herbert took the camera and their guns out the next two days but the gorillas eluded them. Finally, they came upon a large group. Akeley was thrilled to see that there was not one silverback in the group, but three. He felt relieved that he could tell the truthful story about the gorillas with the animals he had already collected. While it is rare to find so many silverbacks in one group, it is not unusual to find two, though one is always clearly dominant. Akeley felt "extreme satisfaction at seeing that band of gorillas disappear over the crest . . . none the worst for having met with white men that morning."[19] He and Herbert descended the mountain just in time to celebrate Thanksgiving dinner with the women, Alice, and the fathers.

Akeley had changed in the Virungas; he had come to a new level of understanding about and acceptance of himself. Age and experience prepared him for his metanoia and the mountains themselves formed a catalyst. Mikeno means "the naked one," or the "poor one"—man laid bare and vulnerable. Akeley was not the first man to be affected by the mystery and sacredness of mountains.

Of greatest importance, however, were the gorillas themselves. The story of Akeley's thinking about gorillas is itself an allegory. If J. T. Jr., the vervet monkey, represented for Mickie some element of chaos or anarchy, gorillas symbolized for Akeley a sense of order, or a coming together of his own disparate sides. He too was both ferocious and gentle, but he had been incapable of embracing those seemingly antithetical aspects of himself and, split, he would act out one or the other, torn apart by his inability to change or control them. In gorillas, and their unself-conscious embodiment of opposites, Akeley found permission for his own humanity.

If Akeley found God on Mt. Kenya, he found himself in the Virungas.

His relationship with the animals resonates with a kind of release or freedom, witnessed further in his sculpture of *The Chrysalis*. The man emerging from the gorilla skin is freed from the cocoon, astonished at his own birth. The work itself not only expresses evolution on a philosophical level, but also gives a personal statement of Akeley's exuberance. The man is familiar, the sculpture is almost a self-portrait.

We can, therefore, understand Akeley's efforts to save the gorilla as a function of his emotional involvement with the species as well as of his scientific ardor. Akeley was the first to utter the sentiments *"Kweli nudugu yangu"*—"Surely God, this is my kin"—quoted by Dian Fossey; he was the first to feel what George Schaller would feel when he wrote that the extinction of the gorillas would be "like a death in the family." Akeley was the first to write about gorillas in ways that reflect contemporary research. He began to reveal their nature to the world. Like Akeley, we are comfortable in accepting the gorilla as our relative. The gorilla has qualities that we like to see in ourselves—gentility, shyness, curiosity, strength, and a powerful kinship to family—and Akeley first helped us to recognize those qualities.

Akeley quickly became very concerned for the survival of the gorillas. He could think of little else as the expedition wound up its time in the Virungas. Akeley and company camped near the live volcano Nymulagira, making movies of it at night. They journeyed through British East Africa towards Mombasa for their homeward voyage. Akeley, distracted throughout, paid little attention to the sights. By the time the group reached the east coast of Africa, he had a full-blown plan for saving the primates from extinction. He worked out the details with the same precision with which he worked out the plans for the African Hall.

By January 1922, the expedition was aboard a steamer heading home; they had been in Africa about five months, the shortest of Akeley's African sojourns. During the voyage, Akeley wrote to Judge Paul Salkin in Elisabethville, Belgian Congo that he found the gorilla "a wholly acceptable citizen and not the wicked villain of popular belief." He added that he would communicate with Belgian officials, suggesting that they establish a sanctuary in the Virungas where the animals could have protection in perpetuity. Akeley was convinced that if this was not done "very soon they are in positive danger of being exterminated. I do not think it is fair to future generations to exterminate an animal of such intense human interest as the gorilla . . . I not only want to establish a sanctuary but also a Biological Research Station where students of animal psychology and kindred subjects may carry on their research work under most advantageous conditions."[20]

Although it is hubris to determine a species's survival based on its interest to human beings, Akeley's mind and indefatigable energy were focused on saving the gorilla from extinction. Less than a year later, his formulated plans were presented to John C. Merriam of the Carnegie Institution in Washington, D.C. Merriam was an avid supporter of the Akeley idea. Akeley envisioned an absolute sanctuary surrounded by a "dead line," or African police–patrolled roadway, within which the gorillas would be safe. Merriam turned to Baron Emile de Cartier de Marchienne, the Belgian ambassador to the United States, with the Akeley ideas and maps.

While Akeley's efforts can not be underestimated, it is important to remember that another force played a part in the creation of the park. The stage was set by King Albert of Belgium's visit to the American national parks in 1919. His companions on the visit were John Merriam and Akeley's boss, Henry Fairfield Osborn. The United States was the first country to see the need for preserving and protecting wildlife and wilderness, and the scientists impressed the king with the importance of national parks like Yellowstone (founded in 1872) and Yosemite (founded in 1890).

Albert came away from the visit inspired to create a national park for his own country. The Belgian's dilemma, however, was that there was no real wilderness left in his country. He turned his thoughts to the enormous tract of land he ruled in Africa. That same region had brought negative public attention to his country only twenty years before, through Leopold's Congo Free State. And so, Akeley's plan greatly interested King Albert.

The park's boundary was initially the triangle formed by the three volcanoes, Mikeno, Karisimbi, and Visoke. It was to be set aside for the serious study of science in an established biological field station where international scientists could convene and conduct their research. Recreational tourism would not be permitted.

When Akeley returned home from the expedition, he concentrated his efforts on raising the consciousness of the American people to the plight of the gorilla. He wrote articles that were syndicated in newspapers and magazines throughout the country. He went on a lecture tour, something he normally hated, showing his movie of the gorilla trip. And, of course, he created his famous sculpture *The Chrysalis*, with its attendant publicity for the gorilla and human evolution.

Akeley's efforts were rewarded on March 2, 1925, when King Albert created the Parc National Albert by royal decree. The Belgians held that the gorilla was an animal of "extreme interest to scientists," and that while in the past they had permitted the animals to be captured or killed, "the time has come when, in the interests of humanity, as well as the interests of Science itself, steps must be taken to preserve the remaining gorillas from extermination." Therefore, no gorillas were allowed to be taken from the park, dead or alive. This seemed like an overreaction to Akeley. He saw no problem with "the killing of a reasonable number of specimens for scientific institutions." This statement further illustrates the complexity of Carl Akeley, who, as we have seen, could be inconsistent in word and action.

Before the decree was set down, hunters burst forth with a violent outcry against it. After all, the gorilla was just beginning to be popularized as quarry. The international press publicized this debate with Akeley and his friend-turned-rival, T. Alexander Barns, at the center of it. Barns, formerly a rancher in Rhodesia, had gone into the hunting business in the Congo, basing himself in Gisenyi. He felt that Akeley was "making a mountain out of a molehill," and proclaimed that there were "thousands" of gorillas in the volcanoes, advocating that hunters be allowed to take two gorillas each.[21] Akeley, who had a license to take ten gorillas but only took five, was appalled at the idea, even though he felt that the decree went too far in the other direction. Barns's argument could be viewed as self-interest, as he was trying to nurse along a new business called "Alexander Barns Adventure Tours," offering gorillas as one of the inducements to prospective clients. Akeley recognized the possibility that he himself might have been an "alarmist," but felt that it was better to "play it safe." Akeley won the debate, and influenced the Belgians to err on the side of tougher conservation measures.

Akeley also urged the Belgian government to enlarge the park boundaries, feeling that the original scope was too narrow and that the gorillas would be shot by hunters or settlers if they left the specified area. He envisioned the park reaching as far north as Lake Edward. He corresponded with James Gustavus Whitley, the Belgian consul-general at Baltimore, in this regard. Whitley's response was that the park should be rounded out on the Rwandan side by including the territory between Lake Kivu and the park's southwestern corner. He wrote: "This would provide a safe 'corridor' for animals living on the southern slopes of Karissimbi [sic] who might want to go down to the lake to drink, bathe, or spend the week-end at the shore. Otherwise the poor devils would have to make a long detour in order to keep within bounds and we would have to provide them with road-maps as well as with copies of the Parc Rules and Regulations, printed in French, Flemish, Congolese and Gorilla."[23] The park was eventually expanded from the original area, encompassing 24,000 hectares, to 200,000 hectares (500,000 acres).

In the years between 1925, when the original decree established the park, and 1929, when the final documents were in place, the Belgian government revised the concepts and design of the park. While most of the volcanoes where the gorillas ranged were in Belgian territory or in an area mandated to Belgium (Rwanda), some of them spilled over into Uganda, necessitating cooperation with the British. The governments had to work together toward a nonpartisan end—wildlife conservation. Endless details had to be negotiated.

The most serious problem to address was financial. Who was to pay for the park? Belgium ultimately abolished the original idea of the park as a game reserve, and reordered it as a fully administered wildlife sanctuary that would "in no way run counter to the economic development of the country." It would be an expensive proposition, especially if it was not a park dedicated to recreational tourism, which would bring in monies through admission fees. It must be remembered that there was no precedent; Parc National Albert was the first of its kind on the continent, and the first national park in the world established for scientific research as well as conservation. The form the park took is fascinating.

The main focus of the sanctuary was scientific- and research-oriented. The sanctuary would protect not only the gorillas and the indigenous flora and fauna, but also the African pygmies living within its boundaries. The park was divided into four sectors, or reserves, with less rigidly controlled adjacent territories that were considered "protected." Africans were allowed to continue living in these protected areas and to continue hunting (except for gorillas), fishing, and collecting firewood. These privileges could only be exercised through traditional methods, using primitive weapons and tools. The park was to be administered by a commissioner and by a "Committee of Direction," comprising eighteen members. Two-thirds of this body was appointed or selected by the King of Belgium—the remaining third chosen from the international scientific community—and it was Belgium that assumed the immediate operating costs of the park. The commission was authorized to accept gifts, legacies, and donations to further the scientific purposes of the Parc National Albert. So it was to the scientific community throughout the world that Belgium looked for sustaining financial support for the park.

Both the American Museum of Natural History's Henry Fairfield Osborn and John C. Merriam were appointed to the commission. These appointments paved the way for American institutions to receive preferential treatment vis-à-vis primate research in the volcanoes. In fact, the first serious gorilla research was performed by George Schaller in 1959, under the auspices of the New York Zoological Society, whose president was Fairfield Osborn, son of the AMNH president. Akeley was accused, during his lifetime, of establishing the park as his own private reserve, or at least the private reserve of the Americans. Akeley did have a personal interest in seeing the park established and the gorillas protected, but his motives were hardly greedy, as suggested by his accusers.

Today the original park has been broken up into three parks, reflecting the African governments born of independence. The Virunga volcanoes conservation area is comprised of the Parc National de Virunga in Zaire, the Parc National des Volcans in Rwanda, and Kigezi Gorilla Sanctuary in Uganda. Most of the extant animals live in Rwanda, and are studied by international scientists, just as Akeley had hoped. In 1967 Dian Fossey finally founded the station Akeley longed to see established, a research station named Karisoke for its location on the saddle between Mt. Karisimbi and Mt. Visoke. Akeley wanted to see gorilla groups become accustomed to humans so that they could be closely studied. This too came to pass with Schaller's and Fossey's work. Akeley would never have predicted habituation for tourists, but he would have approved of the idea if it were a valid method of procuring funds for their protection.

Today, the gorilla population is growing slowly after decades of abuse. While the 1940s and 1950s were somewhat stable for the gorilla populations, the anarchy resulting from the Africans' fight for independence carried over into the world of the pristine forest. The 1960s and 1970s saw a resurgence of illegal activities in the park; gorillas were killed for grisly trophies, including ashtrays made of gorilla hands. Gorilla skulls were collected for desk decorations. Whole gorilla families were killed to obtain one zoo specimen, and usually the infants died en route to their new home.

Today there are probably around about three hundred mountain gorillas living in Rwanda and Zaire, and possibly another two hundred in Uganda. It is a positive sign that their populations are slowly swelling. There can be no doubt that these numbers would not exist at all were it not for those first efforts to save them, so passionately promulgated by Carl Akeley.

AT THE PEAK

Ha, I was a blaze leaping up!
I was a tiger bursting into sunlight.
I was greedy, I was mad for the unknown.
I, new-risen, resurrected, starved from the tomb,
starved from a life of devouring always myself,
now here was I, new-awakened, with my hand stretching out
and touching the unknown, the real unknown, the unknown
unknown.

    —D.H. LAWRENCE, "New Heaven and Earth"

DURING THE DECADE before the gorilla trip, the American Museum of Natural History suffered from economic woes caused by the First World War, rising costs, and a drop in major endowments. The 1920s, on the other hand, were times of great prosperity, during which the AMNH reached the height of its public reputation through mass publicity. AMNH scientists were nationally recognized personalities. They were "explorers" whose daring exploits were weighted by the seriousness of their scientific mission. Rotogravure sections of Sunday newspapers featured the marriage of adventure and science through the photographs of museum men in the field with wild dangerous animals and exotic peoples. Tales were told of encounters with bandits, cannibals, and rare and prehistoric animals. The museum began sending out as many as thirty or forty expeditions a year to find the "unknown facts of nature." These expeditions became the source of "incessant and nationwide publicity." It is from the press coverage of these real-life audacious and dramatic characterizations that tales like Hollywood's "Indiana Jones" found their inspiration.

The two most promoted figures in the public arena were Carl Akeley and Roy Chapman Andrews. Henry Fairfield Osborn had much to gain from the promulgation of the work of these men. Osborn saw in Roy Chapman Andrews the promise of the museum's reputation as the best in the field of paleontology and evolutionary studies. The flip side of research and exploration is education and exhibition, and Osborn saw in Carl Akeley the realization of the ultimate public exhibition techniques. Akeley and Andrews were friends, colleagues, and brother puppets in Osborn's scheme: to create the finest natural history institution in the world. With this lofty mission in mind, Osborn sent Andrews into the Gobi Desert of Outer Mongolia in 1921 to lead the most extensive and ambitious collective expeditions in the museum's history.

The Central Asiatic Expeditions, as they were called, took place throughout most of the 1920s. Scientists from various paleontological fields traveled to and from the remote regions of central Asia throughout the decade, seeking the truth about the evolution of man and animals. Andrews, as leader, cut a dashing figure, in contrast to the more staid, hard-line scientific work of the expedition. He was handsome and charming, audacious and almost foolhardy. He spoke infectiously of exciting places with names like the Flaming Cliffs at Shabarakh Usu; of extinct creatures like Baluchitherium; and of fending off brigands in pursuit of precious fossils. His team discovered a clutch of dinosaur eggs and more importantly, a tiny mammal skull that recorded the evolution of placental animals to a date millions of years earlier than previous finds had indicated. But they did not find evidence of early man, as Osborn had hoped.

The photographs generated by the expedition and exploited by the press, still some of the most exquisite and romantic images ever taken of these exotic places, speak poignantly of the past. They portray long lines of camel caravans silhouetted against the dusky sky, exaggerated by striking shadows rippling across sand dunes, as well as Mongol camel drivers, horsemen, women and children, and conspicuous car convoys before the Gobi's rocky outcrops. Through them all stands the handsome Andrews, ever planning, thinking and brooding before the desert's stunning vistas.

The expeditions cost a great deal—about forty thousand dollars a year. Osborn used every opportunity at his disposal to publicize the enterprise. Money poured in from all corners to help defray the cost of the expeditions that had captured the imagination of the country.

Osborn sent Akeley to Africa for the fulfillment of his other goal. He looked to Akeley to deliver a state-of-the-art exhibition, surpassing even the British Museum, in the form of the African Hall. Osborn felt that the "splendor and conception of the hall" would match the "grandeur which we desire for the American Museum."[1] Museum press releases exploited Akeley and his work in the jungles of Africa just as vigorously as they did Andrews's adventures.

Where Roy Chapman Andrews was an exciting and effective writer and a brilliant speaker, Carl Akeley was more reclusive in his habits, preferring to work long hours in his studio. He too promoted his own work, but it was in intimate surroundings, often in his studio or office over a glass of scotch and a smoke or at a private dinner given in his honor. He hated lecturing and accepted engagements only when he felt compelled to do so by his own beliefs, as he had with his gorilla lecture tour, which publicized the nature and plight of the animals. He also found writing difficult, even though he had produced a few periodical articles. But he was a great, enthusiastic, and convincing raconteur. Osborn urged him to publish his African exploits, which would not only promote him as a personality, but also advertise his greatest dream and bring money and publicity to his African Hall.

Akeley had been approached by Doubleday, Page & Company in 1919, but was dragging his feet about accepting a publishing commitment. He had met Arthur Page socially and impressed him with his various African tales, yet the notion of sitting at a typewriter unsettled him. If Page wanted a book, he would have to find a way to produce it that would cost Akeley little in time and energy.

Page did so via stealth. During a dinner party, as guests enjoyed brandy before the fire, and unknown to Akeley, Page hid a stenographer behind a curtain. He then encouraged Akeley to tell his stories. On cue, Akeley performed with aplomb, swept up by the vivid memories of his African adventures. The hidden scribe recorded every word. Later, Page and Akeley edited the transcripts together, producing a series of articles for *World's Work*. In this odd fashion Akeley became a writer.

Dorothy S. Greene (later Dorothy Ross) had a particularly fine knack for rendering Akeley's stories in print. A Wellesley College graduate, Greene had majored in English composition and literature, and also had experience reporting and writing for the local newspaper. She had been hired as a record librarian by George Sherwood in 1921. She was an enthusiastic scribe for Akeley's stories, bringing to them a finesse and, occasionally, an arch literary quality. Akeley liked what he read and hired her on a full-time basis. He wrote one book, *In Brightest Africa*, which consisted largely of a compilation of articles published in *World's Work* and other publications. He also produced articles for the AMNH's magazine, the *American Museum Journal*, forerunner to *Natural History* magazine.

By the early 1920s, while in his late fifties, Akeley was a national celebrity, a published author, a respected authority in several scholarly and artistic arenas, and deeply involved in his love affair with Mary Jobe. His life was going very well indeed.

★ ★ ★

There had been another element at play in Akeley's pilgrimage in the Virungas—one that cannot be overlooked in terms of his emotional sensitivity on Mikeno. He was in love again. At fifty-seven years of age, Akeley had passed through the volatile, passionate side of romance and settled on a more stable, educated woman than Mickie—the type of adulating and cherishing companion that Mickie had been in her youth, but was no longer. While Mickie served in Nancy, France, Carl's friends Olive and Warren Howe, concerned about the depth of Akeley's sadness, encouraged him to get out and "circulate." During a visit to Chicago in 1918, Carl accepted an invitation to a party hosted by Dr. and Mrs. Teakin. There he met a woman named Mary Leonore Jobe.[2] As he had with Mickie, Akeley found this younger, adoring woman irresistible.

Mary was born in 1878 on a farm in Tappan, Ohio. Only three years younger than Mickie (actually she lied about her age—she was eight years older than she professed to be), she was looked upon as a much younger woman by Akeley's colleagues, who joked about her sexual demands on the older Carl. Jobe was well educated; she received her degree from Scio College in Alliance, Ohio in 1897, did two years of graduate work at Bryn Mawr from 1901 to 1903, and received a masters degree from Columbia University in New York in 1909. She continued working on her doctorate in history and english, and taught school as well, first on the secondary level, then at Temple University in Philadelphia.

By the time that Akeley met Jobe in 1918, she had gained a fine reputation as an explorer in British Columbia. She had made a series of expeditions to British Columbia from 1905 through the winter of 1917/18, studying first the indigenous flora of the region, then ethnology, especially the Athabascan or "Carrier" Indians living along the Skeena and Peace Rivers; and finally mapping previously unexplored areas around the Fraser River.

When Carl and Mary met, Mary had just completed a successful exploratory and mapping expedition in the region around Mt. Robson, the highest peak in the Canadian Rockies. She had made three expeditions to the area with a companion named Donald Phillips, who had been her lover for years. Together they had attempted to climb Mt. Sir Alexander, but had failed. (The peak of the mountain was not successfully reached until 1929.) As a result of Mary Jobe's efforts in the area, the Canadian government named a peak in the Canadian Rockies in her honor—Mt. Jobe.

Donald Phillips, also known as Curlie, was a small, handsome, and charming man. Known throughout the area as a respected trapper and mountaineer, he supported himself by outfitting and guiding trips into the Rockies. Jobe and Phillips collaborated equally and with mutual respect. They saw each other for an extended period of time once a year for several consecutive years.

Mary Jobe was a powerful, independent, and assertive woman who had published extensively and been made a Fellow of the Royal Geographic Society in London, only two years after the society was opened to female enrollment. In 1914, Mary established a girls' camp in Mystic, Connecticut to instill in young women a love of outdoor life and a sense of self-reliance in what was traditionally a masculine venue. She felt strongly that girls' physical, mental, and spiritual development should progress simultaneously. Camp Mystic attracted mainly wealthy young women from enlightened families that wanted to see their daughters succeed in a holistic way. In addition to being introduced to the outdoor life, the girls were addressed by many renowned explorers and celebrities, who extolled the virtues of fitness and the exhilaration of the open sky. One of these explorers was Akeley's close friend, Vilhjalmur Stefansson.

Stefannson introduced Carl and Mary, probably at Teakin's party. This fact should be noted because Mary Jobe publicly contended that she did not meet Carl until after his divorce from Mickie in 1923. It is also important to note that Curlie came to the East Coast in 1919 to ask Mary to marry him. She refused, most likely because of her relationship with Akeley.[3] Theirs was a clandestine affair for years. During the gorilla trip, Akeley wrote to George Sherwood, then director of the AMNH, in his characteristic scribble, and requested that Sherwood pass on information to Jobe. When the letter, which also contained information on the expedition, was transcribed for the museum records, the references to Jobe were deleted in an effort to conceal Akeley's affair.[4] More importantly, when Akeley was in Cape Town on August 21, 1921, en route to the Kivu for gorillas, he had a new will drawn up, designating Mary Jobe as his sole beneficiary. No doubt he remembered too well his serious scrape with death on the 1910 expedition. Mary and Herbert Bradley and Priscilla Hall witnessed the new will. Akeley's motives had less to do with giving Jobe his estate than with disinheriting Mickie. Carl had written the will in longhand, on AMNH stationery, and stated, "This will is made with the full purpose and intent that none of my estate shall be taken or received by my wife, Delia Akeley, who deserted me in July, 1918, after having received as a settlement and provision for the future all the property that I then possessed."[5]

Gossip spread about Akeley's affair with Mary, some of it confusing Mary Jobe with Mary Bradley, which amused Herbert. Mickie, however, was not amused, and Akeley was correct in his assumption that she would "start things" that would prove extremely unpleasant. Mickie had returned home from France and discovered Akeley's love affair with Jobe, which infuriated her and killed any possibility of their reconciliation. While Akeley had sued for divorce first when he returned from the gorilla expedition, charging Mickie with desertion, Mickie now countersued, charging Carl with cruelty and making outrageous and damaging allegations.

Carl's lawyers urged him to make a swift and peaceable settlement, as

Mickie's countersuit would produce "extra papers with red headlines." Mickie and Carl had supposedly reached an amicable and fair agreement before Carl left for Africa. The more public the relationship between Jobe and Akeley became, the more Mickie's humiliation and vindictiveness intensified. By early 1922 the agreement seemed aborted and the mudslinging began. Mickie accused Carl of leaving her to die of blood poisoning (following J. T. Jr.'s bite), of tying her to the bed and turning on the gas, of threatening to kill her with a razor, and of infidelity. He had openly confessed to the last allegation.[6] Even Mickie's close friends and relatives felt these accusations were exaggerated, except for the infidelity, which was at the crux of the pain anyway. The divorce, bitter and excruciating for both of them, was finalized in March of 1923, with the first monthly alimony check paid to Mickie in the amount of $250.

Mary Jobe hated Mickie and did everything in her power to cripple her professionally. After Carl's death, the feud between the two women began in earnest. Jobe had the upper hand, not only because she was "Mrs. Carl Akeley," but also because she had the weight of her position on the AMNH staff behind her. She eliminated every reference to Mickie in her biography of Akeley and in her numerous articles about him, and even made Bill the authority central to the rescue mission on Mt. Kenya.

Even more outrageous was Jobe's visit, with lawyer in tow, to Mickie's publisher, MacMillan & Co., in an attempt to stop publication of *J. T. Jr., The Biography of an African Monkey*, presumably because it would contain accounts of Mickie's life with Akeley. Mickie wrote to the AMNH's president, F. Trubee Davison: "Coming as a member of the Museum staff, she was taken seriously by the Editor who took the matter up with his attorneys. After reading my manuscript the attorneys pronounced her efforts a vicious attempt to libel, and advised the publishers to proceed with the book."[7] Mickie further implored Davison to "rectify this vicious and harmful propaganda," because her own "veracity, in fact [her] living, [was] at stake." Mickie continued: "I have never falsified or exaggerated in my accounts of our experiences in Africa and I cannot afford to have my work challenged now." Then, at the end of 1936, Mickie wanted to write a biography of Carl and was thwarted by Lewis Akeley, who, urged on by Mary Jobe, appealed to the AMNH and the Field Museum to render Mickie no assistance. Lewis wrote that a biography by her would be "the last word . . . in the undesirable, the unbecoming, and the ultimately damnable . . . [because] I can't forgive nor forget the thing she did to Carl."[8]

Mickie stayed remarkably subdued for such a highly charged woman and, with the exception of the letter to Davison, did not retaliate against Jobe's barbs in any way. Mickie maintained that she ignored these incidents because she did not "want to break the fine thing that I had helped to make," referring to Carl's accomplishments, especially the African Hall. However, Mickie was also acutely aware of the fact that Jobe was educated, while she was not. Mickie felt terribly sensitive about this disadvantage, and tried to conceal it throughout her life. She carried with her a small notebook on correct word usage to which she often referred. She was intimidated by Jobe in this respect, and probably felt that she could not compete with her in the public arena of literature.

Both Mickie and Mary maintained the Akeley name, often causing confusion in the press and in the lecture halls. Several articles following Carl's death discussed Jobe's work, but were accompanied by photographs of Mickie.

Mickie recovered from her downward spiral with astonishing strength and vitality. Six weeks after the divorce, the Brooklyn Museum of Arts and Sciences announced that Mickie would lead an expedition, under their auspices, to eastern and central Africa—the first such expedition led by a woman. Her mission was to collect artifacts and big game and to study the daily lives of Africans, especially women. Mickie would travel with only her African staff, a fact that shocked "civilized" New Yorkers. A headline in the *New York World* that summed up the tone of her publicity: "Woman to Forget Marital Woe by Fighting African Jungle Beasts; Mrs. Akeley Going Alone to Land Where She Saved Husband, Now Divorced."

It took Mickie over a year to raise the necessary funds for her expedition. She finally disembarked on August 23, 1924 and was in British East Africa on her way to the Tana River on October 18, 1924, the day Carl married Mary Jobe. Carl took his bride to his friend Warren Howe's estate in Dorest, Vermont, for their honeymoon. The Howe children, who remembered "Aunt Mickie," never warmed up to Akeley's second wife. They continued to love Mickie and followed her adventures with avid interest and pride.

Mickie's expedition was a huge success; she was dispatched to Africa again by the Brooklyn Museum in 1929, this time crossing the continent from east to west, again traveling with only her African companions. Her exploits are recorded in her book *Jungle Portraits*, a wonderful account that not only tells of her adventures, but also reveals much about her personality and character. She wrote numerous articles and two books after these African sojourns.

In a fascinating turn of events, Mary Jobe's honeymoon cottage became Mickie's as well. Following the death of his wife Olive, Warren Howe married Mickie in 1939. Warren was a domineering man, a "tyrant," but he loved Mickie, who took good care of him. He also feared her vicious tongue, which could bring him to his knees. As she had with Akeley before, Mickie could humiliate her husband with well-placed words spoken before strangers. She had once ridiculed Akeley in front of the Howes and other audience members following a public lecture, declaring, "You made a real ass of yourself tonight, Carl."

207

While fights raged between Warren and Mickie due to their volatile, controlling natures, the marriage was a good one—better than either of their respective earlier unions. Howe died in 1951, leaving Mickie a very wealthy woman. Mickie lived the rest of her life in comfort, in a Daytona Beach hotel, until she died at age ninety-five on May 22, 1970, outliving both Akeley and Jobe. According to her step-grandchildren, she continued loving Akeley to the end of her life.

With his domestic problems now settled, Akeley threw the full force of his energy behind saving gorillas and making the African Hall a reality. He was more convinced than ever of the urgency of its creation. Yet the museum still moved towards the hall's realization with exasperating inertia, even though the administration fully appreciated its value. For while the African Hall dominated Akeley's concerns, the museum had other things to consider.

As mentioned previously, the AMNH sent out more expeditions during the 1920s than at any other time in its history. While many of these expeditions were paid for by wealthy benefactors who wanted to travel for the museum, the two largest expeditions—the Central Asiatic and Whitney South Seas Expeditions—were being financed primarily by the museum. Osborn and his administration fully realized that a project as large and appealing as the African Hall would be able to pay for itself by attracting its own benefactors. Consequently, they decided the African Hall had to be funded principally by subscription. If Akeley wanted to see its full realization, it was necessary that he take a more active role in raising money for it. Akeley had used sculpture, publishing, lecturing, and anything else he could envision to further his goal of creating the African Hall. Now, a new source of publicity and income occurred to him—movies.

He was not considering typically dull documentary films, but good, adventurous, popular, and commercial movies. He believed that if the AMNH promoted an educational film series, about seventy-five thousand dollars a year could be netted for the hall. The concept caught the museum's interest.

Akeley's idea found focus through a chance meeting. In 1921 a cinematographer named Martin Johnson was elected to the Explorers Club; Carl served the club as vice-president. The two met at a reception and formed an immediate friendship. Johnson was a young adventurer, twenty years Akeley's junior, whose films had already won some popular acclaim. Akeley actively engaged his young colleague, who openly accepted Akeley's friendship and advice.

Martin Johnson and his wife, Osa, had traveled to Melanesia and returned with some exciting film footage of the islanders. Of special note was a dramatic encounter with the head-hunter, Nagapate, a chieftain in Malekula, New Hebrides.

The release of three new films about their exciting South Seas adventures virtually assured Johnson's election into the Explorers Club in 1921, where he met Akeley. Johnson had also authored *Cannibal-Land*, which was serialized in *Asia*, a magazine that was sponsoring the Central Asiatic Expeditions with the AMNH.

The publisher of *Asia* was negotiating with Martin Johnson to film Roy Chapman Andrews's popular expedition. But Akeley, who saw Johnson as a valuable asset, stepped in. He knew that the kind of movies Johnson could make meant visibility and profits—money that was needed for Akeley's very expensive hall. He convinced Johnson to go to Africa instead of Asia, just as he had convinced TR to abandon his Alaska plans and go to Africa instead to collect elephants for the AMNH. Both were self-serving moves. Negotiations with *Asia* ceased and the Johnsons prepared for an African adventure.

Akeley and George Sherwood (who besides serving as secretary for the AMNH, sat on the board of directors of the Akeley Camera Corp.) then promoted J. B. Shackelford, an Akeley camera specialist, to replace Johnson as the official cameraman for the AMNH expedition to the Gobi Desert. Roy Chapman Andrews expressed only slight disappointment, as he felt that even though Johnson was a great photographer, he would turn the expedition into a mere "motion picture show." Shackelford created movies that were beautifully shot and fascinating.

Akeley saw African films shown commercially as a way not only to raise money for the new hall, but also to popularize Africa. Audiences already familiar with the continent's fauna and charm would be more interested in seeing the museum's African Hall. Akeley had made his own film on the gorilla expedition, using his own camera. The film served him well when he lectured about Africa in general and gorillas in particular, but he did not think it was sensational enough to be a commercial success. While Akeley took some beautiful images, he basically saw film and photography as a means to enhance his scientific information, in the same vein as measurements, sketches, and field notes. He modestly wrote of himself, "I am only an amateur who uses photography as one of my tools."[10] His film material was an accurate record of people and animals going about their daily lives. They portrayed no flimflam or nature-faking. Akeley did not expect his pictures to compete in a theatrical market.

Herbert Bradley, Akeley's companion on the gorilla trip, wanted very much to see their film, entitled *Meandering in Africa*, released commercially. In an unusual agreement with the AMNH, Akeley and Bradley had maintained rights to the film material. As a matter of course, the AMNH usually shared with expedition leaders or backers all rights, commercial and otherwise, to film and photographs made on expeditions under its auspices. This suggests that Akeley and Bradley had considered promoting *Meandering in Africa* in a competitive market even before they went to Africa.

Meanwhile Martin and Osa filmed their first African movie in British

East Africa. They were pleased with the result, and showed the film to Akeley upon their return home. Akeley was impressed with *Trailing African Wild Animals*, recommending that they let the AMNH approve the film's titles in order to obtain an unprecedented endorsement from the museum. It was a clever move on Akeley's part, and a first step toward a mutually cooperative and dependent relationship between himself and the Johnsons.

Both Akeley and his champion, Henry Fairfield Osborn, fixed their signatures to an unusual testimonial:

> We all recognize that from the scientific and educational standpoint a motion picture record is one of the most important that can be made of the life histories of wild animals. The Museum is particularly anxious to encourage the making of such records. To be of value they must be accurate and truthful and presented to the public free from misleading titles, staging, misinterpretation, or any form of faking or sensationalism. As for Martin Johnson himself, he has demonstrated that he has no superior in wild-life cinematography. His work is technically unsurpassed and in composition, lighting and so forth, he is without a peer. He is ingenious and resourceful and blessed with physical strength and unlimited energy. It seems to us all that he has all of the necessary equipment including a partner, Mrs. Johnson, who is everything that a partner in such an undertaking should be. In short, we believe in Martin Johnson.

With this glowing recommendation by a world-class institution, Johnson's film would find a wider audience. He thereby became indebted to the museum, yet nothing was requested of him in return, other than that he continue to bring Africa to the American people. Whether or not he consciously planned it, Akeley had manipulated Johnson into a situation that would help Akeley realize the birth of his greatest dream, and into a relationship that would profit them both. Johnson would be supported by a great institution, and Akeley would gain from a liaison that he believed would bring attention, popular support, and eventually money, to the achievement of his goal.

Johnson's film and other African films finding their way into the popular market generated a surge of excitement and curiosity. One of them, *Hunting Big Game in Africa with Gun and Camera*, produced by H.A. Snow and his son Sidney, did extremely well, enjoying a three-month run at New York's Lyric Theatre. These successes further convinced Herbert Bradley that his and Akeley's gorilla film was still a viable commercial property. Akeley refused to release it, knowing that it would profit his cause more to have genuinely exciting films turning the hearts and minds of America toward Africa, rather than his own unexciting, albeit innovative movie.

Bradley had heard that the Snows had offered Johnson thirty thousand dollars to keep his picture off the market for six months and questioned Akeley about the rumor. Akeley confirmed it, and added that when Johnson had held out for fifty thousand, Snow's people had rescinded the offer.[11] With interest and amusement, Akeley followed the events, realizing that the more popular Africa became in the U.S., the more likely it grew that greater support and funds would arrive for his hall. *Trailing African Wild Animals* proved to be a lucrative venture, and Akeley was more sure than ever that his instincts in choosing Johnson had been correct.

Martin and Osa Johnson, based on their film's success, approached several key capitalists, including George Eastman and Daniel M. Pomeroy, to back them on their next expedition. With the addition of these 'heavy players,' Akeley, the AMNH, and the Johnsons realized a real convergence of vision and energy.

After an unsuccessful initial effort, the Johnsons succeeded in convincing Eastman, of the Eastman Kodak Company, to help back their next film. He pledged ten thousand dollars to the couple and expected a return on his investment. During that same year, 1923, the Johnsons were introduced— probably by Akeley—to Dan Pomeroy, an AMNH trustee and a partner in J.P. Morgan and Company.

President Osborn had convinced Pomeroy to take on the responsibility for raising funds for the African Hall. Akeley worked closely with Pomeroy, and soon a respect and affection developed between them that would sustain Akeley's belief in the realization of the Hall. The joint efforts of the Johnsons, Akeley, and Pomeroy merged into one of the strangest enterprises ever promoted by the American Museum of Natural History. The museum would back not only an expedition to Africa, but a film about the continent as well. It would cost the AMNH a relatively small amount of money for a potentially great return through good publicity, public education about Africa, and money. Everyone was satisfied. The Johnsons got backing for their adventure, Dan Pomeroy got backing for the hall, Akeley got backing both directly from Eastman and indirectly from all the exciting films that the Johnsons would create, and Eastman would ultimately travel to Africa to hunt with movie celebrities and Carl Akeley.

The fund-raising scheme was created at arm's length from the museum, as some of the trustees, fearing the impact on the museum's non-profit status, worried about the AMNH's direct involvement in a commercial enterprise. A group of trustees, led by Daniel Pomeroy, formed the Martin Johnson Expedition Corporation. In theory, the idea was a good, simple one, and should have worked: The net proceeds from three forthcoming, specially commissioned films were to be placed in a fund for the costly Hall of African Mammals.

The Johnsons, with a thirty-seven-thousand-dollar advance given to them by the Johnson Expedition Corporation, left almost immediately after the contracts were signed and the expedition capitalized. They headed for their idyllic home at Lake Paradise in Kenya's Northern Frontier Province (now in Marsabit National Park) with two Ford trucks, one two-ton truck, four Hupmobiles, one Willis Knight automobile, one ox wagon, a train of camels, scores of African porters, an arsenal of firearms, three Akeley cameras plus other movie and still cameras, photo-developing chemicals, and enough food to feed their small army.

The agreement committed the Johnsons to producing the three films within a five-year period. The pictures were to prove "a sincere reputation of the life of Africa in all its phases." The first was to be based on the indigenous people surrounding their home. It was to be called *Songa, the Tale Bearer*. While Johnson did film many of the tribal people in Kenya, he abandoned that project for another, *Wanderings of an Elephant*. He didn't complete this one either; rather, he moved on to yet another film, *African Babies*, which, again, he left unfinished. None of these movies was made and the terms of the contract remained unfulfilled.

Ten years after the fact, Johnson addressed the multiple problems that they encountered during the expedition. Several species, including the coveted elephants, were nearly nocturnal, he noted, making it very hard to film them. The constant rains and humidity-evoking fogs also stifled shooting. Sickness ravaged the party as well. It is easy to imagine such hardships, but difficult to believe they lasted for four years, especially in light of Martin's journal in which he claimed success on a daily basis. Akeley corresponded with Johnson, directing, encouraging, advising, and trouble-shooting for him, but the venture was ultimately a failure. Johnson was a talented filmmaker, whose best work came from hungry times when he and Osa scrambled to make a living. It was the excitement and challenge that kept them in the game. Perhaps the AMNH opportunity was too fat, too easy, too free of risk. The Johnsons grew unfocused, incapable of making a decision about what to film when they had such a plethora of choices.

For whatever reasons, after four years in Africa the Johnsons returned home to their backers in 1928 with less than one full evening's entertainment, much less the promised series of movies. Dan Pomeroy, President Osborn, and George Sherwood, keenly upset, took Johnson to task.[12] Akeley never shared their anger and disappointment.

The Martin Johnson Expedition Corporation decided to salvage the project by augmenting the film material with footage taken by other cinematographers, including Akeley. They purchased the film *Equatorial Africa: Roosevelt's Hunting Grounds*, made by a friend of Akeley's, Alfred J. Klein—the "lion-killer," as he liked to be called. He was a former AMNH preparator who had moved to Africa and become a safari leader for the rich and famous, a movie consultant for studios filming in Africa, and a filmmaker himself.

The corporation purchased the film for thirty thousand dollars, adding this vast sum to the already expensive expedition. *Equatorial Africa* was cut up and edited into the Johnson footage. The Johnsons also added a "talkie" prologue, which further lengthened the film. (They later quibbled with the museum over this prologue, maintaining that it did not belong to the museum.)

The resulting film, *Simba, King of the Beasts: Saga of the African Veldt*, is a loosely knit tale about how the Johnsons went to Africa to make movies. They used the *Songa* footage; they used the *Wandering* footage; they used the *African Babies* footage. Even George Eastman and Daniel Pomeroy are in *Simba*, in scenes filmed when they were all together in the field. Over all is a soundtrack heavily laced with Richard Wagner's *Der Ring des Nibelungen*, as well as ditties popular at the time, like "How Dry I Am." The film also includes faked footage, an outrage given Akeley's blatant hatred for "nature faking" of any kind. The film is often rude in its ethnocentricity and racism. But it is a piece of Americana, caught in a time warp, and has its charming, if "campy" moments, always beautifully shot.

The truly breathtaking climax of *Simba* holds sophisticated audiences enthralled even today. Carl Akeley met Johnson on the plains of Tanganyika in June 1926, during their respective expeditions, to carry out a collaboration promised for so long. This time Akeley had his Akeley camera, and Johnson had his Akeley camera. They were there to film the lion spearing ritual that had eluded Akeley in 1910. This time they would film it together, working in harmony like the brave men they would film.

The lion bolted from the bush, crashing through the Kipsigi *moran* line. The young warriors gave chase, whooping and hollering. It was, as it had been before, a stunning event. Akeley knew the ritual. Though sense memories returned and adrenalin surged through him, there were no surprises for him. When it was all over, a tired Akeley stood on the hot field content in the knowledge that this time he had caught the event on celluloid.

The footage was a triumph for Akeley. And it happened soon after he had been awarded the prestigious John Price Wetherill Medal of the Franklin Institute in Philadelphia, presented for his important contributions to science and technology through the camera he had invented. His successes must have warmed him. They must have made him speculate about future cinematic ventures, with or without Johnson. But Akeley was ill, and this dampened his enthusiasm; in a few months he would be dead.

THE WHITE HUNTER

He loved the great game as if he were their father.
—Anglo-Saxon Chronicle

M OST OF THE EARLY professional hunters in East Africa were farmers and settlers, adept at shooting and bushcraft. They loved the sport and excitement of hunting, and needed to supplement their incomes to pay off their bank notes. Many hunted elephants for the ready cash brought from ivory. Others had enjoyed hunting in India and sought new opportunities to vent their energies. Still others found hunting a suitable substitute for their proficiency in war which used many of the same talents, such as use of weapons and strategy. Having shared their expertise with friends for the sheer joy of it, these men soon turned their avocation to profit by hiring themselves out to paying clients. They took sportsmen into the bush to coach and advise them through the process and ritual of hunting the desired animal.

Carl Akeley was one of the first Americans in East Africa to be thought of as a "white hunter." He joined the ranks of other professional hunters by taking paying clients into the field, even though they were not paying him directly, but rather paying for the realization of his dream. Furthermore, Akeley provides an excellent focal point in a larger, philosophical picture, illuminating the role of the white hunter as a hunter of animals, a saver of animals, and a friend/foe to his African companions/servants. And so, we will digress for a few pages to look at typical white hunters in East Africa who were contemporaries of Akeley, setting his place among them so that we can better understand how he was set apart from them.

The widespread publicity surrounding Roosevelt's 1909 safari stirred the imagination of a vast American public, eager for the excitement and exotica of wild places. In fact, the safari did more to ignite the enormous popularity of shooting trips in East Africa than any other single event. As already noted, the young colony of British East Africa promulgated itself as a hunter's paradise as a way of bringing in needed money. The licenses issued to European and American sportsmen granted generous game allowances, as we saw on Akeley's British East African expedition, almost guaranteeing the sportsman a superb collection of trophies. Newland and Tarlton (Leslie Tarlton was also a great hunter), Akeley's friends and Kenya's first safari outfitters, did a booming business during the heyday of hunting safaris, roughly between 1910 and 1940. BEA was indeed a shooter's Eden until World War II, with an abeyance of activity only during World War I. Who were these white hunters, who provided the link between the sportsmen and the promises of the African bush?

The expression "white hunter," like "explorer," smacks of a time when the world was emptier, less complex, and populated with a mankind more surefooted than today. The term conjures images of mysterious epic heroes— silent, committed, brave, near-tragic men (and, yes, there were a few women), often sacrificing their lives on the altar of science and/or exploration. They were never more alive than when facing down a charging animal, holding steady and overcoming the adversary with the finesse and calm of a bullfighter lightly grazed on a pass. The myth further demands of them a detached but provocative sensuality, irresistible to women. But only their dark, loyal, ubiquitous companions/gun bearers, ever in their shadows, shared the mystery and, therefore, penetrated the wall of understanding between the inner circle of white hunters and those on the outside. White hunters were the stuff of romance and Hollywood movies. And rightly so; after all, they made a good story.

But what of the reality? They, like Akeley, were only men—often afraid, usually courageous, always flawed. We will confine our examination of hunters to East Africa during Akeley's time, even though the trade then had strongholds in South Africa, Somaliland, and Rhodesia as well. According to legend, the expression "white hunter" was coined by Lord Delamere. He needed two hunters to keep enough game in the pot for his porters. One of them was his Somali headman, the other a young European, Alan Black. To distinguish between them, because of the confusion caused by Black's surname, the two men became the "black hunter" and the "white hunter." The term "white hunter" caught on.

Some of the most famous of these early professional hunters in East Africa include Frederick Courteney Selous, R.J. Cunninghame, William Judd, J.A. Hunter, Donald Seth-Smith, Philip Percival, Baron Bror von Blixen, Denys Finch Hatton and the Americans Al Klein and Charles Cottar. Of these, Cunninghame and Percival (the latter of whom served Roosevelt

215

and George Eastman) hunted with Akeley himself, while Hunter and Klein hunted for the Akeley Hall of African Mammals after Akeley's death.

Blixen and Finch Hatton need no introduction to a contemporary audience recently touched by the rediscovery of Isak Dinesen (a.k.a. Karen Blixen), author of *Out of Africa*, who was married to Blixen; and of the equestrian/aviatrix Beryl Markham, author of *West With the Night*. These women commonly shared hunting experiences and love affairs with both Blixen and Finch Hatton, and both give us stirring portraits of the hunters and their modus operandi.

There are several fine books, both recent and out-of-print, that illuminate the personalities of individual white hunters. Among the recent publications are John Heminway's *No Man's Land: The Last of White Africa*; Bartle Bull's *Safari: a Chronicle of Adventure*, and Peter Beard's *End of the Game* to name a few. These profiles are fascinating. Sir Alfred Pease, settler/hunter who hosted Roosevelt during part of his African sojourn, wrote: "We have lived in the best time and seen the wonders of wildlife . . . and belong to a brotherhood the members of which have memories that cannot be matched." It is, indeed, easy for modern readers to believe that these men and women shared mysteries from which we are shut out.

Yet, if we wish to understand white hunters as a class of people, we nonhunters should first try to understand what the excitement was all about. To many, the hunting experience seems an arrogant, absurd adventure—a squandering of life that is at once decadent and uncivilized. To others, it is magic, and fraught with life, not death. Why? Rather than turn to a hunter, let us turn to a philosopher who hunted, José Ortega y Gasset, and his *Meditations on Hunting*. This 1943 classic, only recently translated into English in 1986, is an illuminating treatment of the subject by a far-sighted and astute mind. In his work, Ortega y Gasset posits that man, sadly disengaged from the earth and her living things, can be reunited with nature, both internal and external, through hunting. He can take "a vacation from his human condition" and rejoin his inner "Paleolithic" man, "who was still an animal," albeit in an artificial way.[1] (It is for the reader to decide whether this is an attractive option.)

The hunter must be entirely present in the moment, senses and instincts sharpened, conscious of the most minute detail in the world around him. His life force is heightened, according to Ortega y Gasset as "the hunter's soul leaps out and spreads over the hunting ground like a net." He inhales and exhales with the earth itself, bound by the animal he pursues. Finally, in the last stage of the hunt, a glorious "mystical union" of moving, thinking, and "feeling" the animal in the air evolves as he nears his prey. Then, all the universe is focused in the eyepiece of a rifle, like a pin spot of light and knowledge. All else falls away, breathing becomes even and deep, and "the idea that such a slender life is going to be annulled surprises him for an instant. *Every good hunter is uneasy in the depths of his conscience when faced with the death he is about to inflict on the enchanting animal.* [emphasis Ortega y Gasset's] He does not have the final and firm conviction that his conduct is correct."[2] But he kills, and after the initial "bitter impression"—a "reaction of disgust and terror"—at the spilled blood on the animal whose soul has escaped, the blood "intoxicates, excites and maddens," having an "unequaled orgiastic power."[3] In a way, hunting is anticipating, producing, and manipulating the inevitability of the hunter's own death, through killing.

Good hunters have an unwritten code of ethics and honor. They are accountable to their prey and their own hearts, and are often seen and judged by none but themselves and the countryside. To violate these codes is to violate something sacred. One such code, critical for two reasons, was to *never* leave an animal merely wounded. First, an animal in pain is extremely dangerous and, less apt to walk away from a fight, it often pursues humans (any human, not only the hunter) with intent to kill. And second, a good hunter does not want to cause an animal a slow and painful death. As we have seen, Akeley violated this rule himself, albeit under extraordinary circumstances, when he wounded an elephant and did not pursue it because of his own terror of the animals following the Mt. Kenya smashup. If a paying client wounded an animal, the dirty task of locating and killing it fell to the hunter. Often the wounded beast hid in dense bush or high grass, further complicating a dangerous situation.

White hunters, themselves mostly ethical, modest men, tended to witness the seedier side of the sport: Sportsmen breezing into Africa for a limited time, intent on killing everything their time and license would allow, their rifles never cooling off between shots. And a white hunter constantly feared that, while he could usually survive the game, he would not survive the client's incompetence. When the hunters convened over a campfire and a whiskey, it was the adventures and antics of the clients that dominated conversation. Al Klein complained that one wealthy photographer and sportsman was a "real pig," violating every rule of the bush. J.A. Hunter told a marvelous story about two Americans trying to bag an impala with a record set of horns. After finally locating the impala, they shot the wrong animal and asked Hunter if he would be willing to artifically lengthen the horns by steaming them, so that the sportsmen could still claim the record. Many a trophy cache displayed with pride in a sportsman's den was collected by the paid hunter, not the client.

Some of the hunters' stories were amusing, populated with adulterous players using the safari to indulge their appetites far away from home, hardly looking up to notice the magical world around them. But many stories ended in tragedy, with stupid clients violating not only the rules of the bush, but the instructions of the hunter. Too often the hunter had to step in to save the client from disaster. One of the hunter's codes was that if only one person should return from the bush, it had better be the client. White hunters were gored, mauled, and bitten by wild animals and accidently shot by their own clients. But they wore their scars like badges.

Another important code of ethics for white hunters concerned real conservation versus maudlin sentimentality. In a world more focused on conservation issues we also find swelling ranks of the cute-lovers, those who mistake feeling touched by bambi-faced infant animals for a genuine appreciation of wildlife and concern for its conservation. This attitude results in the person who screams a warning to the prey of a lioness when watching her stalk on safari. The whole event fizzles in confusion, disrupting the natural order of life. Under the guise of tenderness, such "nature lovers" display an arrogance of attitude, believing they alone have the absolute truth.

Though seemingly contradictory, the best hunters were, and are, lovers and passionate advocates of conserving nature—and not simply because of a desire to control their own dwindling resources. They understand and respect the animals they hunt better than nonhunters do. They were, according to elephant scientist and hunter Sylvia Sikes, "sincere hunters whose first love [was] the wilds of Africa and whose greatest hate [was] the destruction of what [was] best in it."[4] Ample evidence exists to prove that when hunting is banned, as it was in Kenya in 1977, and hunters discontinue a type of (admittedly self-interested) vigilant patrol, poachers take over. This debate has been raging for years and will not be indulged here. As early as 1900, conservation of game was an issue in Africa, which is why game licenses were developed in the first place. Even then, hunters were well aware of the necessity for game control and conservation.

Carl Akeley was a highly respected member of "the club." Fred Stephenson, J.T. McCutcheon, Herbert Bradley, and others can easily be viewed as his clients—men who paid a great deal of money to hunt in Africa with him. Many others (including Paul Rainey) wanted to hunt with Akeley, and he refused for personal or professional reasons. Akeley was regarded as a hunter's hunter. Alan Black offered to take him to one of his secret haunts after elephants. Cunninghame offered to serve him at no cost. Where mutual respect existed, the white hunters knew no end to generosity.

For Akeley, when it came to hunting, the term respect was paramount. As we have seen over and over again, and will see most graphically on his last expedition, Akeley's modus operandi when hunting animals depended on the level of respect that they exacted of him. He played by the rules when he accepted an animal's position as only a notch below his own, a near-equal adversary. The Latin expression *"Aquila non capit muscas"*—"the eagle does not hunt flies"—well describes Akeley's hunting ethic. Only the wiley, clever animal, aware that its life was at stake and with opportunity to escape, became a worthy opponent to be stalked and killed. A stupid, uninspired brute became less worthy of the effort expended in killing it. For Akeley, the question that determined his actions as a hunter was not whether life is meaningless or meaningful, but the degree to which it possesses quality. His attitude took anthropomorphism to new heights.

Yet it was the hunter Carl Akeley who also took *conservation* to new heights by initiating the creation of the first national park in Africa. True, he loved the hunt, for all the reasons expounded by Ortega y Gasset. But he made the choice to put down his gun in the wake of his conversion on Mt. Mikeno. There he experienced a closing of the gap between hunter and prey. Akeley no longer perceived the gorilla as merely a worthy, albeit inferior, animal to dominate and kill. For him, the distance between man and primate slipped, creating a near-equal status. Killing, then, became murder. The rules of the game changed. His sentiments shifted. The blood of gorillas held little "orgiastic power" for him, and he came to prefer the camera over the gun. If he saw himself committing an immoral act—murder—then restitution, even subconsciously, was essential. Instead of merely railing about the decimation of gorillas he needed to personally do something about it. He became their savior, their hunter-turned-protector.

One other important aspect of Akeley the white hunter is his relationship to his gun bearer, Bill. In *Out of Africa*, Isak Dinesen wrote: "Sometimes on safari . . . I have met the eyes of my native companions, and have felt that we were at a great distance from one another . . . It made me reflect that perhaps they were, in life itself, within their own element, such as we can never be, like fishes in deep water which for the life of them cannot understand our fear of drowning. This assurance, this art of swimming, they had, I thought, because they had preserved a knowledge that was lost by our first parents; Africa will teach it to you; that God and the Devil are one."[5]

Akeley, Mickie and Mary Jobe all wrote about Bill, Carl's "faithful gun boy." He became a vehicle through which all of them could relate their thoughts and feelings about "native" and white relationships. For Mickie and Mary Jobe, he became an object of their rivalry, as each vied for his devotion and affection. Carl gave him a whole chapter in *In Brightest Africa*, and at one point wrote, "I continually felt the need and frequently an actual longing for Bill . . . [he was] like a faithful dog."[6] The story of Bill illuminates the conflicted feelings that underscored Carl's struggle with racism. Historical veracity demands that the sensitive issue be dealt with honestly, and so I have recorded many racist terms and attitudes he espoused here. They are often abhorrent, always distasteful, and must make the reader alternately uncomfortable and angry. They undeniably reflect our own terrible history of racism. But his comments and reflections are relevant to the Akeley story—to how he saw and experienced the world in which he lived—and so must be examined.

Akeley's attitude towards the native Africans mirrors the racial climate present during the first few decades of East Africa's colonization. Sir Charles

Eliot, appointed Her Majesty's Commissioner of British Africa in 1900, exposited the philosophy about whites in Africa prevalent during the period of Akeley's safaris. Elspeth Huxley quotes him in her book, *White Man's Country*: "We are not destroying any old or interesting system, but simply introducing order into a blank, uninteresting, brutal barbarism." The white man's goal was to create a white man's country out of black Africa. Huxley further illuminates the white colonial line of reasoning: "If civilization were superior to savagery then obviously a civilized race must be superior to a savage one. There could be no question, therefore that the white man was paramount, and must remain so until the native became—if he ever did—the intellectual equal of the European . . . The African, that is to say, must be able to design an engine, not only to run it; to create literature, and not only to read it. Until he could do these things as well as a European . . . the white man must be paramount; though he should temper his paramountcy with justice, consideration and generosity."[7]

Theodore Roosevelt also addressed this issue of justice when he spoke to a gathering of leading citizens in Nairobi in 1909. "In making this a white man's country," he said, "remember that not only the laws of righteousness but your own real and ultimate self-interest demand that the black man be treated with scrupulous justice . . . and helped upward and not pressed downward."[8]

One of the lessons to be learned from TR's words is that the use of benevolence and justice made good sense in terms of enlightened self-interest. Whites were given an invisible list of rules and regulations to follow to "standardize" relationships between whites and blacks.

And what of the black counterpart to the black/white contract? The other side of "boy," the common name for African assistants, was the image of "adult" or "father." The "boy," the "childlike native" was placed in the position of needing a "father." The white man became his provider, benefactor, mentor—the father doling out both discipline and affection. It is interesting that only the Africans who chose to work for the white man became "boys." The warlike, independent, and "arrogant" tribes like the Nandi and the Maasai were considered "savages," but not "boys." Many of the Bantu people, like the Kamba and the Kikuyu, found employment with the whites. While initially resentful of the unwelcomed employer/employee relationship thrust upon them, many Africans quickly saw the advantages of the relationship and found ways to use it effectively.

A whole group of Africans became experts in safari logistics. The men who were best in their fields—headmen, gun bearers, askaris, cooks, etc.— were in demand by the white hunters, who had little time to spend in the field and needed their safaris to move smoothly. These Africans were self-possessed, competent men who played by the white man's rules, becoming "loyal servants" when in reality they were equal, and often superior, colleagues. They acted out their part in the "Bwana/boy" contract, often finding much to gain from the relationship. They became respected and envied members of their own communities. Many were elected village headmen. They were wealthier than the average African by virtue of the pay and gifts given by white hunters. Ever the pragmatists, these Africans used the Bwana/boy relationship as effectively as the white hunter did.

In classic safari literature the white hunter was called "Bwana," which was translated by those same hunters from the Kiswahili as "Master." Actually, the word "Bwana" simply means "Mister," and is an address of respect first used with fellow Africans, and later with white Europeans. This misinterpretation tells a good deal about the way the white hunters saw themselves; they set up the tone of inequality in such relationships.

These observations generally applied to many "Bwana/boy" relationships, and played a specific role in Akeley's relationship with Bill. Theirs was a friendship and Bwana/boy relationship that lasted twenty-one years—Bill was with Carl when he died—and their association remained complicated throughout. As we've seen, Akeley possessed a powerful, willful, hot-tempered, and indefatigable personality. Bill, a Kikuyu from the heart of Kikuyu country near Mt. Kenya, matched him in all these traits.

Gikungu Mbiru, or Bill, as the whites called him, was quite literally a boy when first hired by Mickie in 1905. Mickie writes that he was about nine years old at the time. Carl, on the other hand, writes that Bill was about thirteen when first hired as assistant to Mickie's tent boy, Ali, the same African who served as J.T. Jr.'s valet. Bill had a difficult time with Ali, a Swahili whose father had made a fortune in the slave trade and who treated Bill like his own personal servant. Bill was at the lowest level of the camp staff. Mickie loved Bill, and discussed adopting him early on. But his incompetence and slovenly habits often exasperated her. Nicknamed "Longonza Mukazi"—clean woman—by the staff, she was finicky about her personal hygiene. Bill hated doing laundry, and bribed porters to do it for him. Mickie was often disgusted with Bill, who "possessed no instinct for orderliness."

Bill had a reputation for being a "bad boy" because of his gambling, bickering with fellow Africans, and insubordination. He had words with Mickie on several occasions. Once his sharp retort to one of her orders was overheard by a white companion, who urged her to beat Bill for his arrogance. She responded that "he was just a little savage, a lovable growing child, trying to learn the complex ways of the white man."[9]

Bill and Mickie's relationship had its stormy moments, for Mickie could be both loving and imperious. Once one of Bill's friends wanted to use a cooking pot as a tub. Mickie refused the request, angering Bill, who left camp abruptly. She too left camp, leaving Carl to recuperate from one of his many bouts of illness, as she had to attend to expedition business in Nairobi and Mombasa. When Mickie and Bill met in Nairobi several days later, he, still angry, refused to speak to her. Yet, as her train left the station, he dashed after it calling out his farewells.

When Mickie returned to Africa on her own expeditions after Carl's death, she did not bother to find Bill. By that time, Mary Jobe had taken him as her own. Mickie writes that she wanted to remember him as he was, before he was "ruined" by white men. But she was also hurt by Bill's change of allegiance from her to Mary.

Mary Jobe had a tight, trusting relationship with Bill; he would see her through the very painful events of Akeley's death, and they would forge a true friendship, apparently void of racial distinctions. After Carl's death, Mary sold Bill one of the expedition lorries at very low cost to help him begin a transport business. She also sent him the equivalent of about two dollars monthly, until his death in 1940.[10] Mary never advertised this generous monthly stipend, which was unusual for someone who normally took every opportunity to promote her generosity and accomplishments.

Carl Akeley took Bill from Mickie as his own assistant. He probably did this to stop the constant bickering between Bill and his manager, Ali. Akeley felt that Ali was one of the most efficient tent boys and camp assistants he had ever had in Africa, and he did not want to lose him. Ali was also adept at entertaining his fellow staff members at night around the fire, bringing a sense of conviviality and comradeship to the expedition. The new position worked out very well for both Bill and Akeley. In fact, Akeley came to say that Bill was "the best tent boy, the best gun-boy, the best tracker, and the best headman that it has ever been my lot to know—a man who, I know, would go into practically certain death to serve me." Akeley also wrote that Bill "earned our everlasting gratitude and immunity from punishment"[11] for his courageous actions with Mickie surrounding the smashup on Mt. Kenya.

One of the most illuminating events of their long relationship took place, in fact, when Akeley did punish Bill in spite of the "immunity." They were hunting elephants. Akeley had a bull in his sights but also saw a cow nearby. He showed no indication, however, that he was aware of her presence. Bill assumed that Akeley had not seen the cow and, believing she was about to charge, he shot at the elephant, causing both animals to bolt. An infuriated Akeley wheeled around and slapped Bill "because he had broken one of the rules of the game, which is that a black boy must never shoot without orders unless his master is down and at the mercy of the beast."[12] Bill was humiliated and angry. Akeley writes that he was "heartbroken." Both men fell into a dark mood. Several hours later, Carl, who was clearly upset by his actions, sought Bill out to apologize with as much humility "as the dignity of a white man would permit."[13]

Confused, Akeley juggled the external behavioral rules of accepted black/white relationships and his internal feelings of guilt and sense of justice. He knew he was wrong, and that he had hurt Bill more spiritually than physically. He loved Bill as a friend, and though Akeley was hot-tempered, he would never have hit a white man under the same circumstances. Akeley's temper often got the best of him. He had humiliated Mickie in front of the staff during another elephant incident, but he had not hit her. Instinctively, he had hit Bill, yet he felt genuinely remorseful about it.

Bill wanted to quit after the incident; Akeley convinced him to stay on. Akeley did record the incident in his later writings, a fact that reveals much about his unique feelings for Bill. Embarrassed by his own sense of shame, he distorted his role by casting himself as the sensitive, benevolent disciplinarian. Yet he did write about it, exposing an ugly side of himself that he could have easily omitted. For his part, Bill did not even tell his son about the incident, considering it a private affair between him and Akeley.

Bwana Akeley respected Bill for his abilities and accepted his personality quirks. Bill was a "dandy," sometimes going into the bush with a straw hat and cane, strutting and preening, but at the same time, never losing the track of an elephant in a web of crisscrossing trails. Akeley probably saw something of himself in Bill—marked individualism, for one thing.

Bill's son, Joseph Gikungu Mbiru, was quite impressed by the fact that when Akeley visited their village, he stayed with the family in their homestead rather than at the mission where the whites usually stayed. White men who were too intimate with blacks were accused of "going native." It was a difficult line to walk for men like Akeley, who loved their companions as fellow men, yet bowed to accepted public behavior because, on some level, they believed in it themselves. Akeley felt twisted and often acted inconsistently, vacillating between his respect for the "noble savage" who lived in perfect communion with nature, and arrogant intolerance for him. Bill's son also felt that there was no racial discrimination between the men. He added that Bill lived as a son with Akeley and that there was a great love between them. This may reflect the colonial Bwana/boy relationship, but more likely was based on something deeper. Akeley was about thirty years older than Bill, had no children himself, and watched Bill grow up. He did love Bill as a son. If he had had children of his own, he would have demanded the same level of devotion and loyalty from them.

On the other hand, Bill's loyalty and competence paid off in his own life. As mentioned previously, during his recovery from the mauling, Akeley shot and wounded an elephant. Because of Akeley's relapse, Bill was sent out to locate it, but the animal was never found. Bill conducted his own investigation into the elephant's outcome over a year after the incident. He discovered that the carcass had been found by another Kikuyu who had illegally sold one of the tusks. As a fine, the district officer assessed the Kikuyu several cattle and confiscated the remaining tusk. Bill notified Akeley, who was back in New York, and Akeley ordered the cattle to be given to Bill. The Kikuyu from Bill's village still remember his arriving home with his valuable prizes.

Like Akeley, Bill was hotheaded. On two occasions he pulled knives on fellow Africans and served time in local jails. Bill held an irresistible quality for Akeley, much like Mickie. They were both wild, devoted companions, but ultimately could not be possessed or controlled. Akeley felt attracted to this trait as a moth to the flame. He wrote during one of Bill's sojourns in prison: "I frequently had an actual longing for Bill." When he saw him after his release, he "wanted to hug him."[14]

Akeley loved Bill as a man and a friend, in spite of the racial overtones that leak into his writing about him. But how did he feel about Africans in general? It is interesting to note that in his journals and lectures, he used the expression "niggers" for Africans whom he did not respect. He was obviously sensitive to the racism involved in the word because he rarely used it in print. Carl was not given to recording his reflections about incidents he saw or experienced. His journals are markedly devoid of personal observations. Yet in his first Uganda journal (1910), he wrote several pages about the "natives." The writing is uncharacteristic of Akeley. It is clear that he had been thinking about Africans and felt compelled to organize his thoughts on paper. In articulating them he could better understand them himself. An excerpt from that journal reads:

> We read and hear of the "Belgian atrocities in the Congo." We shudder a little, . . . rave a little, . . . and forget all about it. Forgetting is the wisest thing of all. People, some people tell truthfully about the Congo, others tell lies . . . but fail to label them. The truth tellers and the liars may continue to tell the truth and lies about the Congo till doom's day and still not tell all the truths and all the lies possible. Bob Ingersoll said "An Honest God is the noblest work of man." The poor natives of the Congo have no gods except of their own making—likewise devils I presume. I don't know how they would go to work to create a god but I can imagine a single Congo savage transforming an honest man into a fiend incarnate.
>
> We have ridden 20 miles on bicycles . . . and are sitting in the shade of a lovely tree—beside us are a lot of delicious bananas and papyrus fresh from the nearby shamba brought to us in a great cool plaintain leaf. We have eaten all we possibly could . . . The porters are coming in hot and tired, laying their heavy loads down with groans; some of them smile and greet you respectfully and you say to your companion—What a fool one is to ever become angry with these creatures, only grown-up children, simple gentle Bagandas. Best of all EA natives, many of them, for the missionaries have labored long and successfully with them. And these porters laying their packs down with a groan for the load and a smile for you. All for 5 rupees a month and to find [themselves] our friends. And here comes one you have said harsh words to because he seemed lazy, but it was only because he was the headman's favorite and he had been made cook's favorite and as a result carried no load on the march. But one day he has a stack of empty water buckets. Empty all but the top one and that is filled with half-cooked meat—quite a load for a lazy boy! As he passes you notice feathers sticking out of the top of the pail and go over to see it unpacked . . . When half the

meat is taken from the pail a pair of fowl are uncovered, legs tied to head and neck to neck. One is dead, the other only just alive. Doubtless they made less trouble this way than when carried humanely . . . The muffled squawking of the tortured birds would not trouble the porter in the least during the 2-day march. As he tumbles the poor birds fall out on the ground a crushed mass of misery and unconcernedly he goes on with his unpacking. The Belgian devil begins to rise in you and as the nigger measures his length on the ground you regret that there is a white man's law in the land. When it is all over you are grateful that the nigger is alive and you marvel that you have let him live.

The next day the same nigger does the same thing but it is a different chicken. After the punishment he wouldn't do it to the same chicken. Mild gentle Bagandas—I can't help wondering what atrocities some of the hideous barbarians of the Congo would drive a peace loving [man] to perpetuate where he could not dole out simple justice without the danger of being unjustly punished. [15]

It is considered a mark of civilization and enlightenment to not only treat animals humanely, but befriend them. The patricians of ancient Rome exaggerated their civility by dining with their dogs, while the lower-class Philistines ate them. It is the luxury of a wealthy, comfortable society to treat animals humanely. It was not a high priority for the Africans during Akeley's time. The Africans had a hard life. Sylvia Sikes wrote that theirs was a culture "where human pain, hunger and death [were] patent everyday experiences, [and where] little attempt [was] generally made to ease those experiences in the lives of others who [did] not belong to the immediate family or clan. Thus, since wild animals [were] outside these limits, no consideration would be accorded them in terms of concepts such as the alleviation of 'pain' or 'suffering.' "[16] Why, then, should they worry about the well-being of a chicken? They would repeat their "inhumane" actions the next day because they did not understand what the fuss had been about. The beatings resulted from a deep frustration. It was not color that separated Akeley from the Africans; it was a lack of understanding and a distance of time that separated them. The Italian historian, Alfredo Oriani, trying to make sense of this separation wrote: "To this Africa, everything that had happened in the history of the world is as if it had never taken place; its existence is still in the sun, which burns the blood and dries up any sentiment in the soul; its people, naked like the deserts and with just as arid conscience, represent the cruelest beast of its fauna."[17]

Neither Akeley nor the Africans could understand the modus operandi of the other. The quotation from Dinesen's *Out of Africa* which opens this tangent romanticizes the perceived knowledge of the African. But Akeley, too, attributed to the African some secret understanding that he felt he could never possess. When Akeley reached the edge of the chasm that existed between them, his frustration became physical—he lashed out.

Akeley appeared to be the beau ideal of white hunter mythology during his lifetime. Kermit Roosevelt suggested that even in New York he looked as if he belonged in the jungle, and in the jungle he appeared to be part of his surroundings. Akeley loved the game—the "game" of hunting—"as if he were their father," and he loved his African companions.

He shared those qualities with his hunter colleagues. He shared their passion for Africa, their courage, self-control, decisiveness, and their self-effacement and acquiescence to nature. He also shared their intolerance and arrogance. Where Akeley stood apart from them was in the extreme aspects of both the best and the worst characteristics found in white hunters.

He made serious errors of judgement in the bush, showing a loss of integrity in his dealings with both men and animals. On the other hand, when he decided to actively fight for the preservation of the gorilla, pitting himself against hunters who had previously been his friends, he did so with a passion and vengeance that was stunning. His conservation efforts far outdistanced him from his fellow hunters, even those who joined the ranks of conservationists.

AKELEY'S LAST
AFRICAN ADVENTURE

*Today I am again preparing to enter Africa. The forthcoming expedition
means more to me than any that has gone before, not merely because it
enables me to return to the country I love, but because it is the actual
beginning of Africa Hall—the realization of my fondest dream. I am
always dreaming dreams; many of them have been forgotten. But the dream
of Africa Hall—of a great museum exhibition, artistic in form, permanent
in construction, faithful to the scenery and the wild life of the continent it
portrays—that dream has lived to become the unifying purpose of my work.
Soon I shall be on my way to Africa, this time accompanied by artists and
taxidermists, happy in the knowledge that my years of preparation are ended
and my big work actually begun!*

—CARL AKELEY, quoted by Mary Jobe Akeley in *Carl Akeley's Africa*

B Y 1925 SEVENTY-YEAR-OLD George Eastman, no doubt stimulated by
Martin and Osa Johnson's tales and excitement for Africa, wanted to
visit the continent himself—and he wanted Carl Akeley to be his personal
guide. Dan Pomeroy's mandate to raise money for the American Museum of
Natural History's African Hall could be expedited if Akeley would cooperate.
Osborn had tried the same tactic earlier, as Carl's services had been requested
by other affluent big game hunters. Akeley felt strongly about choosing his
safari companions himself, always balancing the financial rewards with potential problems. He had refused to allow museum benefactors to accompany
him in the past. Pomeroy carefully approached Akeley with the Eastman idea.

Instead of the anticipated resistance, Pomeroy received enthusiasm from Akeley. Akeley's desire to see the African Hall realized blinded him to any possible problems.

George Eastman had revolutionized photography worldwide, making it accessible to amateurs and professionals alike. After inventing the portable hand camera known as Kodak in 1888, Eastman became a multimillionaire as president and general manager of Eastman Kodak Company. He and Akeley had a tenuous personal connection that went back to the late 1890s in Rochester, growing from a mutual interest in photography. By 1909, Eastman was interested in Carl's photographic work in Africa. He and Akeley held each other in respect, if not in affection. Now Dan Pomeroy was suggesting that the two men travel together to Africa. Expedition life at its best could still induce strained relations among its members. The new, strange environment of African life in the field tended to bring out both the best and the worst in people.

Akeley hoped that Eastman would finance the entire project, greedily seizing the opportunity to discuss both the African Hall and the proposed trip with him. Akeley and Pomeroy traveled to Rochester to see Eastman. During their journey, Akeley, so excited by the fantasy that Eastman would finance the hall, alarmed Pomeroy, who warned him "not to kill the goose who laid the golden egg."[1]

Nonetheless, Akeley arrived at Eastman's office larger than life and asked for one million dollars. The unflappable Eastman refused. He did, however, commit to a sum large enough to actually begin work on the hall. The negotiations resulted in a promise to finance two of the four large corner groups and one of the small groups, and to share in the expedition expenses. Akeley was thrilled. Eastman may have also suggested that he would consider giving further support—or Akeley might have hoped that the magic of Africa would help loosen Eastman's purse strings even more. A particular conversation at the meeting would have grave consequences later on when the two men were together in Africa.

Pomeroy also decided to join the expedition himself, pledging additional funds and a commitment to collect greater kudu for the hall. He succeeded in convincing a friend in Philadelphia, Colonel Daniel B. Wentz, to give further financial support. Altogether it was a red-letter day for Akeley. The month was August 1925; Akeley was sixty-one years old. It had been thirteen years since the museum had approved the plans for the African Hall. After over a decade of anticipation, dashed hopes, broken promises, and false starts, Akeley could finally see a real beginning in sight.

The first thing he had to do was to "whip up" a temporary African Hall exhibit so that the museum could promote the new hall in his absence. President Osborn had only recently convinced the City of New York to appropriate the initial funds for the construction of the African Hall. He had also successfully persuaded New York's governor, Alfred E. Smith, and the

New York legislators to give the museum $3.5 million to build a massive entrance hall to the museum on its Central Park side that would be a great monument to Theodore Roosevelt. The new rotunda would join the African Hall, which was also to be named for TR.

The building work would proceed while the expedition was in Africa securing specimens and accessories. The museum wanted the temporary exhibit to hold the promise of the future hall so that visitors would anticipate the completed wing. Osborn had urged Akeley to create such an exhibit before, but Akeley, demoralized and reluctant, had declined. Now his enthusiasm was roused by a real sense of purpose. Akeley assembled his four elephants, his five gorillas, and his bronze masterpiece of the Nandi lion spearing in the corner of the old North American Mammal Hall. He added a full-scale, hastily executed diorama featuring lions. Akeley had mounted the two lions killed by Paul Rainey several years before, and now secured the services of an AMNH artist, A.A. Jansson, to paint the background. He added accessories, randomly obtained, that suggested a habitat in western Kenya. The exhibit was primitive but succeeded in hinting at the potential of Akeley's conceptualization. President Osborn, the trustees, and several hundred guests were invited to the opening of the exhibit. Everything was finally coming together for Carl Akeley.

The next few months were possibly the most fulfilling in Akeley's life. As he prepared for the expedition he had full, undiluted support from the museum: Whatever he wanted seemed forthcoming, including staff members for his African field work. Akeley began assessing the talents and abilities of AMNH colleagues to determine who would accompany him. He had difficult choices to make from a pool of so many competent and eager staff members.

Akeley eventually chose a brilliant team of museum craftsmen and artists. Robert H. Rockwell, a newly hired taxidermist, was chosen as his first assistant. Rockwell was a Ward's "graduate" who had studied Akeley's method of taxidermy and become especially proficient at it. Akeley's principal advice to him was to take along his rifle and to buy some new clothes in London, as he had to "dress up" for safari. He also insisted that Rockwell buy a tuxedo for special occasions. Akeley gave the same advice to his old friend and Field Museum associate, Richard Raddatz, whom he invited as second assistant. On this expedition they would not only accomplish serious work in the field, but enjoy themselves as well. Raddatz's duties were to include taxidermy, preservation and casting of accessories, vehicle maintenance, and general camp handy work.

The most unusual staff additions were professional artists. Before the development of color photography it was impossible to accurately capture a vista or landscape in all its nuance and depth of field, shimmering with the unusual light of Africa—the *genii loci* "spirit of a place." In the same way that Akeley would not accept a generic mounting of an animal and demanded, of himself and others, a specific portrait of the individual, he would not accept a generalized background for any of his dioramas. Part of his African Hall concept was to illustrate locations, from the jungles and forest to the deserts and plains, stretching across the length and width of the continent. The locations had to be carefully chosen and truthfully represented. Akeley felt that the only way this could be successfully accomplished was to take artists with him to paint studies of these locations. He knew that the spirit of the continent was infectious. His artists would understand the magic and mystery of the landscape if they lived and breathed it. That experience would give birth to Africa's realistic representation on canvas. Back at the museum months or even years later, these studies would be invaluable tools with which to render the finished background.

Pleased with Jansson's work on the temporary lion group background, Akeley invited him to accompany the expedition. Jansson knew that Akeley was seeking a highly qualified artist to head the artistic work of the expedition and introduced him to William R. Leigh, who had been his teacher at New York's Art Students' League. Leigh was not Akeley's first choice. He had tried to secure the mural painter Ezra Winter, but they had not been able to reach acceptable financial terms. Akeley then invited Willard L. Metcalf, an American landscape painter, who died shortly before the expedition was to leave. Under pressure to fill the position quickly, Akeley accompanied Leigh to the artist's studio.

Carl was so impressed with Leigh's masterful paintings of the Grand Canyon that he offered him the job on the spot. Leigh had studied mural painting in Germany and was not only a specialist in cycloramas, but was able to capture the intangible quality of light as well. He was an established artist, well-known nationally for his illustrations published in *Scribner's* and *Collier's* magazines. His exquisite depictions of western scenes, Indians, cowboys, and animals won him the nickname "the Sagebush Rembrandt." Leigh's services were expensive: $10,000, as opposed to $3,600 for Jansson. But Akeley wanted him, and Osborn saw the realization of the African Hall as one of the most valuable investments the museum could make. To his scientific staff, he justified the spending of these massive sums by assuring them that the financial rewards would trickle down to their own research and curatorial needs. (During this period and following Akeley's death, taxidermists and preparators were often taking home higher salaries than curators and administrators.)

Mary Jobe would work as well. Her bailiwick was the accounting department, and she would also help drive the vehicles. Mary was excited to be going to Africa with Akeley on what would be the most extensive and important expedition of his career. Yet Carl knew that she brought more than enthusiasm to the adventure, for Jobe had spent a great deal of time in the wilderness and had proven herself brave and able. She had taken Akeley to the

American West for a short trip following their wedding, where he had seen firsthand her competence in negotiating the wilderness. Akeley admired her independence, abilities, and pluck. These characteristics had, no doubt, attracted him initially. Yet he asked her if she would give up her own work and assist him with his. Though he had asked the same of Mickie, Mickie had not had Jobe's sense of independence in her early life with Akeley (in fact, she would find her own power and career only after the divorce). Mary Jobe was old enough to have both a successful career and a business, the girl's camp in Mystic, and so Akeley was asking her for a much larger sacrifice. Ironically, while Mary felt indignant at the suggestion that she repress her own career in deference to his, she ultimately did just that, becoming "Mrs. Carl Akeley" for the rest of her life, living through his accomplishments and leaving her own behind. Akeley had a devouring power over his wives.

In Africa, the expedition would join forces with Martin and Osa Johnson, George Eastman, and Daniel Pomeroy, forming the largest company of people with whom Akeley had entered the field. The organizational aspects of such an expedition proved challenging in themselves. To exacerbate the difficult numbers, only one of Akeley's working staff had been in Africa before and gained a sense of the attendant problems they could encounter. Rockwell had collected in Senegal, West Africa. Martin and Osa were on their own expedition and of little assistance to Akeley. His spirits were high, however, and he was undaunted by the amount of work that fell to him. Akeley and his assistants assembled fifty-two cases of supplies before they ever left New York. Artist supplies, photographic equipment and film stock, preservation chemicals and containers, and food to suit American palates comprised the bulk of the shipment. Most of the camping equipment, medicine, and clothing would be purchased in London, as in the past at Silver and Edgington, experts in outfitting expeditions for the tropics.

Automobiles and lorries were custom-designed and shipped out from Canada. The days of porterage in East Africa were over. Akeley's safari would use vehicles until it reached the mountains of central Africa. This was a first for Akeley. All of his previous expeditions had been foot safaris requiring hundreds of porters. Akeley hoped to accomplish so much more on this journey partly because of the vehicles, as staff and supplies could reach destinations more easily and much more quickly, allowing more time for the work itself.

Carl and Mary set sail on the *Aquitania* on January 30, 1926. Eastman, Pomeroy, Leigh, Jansson, Rockwell, and Raddatz were to follow later. The Akeleys stayed in London only a few days to finish ordering supplies and proceeded to Belgium. Akeley had been invited by King Albert to discuss the specifics of the gorilla sanctuary. He also had to obtain permission for his expedition to enter the new sanctuary to collect accessories, make paintings and photographs, and study the gorillas. It was agreed that while in the

Belgian Congo, Akeley would accompany the king's representative, Jean Marie Derscheid, a zoologist. He would assist Derscheid in his mission to explore and map out the topography of the three Virunga mountains on which Parc National Albert was located. After the meetings, the Akeleys left Brussels for Genoa where they boarded a steamer, the *Glochester Castle*, that took them to Africa.

Akeley had come down with a common cold in London that was exacerbated by a flu epidemic on ship. He never recovered his full resistance and strength. When they landed in Mombasa, Akeley was already in a physically weakened state. His spirits, however, had never been higher. He was in Africa again, this time to fulfill his most important mission. And he felt delighted to be sharing the experience with his wife.

Mary was thrilled to be in Mombasa, and Akeley experienced it with fresh eyes through her ebullience and attention to detail. Her exuberant writing about every aspect of the visit reflected her genuine delight.

Akeley and Mary had much to do before the arrival of the rest of the expedition members. One of their main tasks was to find acceptable housing for the expedition staff members. Besides being large enough to house so many, it also had to be located on property spacious enough to accommodate expedition supplies, equipment, and motor vehicles. And it had to be elegant enough to house George Eastman, his physician and traveling companion Audley Stewart, and Dan Pomeroy, as well. To find such a house on a short-term lease was difficult, and with so much expedition business already on his mind, making these types of arrangements became quite tedious for Akeley.

The Akeleys settled on a house in the Nairobi suburb of Parklands. They would grow very fond of the house, and try to buy it as the expedition base for future African Hall collecting trips. The owner was willing to sell, but at fifteen thousand dollars the non-negotiable price tag was too high. The expedition would use the Parklands house at present, and find other accommodations for the future. Until the house was available for occupancy, the Akeleys stayed at the Norfolk Hotel. It was a time for pleasure as well as business. Akeley renewed old friendships and presented his new wife to Nairobi society.

They were entertained by the Tarltons, various game wardens including A. Blayney Percival, Keith Campbell, Captain A.T.A. Richie, Sir Edward Grigg, governor of Kenya Colony, and Lady MacMillan. Akeley had arranged for Philip Percival, Blayney's brother, to serve as Eastman's white hunter. Percival was one of the best hunters British East Africa had to offer. The Akeleys spent several days at his large ranch, Potha, in Machakos, planning and replanning Eastman's hunting trip.

The logistics and organizational details demanded most of Akeley's energies. He tried to find Bill, knowing that he would provide invaluable help. He also just wanted to see his old friend, but no one knew Bill's whereabouts. Just when Akeley was ready to abandon the search, Bill appeared in grinning splendor on his doorstep in Parklands. They had not seen each other since 1912, as Akeley had not used Bill on his gorilla trip. The fourteen years had transformed Bill into a man and Akeley into an old man. Bill had become a professional safari hand, having worked for many white hunters in the interim. But he still kept his deepest loyalty for Akeley. The two men rejoiced to be reunited again.

Bill's fortuitous arrival at the Parklands house relieved Akeley somewhat of the logistical responsibilities overwhelming him. Bill assisted Mary Jobe in hiring staff for the first leg of the expedition.

During the Nairobi sojourn, there were was a major snag in receiving the supply shipment sent from the United States. The freight was detained in Mombasa until the governor graciously intervened. (In gratitude for his efforts, the governor would receive a habitat study painted by Leigh.) Akeley found some further assistance with the arrival of Raddatz, Jansson, and Leigh. He barely allowed the men to alight in Nairobi before proceeding to the field. He was anxious to get the expedition going, starting out for the Lukenia Hills near the Athi Plains before Eastman, Pomeroy, and Rockwell arrived. Only forty miles from Nairobi, the hills were a convenient location to begin collecting the six groups Akeley hoped to assemble during their year-long expedition. Their proximity to town enabled Akeley's easy return to meet Eastman and his companions.

The klipspringer group was the first to be collected for the hall. These small delicate antelopes have adapted to a rocky habitat, leaping in and out of the craggy granite *kopjes*, or rocky outcrops, with the dexterity and elegance of ballet dancers on toe. They shared the Lukenia Hills with hyraxes and baboons, among other animals. While Akeley wanted to show the animals at home with their families, it was of equal importance to capture a piece of Africa's landscape.

Akeley had been in the hills before and had been struck by the beauty and mystery of their rocky mass breaking ground at the edge of the vast golden plains. The wonder of the Athi Plains was described by C.G. Jung as "the stillness of the eternal beginning, the world as it had always been."[2] Jung, the noted psychologist, had met with Akeley in New York and discussed East Africa, just before the two of them left on their respective expeditions. Jung was going to study the religion, myths, and dreams of the peoples that inhabited Mt. Elgon, where Akeley had visited in 1910. They were both in the Athi Plains within months of one another.

Akeley hoped that the artists could capture something of the magic and pristine beauty of the location for the background of the klipspringer group. Everyone was taken with the loveliness and the clean pure light of Lukenia. Akeley felt exuberant as he set the artists to work painting the vista he had chosen. Initially everyone was happy to be in this camp. Mary Jobe finalized housekeeping logistics in Parklands and joined the staff in the field. She wrote rapturously of the hills and the animals that called them home.

Akeley left camp on schedule for Nairobi, then Mombasa, to meet Eastman, Pomeroy, and Rockwell. In his absence, the remaining staff started getting on each others nerves. Relationships between the men started breaking down. At one point Leigh ordered Raddatz to repair a broken case for him. Though Raddatz's job was general handyman, he resented being thought of as Leigh's lackey, and told Leigh to fix it himself. When Leigh attempted to do so, Raddatz denied him access to the toolbox.[3] This was petty business, but might grow into hostilities that could tear an expedition apart.

Jansson, on the other hand, was nervous and overly sensitive. The African nocturnal sounds of hyenas and lions terrified him. He gave voice to his fears, annoying his companions. Jansson left Africa after a few months, quitting the expedition. It was clear from the ambiance in the first campsite that the expedition members would find it difficult to cooperate as a team able to accomplish the strenuous tasks that lay ahead.

While Akeley left his staff working in the Lukenia Hills, he was negotiating the personalities of his backers, playing host to Eastman and Pomeroy. He had arranged for a special train to bring the party from Mombasa to Nairobi. A ride in the cowcatcher on the train's engine never failed to impress newcomers to Africa. Because it was a private train, they could stop at any time en route to watch the antelope herds mill across the plains. Though Pomeroy, Stewart, and Rockwell enjoyed the fine start to their African adventure, Eastman complained that he did not see enough game from the train.

Martin and Osa Johnson were in Nairobi with Mary Jobe to meet the entourage. Osa was especially brilliant in her dealings with Eastman. Even though she looked and acted "frivolous," Eastman found Osa "just about perfect."[4] He respected the level of competence with which she fished, shot game, managed camp, photographed, and whipped up excellent meals in the bush. Their time spent in the kitchen together seems to have been as satisfying to him as the hunting. His delight in cooking lemon pies resonates throughout Eastman's letters from Africa.

Akeley, however, immediately found him cantankerous and was less able to curb his tongue or take Eastman's criticisms lightly. Eastman complained about things outside of Akeley's control, like the weather or the Nairobi road conditions. Akeley's good humor began to fade. Where Dan Pomeroy was a jovial and helpful companion, Eastman "had no capacity for conviviality, was an extremely hard man to get to know, and always maintained an air of aloofness and reserve," according to Rockwell. He continued, "Eastman was a bachelor, a lonesome man seared by the battle he fought with the world while creating his photographic empire."[5]

Eastman, Stewart, Percival, and the Johnsons went to the Kidong Valley to hunt for personal trophies. Akeley brought Rockwell back to the Lukenia Hills work camp, and Pomeroy followed later for a short visit. Akeley's mood had darkened while he was away. It worsened when he saw that the esprit de corps among his assistants had disintegrated. Leigh complained to Akeley about Raddatz's lack of cooperation. If Akeley had not been in a foul temper he might have handled the problem more diplomatically, but as it was he sent for Raddatz and demanded an explanation for his actions. Before hearing the answer, Akeley told Raddatz that in the future Rockwell would be in charge of camp in his absence. "Raddatz asked what this had to do with him, and Akeley cut him off tersely by saying, 'Everything—up to a kick in the pants.' "6 Raddatz, a long time friend of Akeley, was able to overlook his harsh words. While Akeley felt he had cleared the air, tension on the expedition continued to mount.

Akeley had always overworked himself, but there was a frantic quality to his efforts on the 1926 expedition. He was a notoriously fast driver, but his driving deteriorated even more on this trip. Impatient, he would push the car into impossible situations, miring the vehicle in mud. Trapped, he would have to spend the night in the car awaiting help. He carried cans of beans and sardines in the vehicle to cover such contingencies. At one point Akeley had a road accident, tearing some cartilage from his breastbone and injuring his ribs. Audley Stewart had to strap his chest. Though obviously fatigued, Akeley never mitigated his efforts, rising at four o'clock in the morning and working until late at night. He worked "like a demon" on his photographs. His photographic work was more complicated than in the past, as he was making circuit photographs as well as stereo prints. The two forms enabled him to record more accurately the African landscapes and the people and animals inhabiting them. Akeley spent hours devising new equipment in the field to develop the prints properly. He also worked on a small diorama study for his klipspringer group. The work demanded patience and meticulous attention to detail.

Part of Akeley's growing fatigue and depression was metaphysical. He was witnessing firsthand, more dramatically than ever, the disappearance of the Africa he knew and loved. He was running out of time, both literally and figuratively. Even in Lukenia, the game was dissipated; some species had vanished from the hills entirely. Mary Jobe was a devoted companion to him, deferring to his needs and attempting to keep the atmosphere balanced.

This was not an expedition of young men. Eastman was seventy-one, Leigh fifty-nine, Pomeroy fifty-seven, and Raddatz forty-nine. Akeley turned sixty-two years old on May 19, 1926, in the Lukenia camp. Mary planned a surprise birthday party for him. The staff in camp pulled together to make it a special event. Leigh had gathered a beautiful bouquet of flowers, Jansson had created clever place cards, Raddatz had concocted an exotic drink, and Mary had made a cake. Akeley had high spirits for a change.

At dinner, he told his companions a story about an incident that had taken place many years before. On an earlier expedition, Akeley had shot some guinea hens for dinner, but was so exhausted that he fell asleep on his camp cot without properly disposing of the fowl. During the night a hyena stole the hens, but not without snarling and laughing in his face, awakening him from his stuporous sleep. Hyenas have been known to bite off the faces of sleeping men. Akeley said that he "never felt so startled or helpless in his life."[7] Given his notorious encounters with wild animals, the hyena incident seems second-rate. What is significant about the story is that Akeley gave it voice on this expedition. The tone of incident is like a recurring nightmare that haunts one for years, without ever revealing its meaning or importance. Akeley's inability to cover all the bases was not only showing but wearing him out. He was more frustrated and vulnerable than during any of his previous African trips. He was older and less vital, and already exhausted. The most important expedition of his life was not panning out the way he had envisioned it. He felt weakened.

Both Rockwell and Leigh reported that Akeley asked Eastman for $500,000 while he was in Nairobi. Eastman flatly refused. Akeley felt demoralized and angry, calling Eastman a "tightwad."[8] Eastman may have been difficult and antisocial, but he was no tightwad, ultimately giving away about $65 million to various charities and institutions. But he said no to Akeley, who was feeling terrible financial pressure. Akeley confided to Leigh that he was not sure how he would pay for the expedition. The mystery here is why he thought that Eastman would be forthcoming with funds. Much later, Raddatz implied that Eastman reneged on a promise, which may mean that a verbal agreement for additional funds had been made back at the meeting in Rochester. In any case, Eastman's refusal, on African soil in the midst of an expensive expedition, dashed Akeley's spirits. He grew more nervous and irritable.

After six weeks in the Lukenia Hills, the expedition had the animal and plant specimens and painted habitat studies needed to complete the klipspringer group. On June 1, they returned to Nairobi, where they heard the good news that Eastman had bagged a lion and was in good spirits. Pomeroy's hunting foray had also been successful; he had shot a lesser kudu. Pomeroy was sensitive to the strain evidenced in Akeley. He bought a five-hundred-dollar hunting license for Rockwell, hoping that he could relieve some of the collecting responsibilities that burdened Akeley.

On the way to the semiarid Northern Frontier District, north of Mt. Kenya, Akeley and his party stopped at the *tinga-tinga kubwa*—"big swamp"—near Muranga, at the southwest corner of Mt. Kenya. They were after buffalos. Rockwell and Akeley, both annoyed and tired, killed three animals indiscriminately. None was an appropriate specimen for the hall, as they had darkened and singed feet from a bush fire. Again we see the dichotomy in Akeley's sense of good sportsmanship. He professed always to want only perfect specimens, and was resolved never to "waste" life. Yet there were different rules for different animals and even those rules could be dismissed in a moment of anger. The buffalo carcasses were abandoned. Akeley wanted to move on with the understanding that they would return to the swamp later on. The expedition rushed on northward to the Northern Frontier District. Eastman, Pomeroy, and company had gone to visit the Johnson home at Lake Paradise in what is now Marsabit National Park. The whole expedition would reconvene later in the Northern Frontier.

The area known as the Northern Frontier District is cut through with a muddy river called the Ewaso Ng'iro. One of the most dramatic aspects of the topography is a great table mountain called Ololoke, rock–ribbed and magnificent, glowing purple and gold. It is one of the most beautiful locations in East Africa, vibrating with radiance and light. Enormous acacias and doum palms line the river itself, creating a dense oasis along its banks. The yellows, greys, and purples of the drier region beyond shimmer through the delicate heat haze. It is a location remarkable for its light, a light so palpable that it penetrates one like a spirit. The area is also home to several northern species of animals that exist no where else. Of these, the reticulated giraffe is the most spectacular. Unlike his southern relatives, his spots are a rich red–chocolate, laced with a web of pure white.

The expedition sought to collect a giraffe family and antelopes for an African water hole group. They passed through Archer's Post, a small settlement, and camped about nine miles from the river to complete their assignments. Leigh was touched by the region's quality, likening it to Arizona's Painted Desert. His and Jansson's work was going well, for they were capturing the ephemeral aspects of Africa, just as Akeley had hoped.

Akeley wanted the biggest and finest bull giraffe specimen that they could find. He wanted the animal to be sixteen feet tall. This height requirement created a problem, as they were unable to judge how tall the animals were. Akeley settled on one male that was most impressive, with beautiful markings, and followed him for a couple of days. He did not want to shoot him, however, until he was certain that the giraffe was the perfect specimen. Akeley rigged up a device to determine a giraffe's height. He knew that his own upward reach was eight feet, and with his gun he could touch a spot three feet higher. He attached a piece of cord, weighted on one end, to the gun barrel of his rifle. He could then sling the weighted cord over a branch from which a giraffe had been feeding and be able to determine its height by calculating the combined footage of man, gun and string. By this method, Akeley realized that the bull was precisely the animal he wanted for the hall. He had to shoot him, but after days of searching, he could not find him.

To make his task easier, he waited by a water hole until the giraffe came in to drink. As the water hole was evaporating in the equatorial sun, Akeley decided to replenish its waters. With Raddatz, he hauled several barrels of water to the hole, after they had lined its bottom with a tarpaulin. It was hard labor for Akeley, who was tired and still weak in his chest from the motor accident, but he never let up on himself. The renewed water source attracted a great variety of game, but not the elusive bull giraffe.

Finally, Rockwell and Akeley located the bull and stalked it. Akeley "gave" the shot to Rockwell with a promise of backup. The rifle's report shattered the air, scattering the small herd, sending the giraffes loping off in every direction. Both men emptied their guns in the direction of the bull, who was retreating with the others. They followed him. Just as Akeley was about to deliver the merciful brain shot, the animal fell over dead. Akeley was shocked to realize that not one of his shots had hit the animal. Only one cartridge from Rockwell's small Springfield .30-.30 caliber rifle had found its mark. The realization that he was not shooting well was disturbing to Carl Akeley, the white hunter. He had "given" the shot to Rockwell out of magnanimity, not because he felt that he could not do it himself. His poor aim and total miss alarmed him.

They made numerous photographs of the animal, took the sixty measurements needed for the mounting process, and began to skin the bull. Because of the sun's deleterious effect on the hide, a tarpaulin was rigged as a tent above the carcass. The giraffe was magnificent. As it lay there at its full length, it was easy to understand the fascination it held for the first foreign visitors to East Africa. The Chinese had taken a live giraffe home in 1419, celebrating it as an auspicious symbol and "celestial unicorn." This giraffe, too, was an omen of good fortune, a beautiful beast that would dominate the water hole group. The men skinned the animal, casing the legs as Akeley had done as an experiment with his zebra when he was a young man at Ward's. It took Rockwell, Raddatz, and Akeley three days to shave down the skin from the nearly one ton animal.

It took three more weeks—an inordinately long time—to collect a female and a calf for the giraffe family. Akeley was losing his touch. Putting his pride aside, he was willing to let Rockwell lend a hand. Rockwell had been assigned to collect Grevy zebras and oryxes, which he accomplished quickly. Rockwell was anxious about collecting the animals without Akeley's immediate direction as Akeley was so definite about what he would and would not accept. Nonetheless, Rockwell located and shot a young giraffe about 8½ feet high. Rockwell wrote:

> When the truck brought it into camp I was dismayed to find Carl not at all pleased. Apparently he wanted a tiny calf, perhaps just a day old, but in his preoccupation he had never told me that. There was a tenseness in the air as he looked at me and then the carcass. He kept so quiet I knew he was boiling inside.
> "What's the trouble?" I said heatedly. "You know I'm trying to do my best for the expedition. I misunderstood your orders. I made a mistake—but what can I do about it now?"
> Something more than this seemed to be riling Carl as he retorted, "That calf is much too large, you ought to have known that. But I'll have to accept it." He

glared at the truck again and then at me, finally spitting out, "The trouble with you, Rockwell, is that you're putting your judgement above mine."

The injustice of this hurt me more than a little. My Irish, hot-headed temper was hard to control and liable to explode. Silently I stood there, cutting phrases shaping up in my mind, but as I looked levelly at Carl it came to me that here was a tired, aging man, beset by difficulties, yet furiously intent on carrying out the vision of a lifetime. He and George Eastman had not hit it off as well as had been expected. A coldness had developed between the two men, which tended to make Carl irritable.[9]

The giraffe incident illustrates the growing strain on Akeley. He was unwilling to relinquish any control over any aspect of the expedition or his African Hall. Yet it became more and more clear to him that he was incapable of doing everything himself. His tension permeated the expedition. His inaccurate aim at the bull giraffe had exacerbated his feelings of impotence. Stress and fatigue were making him buckle. He attempted to keep his spirits high and hopeful, but it was becoming more difficult. Everyone began to notice how frayed he was getting.

Eastman, Pomeroy, and company met and stayed with the expedition at this campsite for several days before moving on to the Serengeti Plains in Tanganyika (now Tanzania). Akeley, Mary Jobe, and Raddatz would join them while the artists and preparators remained in the Northern Frontier. When they completed their assignments, they were to return to the great swamp where they were to collect and paint environmental studies. Raddatz would meet them at the swamp, help them move on to the Kidong Valley, and bring Leigh back to Tanganyika. Rockwell and Jansson were to collect and paint as they awaited Akeley. Unlike any previous expedition, there was a lot of coming and going, meeting and missing, among its members. Their trails were like a jumble of tracks traced in the sand, difficult to follow. Keeping the schedule moving smoothly was an arduous task in itself, demanding flexibility of everyone.

Akeley, Mary, and Raddatz arrived in Tanganyika at the end of July. They stayed near Simpson's Camp. Leslie Simpson, a California mining engineer, had established the camp some years before, and it was often used by prestigious visitors and white hunters. Alfred Klein's camp was not far away. At the same time that Eastman's company was at Simpson's, Klein was leading a safari for Ralph Pulitzer. These camps were located in the northern Serengeti, not far from Kenya's border near the Grumeti River. The area is dotted with acacia woodlands. One need not travel far, however, to reach the vast open expanse of the plains. Millions of animals were milling about when Akeley was there in 1926—so many, in fact, that travel by motor was difficult, as the walls of wildebeest barely parted to let vehicles pass.

There were two tasks to be accomplished in the Serengeti. The most important mission was to collect the animals for another one of the African Hall's corner exhibits. The plains group would feature the main plains ungulants at rest or feeding, clumped together in the corner of the Serengeti. Akeley and Leigh had to determine a location that would best illustrate the topography of the Serengeti for the background. The second mission was to collaborate with Martin Johnson on making motion pictures of the lion-spearing ritual that Akeley had unsuccessfully attempted to film so many years before. The footage would be used in the film *Simba*, discussed in an earlier chapter.

Akeley spent the first few days at Simpson's rigging the Akeley camera to his Chevrolet. Johnson did the same with his. With the cameras fixed to the open automobiles they could easily follow the quick action of the lions and the men pursuing them. Mary drove Carl's car while Pat Ayre, Pomeroy's hunter, drove Johnson's. The cinematographers were then free to concentrate solely on making movies. Even George Eastman, with his Cine-Kodak, was pre-pared to capture the exciting man-to-cat challenge on film. The men hired a group of Lumbwa (now called Kipsigi), to perform the lion-spearing ritual for the cameras. From August 2 through 15, with a day or two off for bad weather, they made movies. The day after the Lumbwa returned to their normal pastoral life and duties following the excitement and fanfare of the hunt, Eastman, too left the expedition. He returned to Nairobi and proceeded north to the Tana River to hunt elephants. Pomeroy stayed on.

The Serengeti was the place for lions. Bill introduced the Akeleys to a valley previously undisturbed by white hunters. Lions abounded, and seemed remarkably nonchalant about human invaders. Mary Jobe killed a large male at Akeley's urging. Akeley saw these events as rites of passage. He had pushed Mickie, as well, to kill elephants. The difference was that Mickie took well to the game and became very proficient at it. Mary, too, wanted to please her husband and prove that she was worthy of his respect, but one killing was enough for her. She had mixed feelings about it. She was proud to have bagged the lion, but she did not enjoy the hunt, and refrained from shooting any other animals.

Akeley brought Pomeroy and the Johnsons to see the animals in the lion valley. They decided to make close-up movies of the unusually large prides. Because the lions had no fear of men, the cars would theoretically enable them to get quite close for their pictures. They fitted one of the Overlands with a makeshift cage, for protection in the event one of the lions charged them. Akeley, Johnson, and the camera emerged from an opening at the top of the cage. They approached the animals within twenty-five feet, Martin filming as Akeley guarded him with his elephant gun. The lions were excellent subjects, playing, stretching, preening, and grooming each other. They seemed unconcerned about the humans in the Overland. The film shot was exceptional even by modern standards.

One afternoon in Serengeti, when Akeley was returning from an unsuc-cessful photographic venture, he spotted a group of wild dogs on the horizon. Slightly larger than jackals, the dogs have orange, black, and white splotchy markings. Their most notable physical characteristic is their large rounded ears. Wild dogs, exceedingly clever creatures, are usually unkempt and give off a foul odor. The animals tend to make people squirm with discomfort and disgust. Like hyenas, they eat their prey alive, the dying animal suffering during the several minutes it is held by its nose or muzzle while being disemboweled and ripped apart by the pack. Some scientists now suggest that the victim feels little pain, as shock takes over instantly. Nonetheless, wild dogs are often judged as less "honorable" than other predators because of their hunting methods. Considered the "wolves of Africa," they have been despised and slaughtered.

Today, we understand them better than Carl Akeley did. We respect them for their unique position in the ecosystem. Wild dogs are one of nature's most social, bonded, and cohesive animal groups. Unlike most animals, they take care of their own, feeding not only their young but their old and lame as well. They wait politely for their turn at a carcass, confident that every animal will receive its fair share. One of nature's great rituals is the ceremony performed by wild dogs before a hunt. They gather together in a frenzy, licking each others' mouths and genitals, nuzzling, urinating, defecating, and tail-wagging, making sounds more like insects than canines. Through this ritual they seem to synchronize and peak their excitement, like athletes "psyching each other up" in a pregame locker room. And then they head out in single file, committed, silent, in earnest—an efficient killing machine. In perfect harmony, they orchestrate the cutting from the herd of an animal they have chosen as victim. Away from the security of the group, the animal dashes frantically across the plains, zigzagging in panic with the pack of dogs in pursuit. The dogs rarely fail.

Wild dogs are on the locomotive headed for extinction. There are only ninety to two hundred dogs left in Serengeti, their numbers decimated by distemper, as well as other causes. They are not "charismatic genotypes"— animals thought of as endearing to humans and therefore fought for and supported politically and financially—like gorillas and harp seals, though there are a handful of conservationists fighting for their survival. But they are fantastic creatures. Akeley wanted them for his hall, and they were easy prey for his gun. He directed Mary to drive close to them and shot them from the car. Akeley normally found this custom reprehensible and unsportsmanlike. Again his actions point up the dichotomy in his hunting ethic. "Nine dogs, eight shots, seven minutes," Bill reported rather flippantly. Akeley had actually killed two dogs with the same shot, the bullet passing through the first dog and lodging in the second. After they collected the dog bodies and put them in the back of the car Akeley was worn out. He would never spend another active day in the field. That he performed his last collecting effort without his customary sense of honor and sportsmanship suggested the growing disturbance in his heart and mind.

Akeley showed signs of terrible fatigue as he worked on the dog skins and some wildebeests he collected. Raddatz helped him, and felt alarm when Akeley suddenly went to bed one noon with a high fever. His illness worsened when he left his cot to help Martin Johnson with a trivial task. Raddatz reported that "his fever became very much worse after this, but he was always worrying about his work and it was very hard for him to give in to being sick at all." As if symbolic of Akeley's condition, there was a raging grass and woodlands fire burning close to the camp's northern perimeter. The smokey haze inundated his tent, heating the air and burning the eyes. On September 3, Mary and Dan Pomeroy decided the only thing to do was to take him to Nairobi for medical attention. They put Carl's bed in the lorry and the Akeleys started for Nairobi. It would take them three days to get there over the rough roads that made for excruciating travel conditions. Pomeroy, Leigh, Raddatz, and the rest of the company stayed behind to finish their assignments.

En route to Nairobi, Akeley wanted to stop in the Kidong Valley to see how Rockwell and Jansson were doing. Rockwell found Carl on a cot in the back of the truck. He wrote that he was "shocked beyond word's at Carl's drawn, emaciated appearance . . . his once powerful hands were thin, with the tendons showing plainly." As if it were not obvious, Akeley explained to him that he was ill and on his way to the Nairobi Hospital. He outlined for Rockwell what assignments were to be completed in his absence.

Even though Mary had wired ahead requesting a room for her sick husband, when they arrived at the Nairobi Hospital, there were no accommodations for Carl. She took him on to the Kenya Nursing Home, placing him under the care of Dr. G. W. S. Anderson. While Leigh suggests in his book that Akeley might have had a slight case of typhoid fever, Mary writes that Anderson found no reason to believe that Akeley suffered from pathogenic bacteria. According to her, Dr. Anderson pronounced Akeley's illness as "complete exhaustion from strain and overwork."[10] His illness was also described as "nervous exhaustion," which we interpret today as a nervous breakdown. Certainly, sheer exhaustion played an enormous part in the illness. But a lion's share of Akeley's collapse was caused by stress. It was an exceedingly complicated expedition, as we have seen, made more painful by his lost illusion that Eastman would assume more of the financial burden of the African Hall.

After George Eastman's unsuccessful elephant hunt was completed he returned to Nairobi, not bothering to visit Akeley in the nursing home. He stayed at the Parklands house. In a letter dated September 12, he stated "Audley does not think there is anything serious the matter with him [Akeley]. He worries a good deal about his work and his wife says he does not take any care of himself."[11] Eastman had little patience with human weakness, physical or emotional, including his own. A few years later, when he himself suffered a degenerative spinal disease, he shot himself through the heart, leaving a note which stated simply: "To my friends: My work is done. Why wait? G.E."

Akeley was in the nursing home for three weeks. During that time friends visited him and revived his spirits. Rest and a good diet strengthened his body. He read extensively during this period and Llewelyn Powys's book *Black Laughter*, was one of his favorites. He felt it captured the real essence of life and hunting in Africa at that time. While Akeley's health was improving, according to Dr. Anderson, it was Mary Jobe who pushed Carl to leave the nursing home. Anderson felt that the move was premature, and that Akeley was not yet strong enough. He also sensed Akeley's reluctance and felt that he was bowing to his wife's pressure.[12] Perhaps Mary felt that Carl would get better if he got back "in the saddle," knowing how important the expedition business was to him. More likely, she wanted to subdue the Nairobi gossip about her husband's collapse. Akeley's "nervous breakdown" was even reported in American newspapers.

After Eastman left Africa, Akeley returned to the Parklands house to continue his recuperation in more comfortable surroundings. While he was there, Leigh and Raddatz returned from Tanganyika and Rockwell and Jansson returned from Kidong. They awaited further instructions. After two more weeks of rest, Akeley felt he had lost too much time and decided to reschedule the expedition.

Originally he was to accompany Dan Pomeroy on a Tanganyika hunt for greater kudu. He was looking forward to the time they would spend together in the field, as Akeley cherished Pomeroy's friendship and companionship as much as he did his support. But the hunt would not materialize. Pomeroy would continue without Akeley, the two friends parting in disappointment and sadness. Rockwell was dispatched with Pomeroy and Pat Ayre because Akeley himself wanted to move on quickly to the Congo.

While the Akeleys were in Brussels at the beginning of the expedition, they had arranged to meet with the Belgian zoologist Jean Marie Derscheid in Nairobi. Derscheid arrived at the end of September as plans were being finalized for the Congo leg of the expedition. Derscheid and Akeley conferred on the objectives they wished to accomplish, in addition to those of the AMNH expedition. Theirs would be an expedition within an expedition, which needed plans as finely tuned as the larger effort. Besides making a general survey of the gorilla sanctuary around the volcanoes, the men were to determine appropriate locations for the research laboratories Akeley hoped would be established. Once again Akeley was taking on an enormous amount of work—work in a difficult environment that would try the endurance of a young man in perfect physical condition. By then Akeley looked like an old and feeble man just returning from a serious illness. However, his eyes still gleamed with the youthful spirit that rarely left him. These briefings with Derscheid in Nairobi stimulated Akeley, making him more anxious to move along to the Congo. Derscheid, only twenty-five years old, deferred to Akeley's wishes and advice like a grandson to his elder.

The trip would be the culmination of Akeley's work, a perfect marriage between his physical artistic work, manifested in the gorilla diorama, and his spiritual work to save the gorilla, born of his hunter-turned-conservationist epiphany on Mt. Mikeno. One single expedition would epitomize the greatest achievements of his life. Akeley and his staff would study the primate, collect accessories from his home, and paint his primeval habitat for the finest group in his African Hall. And at the same time, he and Derscheid would further secure the well-being and preservation of the gorilla through expanding data on his sanctuary, the Parc National Albert.

Akeley was also travelling to a place where he had made a kind of peace with himself and his demons. In his fragile mental state, Akeley felt a real need to get to the Virungas, the most beautiful place he had ever seen. He had experienced the "high spot" of his African experiences there, a change of heart and hope. His memories of the environment's hostility did not deter him. It was that almost violent, primordial, sodden, and back-breaking environment that pushed him to his limit. It was not a place for puny hearts. An urgency to push on to the Congo compelled him.

On October 14, 1926, Akeley, Mary, Raddatz, Leigh, Derscheid, and Bill left for the Belgian Congo and the gorilla sanctuary. Akeley had a buoyant heart as they set out across the southern route from Nairobi to Uganda. The brief rains had begun making the roads difficult to traverse. They traveled through the Kidong Valley, past Lake Naivasha and up into the Uasin Gishu, where Akeley had hunted with Theodore Roosevelt. It was also where Mickie had brought him to recover in the healthful sun after the first Uganda expedition for elephants in 1910, when Akeley had gone down with a violent attack of malaria, and they had both gone mad from the gloominess of the dense, wet forests.

The plateau was almost unrecognizable. The game had disappeared, their homeland now covered with vast expanses of Boer wheat farms. They paused at the Uasin Gishu to celebrate the Akeleys' second anniversary. Carl was happy with Mary. It had not been an easy expedition and Mary had been very supportive throughout. She had not had an easy time either. Africa itself and the negotiations between so many people and so many egos had tried her patience and competence. She had managed well, focused especially on Akeley and his needs. Akeley was looking forward to sharing the Kivu and its beauty with his wife. The anniversary party was a celebration and held the promise of all they would accomplish together in the future. Mt. Elgon was a looming mass above them, straddling the Uganda border. Uganda promised better roads and access to the Virungas, their goal.

Once in Uganda, the expedition was halted because of a small-pox epidemic localized in Jinja. No one was permitted to move on to western

Uganda. The Akeleys negotiated with the district commissioner and the medical officer to make an exception in their case, assuring the officials that none of the staff was contaminated and offering to take the necessary vaccinations. Because of Akeley's reputation and the seriousness of his mission, the expedition was allowed to continue.

They continued on the old caravan routes established between Mombasa and the Nile headwaters, now widened and easily accessible. These were the same roads Akeley and Mickie had traveled on bicycle so many years before. Akeley had promised his friend, the sculptor Bessie Potter Vonnoh, that he would make photographs of the indigenous Baganda men and women to be used as studies for bronzes. He hoped that the pieces would be used in the African Hall. Along the way to Kampala, Akeley made many photographs to this end. His mind was full of endless details and self-assigned tasks to be completed. The trip through Uganda must have dredged up memories of fulfilled hopes, broken promises, and endless dreams in his life with Mickie.

At Kampala they received assistance from the provincial commissioner, who advised them on the route to Kabale and the possibility of securing porters there. Kabale was the end of the road. After that they would have to march into the Kivu. The commissioner gave them letters of introduction to make their task easier. He offered to wire the district commissioner at Kabale to alert him to their impending arrival. His gracious offer proved impossible, however, as elephants had walked through the telegraph lines the day before, breaking down communication between the two cities. The expedition would have to arrive unannounced.

The roads were excellent from Kampala to Masaka and Mbarara, and their motor convoy made fine progress. The situation changed dramatically between Mbarara and Kabale. The rains had washed away many road sections and the bridges were often in disrepair. One of the lorries snapped a crosspiece on a bridge, lodging its heavy mass between newer, sturdier pieces of timber. Akeley himself jacked the truck up. It took hours of hard labor in the scorching sun to remove the old broken bridge logs and replace them with new ones. Finally they extricated the lorry from the bridge vise, and were on their way once more. Akeley was not up to such physical exertion, but as Raddatz put it, "He never spared himself but took the rough end of things."[13] There were other problems with the vehicles. The most pronounced involved hiring scores of local Africans to push the lorry and the touring car up a steep hill. It was agonizing work in itself, and then a sudden storm broke over them, drenching everyone to the bone.

A night of relative luxury awaited them in Kabale: a good meal served in the company of the charming and bright assistant district officer, Captain Vaughan Jenkins; a hot fire to dry their cold and rain-soaked clothes; and warm comfortable beds. They spent a few days in Kabale to store their vehicles, organize their supplies, and recruit porters for the final push, on foot, to the Virunga Mountains. The foot safari was old hat to Akeley, but a new experience for his companions. Mary was taken aback by the two hundred "naked savages" that would accompany them.

The first leg of their safari was not made on foot at all, but in dugout canoes over Lake Bunyonyi. The lake was beautiful and pristine, blanketed in places with large fragrant lotus that parted as the canoes silently glided through them en route to the campsite on the other side. They rested in the afternoon to prepare for the next two days' hard march to Behungi—fifteen miles of mostly uphill travel. Back at Kabale, the officers, appraised of Akeley's recent illness, offered him sedan chairs so that he could be carried by the African porters. Carl declined. The expedition traveled with a stretcher in case of emergency.

At Behungi the porters were discharged and new ones taken on for the march to the border of the Belgian Congo. From Behungi, the expedition could see the Virungas rising before them and knew that they were finally near their destination. Everyone marched at his or her own pace during the next days: Raddatz and Akeley in front, Mary, Leigh, and Derscheid straggling behind. Akeley advised his companions that the only way to make it was to "just put your head down and go."

They all suffered terribly from exhaustion, exertion, and heat. Willpower was pushing Akeley onward, but it was not enough. Akeley collapsed on the trail, feeling "strange and dizzy."[14] His companions helped him to the shade of a tree and sent for the stretcher. They traveled another three miles before they found an appropriate place to set up camp. Then it rained nonstop, exacerbating their anxiety over Akeley's health, as well as their own misery.

The next morning, Akeley felt better and insisted on walking into Rutshuru. Until just before their arrival, Rutshuru had been the Kivu administrative headquarters, which had relocated to Bukavu on the southern shores of Lake Kivu. This was a fortunate turn of events, as the headquarters' vacated house was offered to the expedition for rest and recuperation. Akeley was still very weak and needed a break. Four days were spent at Rutshuru amid attendant festivities surrounding the dedication of a new Catholic church. Akeley was invited to speak at the dedication. He addressed his belief that the Virunga gorilla sanctuary was also a great cathedral that brought one closer to God. He was a spiritual man addressing the existence of God throughout his life—seeing God in the goodness, truth, and beauty of the natural world. On his last expedition his spirituality was more pronounced; at least it was given a louder voice through Mary Jobe when she wrote about the expedition in *Carl Akeley's Africa* and in her personal journal. Whether it was simply age, or the renowned wager of Blaise Pascal, Akeley was apparently closest to God in these last months of his life.

At the dedication Akeley saw the White Fathers who had offered him hospitality on his previous expedition. Their greeting was cordial, if not overly friendly. Their misunderstandings about Akeley, derived from Herbert Bradley in 1921, were finally dismissed by Derscheid, who spent time with the Fathers. The priests then invited the expedition for lunch at their mission at Lulenga. But the days of celebration provided little rest for Akeley, who assumed the position of official photographer for the ceremonies and the attendant African tribal celebrations.

The Watusi, Bahutu, and Batwa pygmies were present in the thousands, celebrating the opening of the new church. The swirl of color and movement, the drums and the cacophony of African sounds and music were everywhere, charging the atmosphere with vitality at Africa's heart.

The easy march from Rutshuru to the White Fathers' mission took only a day and a half. The Fathers assisted them in buying provisions for the mountain. Akeley and Raddatz spent their time there fixing the Fathers' disabled motorbike. Again, Akeley refused to rest. Stopping only for lunch at the mission, the expedition left in pouring rain for their next destination four miles away, the village of Burunga (now Kibumba). Akeley had hoped to see the chief of the village, who had assisted him in finding good gorilla guides in 1921, but the chief had been banished from the area because of "crimes and misdemeanors"—he had been killing the mail carriers and stealing the mail. They set up camp near the village. Mary went down with fever. Akeley gave her some quinine, but did not lighten up on the schedule. They broke camp at dawn and moved out for another day of hard marching.

Mary was weakened and fell behind, winning Akeley's sympathy tinged with impatience. He fell back with her and brought up the rear of the column. They were on the lower slopes of Mt. Mikeno. Akeley found the black, mired, slippery trails familiar. It was cold and raining as they made their way slowly up the mountain. Fresh spoor from elephants and buffalos gave evidence of their presence all around, signaling a need for caution. In spite of her fever and the difficult trek, Mary was struck with the beauty of the mountain. They pitched camp on Rweru, one of Mikeno's peaks, near where Akeley had camped before. The site was magnificent when the mist cleared momentarily, revealing the valley that stretched below them, with Lake Kivu, Nyamulagira, and Nyiragongo in full view on the other side. These live volcanoes dominated the nights as their red glow shone like beacons in the western sky. Thick clouds of mist swathed the camp by day. The dense mist made the travelers feel like they were standing on the edge of the earth—one badly placed step and they could fall off the planet, never to be seen again. Moving through the fog was like moving through a dream, in slow motion. Between the elements and illness, the stay in Rweru camp took on a surreal quality.

They remained in this camp for four days, during which time Mary's health improved and Akeley's worsened. Derscheid, anxious to proceed with his own assignment, began exploring the mountain and filming the valley below. Porters were sent ahead to clear a path to Kabara, a meadow on the saddle between Mt. Mikeno and Mt. Karisimbi. "*Kabara*" means "place of rest" in Kinyrwanda, the local language.

On the second morning at Rweru Camp, Akeley awoke with nausea and fever. He felt somewhat better that afternoon, and sat by the fire chatting with his wife. He entertained himself by reading a tribute to O. Henry written by his own publisher and friend, Arthur Page. Raddatz took charge of the porters and had moved most of the equipment and supplies to the Kabara Camp. Derscheid had followed. Muguru, Akeley's old gorilla tracker, arrived at Rweru Camp, offering his services to his old boss. Muguru was alarmed at how much Akeley had changed in five years; he had grown old.

When Akeley woke the fourth morning he felt much better and wanted to move to Kabara later in the day. His spirits were high. He sent for Leigh, advising him to move on immediately. It was of prime importance to Akeley that Leigh find the spot where the "Lone Male of Karisimbi" had fallen in 1921. From that precise location Akeley wanted Leigh to illustrate the panorama for the gorilla diorama background. Akeley promised Leigh that it would be a place "so fantastic and strange that you would not be surprised if you saw gnomes and fairies among the trees." Akeley, though wan and shadowy, wished to accompany him to the spot.

That afternoon Akeley was ready to leave for Kabara. Mary urged him to use the hammock, but the trail was so steep that negotiating the near-vertical slopes in a hammock seemed almost impossible, so he opted to climb at least part of the way. At the ridge's summit, however, his companions forced the issue and Akeley was carried for some distance. He felt cold and wanted to walk the last two miles to Kabara. Although it rained incessantly, his spirits remained excellent. He felt overjoyed to be on Mikeno again. He and Mary startled a group of gorillas, who fled from their dinner of wild celery as the Akeley's passed. Carl was happy to introduce Mary to the unseen primates, in the knowledge that they were safe. He pointed out other faunal and floral treasures to her—a sunbird's nest here, an orchid there—as he reminisced on the way to Kabara. Raddatz and Derscheid were awaiting them. Camp was sited to face the snowy peak of Karisimbi. Behind them, supporting them, rose the peak of Mikeno—"the naked one," "the poor one," the mountain that strips away everything but the most essential, at once vicious and grand. And in that essence, that cleanness, that "place of rest," Akeley was ready to die.

CARL AKELEY DIES

When fulfilled people die
the essential oil of their experience enters
the veins of living space, and adds a glisten
to the atom, to the body of immortal chaos.
> —D.H. LAWRENCE,
> "When The Ripe Fruit Dies"

From the diary of Jean Marie Derscheid:

Monday, 15th—Kabara Camp:
 Mr. Akeley shows no improvement whatever. Violent dysentery; the stomach refuses all nourishment. I had a long conversation with him in his tent, and he explained to me all his ideas regarding the "Parc National Albert."

Tuesday, 16th:
 On my return from an inspection tour to one of the neighboring hills, Mrs. Akeley sent for me. Mr. Akeley, in effect, is growing worse and worse, and I was overwhelmed by the change in his appearance. We try with every means at our disposal to keep him warm and to sustain him. He has had one hemorrhage after another today, and is dreadfully weak and pale. In the last hemorrhage he lost more than a quart of blood. While this was happening he pronounced several words: "I think that I shall not be able to support more than another one . . ." He breathes with great difficulty and groans unceasingly. It is evidently this terrible climate that is killing him; we ourselves, in good health, constantly feel the distressing effect of breathing this thin air, and the heart beats with difficulty after so brusk a change in the pressure of the atmosphere. The humidity with which

the atmosphere is over saturated is so terribly depressing. During the evening he has been delirious several times, and speaks of the Museum, of electrical projects, etc. etc. At his request we have given him several doses of chlorodyne, a drug which he has frequently administered to certain of his African companions in case of dysentery. His pulse is almost imperceptible, but he is reposing more tranquilly. We take turns in watching over him. Outside, the snow-covered Karisimbi glitters in the moonlight.

Wednesday, 17th:

About three o'clock in the morning Mr. Akeley recognized Mr. Raddatz, who came in to refill the little stove, and said to him: "I feel quite all right, and comfortable." However, his heart action continued to grow weaker. Mrs. Akeley gave him four teaspoons of Bovril. I sent a courier to request the Administrator at Kisengi [sic] to have the Ruanda Doctor sent in all possible haste. At eight o'clock I found the pulse practically imperceptible. I asked Mr. Akeley if we might give him a hypodermic injection; he consented and I gave him a dose of caffeine. At about nine o'clock the pulse became strong again, but the respiration remained abrupt, short and noisy. He groaned unceasingly and was entirely unconscious. About eleven o'clock the heart action fell again. I gave him another injection of caffeine, but this time without result. About 11:35 there was no pulse or respiration perceptible. I had the impression that he was dead. I held his hand in both of mine, watching for any sign of life. The mouth was wide open, the muscles stiffened, the eyes open in a fixed stare. As it was quite cold outside (the frost had not yet melted), I had the little tent kept very warm. I made two more injections of caffeine, but in vain. The head and the hands were growing cold, and the complexion was becoming a dull white, but it was not until about four-thirty that Mr. Raddatz and I were able to convince ourselves of the reality. We had to decide which of us would announce the terrible news to Mrs. Akeley. Finally I was charged with this cruel mission. Impossible to describe the state into which it plunged the widow, and the whole camp. I was apprehensive lest the natives, terribly affected, should desert us during the night. I remained near the corpse with the boy Bill and Mr. Raddatz, and we shared the night's watch. I was literally broken with fatigue. I closed the mouth and eyes of the deceased.

Thursday, 18—Kabara:

The pale, cold dawn which descended over camp found us sitting together, overwhelmed by the unforeseen end of this friend of us all. Back in 1912 [sic], he had been crushed by a charging elephant, and had never entirely recovered his strength. His mind, on the other hand, had remained young and enthusiastic, his ideal ever lofty, and, with age, the disproportion between his physical resistance and the task imposed upon him by his conception of a work to be realized and his iron will, became more and more accentuated. In his own words, all of his recent excursions into East Africa were mere child's play compared with the present expedition, fraught with difficulties due to the special nature of the country. Ever since our departure from Kobale [sic], each day we had seen the energy of his body diminish, but not that of his mind, clear and firm. His death was really caused from overexhaustion, from which his body, already tired, was unable to recupe-rate. He saw in the present expedition the coronation of his African work. His strength supported him until he had reached the Virunga volcanoes, which he considered the most splendid part of Africa, this "Parc National Albert," which had been created on his initiative, and in large part, according to his advice. He held out on the steep declivities of the bamboo forest, and in the mud of the marshes, across the thickest of the jungles, until he reached his old camp in the pass separating the two majestic volcanoes, until he had been able, in a long last glance, to recognize the trail, the rocks, the trees which were familiar to him, and there on the very spot, where his eyes embraced avidly, as if to regain possession, the forest, the lofty summits, the cloudy and tragic sky of this fading afternoon; there on this very spot where staggering with fatigue, he refused to sit down until his eyes had drunk in a long draught of light; there is where his mortal remains must repose. His anxious impatience to reach this old camp as quickly as possible, his insistent desire, in spite of all obstacles, to push on from the Rueru [sic] camp and to climb always higher, the energy which his almost strengthless members were still able to find for the final lap, all show the powerful attraction which this locality had for him. He had, at the prime of many difficulties, brought the best painter he was able to find, in order to record on canvas the image of the incomparable site. This was the final point, the goal he was deter-mined to reach, from which he would permit nothing, throughout the course of the whole long route, to hold him back, and this is where we shall leave him to sleep.

I have just been once more to sit beside his bed. His flesh has taken on the colour of purest ivory and all wrinkles have disappeared from his countenance, excessively calm and peaceful. His features, fine and regular, his broad, serene forehead, his fine, soft hands crossed on his breast, all express repose at last. The rings beneath his eyes, now closed, have completely disappeared, and his mouth, slightly open, seems to breathe so much more easily the rarefied air which surrounds us; he seems at last to be entirely accustomed to this terrible climate of the high altitudes and all trace of struggle has disappeared.

I have written to the territorial Administrator at Rutshuru to inform him and to request his instructions with regard to the necessary formalities; also to the T.A. at Kisengi [sic], to tell him not to send the Doctor whom I had requested in my previous letter; also to the Mission at Lulenga. I am sending six carriers and one of the soldiers to requisition ten planks at Burunga, where Mr. Block has a stock of lumber. We are preparing, Mr. Raddatz and myself, the tent where we shall place him until the last moment.

In the afternoon, after having rendered the last respects to our friend, aided by Mr. Raddatz, I dressed him in fresh clothing. We dressed him in the pyjamas which he preferred, his finest silk shirt, his best costume, the belt of elephant leather which he liked so much, several objects of jewelry, etc. We laid him on the bed, covered with a great white cloth, and I placed on a table near him two candles and a bouquet of wild roses gathered on the side of Mikeno.

All this has been very long and most painful, and our nerves are at an end. But we are able to feel that we have done the best we could, and in the most appropriate manner possible, if one takes into account the circumstances. Raddatz is wholly exhausted, which will soon leave me alone to watch over the corpse during the night. At about one-thirty in the morning my carriers returned from Burunga with the planks for the coffin. The poor devils came in one by one, in the obscurity, frozen and starved, having made in one day, there and back, a trip for which we required two days of marching to cover one way. I cannot but be touched by the devotion of these miserable creatures, who have just been marching for more than seven hours in the dark, and in the forest infested with elephants, buffalos and leopards. Our leopard, by the way, has just come down from the neighboring hill, and passes and repasses with his incessant guttural noises, some sixty yards from here. About five o'clock, Bill, Mr. Akeley's favorite servant, came to relieve me, and I went and laid down for awhile in my tent, but was unable to sleep.

Saturday, November 20, 1926—Kabara:

We passed the entire day in preparing for the interment, in cleaning the site, cutting down trees, digging the grave. At the depth of a spade and a half we encountered lava, fortunately in fragments, and were therefore able to dig quite a deep grave. Raddatz was busy making the coffin. In the evening Leigh took the watch with a boy until one o'clock in the morning. The boy then came to wake me up and I watched over the corpse until seven o'clock.

We passed the entire time from the 20th to the 21th [*sic*] in preparing the grave and the coffin of Mr. Akeley, whom we buried on the 21th at five o'clock in a large excavation nine-feet deep, dug, not without difficulty, in the lava of Mikeno; the coffin, made of heavy planks, lined with a strong waterproof cloth, covered over with thin sheet-iron soldered together, and with blankets inside, weighed about 600 pounds, and a thick wall of logs was arranged at the bottom of the grave to protect it from exterior pressure. All this has been sad and very tiring. In addition, I have had to write a mass of letters and notices to the authorities at Rutshuru, Kisengi etc.

The 22nd

Very heavy frost during the night. I spent the morning wandering over the parts of Mikeno which overhang the camp, up to where the forest is composed of giant laurel-trees and junipers. In the evening I completed my map of the pass between Mikeno and Karisimbi. During dinner the boys came to call us—the leopard was sitting in the grass some ten yards from us, but be decamped as soon as we arrived with the rifles.

Today, 23rd:

I am making my preparations to depart. My paper is almost finished. A gorilla has just barked on the hill nearby.[1]

We will never know exactly what killed Carl Akeley. Dysentery, malaria, exhaustion, even typhoid fever have been suggested. There is no way of knowing for sure. It was simply time for him to die.

Everyone at the time spoke in terms such as "unexpected," "shocking," "sudden," "unanticipated." Yet Akeley expressed subtle and overt presentiments to his passing. In 1921, when he said, "I envy that chap his funeral pyre,"[2] about the death of Bradley's gorilla, he gave voice to his desires to "die in the harness," to die in Africa, and, specifically, to die in the Virungas. It was with a real sense of urgency that he needed to return to the volcanoes after he left the Kenya Nursing Home. And he did, in fact, die, five years later to the day, near that very spot where he envied the Lone Male of Karisimbi his funeral pyre.

When Raddatz was preparing the supplies for the expedition, Akeley had insisted that he include a box of small nails. When Raddatz had balked at the extraneous baggage, Akeley had suggested that they might come in handy. The nails were used to build the coffin. There were other subtle intimations, such as a letter to Will Wheeler asking him to come along so that the two old friends could die together in Africa.[3] Another coincidental indication was the fact that Akeley carried a poem given to him by his friend Ernest Harold Baynes, entitled "The Last Race."[4] The last stanza sums up Akeley's attitude about his life, death, and accomplishments: "Death wins! Bravo!—But I laugh in his face as he noses me out at the wire."

Akeley's death on Mt. Mikeno came as a terrible shock to the rest of the expedition. Derscheid's account is important because it is written in the present tense and is the most levelheaded rendition of the events leading up to the death itself. He had nothing to gain from the notations in his diary. The other accounts—and all four white members of the expedition wrote about or gave oral accounts of the death—were presented after the fact. This is significant, because the other versions are often inconsistent with Derscheid's.

The situation was charged emotionally, coloring the way each person interpreted what happened. Mary Jobe and William R. Leigh inflated their roles in the awful events. Their presence is noticably lacking in Derscheid's account. Raddatz, on the other hand, underplayed his efforts in the death and burial of his friend. He had the grisly task of embalming Akeley's body. He used the formalin brought to preserve plant specimens and animal organs. They felt the embalming necessary to buy time so that the grave could be properly constructed. Mary Jobe, who was publicly central to the tragic events at Kabara, implies in her account that she was with Akeley when he died, but the sad fact was that, in spite of the dire physical condition that Akeley was in, no one was with him at the moment of death. We know this from an interview that Richard Raddatz gave Delia Akeley after the expedition. The meeting took place at the suggestion of the director of the Field Museum in the spring of 1927. Raddatz told Mickie that Derscheid "discovered the body two hours after his death."[5]

Yet Mary Jobe writes: "We were with him day and night;" "We used our remedies available to stop the hemorrhages;" "Dr. Dersheid, [sic] a graduate M.D. of Brussels, was with us, and I had his skill and knowledge at com-

253

mand;" and "We were able to embalm him, so that he could stay with us four days." Mary admits that she did not realize how ill he was: "To me he seemed far less ill than in Tanganyika," she wrote, and, "We had no warning."[6] The emotional and physical stress, aggravated by her guilt at not being with Akeley when he died, compelled her to rewrite the events, putting herself in a better light. No one can deny how horrible it was for her. She changed the cotton pads under Akeley's body after his bowels exploded with waste and blood. Her terror alone would have made less courageous women freeze. But in spite of the physical violence that ravaged Akeley's body, Mary wrote that she "had no warning," and Akeley died alone.

Mary's writings about the death are poignant not only because of Akeley's pain, but because her own terrors and insecurities are evident in her rendering. She had, in the past, "beg[ged] admission into Mr. Akeley's tent"[7]—permission that he often refused, preferring to be alone. Mary was a warm, affectionate woman who idolized Carl Akeley, and enjoyed putting her arms around him and holding him. He took for granted her affection and coddling, accepting it, with a cavalier air, only when it suited him. He just as often denied her the closeness she longed for, when he himself needed to be alone. She writes that in Kabara he did not want her to stay with him when he was so ill. Akeley was like a dog in that he suffered stoically and alone as his "insides boiled." He was perhaps embarrassed by his own physical degeneration and mortality, not to mention the humiliating breakdown of control over his bowels. If indeed Akeley did not permit Mary's closeness in his worst hour, this was double agony for her: to witness her husband's suffering and also feel the humiliation of having him turn away her assistance and her love and tenderness.

When reading Mary's journal, one is struck with the almost naive, schoolgirl quality of her regard for her famous husband. One is just as taken with her effort to insinuate her profound importance to Akeley. Over and over again she tells the reader what Akeley said of her influence on and value to him, inflating her own position in the scheme of things. Mary was devastated by Akeley's death; she felt a panic shooting through her that went beyond the awful events. She buried with him her own wedding ring, engraved "Mary and Carl, October 28, 1924," and the wool blanket they had shared during their nights together. A space was left at Akeley's right hand where Mary wanted her ashes to be buried after her own death. It was not to be. Mary, who died in 1968, was buried in Ohio. Along with her ring, she seemed to have buried something of herself with Akeley—a resilience and determination to regroup her own powers for personal fulfillment. Mary and Carl were only married for two years. Mary lived another forty years after Akeley died. She lived through his name and his accomplishments, never realizing the potential promised in her youth.

Mary detested William Leigh, and accused him of being no help at all in her great hour of need. She felt he was a self-serving publicity monger.[8] Mary wrote to the museum that Leigh had not seen Carl for the several days before his death, and further, that he had not even bothered to pay greetings at Carl's tent, much less to offer assistance. Leigh did not even attend the funeral service, choosing rather to trek up Karisimbi and pitch his painting camp. Mary wrote that she "was devotely glad that he did not come, because I do not think I would have had the strength to go through the service in the face and knowledge of his irreligious, sacriligious [sic] cynicism—His feelings about God, about the things which Carl and I have always considered best and finest in human relationship are so diametrically opposed to that of right thinking people that I find it impossible to tolerate his expressed thoughts."[9] Yet Leigh, too, wrote intimately of the events that moved their lives at Kabara. He boasted about sensing a terrible foreboding concerning Akeley's end, placing himself in the position of expedition savior: "I felt . . . the whole [success] of this costly expedition hinged upon myself and my studies and sketches."[10]

Mary was cross with Derscheid as well. She felt he was thoughtless and inconsiderate of her, "leaving [her] alone with just Nature."[11] Derscheid himself was grief-stricken, and, like Mary, spent a good deal of the time in tears, bereft at Akeley's passing. These inconsistencies reveal the hysterical and emotional ambiance of the camp. The image, as Derscheid recounts it, of the white members huddled together outside the tent with the ghoulish, open-mouthed, open-eyed corpse of Akeley lying on his cot, is poignant. They thought—indeed, hoped—that he was merely in a stupor; they were incapable of accepting the truth that Akeley had died.

And what of the black members of the expedition? Bill was devastated, and went into a period of mourning that lasted a couple of years, according to his son. Muguru, according to his wives, became physically ill with grief. The survivors of both Bill and Muguru spoke of the men as having lost their "father." One of Muguru's wives gave birth to a son the day Akeley was buried while her husband attended the funeral. That son to this day speaks of Akeley's importance to his father. The white members feared that the black staff would desert them on the mountain. Many of the porters grew ill in the freezing rain with little cover and dwindling provisions. But the Africans were loyal and everyone managed as best as the dire circumstances would allow. Palpable fear and misery descended on Kabara.

The expedition was on the verge of being aborted. Mary Jobe seized control of the situation and decided to complete the work of the expedition, assuming the role of leader. Leigh suggests that this was requested of her by Dan Pomeroy. She, more than anyone else, was acutely aware of Carl's finite and ultimate goals. She wrote to the museum seeking permission to carry on and was encouraged to do so. The strain on Mary was extreme. She had just lost her husband and was reeling from grief, and she had taken on an almost impossible task. Even Carl with his years of experience had difficulty negotiating the personalities and logistics of the expedition. It was a brave undertaking on Mary's part.

They stayed in Kabara for several weeks. Leigh had to complete the paintings of the gorilla habitat. With Muguru's assistance they had found the spot Akeley had wanted for the background. Ironically, they located it the day Akeley died, so he was denied the knowledge that his dream could be accomplished. The habitat studies and the finished painting in the museum are magnificent. Akeley felt that Leigh was "the best investment of the expedition,"[12] and Leigh proved to be the artist that Akeley had dreamed of. A copy of the gorilla habitat study was given to King Albert of Belgium. They finished the arduous task of collecting plant accessories—over fifty varieties—in the sodden volcanoes. The sun shone only seven times in as many weeks. The night temperature hovered just above thirty-two degrees, with daytime equivalents of forty to forty-five degrees. In addition to plaster casts and formalin specimens, they collected quantities of moss and lichen, dirt, twigs, berries, flowers, part of an old fallen tree, and an entire gorilla nest. Mary recorded every detail photographically, using the stereo and circuit cameras that Akeley had labored over earlier. Nothing would be left to memory when the gorilla diorama was constructed back at the museum. They collected everything they needed to perfectly duplicate every element of the gorilla diorama. If one exhibit would be the ultimate representation of Akeley's dream, it would be the diorama that meant the most to him.

In this sad and trying period, all devoted themselves without reserve to their individual tasks. Mary leaned heavily on Richard Raddatz for support and help. The stamina she manifested under such physical and emotional stress was astounding. Her years of the rigors and hardships of trekking and exploring in the Canadian Rockies sustained her, along with the focused will to realize Akeley's dream. Derscheid and Bill left Kabara for days and weeks at a time to explore the surrounding mountains.

They all left Kabara on December 19. Mary was resolved to return the next year with a copper coffin in which to rebury her husband. In fact, it would be twenty years before she would return to the meadow. Akeley was buried where he wanted to be buried in what was believed to be an impenetrable grave. Mary and the others left Kabara and Akeley "with the homage of our broken hearts and with the outpouring of our tears,"[13] and began the long climb down the mountain and their journey home.

The shock of Akeley's death reverberated beyond Kabara. Wires were sent from Gisenyi to Nairobi and relayed on to the United States. Akeley's death made front page news in the *East African Standard* on December 1, 1926. When Henry Fairfield Osborn received word, he wept, then called a press conference to announce the tragic news. Newspapers across the country ran features on Akeley's life and work. These articles were summarized in the *Atlanta Journal* on December 26, 1926; the *Lexington* (Kentucky) *Leader* recognized him as "a man of great versatility an artist, a scientist, an explorer, whose work in taxidermy stands out as unique of its kind." The *Sacramento* (California) *Union* wrote that his death "brings profound grief to the scientific world in general and the naturalists and geographers in particular." The *Springfield Illinois State Journal* stated that "such men as Akeley are rare in the world. They serve the essential purpose of education. They are the bearers of light and diggers of treasure, by all of which man learns to direct his ways. His spirit of adventure is in all of us, but few persons have the courage and initiative to launch forth the expedition into the unknown." One paper, the *Little Rock Arkansas Democrat*, wrote that without men like Akeley there would be no America. He was likened in importance to Stanley and Livingstone: His exploration, the newspaper said, had allowed millions to understand the world around them, and therefore to be "better fitted to live their own lives."

The *San Francisco Call-Post* wrote that Akeley "made amends to the well-behaved gorillas" that had been misrepresented by Paul Du Chaillu. The *New York World* addressed his art, seeing in it "a sense of the beauty and grandeur of African forests, of the poetry in a crouched lion and magnificence of a stampeding herd of elephant; a scientific knowledge of habitat and of instinct; an unusual ability in sculpture. We have plenty of naturalists and hunters who describe wild life appreciatively; we have always had museum workers who could stuff skins into recognizable imitation of the live animal; but until Carl Akeley we have never had a combination of artist, museum expert and hunter who could bring home visually to the ordinary man the irresistible power of a charging rhinoceros, the beauty of a leaping antelope and the exotic charm of an African river with animals drinking and wildfowl bathing." Each newspaper, in turn, spoke to its readers in terms of the Akeley achievement that best touched their own lives or interests, be it education, exploration, patriotism, or art. With a field of experience as broad as Akeley's, this was a relatively easy task. But even his eulogies fragmented his vast accomplishments. No paper touched the whole story, the story of an uncompromised vision harnessing all the powers, energies, and talents of a single life—a life that burned hot and bright for decades and blew out quietly on a freezing mountain in the middle of Africa.

CARL AKELEY'S
LEGACY—TODAY: 1990

He lives, he wakes—tis Death is dead, not he. . . .
He is made one with Nature: there is heard
His voice in all her music, from the moan
Of thunder to the song of night's sweet bird. . . .
He is a portion of the loveliness
Which once he made more lovely.
      —Percy Bysshe Shelley, "Adonais"

SOON AFTER AKELEY'S DEATH there was a memorial service for him at the American Museum of Natural History. It was an emotional meeting of friends and colleagues; a select few were invited to share their thoughts about Akeley's vast accomplishments. Representatives of diverse fields described him variously as "taxidermist," "conservationist," "sculptor," and "inventor," again fragmenting his achievements. These tributes were published in *Natural History* magazine (Vol. 27, No. 2, 1927), and attest to the impact he had on life around him. George Sherwood spoke of "Akeley, the Man," as if somehow the man was separate from his work. But Sherwood, an affectionate man himself, loved Akeley personally, and imbued his comments with an emotion and poignancy rarely evident in other writings about Akeley. He felt that Akeley's greatest legacy, his "invisible monument," was "the gratitude in the hearts of a host of friends who have thus profited by their contact with him." Sherwood quoted a mutual friend of his and Akeley's: "Whatever there is in me of decency and worth-whileness I owe to Akeley more than to any other man in the world."

Akeley's life and death informed the lives of the living in a dramatic and even inspirational way. His friends and colleagues had the memories of his whimsical and mischievous humor, and of contact with his penetrating eyes—sometimes kind, sometimes hard, always intense. They all mentioned his eyes. They remembered him as youthful, even giddy and goofy, when his life was going well. These memories, recalled and discussed by those personally touched by him, are fascinating to those of us who have no direct knowledge of Akeley. Such memories of Akeley must inevitably die along with those who knew him, and, in 1990, they have almost all gone. His "invisible monument" has evaporated with time.

So what do we have left of Carl Akeley? Why and how does he touch our lives today, and why should we care about him and what he did so long ago? His most famous monument is, of course, his African Hall, which he signified as the "unifying purpose of his work." The hall finally opened on what would have been his 72nd birthday, ten years after his death. It is almost exactly as he envisioned it in 1910, though smaller, with only twenty-eight dioramas instead of his proposed forty. A spectacular and compelling place, the hall is a series of discrete, bright little worlds pulling us in from the darkness and holding our rapt attention. In its regional windows, the hall celebrates Akeley's vision, techniques, artistry, and passion for Africa. Akeley would have loved it.

While it no doubt still possesses style and elegance, we should consider whether, in 1990, the hall remains valid or relevant; after all, it is a time capsule from the 1920s and 1930s. We are instantly reminded of this by the bronze bas-relief panels above the dioramas, executed in perfect art deco style, beautifully designed by John W. Hope. And what of the dioramas themselves? Studies in ethology have intensified; scientists spend years and even decades in the field, concentrating on various species and illuminating their most subtle behaviors. In light of these studies, can the scientific information in the African Hall still be correct? And what about museum exhibition itself? Can the hall still find an important niche in contemporary museology? Akeley wanted to create a timeless exhibit, one that would touch and teach visitors about the wonders of Africa, which he felt were draining away. Is the hall an out-of-date "white elephant" or a treasure?

In the 1920s, one of the museum's anthropologists warned the administration that with the installation of the large animal habitats—those proposed by Akeley—the museum was backing itself into a corner. The famed anthropologist Franz Boas wrote that the exhibits "armored the Museum, like a dinosaur, against change . . . the exposition of one particular aspect of science . . . made it almost impossible for [the museum] to respond to changing scientific interests." Today, the international museum world is taking a hard look at itself to reevaluate its mission and its modus operandi.

The concepts of museum exhibition have changed to accommodate the tastes of people reared in an electronically stimulated society. In general, it is difficult, at best, for museums to keep pace with quicksilver scientific developments. When a museum is "armored like a dinosaur" like the AMNH, the task becomes that much more difficult. On the one hand, the African Hall habitat groups take up a lot of valuable New York real estate; on the other, we have to question whether they can still speak to a generation wired with Walkmans on the head and Gameboys in the pocket. Why not replace the African Hall, or "juice it up" as an exhibit that will blitz the senses—that will engage us by talking to us or inviting us to push, pull, or flip a knob or button that will make something miraculous take place? Perhaps we could animate the central herd of elephant with robotic microchips, like those enormous plastic dinosaurs touring the country. Then they could move and trumpet and scream—as in a carnival's fun house.

I wanted to reach beyond my own emotional connection to the hall to determine whether Akeley's dream was still viable. To this end I sat on the long wooden benches surrounding the elephant herd and tried to let the hall touch me as if it were the first time instead of the hundredth. In its central herd of elephant, we find not only an extraordinary piece of animal sculpture, but a magnificent monument to the species as well. Akeley's obsessive search for the "perfect bull" paid off. The animals are on a pedestal, literally and figuratively. Akeley held the elephant in highest regard—even above the gorilla—for its power and intelligence. Let us just look at the significance of the herd for a minute, vis-à-vis Akeley's legacy.

There was a good deal of talk about elephants in 1989, most of it in an attempt to raise the consciousness of the world to the plight of the species because of the recent drastic and horrifying decimation of the elephant population. The debate centered on whether or not the animals should be reclassified to "Appendix I" status by CITES (Convention on Trade in Endangered Species), a move that would ban the ivory trade worldwide. The issue was emotionally charged for almost anyone entering into discussion about it. The very name "ivory poacher," which would have elicited a shrug or a vacant look a decade ago, suddenly made many people wild with indignation and contempt. There were shocking full-page ads in the *New York Times* showing buckled and decaying elephant carcasses with their faces hacked away. There were stories in national news magazines about the immoral trail of elephant blood staining the earth, from Africa to the Orient to the affluent western countries. And for what? A pretty bracelet or music box—a symbol of our unconscionable greed and vanity, and of our refusal to face our destruction of the world in which we live. The elephant became a standard-bearer for us: lose the elephant and we would lose our universal soul, which many felt was as endangered as the animal itself. The media campaign climaxed with the CITES convention in October 1989, which decided that, indeed, the elephant should be reclassified to Appendix I, the highest conservation category. The complicated issue is hardly resolved, but a battle has been won.

So, we look at Carl Akeley's elephant herd, called "*The Alarm*," as it dominates his hall. Yes, they were collected, but we must remember that they were collected during a time when hundreds of thousands of elephants still ranged over most of Africa. While they are today a sad reminder of our obscene offenses towards the earth's resources, they also hold the hope of our future. The elephants seem poised to stampede out of the museum and into Central Park, and we cannot help but be struck by the grandeur and power of the species as the herd is singly one of the greatest monuments to a vanishing Africa—indeed, a vanishing nature—and it may disturb us to look at it. Our response is bound to be emotional, as we stand in awe of the herd and grow more determined to prevent the destruction of the earth's legacy. We celebrate the fact that this mounted herd exists not only for the charisma of the animals themselves, but also so that we can bring our children to see it, and show them what they—and their children—would be missing if we allowed the species to slip into extinction.

Likewise, in the gorilla diorama, we again find an elegant, truthful exhibit. This one depicts familial warmth and peace among gorillas—another group of extremely endangered animals that has touched us emotionally and intellectually. Yes, Carl Akeley killed these animals—three of them, at least—but if he had not done so, the species would most likely not even exist today. That is a rather staggering thought and imbued with irony, but it is true. The hunter turned into the conservationist in the location represented in this diorama. Akeley's metanoia on the mountain is crystallized in this little world, and reminds us of the human capacity for change and conversion. It reminds us that we can have hope for the future in the midst of the often dark and foreboding messages that surround us. Adding further irony to the diorama is the fact that it also recreates the site of Akeley's death—so the hall becomes an even more personal monument to the man.

When I was meditating on the elephant herd and the gorilla diorama, I began to realize that the entire African Hall tells the same tale. It is a treasure extending far beyond the personal legacy of Carl Akeley. The American Museum of Natural History is curator of this great hall, accepting the responsibility for its continued existence. The museum is in a peculiar position, not unlike that of the African countries that must curate or husband the live animal species represented in the hall. The outside world brings pressure on these countries to save the animals they host. These demands are inordinately expensive for the individual governments involved. Most of the game exists in underdeveloped countries, precisely because they are underdeveloped countries. Game disappears through the very process of development. So it is an accident of nature that these African countries possess a universal treasure, which they must maintain for the world at large—a world growing more conscious of its dwindling natural resources.

The museum fully realizes the great treasure it has in its African Hall. It need not be pressured by the outside world to save it. On the other hand, one could imagine the old-fashioned hall—like African game—disappearing through contemporary development. It occurred to me to discover what the outside world thought of the hall. To this end I requested statements from three experts whose areas of proficiency are represented in the hall: an Africanist/conservationist, a scientist/conservationist, and an art critic. I requested that these statements be written from an intellectual and emotional perspective.

The first person to whom I turned was John Heminway, Chairman of the Board of the African Wildlife Foundation, author, longtime television producer and currently producer and host of the series "Travels" on PBS. Heminway is a passionate Africanist and conservationist, who wrote eloquently about the African Hall's "truth":

> A decade before I ever set foot in Africa I fell under the spell of that continent at the American Museum of Natural History. For me, age six, the African Hall was all I expected of that formidable land. The sepulchral pall on entering, distant footfalls behind the crashing herd of elephants, illuminated kaleidoscopes of danger and resurrection—that must be Africa.
>
> And I never grew tired of it, even when I was a teenager and I had learned that, perhaps, there was more to Africa than a Serengeti waterhole or a pride of lions.
>
> What is so remarkable about Carl Akeley's contribution is that it never fails *anyone*. Here I am today, with three-quarters of my life spent pondering Africa, and my heart still races with his gorillas. I have been on those very volcanoes on the Uganda/Rwanda/Zaire frontier, been threatened by the rank mustard smell of their primacy, but whenever I stroll through the marble foyer of the Roosevelt Rotunda and encounter Carl Akeley's vision, I draw back involuntarily.
>
> So too today's kids—I've watched these veterans of Big Bird and Ninja Turtles stand transfixed by the elephants and the ostriches and the cheetahs. Perhaps like this long-ago six year old the Museum will launch them into the outer space of reality.
>
> It's clear to me that in the 1920s Carl Akeley was well ahead of his time, as are the dioramas today. I believe his achievement was his fidelity to nature. Others haven't been so scrupulous and, somehow, we—even the kids—sense it. In this over stimulated age of ours, truth still sings through.
>
> I don't know whether or not curators "spruce up" a gorilla's expression or "refresh" the grasses or "refine" a lion skin when moths go on a rampage, but I'm convinced that what Carl Akeley intended—a vision of Africa as if you had discovered it yourself—still works.

The second person to whom I turned, to comment on the Hall's value as an art treasure, was an art historian and critic. Such commentary does not merely involve addressing the twenty-eight stunning background paintings by William R. Leigh, Robert Kane, Frederick Scherer, Dudley M. Blakeley, Francis Lee Jaques, James Perry Wilson and Clarence C. Rosenkrantz, all of whom worked directly with habitat studies made in Africa; it involves considering the dioramas as individual works of art.

Again, let us look at the gorilla group. The Leigh painting is magnificent and the accessories are extraordinary. The seventeen-thousand leaves, individually made of wax, cotton fiber, paper, and celluloid, are astounding. Even the tiny white flowers on the wild berry bush were meticulously created from onionskin paper dipped in wax. The long tendrils dangling from the hagenia tree are made of strings dragged through wax and painted. They are suspended over a real gorilla nest brought back from the Virungas. The dead tree trunk, lichens, mosses, bark, twigs, and hypericum tree are also real, having been collected and brought back to the museum by Mary Jobe and Richard Raddatz. To these real elements are added manufactured elements. The marriage of these accessories defies the viewer to discover its secret of natural and chemical synthesis. One can almost smell the crushed wild celery and feel the coolness of Mikeno's misty slopes. And in this fairyland the gorilla sculptures are magnificent.

I requested a statement from Jack Flam, the art critic for the *Wall Street Journal*. Flam has written extensively on modern art, and is professor of art history at Brooklyn College and the Graduate Center of the City University of New York. He is also an expert in African art, his passion ignited by the museum's collections when he was a graduate student. It was during this scholastic sojourn at the museum, studying the Zairian artifacts, that Jack grew even more enchanted with Akeley's Hall:

> The first museum that I came to know was not an art museum but the American Museum of Natural History. It was there that my father regularly brought me on Sunday afternoons during my childhood, and it was there that I was herded on numerous field trips during my grammar school days. It was also there, many years later, that my wife and I frequently took our small daughter—one of the few institutions in the city that had remained fairly constant during the four decades that separated my childhood from hers.
>
> When I was a child, my favorite parts of the Museum were the dinosaur hall and the Hall of African Mammals; the first because it somehow suggested a vastness of time that even then I knew I would never be able to grasp; the second, because it evoked a vast and mysterious place that seemed impossibly far away but which I could hope someday to visit. There were, of course, live African animals at the local zoos, but they were so clearly uprooted from their natural environment that they seemed displaced and freakish, like animals in a circus.
>
> What was so exciting about the dioramas in the African Hall was the sense of place and of empathy that they evoked. When you looked at the lions there, you seemed to be among them, like another lion joined in alertly watching the herd of antelopes that grazed off in the distance. And no other elephants, either in zoos or

263

in the circus, had anything near the same pride of bearing as those that strode so majestically through the center of the Hall.

Years later, as a graduate student, when I became involved in research on the Museum's African sculpture collection, I was delighted by the awareness that the African objects I was working with were housed in the very same building where I had got my first clear idea of Africa.

Over the years, I have continued to be impressed and delighted by the place. The dioramas remain for me marvels of imaginative reconstruction and meaningful detail—at once vivid, dramatic, and accurate. They are wonderful reminders of the heyday of a craft that in its best examples was transformed into an art.

The African Hall is one of the great treasures of New York City. It invites aesthetic contemplation as well as scientific study and it provides a unique link with the past of our own city as well as with the rapidly disappearing natural beauty of the African continent.

The African Hall is a grand monument to Carl Akeley, a real place made of skins, papier-mâché, wood, wax, and paint. Standing in the hall, we are stunned by the realized vision of an obsessed and focused man. It is a wonderful legacy. But the African Hall doesn't even approach his greatest accomplishment. The hooting of living gorillas traveling on the sodden, cool air at dusk above Akeley's grave at Kabara echo in testament to the fact that they are alive and well. This is the greatest legacy of all to Akeley's life and passion. To comment on this area I turned to Dr. George B. Schaller, director of Wildlife Conservation International.

Like many students of nature, I hold Schaller in the highest regard. He is not only a brilliant scientist, but also such an eloquent recorder of that science that his interpretation of data is transformed into something like poetry, so poignantly does it touch the human heart. Schaller lived in Kabara when he did his groundbreaking work on mountain gorillas. He and his wife and colleague, Kay, often sat near Akeley's grave, because it was such a lovely site, when a hard day of tracking gorillas was over. If time and proximity would allow for Akeley's spirit to touch the living, it would be the Schallers who would hold his "essential oil of experience," having lived for over ten months near Akeley's cemetery. This is what George Schaller had to say about Carl Akeley's legacy:

As a teenager, over four decades ago, I at times visited the American Museum of Natural History, where I lingered longest in the Akeley African Hall. So realistic are his dioramas that I was transported to the Serengeti plains, up among the mountain gorillas in the Virunga Volcanoes, and other mysterious and exotic places that fill an adventurous young heart with longing. In an age before zoos emulated natural habitats for their animals, Carl Akeley's dioramas recreated the African wilderness so faithfully that they surpassed the reality of early films . . . When years later I observed wildebeest among the kopjes and flat-topped acacias of the Serengeti and pushed through an undergrowth of wild celery and blackberry brambles in search of gorillas, it all seemed familiar, and I realized that the images of Akeley's dioramas were still with me.

My wife Kay and I settled among the Virunga Volcanoes in 1959 to study the mountain gorilla, an animal reputedly belligerent. Years before, Akeley had raised a lone voice in the gorilla's defense by calling him a "perfectly amiable fellow and decent creature." . . . We lived for months at Kabara in a cabin beside his grave . . . Akeley was a companionable presence in this peaceful and beautiful spot. We were very aware that by studying the gorilla's life we were turning his dream into a reality. And we silently acknowledged our debt to him. Without his vision and initiative, the gorillas here would have been long gone, another victim of humankind, their forests turned to fields.

Now thirty years after we left Kabara, the gorillas still survive. But now, instead of the shadowy creatures far from human consciousness they are viewed by several thousand visitors a year, all enthralled by the most powerful and elegant of our kin. The governments of Rwanda and Zaire, as well as many individuals and several conservation organizations, are dedicated to assuring the gorillas a future. In fact, it is now realized that the well-being of the human population near the Virungas has depended on the gorillas. The volcanoes represent a mere $\frac{1}{2}$% of Rwanda's land area but 10% of the country's water catchment; acting like a sponge, the mountain forests store water during the wet season and supply it as perennial streams during the dry season. The local people would long ago have cut this lifeline if gorillas had not provided the impetus for conservation. Akeley would no doubt be delighted that his solitary vision has had such far-reaching and varied consequences.

Nearly three quarters of a century ago Akeley became a pioneer in African conservation through his art and love of gorillas. Stimulated directly or indirectly by him, many others have over the years accepted the challenge and moral obligation to fight on behalf of Africa's wildlife. The mountain gorilla is Akeley's living monument, and those that follow his lead remain his most enduring legacy.

EPILOGUE
The Akeley Grave Project

But when my mother's son lay dead, had I
Neglected him and left him there unburied,
That would have caused me grief;
And if you think it folly, then perhaps
I am accused of folly by a fool.
                    —SOPHOCLES, *Antigone*

I STILL WONDER why I felt so adamant about securing the remains of Carl Akeley in his death place at Kabara, on the saddle between the volcanoes Karisimbi and Mikeno in Zaire. I still suspect that Akeley was rather enjoying having his bones scattered about the place he thought was the most beautiful in all the world. Perhaps his burial was a selfish act: a way of putting something to rest for myself, something I have yet to understand—a symbolic act. But it had to be done, and I had to do it myself. While I was in Africa on museum business, I would return to Kabara and accomplish the task. Even a small expedition can be costly. I had received contributions from Akeley's family, with whom I had worked on his biography and grown close, and from friends, good friends who supported me by supporting the venture. It is for my supporters that this report is written.

Making arrangements, negotiating, and raising money for what came to be called the "grave project" took about one year. The most important and crucial hurdle to overcome was receiving permission to rebuild the grave, because it was located in a national park. A letter was sent to Makabuza

Kabirizi wa Nzigiye, the chef du conservateur of the IZCN (Zaire national parks), in September 1989, requesting permission to enter Parc National des Virunga and repair the ransacked grave. Makabuza in turn had to obtain permission from his superior, the head of the IZCN. As late as January 1990, permission was still not forthcoming. Through friends of mine who have relatives on the Zaire Desk of the U.S. State Department in Washington, I implored the Central African Desk for assistance. Despite time constraints and difficulties in communication, a series of communiqués were exchanged with the U.S. embassies in both Kinshasa, Zaire and Kigali, Rwanda, and based on unofficial, but positive, feedback, I was encouraged to proceed with my plans.

On arrival in Kigali on January 12, we still had not received official word. I was to receive news from the U.S. embassy in Kinshasa through the U.S. embassy in Kigali. While a low-grade anxiety started enveloping my heart, I resisted it and forged onward. While it would be disappointing for Laurence Bajeneza, my Kabara companion from the year before, and myself to be refused permission, it would be tragic for George Rowbottom, a friend who was flying to Africa for the sole purpose of assisting us in our mission. If the whole affair had to be cancelled, it had to be done quickly, as George would soon be leaving the U.S. On January 19, my last day in Kigali on museum business, I visited the U.S. embassy. Secretary Joseph Cuadrado was most helpful, and promised immediate assistance in trying to wrest permission from Kinshasa.

I had to move on to Tanzania. On January 28, George flew to Nairobi as planned to meet me. I withheld my fears from him, hoping that everything would work out. It is always difficult to negotiate logistics in Africa and one has to be flexible. However, on Thursday, February 1, the worst news came from Laurence: He told us not to bother coming, as there was still no word. We later learned that in mid-January there had been some Zairian governmental reorganization, complicated by ministerial changes. But at the time we assumed that inefficient communication systems were the sole reason for the IZCN's silence. George handled this snafu quite well, and agreed that we should move on to Rwanda and try to solve the problem in situ. We were to fly to Kigali the next day. I sent a fax to Laurence telling him that we were coming regardless, and that he should meet us at the airport. Then I called Joseph Cuadrado, as I knew he would have left the embassy for the weekend by the time we arrived the next day. I asked him for anything he could give us on paper that would suggest the permission we needed. Again he promised assistance.

On our arrival at the Kigali airport, Laurence handed me an official letter from Joseph. It was delicately worded, and did not suggest that permission had been granted. But it did suggest that permission might have been granted at a meeting held that very morning in Kinshasa between U.S. State Department personnel and IZCN, but not yet communicated from the capital. Based on this ambiguous, but very impressive-looking letter, we decided to proceed to Zaire.

We wanted to leave for Gisenyi immediately so that we could cross the border into Zaire the next morning. We had to move quickly, as it was already late in the day and we would have to drive for over three hours. First we had to secure a vehicle. Laurence had rented a pickup truck for us at a reasonable rate. There was one serious drawback to it, however: the truck was open to the pouring rain, and it was really pouring that evening. In addition to our luggage and supplies, we had to transport several bags of cement and sand, and we imagined arriving in Zaire soaking wet, with solid blocks rather than bags of cement. The truck was abandoned and we hired a van, one of the infamous *matatus* of Africa, which cost us a walloping $106 a day! At that point, time was too precious to attempt finding a cheaper vehicle, as both George and I were locked into a departure schedule the following Friday, and we had no idea of what time-consuming problems we might encounter.

We left for Gisenyi, stopping in Ruhengeri en route for dinner and finally reached Gisenyi about 11:00 P.M. The hotel there—the Izuba Meridien—is my favorite in the world, and I was happy to be on the shores of Lake Kivu again and in a comfortable bed. Jean Marc Panossian, the manager of the Izuba, gave us complimentary rooms and meals on our way to and from Zaire for our "pilgrimage." Our hot showers were the last piece of "civilization" we would enjoy for many days.

On Saturday, February 3, Laurence bought supplies as we waited for him at the Izuba. One look at our *muzungu* (white European) faces and the prices would have increased considerably. But our waiting was hard. Wandering on the Kivu beach lent fuel to what was becoming a raging worry that we would meet Makabuzu only to be denied permission.

Most Westerners would find it almost impossible to comprehend the difficulty of communication in Zaire. One might assume that we needed only to pick up the phone and speak with Makabuza. But there is no phone. There is a very temperamental radio linkup, however, between his office at the park headquarters in Rumangabo and an office at Goma. During the endless attempts to communicate with Makabuza in the past, we had paid a friend in Rwanda to ride his motorbike to Goma and deliver a note which then might be successfully radioed to Makabuza at Rumangabo. The situation was aggravated by the fact that Makabuza's radio was working, but the unit at the IZCN's in Kinshasa was not.

We all shopped for food staples—bread, butter, cheese, etc. George had brought dry packaged soups from home which we supplemented in Nairobi with pasta, coffee, tea, and chocolate. We needed provisions for the three of us and for Ndetsetse, the park ranger who had been with us the year before. We would buy the porter's food and our fruit and vegetables at Kibumba, at Mt. Mikeno's base. We left Gisenyi at noon.

Epilogue

The immigration officials at the Goma border crossing were unexpectedly cordial. They usually are not, demanding first your official documents, and, if they are in order, then perhaps your baptism certificate; if you have that, they'll keep going until you don't have what they demand and you end up bribing them to let you pass.

Mt. Mikeno and, right behind it, Mt. Karisimbi were spectacular when we passed en route to Rumangabo. The outlines of their usually cloud-wrapped peaks cut sharply against the grey sky. We pushed on to the park headquarters and the dreaded decision. We arrived about 2:00 P.M. Rangers dressed in camouflage escorted us into the decaying orange and green building as Laurence went to find Makabuza at his home. Swallows flew in and out of the broken windows to their nests on the high wall above us, their guttural but metallic song echoing in the huge room. Snakes and other reptiles, greyed with age, lined a table in half-full formaldehyde jars. They were most bizarre: the parts in liquid were still plump and smooth, the parts hitting air, stringy and parched. Skulls of an elephant and a gorilla were whitened from swallow droppings as they lay without dignity on another old table.

I knew the negotiations with Makabuza could go on for days and I was surprised to realize how nervous I felt. Makabuza arrived and escorted us to his office. He is one of the loveliest, most sincere men I have ever met. I had been expecting a Zairian honcho with his palm up. Instead we found a genuinely concerned, uncorrupted conservation officer. About forty-five years old, Makabuza was slight and neatly dressed. A torn undershirt peeking out at his collar advertised his own less-than-affluent financial state. We brought him gifts of scotch, a calculator, and a watch, all of which he graciously accepted but never exacted. He told us immediately that he had never received permission for us from his boss. He felt very badly about it as he was a great fan of Akeley himself. To prove this, Makabuza produced articles he had written which mentioned Carl Akeley. He also admitted that he would not even have a job if it were not for Akeley as the park might never have been established. He said that the request for permission had gotten too big, that the State Department had become involved and now it was an issue between countries.

George was frozen in disappointment. Laurence and I remained hopeful. Laurence started chatting away about the broken radio and suggested that Kinshasa was probably trying to communicate permission as we sat there. I went into an "Akeley rap," showing Makabuza photos of Muguru, Akeley's gorilla guide, and answering his questions about the death. We produced copies of all the State Department telexes and faxes, in addition to Cuadrado's letter. I told him that we really only wanted to secure the remains. He obviously felt badly that the grave had been ransacked by local Zairians. After a couple of hours, Makabuza decided that because Akeley had actually founded the park, the government itself should erect a monument at his grave. To this end, we were allowed to secure Akeley's remains with a flat, primitive, temporary slab of cement that might conceivably be used as a foundation for a larger monument that the government of Zaire might some-day erect. We all felt comfortable with this arrangement. Makabuza wrote out a letter of permission that we were to bring to Ndetsetse. We were more than relieved; we were ecstatic. Outside, the volcanoes of Nymulagira and Nyiragongo stood magnificent in the afternoon sun. Nymulagira had vented open on the side of the mountain and a wispy grey tendril of smoke found its way to the heavens from its smoldering base. We were so happy.

Now we had to find a place to eat and sleep, as it was getting late. We pushed on to Rutshuru and a mission we had heard about. The rooms seemed clean enough, if primitive, and there was running water in the communal lavatory down the outside corridor. There was a Batwa man in attendance, whom we approached for information. He refused my handshake. As Laurence requested information about rooms and food, a large, yellow, mangy dog approached us for attention. I patted him, which made him hungry for more affection. (Animals are treated horribly in Africa, which could be the subject of another meditation.) As I patted the dog, the Batwa man came over and socked him hard in the face. The dog yelped and I exploded, telling the man to leave him alone. Laurence intervened and told me to calm down as the man was drunk. The dog skulked around waiting for a chance to approach me again. The incident put me off the mission and, even had it had provisions for dinner, which it did not, I would still have insisted that we move on. My obstinacy caused chagrin among my tired, hungry companions who from that time called me "Queen"—short for Queen of the Virungas. They teased me unmercifully for my overbearing ways. We had a marvelous time to-gether.

We ended up in a dreadful but adequate Rutshuru hotel called Gren-frame. It had no running water, single tiny bulbs illuminating dingy little rooms, filthy pillowcases used by hundreds of heads, and animal traps on the floor. We chalked this stay up to adventure. George and I stayed in a room called Uganda, Laurence in one called Zaire. The kitchen, a wooden shed with a dirt floor, was out back. A turkey was tied to a table inside, making a racket as he pulled on his rope. Through an open window we ordered some dinner and beer from a nice man who clearly never saw *wazungu*. Laurence was off to buy cement on the black market as we waited the forty-five minutes for dinner to be served. We retired to another shed. George's scotch arrived in a delicate little liqueur glass; the bottle quickly rushed back to its locked cabinet until the next pour. The meal of stewed goat and potatoes was filling and tasty. Laurence returned successful from his dark dealings and we celebrated our good fortune with beer and scotch. We felt elated. We paid someone to bring us water and doubly rejoiced in clean faces and teeth as we settled in for our last night in a bed. The prostitutes and truckers outside laughed through the cool night.

The next morning we bought sand and backtracked to Kibumba, stopping briefly to see Makabuza. At Kibumba we bought our bananas, beans, carrots, leeks, and cabbage. Ndetsetse met us and told us that he could not join us as he was ill. I felt very badly about this. By the time we reached the ranger station, however, he had changed his mind and was dressed for the trek. He wanted to be part of the pilgrimage. We hired our porters, fifty-three in all, to carry the heavy loads of cement and sand up the mountain. Laurence had divided the bags into small packs but they were still dense and heavy. It began to pour. Those carrying the cement and sand were ordered to follow the next morning. The rest of us pushed out for the ordeal of climbing Mikeno.

I swore that this year we would leave in time to take the trek at a slower pace, without the pressure of darkness falling upon us. I remembered too well how hard it was to negotiate the forest floor in the pitch black of night. But again we were starting out too late—and this time it was pouring as well. George was high-spirited, with a group of children following him. He led them in songs and rhymes as they laughed in sheer delight and tried to touch his blond hair. They soon fell away as we faced the lower slopes of Mikeno. We had all taken altitude medicine to help us in the thinning air. My hands and feet were tingling disembodied members. Laurence decided that because we were so late, we needed to save time by crossing over the top of Rweru peak instead of moving around its side. The news struck me with horror. There was nothing I could do to change his mind. As it was we would be marching over an hour in darkness. I reminded myself of Akeley's words: "Just put your head down and move."

By the time I reached the upper, nearly vertical slopes of Rweru, I stopped, leaned my head against my stick, and couldn't decide whether I wanted to die or just sleep. I was faint and dizzy, and I had ceased to care about anything. The toll the mountain takes on your body cannot be adequately expressed. I felt nauseated, weak, covered with nettle stings, and drenched to the marrow of my bones. I wanted to stop. Laurence later told me that he thought in that moment that he would be burying me with Akeley. I was very pale. Ndetsetse was weak as well, but he had the excuse of already being ill. George was a half-hour ahead of us, but also having a hard time of it. Even Laurence complained that his little money bag was too heavy, and contemplated asking one of the porters to carry it for him. It was all we could do to carry our own pounds up the mountain. I marveled at the porters, barefoot with nothing but a cotton cloth to keep them warm, scrambling up before us carrying heavy packs on their heads. I kept asking myself why I was doing this—and no answers came.

After dark, an African stayed close to me, hitting roots and fallen branches with a stick to alert me to their presence. I stumbled onward in misery. We reached Kabara and were jubilant to have arrived. Any doubts or miseries experienced on the trail soon evaporated into good spirits and righteous pride in our accomplishment. It had taken us less than five hours to make the climb.

We set up house in the Frankfurt Zoological Research Station, where we had stayed before and where Akeley's skull had been found on the table in 1979. After a supper of soup, pasta, and beer, we retired to our sleeping bags. Everything was wet, and stayed wet for the duration of our Kabara visit. The Africans huddled around the charcoal stove in rooms to both sides of us, talking and laughing throughout the night.

The next morning it was still raining. We waited for a break in the weather and began work on the grave. With so many porters the work went very quickly. We cleared the vegetation out of the pit and Laurence started digging around for Akeley's remains. I asked him to refrain from his search and to leave all as it was. A group of men removed the old cement headstone that I wanted to incorporate into the new cement slab. We filled the pit with volcanic rocks, some of which had to be brought from some distance. When we had made the pit level with the ground, we centered the old piece of cement with Akeley's name on it and positioned a form of logs and sticks around the perimeter, within which cement would be poured.

The remaining porters appeared with the cement and sand. Several of them requested headache medicine from *Mama Muzungu*, as they called me, as the trek with their dense packs had been harder than they had expected it to be. The men mixed the cement, sand, and water on a piece of corrugated metal. It was hard work. They took turns in the drizzle until the skies opened up and drenched us again. Laurence and George did all the planning and organizing to complete the work on the grave. The first layer of cement was poured that same afternoon. I was impressed with the enthusiastic effort expended by the Africans as they worked. One of them, Maguru Sebastien Nzabonimba, turned out to be a preacher and the grandson of Muguru. He said he had simply wanted to be a part of the project, and I was touched by his efforts in particular. When everyone ran for cover from the rain, he stayed behind with Laurence and George to assist in whatever way he could. I gave him a photograph of Muguru which seemed to mean a great deal to him. While the cement was wet we had to position the copper plaque we had brought to mark the grave. Makabuza had been very impressed with it, and now the Africans were especially intrigued with the photograph of Akeley that had been acid-etched into it. The plaque had been fabricated through the generosity of Albert Lehman of Lehman Brothers in New Haven, Connecticut. For Akeley's epitaph I chose a line from a poem he had with him when he died: "Death wins. Bravo! But I laugh in his face as he noses me out at the wire."

The next morning the sun was dazzling. George suggested that it was a sign that Akeley was appreciative of our effort. We poured two more layers of cement and attempted to smooth the surface as best we could. I dispatched some men to climb surrounding trees and bring down large pads of moss and epiphytes to decorate the edges of the finished grave. Some of the men planted tall stalks of yellow flowers at the grave's head. We said our silent prayers for the "old gorilla," as Akeley had liked to call himself. Then we covered the grave with a large plastic sheet, which Ndetsetse promised to remove later, so that the cement could cure. Then we started down the greasy mud chutes of Mikeno. Clouds still covered the peaks of Karisimbi and Mikeno, but streaks of sun illuminated the vegetation of the magnificent forest where, according to Akeley, "the faeries dance."

Two notable incidents took place on the lower slopes of Mikeno that illustrate something of the hard lives of the local Africans. We had given the porters the remaining food purchased for them. The porter who carried a bag of string beans back down the mountain felt that the beans should be his alone. He clutched the bag closely as the other porters descended on him to get their share. He defended his small bag of beans with a machete, frantically swinging it at his companions. His face showed total desperation, and terror that the beans would be taken from him. The other porters subdued him and, laughing, took the machete and the beans away from him. The man was broken, and looked as if he would cry. Just then someone else moved a metal gutter piece from which rats came running in every direction. We all started jumping to avoid them. They were as frightened and startled as we were, and chaos erupted in the square at the ranger's station.

The other incident was a *shaurie*, or meeting/negotiation, that took place in the same square when things had settled down after the furor over rats, beans, and machetes. The men were not pleased with the terms previously agreed upon, as the work had been completed so quickly. They demanded pay for three days when they had worked less than two. I refused to be taken advantage of. Ndetsetse and the preacher were on my side and tried to sway the others, but they were firm in their demand. I too was firm, and we sat there at an impasse as the dark clouds forming above us reflected the mood of the men. Makabuza had sent word that they were to assist us for the equivalent of $1.50 per day. I had already increased their salaries to $3.00 per day with a promise of a bonus, and I was not pleased to be taken for a fool. I refused to budge. Laurence, the consummate diplomat, after trying to negotiate, finally told them not to cheat the *muzungu* or they would not get their bonuses. The men finally relented and clapped their hands in thanksgiving. They accepted their pay and bonuses, and we all smiled at each other as if nothing could interfere with our undying friendship. After all, it was just business.

At the base of the mountain another surprise awaited us, this one more pleasant. Two of Muguru's wives and his son had gotten word that Akeley's "granddaughter" was on Mikeno. They had traveled from their home village far away to meet me. I was very touched and impressed by them. The oldest of the wives was over ninety. Her son alarmed me, as he kept marching around and saluting me. I was at a loss to understand what it was he was doing. He had been born the day that Akeley was buried. His mother told me she too would have been at Akeley's funeral had she not just given birth to this man. Their heart-felt sentiments for this man, long dead, rekindled my own emotional attachments. As George kept saying, it was a premier experience.

We finished so quickly that when we returned to Makabuza to report our success, he invited us to see the chimpanzees at Tonga. This we did—what was another day of hard physical exertion to us? We slowly slipped down from the ecstatic mood of our Kabara episode, allowing the various realities of it to dawn on us. We ended the whole grave project with a visit to Rosamond Carr's house outside of Gisenyi. Roz is a lovely friend who moved to Rwanda from the U.S. over forty years ago. At that time she was married to Kenneth Carr who was a white hunter for Prince William of Sweden on his gorilla expedition. More recently she was a close friend to Dian Fossey. In the comfort of her dining room, we recounted the events of the previous days as she listened with rapt attention. She shared her own thoughts on Akeley, his wives, his death, and the gorillas he saved, as hadada ibis screamed outside in her magnificent garden.

Securing Akeley's last resting place provided a poignant and emotional experience for us all. The event meant something very different to each—Laurence, George, and me. Being in Kabara this time helped me to understand better my own emotional connection to Akeley. Kabara helped me somehow to participate in Akeley's life, perhaps because it is unchanged from when he was there, and he loved it so much. I felt that I had calmed down and now held the wonder of his life in my heart in a more measured way than before. I no longer envied his life but allowed Akeley's person and work to inform and inspire my own. If this (albeit one-way) relationship between Akeley and me took on a real, physical form, I would say he was like a brother who encouraged and coached me. I couldn't begin to say thank you for all that Akeley has given to me but I could pay some small homage of gratitude—I could see that his remains were secure in the earth of Kabara. *Kwaheri, ndugu yangu.*

NOTES

Chapter 1

1. Alan J. Isselhard, *Images of Clarendon Past* (Clarendon, NY: 175th Jubilation Committee, 1985), 4.
2. David Sturges Copeland, *History of Clarendon: from 1810–1888* (Buffalo, NY: Courier Co., 1889), 137.
3. Ibid., 357.
4. Carl Akeley to Nettie M.P. Akeley, March 26, 1923, Akeley Collection, Rush Rhees Library, University of Rochester, NY.
5. Copeland, *History of Clarendon*, 144.
6. Lewis Akeley prepared "Early Life of Carl Akeley" at Jobe's request and included it with a letter to her circa 1937, AMNH Archives.
7. Copeland, *History of Clarendon*, 144.
8. Vernette Akeley Armstrong, *Glidden, Our District*, Regina, Saskatchewan Archives.
9. "A Small Man with a Rudder," interview with Lewis Akeley in *Sioux City, Iowa*, 13 October 1957.
10. Elizabeth Martin to Mary Jobe Akeley, January 10, 1929, AMNH Archives.
11. Vernette Akeley Armstrong; interview with author, Eston, Saskatchewan, fall 1989.
12. L. Akeley, "Early Life."
13. Lewis Akeley to Vernette Akeley Armstrong, December 19, 1954, Vernette Akeley Armstrong Collection.
14. Elizabeth Martin to Mary Jobe Akeley, January 10, 1929, AMNH Archives.
15. L. Akeley, "Early Life."

16. Jennie Cowles to Mary Jobe Akeley, September 21, 1928, AMNH Archives.

17. Elizabeth Martin to Mary Jobe Akeley, January 10, 1929, AMNH Archives.

18. L. Akeley, "Early Life."

19. Josephine Glidden Hedin to Mary Jobe Akeley, July 1937, AMNH Archives.

20. Lewis Akeley to Mary Jobe Akeley, August 6, 1937, AMNH Archives.

21. Lewis Akeley to Mary Jobe Akeley, March 27, 1939, AMNH Archives.

22. Lewis Akeley to Mary Jobe Akeley, January 18, 1939, AMNH Archives.

23. "David Bruce was Man of Great Artistic Talents," *Brockport Republic Democrat*, November 25, 1954.

24. Carl E. Akeley, *In Brightest Africa* (Garden City, NY: Doubleday, Page & Co., 1923), 2.

Chapter 2

1. C. Akeley, *In Brightest Africa*, 4.

2. William Morton Wheeler, "Carl Akeley's Early Work and Environment," *Natural History* 27 (April 1927), 135.

3. Mary Jobe Akeley, *The Wilderness Lives Again* (New York: Dodd, Mead & Co., 1940), 15.

4. L. Akeley, "Early Life."

5. Ibid.

6. William R. Leigh, *Frontiers of Enchantment* (London: George C. Harrap & Co. Ltd., 1939), 18.

7. L. Akeley, "Early Life."

8. Ibid.

9. Frederic Lucas, "Akeley as a Taxidermist," *Natural History* 27 (April 1927), 144.

10. C. Akeley, *In Brightest Africa*, 176.

11. Carl Akeley to Henry Ward, November 1883, Ward Collection, Rush Rhees Library.

12. Ibid.

13. Wheeler, "Early Work," 136.

14. Ibid., 136.

15. Ibid., 137.

16. Sylvia Sikes, *The Natural History of the African Elephant* (London: Weidenfeld & Nicolson, 1971), 293–294.

17. Isselhard, *Images of Clarendon Past*, 32.

18. Wheeler, "Early Work," 137.

19. L. Akeley, "Early Life."

20. Ibid.

Chapter 3

1. M.J. Akeley, *Wilderness*, 29.
2. Wheeler, "Early Work," 137.
3. Mary Alice Evans and Howard Evans, *William Morton Wheeler, Biologist* (Cambridge: Harvard University Press, 1970), 9.
4. Ibid., 11.
5. Gertrude Perkins Maxfield to Mary Jobe Akeley, March 29, 1939, AMNH Archives.
6. Letterhead on Carl Akeley's stationery, 189–, Rush Rhees Library.
7. Nancy Oestreich Lurie, *A Special Style: The Milwaukee Public Museum, 1882–1982* (Milwaukee, WI: Milwaukee Public Museum, 1983), 16.
8. Evans and Evans, *William Wheeler*, 46.
9. Elizabeth Fagg Olds, *Women of the Four Winds* (Boston: Houghton Mifflin Co., 1985), 77.
10. "Woman of the Week: Delia Akeley," *The News Review* (Macmillan Company newsletter), 22 February 1932.
11. Milwaukee Public Museum, *Annual Report* (Milwaukee, WI: Milwaukee Public Museum, 1890).
12. C. Akeley, *In Brightest Africa*, 1.
13. Frederic Lucas, *Fifty Years of Museum Work* (New York: The Museum, 1933), 16.
14. Delia Akeley, *Jungle Portraits* (New York: Macmillan, 1930), 87.
15. Carl Akeley to W.H. Holmes and Edward Earll, May 2, 1892 to May 18, 1893, Smithsonian Archives, Washington, D.C.
16. C. Akeley, *In Brightest Africa*, 13.

Chapter 4

1. "Woman of the Week," *The News Review*, 6.
2. Wheeler, "Early Work," 136.
3. Frank Chapman, "Daniel Giraud Elliot," *The Auk* 34 (January 1917).
4. Daniel Giraud Elliot, "Report on the Africa Expedition to the President, Chairman and Members of the Executive Committee of the Field Museum," January 5, 1897, Field Museum Archives, Chicago, IL.

Chapter 5

1. Daniel Giraud Elliot to Director Skiff, April 4, 1896, Field Museum Archives, Chicago, IL.
2. Ibid.
3. Richard F. Burton, *First Footsteps in East Africa* (N.p., n.d.), (London: Constable and Company, Ltd., 1987), 79.

4. Pascal James Imperato, M.D., *Arthur Donaldson Smith and the Exploration of Lake Rudolf* (Buffalo: Medical Society of the State of New York, 1987), 34.

5. Elliot to Skiff, April 27, 1896, Field Museum Archives.

6. Ibid.

7. Ibid.

8. Burton, *Footsteps*, 8.

9. Ibid., 78.

10. Ibid., 55.

11. Elliot, "Report on the Africa Expedition."

12. C. Akeley, *In Brightest Africa*, 114–117.

13. Elliot to Skiff, May 20, 1896, Field Museum Archives.

14. Elliot to Skiff, June 14, 1896, Field Museum Archives.

15. Ibid.

16. Ibid.

17. C. Akeley, *In Brightest Africa*, 100–102.

18. Michael Herr, *Dispatches* (New York: Alfred A. Knopf, 1977), 63.

19. Elliot to Skiff, April 4, 1896, Field Museum Archives.

20. Elliot to Skiff, October 25, 1896, Field Museum Archives.

21. Elliot to Skiff, July 30, 1896, Field Museum Archives.

22. Elliot, "Report on the Africa Expedition."

Chapter 6

1. Elliot to Skiff, October 6, 1896, Field Museum Archives.

2. Daniel Giraud Elliot, "List of Mammals Obtained in the Expedition to the Olympic Mountains, Washington, 1898," *Field Columbian Museum Zoological Series* 1 (1895–99), 241.

3. Ibid., 244.

4. Ibid., 253.

5. Field Museum, Executive Minutes, meeting of January 24, 1900. Field Museum Archives.

6. Charles Brandler to Carl Akeley, April 18, 1901, Rush Rhees Library. Akeley Collection.

7. N.K. Luxton to Carl Akeley, January 13, 1902, Rush Rhees Library. Akeley Collection.

8. William Wheeler to Carl Akeley, January 13, 1902, Rush Rhees Library. Akeley Collection.

9. Herman C. Bumpus, "Report on the Department of Education for 1905," January 1906, AMNH Archives.

10. James Lippitt Clark, notes on Akeley, AMNH Archives.

11. Carl Akeley, "Lecture Given to the New York Assembly Chamber, Albany, New York," March 13, 1923, Rush Rhees Library. Akeley Collection.

12. William Alanson Bryan to Carl Akeley, July 8, 1904, Rush Rhees Library. Akeley Collection.

Chapter 7

1. D. Akeley, *Jungle Portraits*, 135.
2. C. Akeley, *In Brightest Africa*, 150.
3. "Woman of the Week," *The News Review*.
4. Carl Akeley to Thomas Akeley, January 11, 1906, Collection of Vernette Akeley Armstrong, Eston, Saskatchewan.
5. Helen Hulett Searl, "In the Service of Science," *Woman Citizen* n.s. 10 (December 1925), 17.
6. C. Akeley, *In Brightest Africa*, 65–67.
7. Ibid.
8. D. Akeley, *Jungle Portraits*, 84.
9. Carl Akeley, "Elephant Hunting on Mount Kenya: A Woman Wins the Record pair of Elephant Tusks for a Sportsman's License in British East Africa," *American Museum Journal* 15 (November 15, 1915).
10. Ibid.
11. Ibid.
12. Searl, "In the Service of Science," 17.
13. J.M. Greene to Delia and Carl Akeley, February 8, 1907, Rush Rhees Library. Akeley Collection.
14. C. Akeley, *In Brightest Africa*, 114.

Chapter 8

1. Wilfred H. Osgood, "In Memoria: Charles Barney Cory," *The Auk* 34 (April 1922), 158.
2. H.N. Higinbotham to Elliot, August 10, 1905, Field Museum Archives.
3. To Carl Akeley (the last page of this letter with the closing and signature is missing in the collection), January 31, 1907, Rush Rhees Library. Akeley Collection.
4. Ibid.
5. Call Akeley to Osborn, March 17, 1911, AMNH Archives.
6. Clark, notes on Akeley.
7. C.L. Dewey, "My Friend Ake," *Nature Magazine* 10 (1927), 389.
8. Roy Chapman Andrews, "Akeley of Africa," *True Magazine*, 124.
9. Dewey, "My Friend Ake," 389.
10. J.P. Morgan to Osborn, May 17, 1911, AMNH Archives.
11. Osborn, "Report on the Proposed Elephant Hall," March, 1911. AMNH Archives.
12. Andrews, "Akeley of Africa," 124.

Notes

Chapter 9

1. C. Akeley, *In Brightest Africa*, 46–50.
2. D. Akeley, *Jungle Portraits*, 231–242.
3. Ibid.
4. C. Akeley, *In Brightest Africa*, 51.
5. Andrews, "Akeley of Africa," 124.
6. "Boyce to Send Expedition to Congo," *The Leader* (Nairobi), November 27, 1909.
7. Leslie Tarlton to Carl Akeley, November 27, 1909, Rush Rhees Library. Akeley Collection.
8. John T. McCutcheon, *In Africa: Hunting Adventures in the Big Game Country* (Indianapolis: Bobbs-Merrill Co., 1910), 399.
9. Elspeth Huxley and Arnold Curtis, eds., *Pioneers: Scrapbook Reminiscences of Kenya 1890 to 1968* (London: Evans Bros. Ltd., 1980), 40.
10. C. Akeley, *In Brightest Africa*, 106.
11. Ibid., 110.
12. D. Akeley, *J. T. Jr.: The Biography of an African Monkey* (New York: Macmillan, 1928), 26.
13. McCutcheon, *In Africa: Hunting Adventures*, 175.
14. Ibid., 176.
15. Ibid., 137.
16. Ibid., 138.
17. Kermit Roosevelt, *A Sentimental Safari* (New York: Alfred A. Knopf, 1963), 97.
18. C. Akeley, "Lecture Given to the New York Assembly," March 13, 1923, Rush Rhees Library. Akeley Collection.
19. Robert Underwood Johnson, *Remembered Yesterdays* (Boston: n.p., 1923), 388.
20. D. Akeley, *J. T. Jr.*, 38.
21. Ibid., 39.
22. D. Akeley, *Jungle Portraits*, 83.
23. Tarlton to Carl Akeley, November 27, 1909, Rush Rhees Library. Akeley Collection.
24. C. Akeley, *Journal*, 1910 original, Collection of Patricia and Lot Page, Lincoln, MA.
25. D. Akeley, *Journal*, 1910, Page collection.
26. "Lion Killing Galore," *The Leader* (Nairobi), June 11, 1910.
27. D. Akeley, *Jungle Portraits*, 87.
28. Ibid., 135.
29. D. Akeley, *Journal*, 1910.
30. C. Akeley, *Uganda Journal* (#2), AMNH Archives.
31. C. Akeley, *Journal*, 1910 original.

32. C. Akeley, *Uganda Journal* (#2) AMNH Archives.

33. Delia Akeley to Tom Akeley, October 28, 1910, Vernette Akeley Armstrong collection.

34. C. Akeley, *Uganda Journal* (#2).

Chapter 10

1. Carl Akeley to Osborn, May 29, 1912, AMNH Archives.

2. J.P. Morgan to Osborn, May 1912, AMNH Archives.

3. Osborn to Percy Pyne, October 2, 1912, AMNH Archives.

4. Osborn to F.A. Lucas, October 11, 1912, AMNH Archives.

5. Andrews, "Akeley of Africa," 127.

6. Ernest H. Rowe, "Shooting Big Game, Pictures and Cement," *Industry Illustrated*, June 1923.

7. Andrews, "Akeley of Africa," 128.

8. Carl Akeley to Lucas, May 31, 1913, AMNH Archives.

9. Carl Akeley to Osborn, July 2, 1914, AMNH Archives.

10. J.P. Morgan to Osborn, July 2, 1914, AMNH Archives.

11. Andrews, "Akeley of Africa," 126.

12. Osborn to Carl Akeley, July 18, 1911, AMNH Archives.

13. Lucas to Osborn, April 7, 1915, AMNH Archives.

14. Andrews, "Akeley of Africa," 122.

15. Carl Akeley to Osborn, October 30, 1910, AMNH Archives.

16. Andrews, "Akeley of Africa," 126.

17. *Guest Book*, Explorers Club Archives, New York.

18. D. Akeley, *J. T. Jr.*, 185.

19. C. Akeley, *Uganda Journal* (#2).

20. Major O.B. Zimmerman to Mary Jobe Akeley, March 1, 1929, AMNH Archives.

21. Memo, Robin Smith to James A. Oliver, March 27, 1967, AMNH Archives.

22. George Sherwood, "Akeley the Man," *Natural History* 27(2) (1927).

23. Carl Akeley to Osborn, January 12, 1920, AMNH Archives.

Chapter 11

1. C. Akeley, *In Brightest Africa*, 175.

2. Ibid., 176.

3. Charles Francis Potter to Carl Akeley, March 21, 1924, Rush Rhees Library. Akeley Collection.

4. "The Jungle Worshipper," *New Orleans States*, June 15, 1924.

5. C. Akeley, *In Brightest Africa*, 185.

6. William F. Brooks, *The Shrine of the Lion*, unpublished report, AMNH Archives.
7. Carl Akeley to Jim Brite, July 30, 1920, Rush Rhees Library. Akeley Collection.
8. James L. Clark to W.M. Faunce, Dec. 3, 1935. AMNH Archives.
9. C. Akeley to E. Rowe, June, 1923. Rush Rhees Library. Akeley Collection.

Chapter 12

1. Carl Akeley to Osborn, February 7, 1921, AMNH Archives.
2. Carl Akeley to the Bradleys, February 3, 1921, AMNH Archives.
3. Carl Akeley to McCutcheon, date illegible, Rush Rhees Library. Akeley Collection.
4. Carl Akeley to the Bradleys, July 11, 1921, Rush Rhees Library. Akeley Collection.
5. C. Akeley, *In Brightest Africa*, 196–97.
6. Carl Akeley to the Bradleys, February 3, 1929, AMNH Archives.
7. Mary Hastings Bradley, *On the Gorilla Trail* (New York: Appleton & Co., 1922), 22.
8. C. Akeley, *In Brightest Africa*, 202.
9. Ibid., 208.
10. Ibid., 211.
11. Ibid., 217.
12. Mary Hastings Bradley, *Alice in Jungleland* (New York: Appleton & Co., 1927), 100.
13. Mary Jobe Akeley, *Kivu Journal* (1926), AMNH Archives.
14. C. Akeley, "Lecture to the New York Assembly."
15. Bradley, *Gorilla Trail*, 112.
16. C. Akeley, *In Brightest Africa*, 230.
17. "Desired Burial in Africa," *The New York Times*, December 2, 1926.
18. C. Akeley, *In Brightest Africa*, 230.
19. Ibid., 235.
20. M.J. Akeley, *Carl Akeley's Africa*, 239.
21. Ibid., 244.
22. James Gustavus Whiteley to Carl Akeley, September 15, 1925, AMNH Archives.

Chapter 13

1. Osborn to Roy Chapman Andrews, September 2, 1921, AMNH Archives.
2. Patricia and Lot Page, interview with author, Lincoln, MA, fall 1989.
3. Dawn-Starr Crowther (Mary Jobe Akeley's biographer), interview with author, fall 1989. New York.
4. Carl Akeley to Sherwood, September 2, 1921, AMNH Archives.

5. "Akeley Leaves $10,000 Estate to Second Wife," *New York Herald Tribune*, July 30, 1927.

6. Herbert Bradley to Leonard D. Baldwin, September 12, 1922, AMNH Archives.

7. Delia Akeley to Trubee Davison, June 4, 1936, AMNH Archives.

8. Lewis Akeley to Roy Chapman Andrews, December 12, 1936, AMNH Archives.

9. Delia Akeley to Davison, June 4, 1936, AMNH Archives.

10. Carl Akeley to Captain Gyde, September 15, 1923, Rush Rhees Library. Akeley Collection.

11. Herbert Bradley to Carl Akeley, May 29, 1923; Akeley to Bradley, June 12, 1923, AMNH Archives.

12. Summary of meeting between Sherwood, Pomeroy, and Johnson, November 1929, AMNH Archives.

Chapter 14

1. Jose Ortega y Gasset, *Meditations on Hunting* (New York: Macmillan, 1986), 111.

2. Ibid., 88.

3. Ibid., 91.

4. Sylvia Sikes, *The Natural History of the African Elephant* (London: Weidenfeld & Nicolson, 1971), 314.

5. Isak Dinesen, *Out of Africa* (New York: Vintage Books, 1985), 20.

6. C. Akeley, *In Brightest Africa*, 144, 147.

7. Elspeth Huxley, *White Man's Country: Lord Delamere and the Making of Kenya* (London: Chatto and Windus, 1935), 81.

8. Roosevelt, *Sentimental Safari*, 165.

9. D. Akeley, *Jungle Portraits*, 142.

10. Joseph Gikungu Mbiru, interview with author, Muranga, Kenya, March 1989.

11. C. Akeley, *In Brightest Africa*, 131.

12. Ibid., 142.

13. Ibid.

14. Ibid., 145.

15. C. Akeley, *Journal*, Page Collection.

16. S. Sikes, *African Elephant*, 303.

17. Alfredo Oriani, *La Lotta Politica in Italia: Origini della Lotta Attuale, 476–1887*, 3 vols. (Florence: Della Voce, 1913), 3:340.

Chapter 15

1. M.J. Akeley, *Wilderness*, 225.

2. C.G. Jung, *Memories, Dreams, Reflections* (New York: Vintage Books, 1961), 255.

3. Robert H. Rockwell and Jeanne Rockwell, *My Way of Becoming a Hunter* (New York: W.W. Norton & Co., 1955), 213.

4. George Eastman, *Chronicles of an African Trip* (Rochester, NY: Published by the author, 1927), 35.

5. Rockwell and Rockwell, *My Way*, 208–9.

6. Ibid., 214.

7. Ibid., 217.

8. Leigh, *Frontiers*, 133–134.

9. Rockwell and Rockwell, *My Way*, 224.

10. M.J. Akeley, *Carl Akeley's Africa*, 150.

11. Eastman, *Chronicles*, 85.

12. Dr. Pascal Imperato, interview with author regarding his interview with Dr. Anderson in Nairobi before his death, spring 1989. New York.

13. "Statement Given to Mrs. Carl Akeley and Dorothy G. Ross, February 10, 1928, by R.C. Raddatz," AMNH Archives.

14. M.J. Akeley, *Carl Akeley's Africa*, 174.

Chapter 16

1. Excerpt from Derscheid's journal, AMNH Archives.

2. "Desired Burial in Africa," *New York Times*, December 2, 1926.

3. Wheeler, "Early Work."

4. Mary Jobe Akeley, note on poem, AMNH Archives.

5. Delia Akeley to Davis, May 25, 1927, Field Museum Archives.

6. Mary Jobe Akeley, *Kivu Journal*. AMNH Archives.

7. Ibid.

8. Mary Jobe Akeley to Sherwood, February 18, 1927, AMNH Archives.

9. M.J. Akeley, *Kivu Journal*.

10. Leigh, *Frontiers*, 170.

11. M.J. Akeley, *Kivu Journal*.

12. Carl Akeley to Sherwood, May 2, 1926, AMNH Archives.

13. M.J. Akeley, *Carl Akeley's Africa*, 258.

SELECT BIBLIOGRAPHY

Books

Akeley, Carl E. *In Brightest Africa*. Garden City, New York: Doubleday, Page & Co., 1923.

Akeley, Carl E., and Mary L. Jobe Akeley. *Lions, Gorillas and Their Neighbors*. New York: Dodd, Mead & Co., 1934.

Akeley, Delia J. *J. T. Jr.: The Biography of an African Monkey*. New York: Macmillan Co., 1928.

————. *Jungle Portraits*. New York: Macmillan, 1930.

Akeley, Mary L. Jobe. *Carl Akeley's Africa*. New York: Dodd, Mead & Co., 1929.

————. *Congo Eden*. New York: Dodd, Mead & Co., 1950.

————. *The Wilderness Lives Again*. New York: Dodd, Mead & Co., 1940.

Andrews, Roy Chapman. *Beyond Adventure: The Lives of Three Explorers*. New York: Duell, Sloan & Pearce, [1954].

Baumgartel, M. W. *Up Among the Mountain Gorillas*. New York: Hawthorn Books, 1976.

Bourne, George H. and Cohen, Maury. *The Gentle Giants: The Gorilla Story*. New York: Putnam, 1975.

Boyce, William D. *Illustrated Africa, North, Tropical, South*. New York: Rand McNally & Co., 1925.

Bradley, Mary Hastings. *Alice in Jungleland*. New York: Appleton, 1927.

————. *On the Gorilla Trail*. New York: Appleton, 1922.

Brownlow, Kevin. *The War, the West and the Wilderness*. New York: Alfred A. Knopf, 1979.

Select Bibliography

Burton, Richard F. *First Footsteps in East Africa*. N.p., n.d. London: Constable and Company, Ltd., 1987 (first published in 1894).

Coleman, Laurence Vail. *Plants of Wax*. American Museum of Natural History Guide Leaflet Series, no. 54. New York: American Museum of Natural History, 1922.

Copeland, David Sturges. *History of Clarendon: from 1810 to 1888*. Buffalo, NY: Courier Co., printers, 1889.

Crowther, Dawn-Starr. *Mary L. Jobe Akeley*. History of Photography Monograph Series, no. 24. Arizona Board of Regents, 1989.

Dinesen, Isak. *Out of Africa*. New York: Vintage Books, 1985 (first published in 1938).

Dixon, A. *The Natural History of Gorillas*. London: Weidenfeld & Nicolson, 1981.

Dugmore, Arthur Radclyffe. *Camera Adventures in the African Wilds*. London: William Heinemann, 1913.

Eastman, George. *Chronicles of an African Trip*. [Rochester, NY]: Published by the author, 1927.

Evans, Mary Alice, and Howard Ensign Evans. *William Morton Wheeler, Biologist*. Cambridge: Harvard University Press, 1970.

Huxley, Elspeth. *White Man's Country: Lord Delamere and the Making of Kenya*. 2 vols. London: Chatto and Windus, 1935.

Huxley, Elspeth, and Arnold Curtis, eds. *Pioneer's Scrapbook: Reminiscences of Kenya 1890 to 1968*. London: Evans Bros., Ltd., 1980.

Imperato, Pascal James. *Arthur Donaldson Smith and the Exploration of Lake Rudolf*. Lake Success, NY: Medical Society of the State of New York, 1987.

Isselhard, Alan. *Images of Clarendon Past*. Clarendon, NY: 175th Jubilation Committee, 1985.

Johnson, Martin. "Diary and Reports, the Martin Johnson African Expedition." Bulletin Nos. 1–7, December 1923–25 (mimeographed).

————. *Safari: A Saga of the African Blue*. New York: G.P. Putnam's Sons, 1928.

Johnson, Osa. *I Married Adventure*. New York: J.B. Lippincott Co., 1940.

Jung, C.G. *Memories, Dreams, Reflections*. New York: Vintage Books, 1961.

Kennedy, John Michael. "Philanthropy and Science in New York City: The American Museum of Natural History, 1868–1968." Ph.D. diss., Yale University, 1968.

Leigh, William R. *Frontiers of Enchantment*. London: George C. Harrap & Co. Ltd., 1939.

Lucas, Frederic. *Fifty Years of Museum Work*. New York: The Museum, 1933 (mimeographed).

————. *The Story of Museum Groups*. American Museum of Natural History Guide Leaflet Series, no. 53. New York: American Museum of Natural History, 1926.

Lurie, Nancy Oestreich. *A Special Style: The Milwaukee Public Museum, 1882–1982*. Milwaukee, WI: Milwaukee Public Museum, 1983.

Maple, T., and M. Hoff. *Gorilla Behavior*. New York: Van Nostrand Reinhold, 1982.

Matson, A.T. *Nandi Resistance to British Rule 1890–1906*. Nairobi: East Africa Publishing House, 1972.

286

Select Bibliography

McCutcheon, John T. *In Africa: Hunting Adventures in the Big Game Country*. Indianapolis, IN: Bobbs-Merrill Co., 1910.

Meinertzhagen, R. *Kenya Diary 1902–1906*. London: Oliver and Boyd, 1957.

Moss, Cynthia. *Portraits in the Wild: Behavior Studies of East African Mammals*. 2nd ed. Chicago: University of Chicago Press, 1982.

Moyer, John W. *Practical Taxidermy: A Working Guide*. New York: Ronald Press Co., 1953.

Nash, Roderick. *Wilderness and the American Mind*. 3rd ed. New Haven, CT: Yale University Press, 1967.

Olds, Elizabeth Fagg. *Women of the Four Winds*. Boston: Houghton Mifflin Co., 1985.

Ortega y Gasset, Jose. *Meditations on Hunting*. New York: Macmillan Publishing Company, 1986 (first published in 1942).

Pease, Alfred E. *The Book of the Lion*. London: Murray, 1913.

Percival, Arthur Blayney. *A Game Ranger's Note Book*. New York: George H. Doran Co., 1924.

Rockwell, Robert H. and Rockwell, Jeanne. *My Way of Becoming a Hunter*. New York: W.W. Norton & Co., Inc., 1955.

Roosevelt, Kermit. *A Sentimental Safari*. New York: Alfred A. Knopf, 1963.

Roosevelt, Theodore. *African Game Trails*. 2 vols. New York: Charles Scribner's Sons, 1920.

Schaller, G.B. *The Mountain Gorilla: Ecology and Behavior*. Chicago: University of Chicago Press, 1963.

Sikes, Sylvia K. *The Natural History of the African Elephant*. London: Weidenfeld & Nicolson, 1971.

Stott, Kenholm W. *Exploring With Martin and Osa Johnson*. Chanute, KS: Martin and Osa Johnson Safari Museum Press, 1978.

Trzebinski, Errol. *The Kenya Pioneers*. New York: W.W. Norton & Co., 1988.

William, Prince of Sweden. *Among the Pygmies and Gorillas*. New York: Dutton, 1921.

Articles

"Akeley Leaves $10,000 Estate to Second Wife." *New York Herald Tribune*, July 30, 1927.

Akeley Memorial Issue. *Natural History* 27 (March–April 1927).

Akeley, Carl E. "Elephant hunting in Equatorial Africa." *American Museum Journal* 12 (1912): 43–62.

————. "Elephant Hunting in Equatorial Africa with Rifle and Camera." *National Geographic Magazine* 23 (1912): 779–810.

————. "Elephant Hunting on Mount Kenya." *American Museum Journal* 15 (1915): 323–338.

————. "Gorillas—Real and Mythical." *Natural History* 23 (1923): 428–447.

Select Bibliography

_____. "Have a Heart—A Statement and Plea for Fair Game Sport in Africa." *Mentor*, January 1926, 47–50.

_____. "Report of the African Expedition." *Annual Report of the Director of the Field Museum of Natural History*, vol. 3. Chicago: Field Museum of Natural History, 1908.

_____. "Report of Carl Akeley Included in Dr. D.G. Elliot's List of the Mammals Obtained in Somaliland, 1896." *Field Columbian Museum Zoological Series* 1 (1895–99): 135.

_____. "The Wild Ass of Somaliland." *American Museum Journal* 14 (1914): 113–120.

Akeley, Delia J. "My First Elephant." In *All True! The Record of Actual Adventures That Have Happened to Ten Women of Today*. New York: Brewer, Warren & Putnam, 1931.

_____. "Table from Elephant's Ear." *Mentor*, May 1929, p. 33.

Akeley, Mary Jobe. "Africa's Great National Park." *Natural History* 39 (November–December 1929): 638–650.

_____. "Belgian Congo Sanctuaries." *Scientific Monthly* 33 (October 1931): 289–300.

_____. "Carl Akeley's Last Journey." *World's Work* 56(3) (July 1928): 250–259.

_____. "King Albert Inaugurates the Parc National Albert." *Natural History* 30 (March–April 1930): 193–195.

Andrews, Roy Chapman. "Akeley of Africa." *True Magazine* (June 1952): 117–131.

Dewey, C.L. "My Friend Ake." *Nature Magazine* 10 (1927): 387–391.

Eastman, George. "A Safari in Africa." *Natural History* 27 (1927): 533–538.

Greene, D.S. "Carl Akeley—Sculptor-Taxidermist." *American Magazine of Art* 15 (March 1924): 125–130.

_____. "Sculptures of Carl Ethan Akeley." *Country Life* 36 (June 1919): 45–47.

Hopkins, A.A. "Evolution in Museum Technique." *Scientific American*, June 1922, 399.

Hornaday, William Temple. "Masterpiece of American Taxidermy." *Scribner's* 72 (July 1922): 3–17.

Jobe, Mary L. "A Winter Journey Through the Northern Canadian Rockies from Mt. Robson to Mt. Sir Alexander." *Appalachia* 14(3) (June 1918): 223–233.

_____. "A Winter Journey to Mt. Sir Alexander and the Wapih." *The Canadian Alpine Journal* 9 (1918): 79–89.

Lucas, Frederic. "How Elephants are Mounted." *Natural History* 23 (November–December 1923): 597–605.

_____. "The Story of Museum Groups," parts 1 and 2. *The American Museum Journal* 14 (January, February 1914): 3–15, 50–65.

Murphy, Robert Cushman. "Carl Ethan Akeley, 1864–1926." *Curator* 7 (1964): 307–320.

Rockwell, Robert H. "Adventures in Sculpture-Taxidermy." *Asia* 29 (1929): 22–29.

Rowe, Ernest H. "Shooting Big Game, Pictures and Cement." *Industry Illustrated*, June 1923.

Searl, Helen Hulett. "In the Service of Science." *Woman Citizen* n.s. 10 (December 1925): 17.

White, Stewart Edward. "The Making of a Museum." *Mentor* 13 (January 1926): 6–9.

Wilhelm, Donald. "A Wonderful Preserver of Wild Animals." *American Magazine* 79 (June 1915): 56–57.

"Woman of the Week: Delia Akeley." *The News Review* (Macmillan Company newsletter), 22 February 1932.

Archives and Manuscript Collections

American Museum of Natural History, New York. Department of Library Services, Archives and Special Collections.

Armstrong, Vernette Akeley, Eston, Saskatchewan, Canada. Private Collection.

Field Museum of Natural History, Chicago, Illinois. Field Museum Archives.

Kenya National Archives, Nairobi, Kenya.

McMillan Library, Nairobi, Kenya.

Mystic River Historical Society, Mystic, Connecticut. Mary L. Jobe Akeley Collection.

Page, Patricia and Lot, Lincoln, Massachusetts. Private Collection.

Smithsonian Institution, Washington, D.C. Smithsonian Institution Archives.

University of Rochester, Rochester, New York. Rush Rhees Library. Department of Rare Books and Special Collections.

University of Saskatchewan at Regina, Saskatchewan, Canada. Saskatchewan Archives Board.

University of South Dakota, Vermillion, South Dakota. I.D. Weeks Library.

INDEX

291

Index

Index

Index

Index